THE BIBLE
AS LITERATURE
THE OLD TESTAMENT
AND THE APOCRYPHA

BUCKNER B. TRAWICK, *Professor of English*
University of Alabama

BARNES & NOBLE BOOKS
A DIVISION OF HARPER & ROW, PUBLISHERS
New York, Cambridge,
Philadelphia, San Francisco, London,
Mexico City, São Paulo, Sydney

THE BIBLE AS LITERATURE. Copyright © 1963, 1970 by Harper & Row, Publishers, Inc. All rights reserved. Printed in the United States of America. No part of this book may be used or reproduced in any manner whatsoever without written permission except in the case of brief quotations embodied in critical articles and reviews. For information address Harper & Row, Publishers, Inc., 10 East 53rd Street, New York, N.Y. 10022. Published simultaneously in Canada by Fitzhenry & Whiteside Limited, Toronto.

Second BARNES & NOBLE BOOKS edition published 1970.

ISBN: 0-06-460056-4

88 89 90   20 19 18 17 16

Table of Contents

*Part One: Backgrounds of the Old Testament
    and the Apocrypha*   1

  1. Palestine and Its People   3
  2. The Nature, Origin, and Contents of the Bible   18

Part Two: History and Biography   45

  3. The Founding of the Hebrew Nation   49
  4. Rise and Fall of the Monarchy   85
  5. Establishment of a Church State after the Exile   137
  6. The Maccabean Revolt   150

Part Three: Prophetic Literature   163

  7. Eighth-Century Prophets   167
  8. Judah's Pre-Exilic Prophets of the Seventh
       and Sixth Centuries   184
  9. The Exilic Prophets   199
  10. The Post-Exilic Writings   219

Part Four: Lyric Poetry   237

  11. The Psalms: A Hymnbook for Jews and Christians   241
  12. Minor Lyrical Books   262

Part Five: Dramatic Literature   271

  13. Job: A Drama of the Inner Life   273
  14. The Song of Solomon: A Wedding Idyl   287

Part Six: Short Stories and Tales   295

  15. Fourth-Century Stories Advocating Tolerance   297
  16. Second- and First-Century Stories Encouraging Integrity 306

Part Seven: Wisdom Literature   337

  17. Ethical Precepts and Cynical Pessimism   339

Part Eight: An Apocalyptic Literature   357

  18. II Esdras: Visions Attributed to Ezra   359

Notes   363
Bibliography   385
Index   397

Maps

The Old Testament World   7
Palestine: The Period of the Judges   93
Divided Kingdom (ca. 860 B.C.)   123

Preface

The Bible is one of the most fascinating books ever written, and sometimes one of the most puzzling. This Outline is an attempt to catch and to share with others some of its fascination and to help solve some of its puzzling passages. It is hoped that the book will prove useful to the average lay reader as well as to the student primarily interested in the Scriptures as literature.

This edition, which supersedes *The Bible as Literature: Old Testament History and Biography* (Barnes & Noble, 1963), covers *all* the Old Testament and *all* the Apocrypha. To the previous volume have been added discussions of prophetic literature, lyric poetry, dramatic literature, short stories and tales, wisdom literature, and apocalyptic literature. The Bibliographies have been enlarged and brought up to date, and a new map on the Old Testament world has been included.

Although the principal emphasis in this volume is on *literary* rather than religious or ethical qualities, any significant discussion of Biblical literature necessarily deals with content as well as techniques; and it must offer interpretations of some of the content. A determined effort has been made to bring to the reader a compendium of the most up-to-date scholarship on the Bible which will be of value and interest to Protestant, Catholic, Jew, or skeptic; several points of view are presented on controversial matters.

In the belief that the King James Bible is still the best *literary* version, it has been chosen as the basis for this book. It is hoped, however, that readers who prefer the Douay, the Revised Standard, or the Jewish version will find the Outline equally helpful.

The Bible as Literature: The Old Testament and the Apocrypha is supplemented by a companion Outline, *The Bible as Literature: The New Testament* (2nd ed.; Barnes & Noble, 1968), which discusses in similar fashion every book of the New Testament. Thus together the two volumes offer the reader a commentary on all eighty books of the King James Bible.

B.B.T.

About the Author

Buckner B. Trawick is Professor of English at the University of Alabama. He received his B.A. from Emory University and both his M.A. and Ph.D. from Harvard University, where he has undertaken additional study on a Ford Foundation Fellowship. Prior to his present position, Dr. Trawick held teaching positions at Clemson College, the University of Mississippi, and Temple University. He is the author also of *World Literature* (2 vols.) in the Outline Series and of *The Bible as Literature: The New Testament*.

Acknowledgments

The author of this Outline is grateful to The Macmillan Co. for permission to quote four extensive passages (acknowledged again in the footnotes) from Mary Ellen Chase, *The Bible and the Common Reader* (rev. ed., 1952) and from George Sprau, *Literature in the Bible* (1932); and to the Abingdon Press for permission to use the maps on pp. 93 and 123. The author also received much assistance from the numerous sources cited in the Notes on pp. 363-384. Many facts, dates, and discussions were based on *The Interpreter's Bible* (12 vols.) published by the Abingdon Press, Nashville, Tenn., 1951-1957.

Part One
Backgrounds of
the Old Testament
and the Apocrypha

The Old Testament and the Apocrypha provide a record of the history, the religious experiences, the hopes and fears, the thoughts and feelings of the Jewish people over a period of almost two thousand years. The serious student of the Bible will want to know who the ancient Hebrews were, how their Holy Scriptures were written, how these writings were preserved and transmitted through centuries of tribulation, and how they were translated by gifted and painstaking scholars into an English classic—the King James Bible.

Palestine and Its People

Palestine, the home of Biblical literature, is not much larger than the state of Maryland in area and population. Never the seat of a major military or political power, it has nearly always been dominated by one or another mighty neighbor. From the time when the Pharaohs controlled the Mediterranean world down to the era of the Caesars, successive foreign cultures were pressed upon its people, who, nevertheless, persisted in maintaining distinctive national customs and, above all, allegiance to their traditional religion.

BIBLICAL PALESTINE
AND THE MEDITERRANEAN WORLD

Forming part of the eastern coastline of the Mediterranean Sea, Palestine (the land known to the ancient Hebrews as Canaan) extends only about 150 miles from north to south and, at its widest, only about 100 miles from east to west. It is bounded by Lebanon and Syria on the north, Jordan on the east, and the Sinai Peninsula of Egypt on the southwest. Its total area is not more than 11,200 square miles. In Biblical times it was almost encircled by larger and stronger nations. In the ancient world it was subjected, in turn, to the great Egyptian, Assyrian, Babylonian, and Persian empires.

Egypt. Egypt developed an advanced civilization in ancient times which shed a cultural influence on the Hebrews. The Egyptians attained a high level of accomplishment in literature, architecture, sculpture, painting, mathematics, government, medicine, and military science. Their *Book of the Dead*—a collection of prayers, formulas, and charms written at various times prior to the fifteenth century B.C. and designed to sway the decisions of

Osiris, Judge of the Dead—reflects their worship of the gods
(particularly Osiris and the sun god Ra) and their belief in personal immortality. According to some historians, Egyptian ideas
and institutions affected the culture of the Hebrews, who, in due
time, rejected the multiple deities in favor of monotheism.

Assyria and Other Countries of the "Fertile Crescent." Northeast of Palestine is the "Fertile Crescent," an arc of fertile lands
(watered by the great rivers) extending along the eastern Mediterranean through Syria, thence eastward and southward to the
Persian Gulf, thus including the richly productive area between
the Tigris and Euphrates rivers. Here the settlers had access to
the great seas and to Egypt.

Like the Egyptian civilization, the Sumerian, Assyrian, Babylonian, and other civilizations of this fertile area were of great
antiquity. Sumerian leadership in the southern region declined
late in the third millennium B.C.; the Babylonians (originally the
Semitic group called Amorites) gained the ascendancy but were
conquered by the Hittites and Kassites in the eighteenth century B.C. The northern region was dominated by the Assyrians,
who formed a great empire that reached its peak during the reign
of its last famous ruler, Assurbanipal (669-626 B.C.). The extensive library of that monarch contained not only numerous official
documents but also myths, legends, hymns, prayers, proverbs,
early scientific records, and accounts of battles. The poetry resembles that of the Hebrews in its use of proportion, balance,
and parallelism. The Assyrians were skilled in law, sculpture,
and architecture. They were militarily strong enough in the seventh century B.C. to challenge the armies of Egypt. They achieved
a high level of practical skill, exemplified, for instance, in their
fine system of roads. Their main contribution did not consist of
creative or practical works, however, but rather of the transmission of Sumerian and Babylonian culture to the Persians, Greeks,
and Romans. Some of the Old Testament stories—the Creation,
Adam and Eve, and the Flood—can be traced back to these ancient cultures; and some portions of the Hebrew legal code may
have been inherited from the Babylonian code of Hammurabi.

In 612 B.C. the Chaldeans destroyed the Assyrian Empire.
They conquered Israel and carried the Jews off into captivity in
Babylonia. Following the death of their most gifted king, Ne-
buchadrezzar, in 562 B.C., however, the Chaldean Empire went

into a rapid decline; Babylon was captured by Cyrus of Persia in 539 B.C. (Cyrus had conquered the short-lived Median Empire which had been built up by Cyaxares, 625-585 B.C.) Under Cyrus the vast Persian Empire reached from eastern Persia throughout southwestern Asia to the Aegean and Mediterranean. The Persians conquered Egypt in 525 B.C. and then attempted in vain to subdue European Greece.

Greece. Greek culture attained its zenith in the fifth and fourth centuries B.C. The spread of that culture was given new impetus when the Greeks defeated the Persians early in the fifth century B.C.; shortly after Alexander the Great had conquered Persia in 333-331 B.C., Greek civilization, including the language, was forced upon the Hebrews of Palestine, as it was upon the peoples of other parts of the Persian Empire. Thus Hellenic culture, particularly Greek philosophy and drama, was reflected in the thought of the Jews and early Christians as well as in that of the Romans.

Rome. Roman influence was not felt in Palestine until the last Greek resistance to the Roman legions ceased in 146 B.C. In addition to serving Western civilization as a transmitter of Greek culture, Rome contributed numerous scientific and technical innovations, a remarkable legal system, and effective political organization. Roman civilization is reflected in the New Testament, where we may observe many instances of the Caesars' genius for government and for enforcing law, order, and payment of taxes.

Almost encircled by these great powers was the small but tough Hebrew nation, becoming a part of one mighty empire and then of another, absorbing culture from each, yet preserving many of its own customs and traditions and fiercely maintaining its allegiance to the God of Abraham.

IMPORTANCE OF GEOGRAPHY TO BIBLICAL LITERATURE

The location, soil and topography, and climate of Palestine had a profound influence on the intellectual and material life of its inhabitants.

Location. The location of Palestine was of great strategic significance in ancient times. It lies athwart the land route between Africa and Asia; to the west is the Mediterranean, and to the east the vast Arabian Desert. Hence any invasion by land of

either continent by an army from the other required passage
through Palestine. Because it was small and comparatively weak
and because it was a bridge between two continents, Palestine
suffered from numerous military expeditions. From the middle of
the eighth century B.C. until the beginning of the Christian era,
it was overwhelmed by one world power after another. It is not
surprising that the most persistent prayer of its inhabitants was
for deliverance from the indignities and persecutions to which
they had been subjected.

However, frequent military invasion was not the only result of
Palestine's unique position. The road over which armies traveled
was also a commercial route, one of the most ancient on record;
and the Hebrews had the opportunity to learn a great deal from
the civilizations whose caravans crossed their land.

Soil and Topography. A study of the soil and topography of
Palestine discloses striking contrasts. The coastal region and the
narrow strip on each side of the Jordan River Valley are exceedingly fertile (a land of fruits, olives, wheat and other crops, "a
land of milk and honey"), whereas east and south of the Jordan
lies the desert, and much of the area between the Jordan and
the Mediterranean is hilly and rocky. Some of the hilly region is
high above sea level; Mount Hermon rises 9,052 feet, and Mount
Lebanon 10,059 feet. But the Sea of Galilee is 680 feet below
the level of the Mediterranean, and the Dead Sea is 610 feet lower
than that! From its source the Jordan descends 3,000 feet before
emptying into the Dead Sea. Jerusalem, only twenty miles from
the coast of the Dead Sea, is 4,000 feet higher than the level of
water. During the Roman era, the central hilly section of Palestine included Judah—this was the southern portion extending to
Beersheba; Israel—this was the middle section extending north
to the plain of Esdraelon; and Galilee—this was the northern area.

The relatively poor, hard soil facing many of the Hebrews in
the large hilly area was felt to be a severe handicap challenging
their utmost energy and ingenuity, both as individuals and as a
people. The Old Testament reflects the courage of this bold, en-
terprising "chosen people" and their faith that God would bring
justice to them and help them to overcome hardships. Continued
misfortunes were interpreted as merited punishment for misbe-
havior.

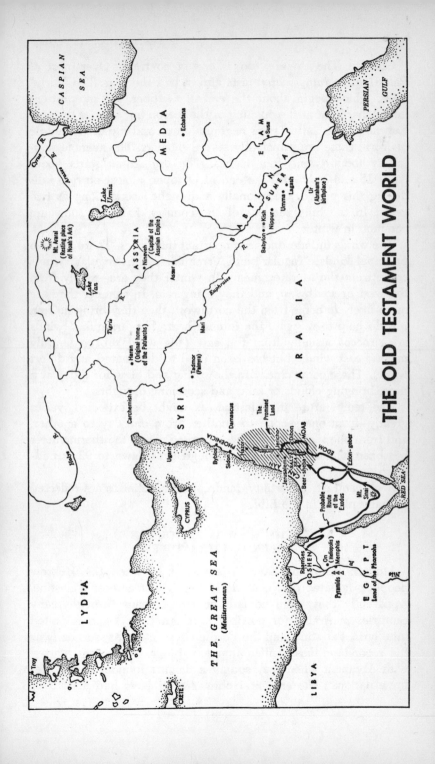

THE OLD TESTAMENT WORLD

Climate. The climate, too, is one of contrasts. Over most of Palestine the *rainy season* lasts almost half the year. The "early" rains, which begin about the end of October, are intermittent and rather light at the opening of the season but heavier through February. The "latter" rains begin in March and end in the middle of April; these are principally severe showers. The average rainfall is about twenty-four inches. The *dry season* starts about April 15 and lasts until the end of October; almost no rain falls during this period. Occasionally a drought lasts as long as two years. In the hilly sections of the country, hail and snow are common in winter.

The winds in Palestine are important influences. There are two principal kinds: "regular" and "irregular." The "regular" winds come from the Mediterranean. In winter they are usually from the west or southwest, and they bring rain. In summer they are more likely to come from the northwest; then they bring no rain but do help to mitigate the intense heat. The "irregular" winds are siroccos, usually from the east (the word *sirocco* literally means "east wind," but has been used to designated any desert wind). These come chiefly in the spring and blow for a day at a time, bringing clouds of sand and scorching droughts.

The temperature in Palestine, as might be expected, varies greatly—from one section to another, from one day to another, and from one season to another. In some places the thermometer has been known to rise from 48 degrees at dawn to 92 at mid-afternoon.

Such contrasts in fertility, landscape, and climate are reflected in many places in the Bible.

JEWISH HISTORY AS TOLD IN
BIBLICAL LITERATURE

Modern historians have little record of when the Hebrew people originated or when the Hebrews first entered Palestine. Apparently they were nomads or semi-nomads through many centuries in Arabia (or possibly northern Egypt) and migrated into Syria, Palestine, and the Fertile Crescent perhaps as early as the second or third millennium B.C. Biblical historians started with Abraham when they sought a definite founder of the Hebrew nation. (The ancient Hebrews must have had notions of time very different from our modern concepts of centuries and millennia. Since little is known about their views of time, we can only guess what they had in mind in setting forth a chronology which seems inconsistent or illogical to us.)

The Hebrew Claim to Palestine; Enslavement of the Hebrews in Egypt. At some time between the twenty-first century B.C. (Biblical chronology) and the sixteenth century B.C. (a favored archaeological date), Abraham wandered from Ur in Chaldea to Haran in the northern part of the Arabian Desert near the Euphrates and then traveled from Haran southwest to Palestine. Genesis confirms the recent evidence of archaeologists as to the Chaldean origin of Abraham,[1] and the Hebrew language shows many Chaldean elements.[*] According to Genesis the land of Palestine was given to Abraham and his descendants by divine covenant. He and his people took possession of the right bank of the Jordan; but a generation later the family of his grandson Jacob was driven by famine into Egypt, and their descendants were eventually enslaved. Biblical scholars doubt that all the Hebrews migrated to Egypt; a few even consider the sojourn in Egypt to be in some respects legendary.[2] Yet, it is entirely reasonable to assume that large numbers of the people were driven by drought and famine into Egypt and were estranged from their kin who remained in Palestine.

Exodus and the Conquest of Canaan. According to the Bible, Pharaoh, the Egyptian king (probably Rameses II, c. 1290-1224 B.C.),[3] oppressed the Hebrews so cruelly that they eventually fled from Egypt—600,000 soldiers and their families if we are to accept Exodus 12:37-38—under the leadership of Moses and his brother Aaron. According to some modern Biblical scholars, this event may have taken place about 1200 B.C. during the reign of Merneptah, successor of Rameses II. (A fragmentary inscription by King Merneptah on a granite stele at Thebes contains in hieroglyphics a reference to the defeat of the Israelites and the curbing of the Hebrew nomads.) The Hebrews probably did not become a nation until the Exodus from Egypt. After a generation of wandering in the wilderness, they finally reached Pales-

[1] For this and all succeeding notes indicated by raised numbers, see pp. 363 ff.

[*] See W. F. Albright in H. H. Rowley, ed., *The Old Testament and Modern Study* (London: Oxford University Press, 1951), pp. 6 ff.

tine. There they were confronted by the hostile Canaanites and, somewhat later, the Ammonites, the Midianites, the Philistines, and other unfriendly tribes. During this period of warfare the military leaders Joshua and Gideon were the rulers of the Hebrews.

The Period of Theocracy (*c.* 1200-1020 B.C.). When they had achieved some degree of peace, the Hebrews placed themselves under the rule of "judges," who were at once religious and military leaders. But religion came first, and all rulers had to be subordinate to God, obedient to his laws. Each of the twelve tribes maintained a large measure of autonomy. The last theocratic ruler was Samuel, a lover of peace. But the war against the Philistines created a demand for a king who would unite the military forces of the tribes.

The United Kingdom. About 1020 B.C., Saul, of the tribe of Benjamin, was proclaimed king. Although he was not recognized as sovereign by all the tribes (possibly only by Manasseh, Ephraim, and Benjamin), he extended his rule to the lands of the tribe of Judah in the south and also eastward across the Jordan. An able military commander, Saul led his followers successfully against many of their enemies, including the Ammonites, Amalekites, and Philistines. His reign lasted until about 1000 B.C.

Saul was succeeded by David, who is said to have ruled for about forty years (*c.* 1000—*c.* 960 B.C.). He was a great warrior; after a series of brilliant victories over the Philistines, Moabites, Ammonites, and Edomites, he established his capital in Jerusalem and ruled over most of Palestine and much of the territory across the Jordan as far north as Damascus.

Note that although a king might sometimes designate his successor, the decision was always attributed to divine action. Women were automatically excluded from kingship.

David's son Solomon succeeded him about 960 B.C.; like David, he also is said to have ruled forty years. Among Solomon's foremost contributions were the building of the Temple at Jerusalem and the expansion of industry and commerce; he brought the kingdom to its highest peak of splendor.

The Divided Kingdom. Upon the death of Solomon in *c.* 922 B.C. (some authorities say 935 B.C.), the kingdom was divided. Solomon's son Rehoboam levied such heavy taxes that the ten northern tribes refused him allegiance; they recognized Jeroboam (a former administrator who had plotted against Solomon) as their king and set up a capital at Shechem. This northern realm was thereafter known as the "Kingdom of Israel." The southern realm, made up of the tribe of Judah and part of the tribe of Benjamin, was called the "Kingdom of Judah."

The history of the Northern Kingdom, Israel, for the next two centuries is principally a record of assassinations, usurpations, and minor wars. Jeroboam I, a strong king, held the throne about twenty years. By encouraging the worship of idols he diverted attention from the Yahweh-worship at the Temple in Jerusalem. Another important ruler, Omri, strengthened his political position by bringing about a marriage between his son Ahab and Jezebel, daughter of the king of Tyre. As Jeroboam had done, Ahab and Jezebel espoused the worship of alien gods in Israel; thus they aroused the antagonism of the prophets Elijah and Elisha, who helped to foment a revolution which led to the end of the Omri dynasty. Jehu, a new and able but most severe ruler, temporarily put an end to the worship of foreign deities. (His slaughter of idol-worshipers was denounced by the later prophet Hosea as an immoral act.) He established a dynasty that ruled about a century (842—c. 745 B.C.). His two sons were incompetent rulers, but they were succeeded by Jeroboam II (786-746 B.C.), who extended the boundaries of Israel and brought it great prosperity. Unfortunately, prosperity and luxury, combined with new customs and religious views imported from abroad, led to dissolute living and numerous social and economic evils, especially in the northern and western regions of Palestine. In vain the contemporaneous prophets Amos and Hosea warned the people sternly against the prevalent immorality.

The five weak successors of Jeroboam II did little to improve the degenerate society. Consequently in 722 B.C. the Assyrians under Shalmaneser V (727-722 B.C.) and Sargon (722-705 B.C.) found it an easy matter to overthrow the Northern Kingdom and to destroy the capital, Samaria; the following year about 27,000 Israelites were carried into captivity. The kingdom of Israel never recovered from the effects of this disaster.

Meanwhile, the kingdom of Judah, its semi-nomadic people strengthened by generations of hardships, danger, and austerity, had continued under the Davidic dynasty, which was destined to endure until the destruction of Jerusalem in 586 B.C. After Rehoboam's severe regime (c. 922—c. 915 B.C.) little of significance occurred until the reign of King Jehoram (c. 845 B.C.), who married Athaliah, the daughter of Jezebel and Ahab of the Northern Kingdom. Upon the death of both Jehoram and his son Ahaziah in 843 B.C., Athaliah seized power and murdered all but one of the sons of Ahaziah; Jehoash alone was saved, and he later became king (c. 837 B.C.). His son Amaziah waged a disastrous war (c. 790 B.C.) against the kingdom of Israel, in which Jerusalem was partially destroyed.

During the forty-year reign of Amaziah's son Uzziah (or Azariah), c. 783—c. 742 B.C., Judah's fortunes were restored. When the Assyrians threatened Palestine, Uzziah agreed to pay tribute and thus temporarily saved his kingdom from the fate of Israel. King Hezekiah (c. 715—c. 687 B.C.) allied himself for a time with Egypt and the Philistines, but later reversed this error and resumed the payment of tribute to Assyria.

Toward the end of the seventh century, Assyria's power began to wane. The Babylonians captured Nineveh from the Assyrians in 612 B.C. and shortly thereafter began to exact tribute from Judah. In 598 B.C. King Jehoiakim, making overtures to Egypt, refused to continue such tribute, whereupon the Babylonians invaded Judah and captured Jerusalem (597 B.C.). They made Jehoiakim's brother Zedekiah king, but he, too, attempted to enlist the aid of Egypt, whereupon the Babylonians returned, this time to destroy Jerusalem and carry off many of the inhabitants of Judah into exile (586 B.C.).

Palestine under Foreign Rule (586 B.C.—A.D. 125). The exile lasted until 536 B.C. when Cyrus the Great of Persia, having conquered Babylon in 539 B.C., allowed the Hebrews to return to their own country. They completed the restoration of the Temple in 516 B.C. Palestine continued under Persian rule for about two centuries. In 444 B.C. Nehemiah received permission to rebuild the walls of Jerusalem. It is also believed that, under the leadership of the priest Ezra, a large contingent (about 1,800) of the exiled Hebrews went back to Jerusalem early in the fourth century B.C.

Alexander the Great defeated the Persians under Darius III at Issus in 333 B.C. and soon brought Palestine within the Macedonian Empire. Despite bitter resistance by the Hebrews, the Greek language and Greek culture superseded their own in some

respects; even the Hebrew Scriptures eventually had to be translated into Greek (c. 250 B.C.) for the benefit of those Hebrews
who could understand no other language.

When Alexander died in 323 B.C., his realm was divided, and
Palestine fell to the Ptolemies, kings of Egypt. In 198 B.C., it was
transferred to the kingdom of Syria, ruled by the Seleucids (the
Macedonian general Seleucus and his descendants). When Antiochus IV (Epiphanes), the Syrian king from 175 to 163 B.C.,
made vigorous efforts to Hellenize the Hebrews, the priest Mattathias and his five sons (especially the eldest, Judas Maccabeus)
led a successful revolt (167-160 B.C.). By 142 B.C. the Hebrews
had not only won religious freedom but also regained almost
complete political independence. The Maccabeans (or Hasmonaeans) held the throne until 67 B.C. Then internal squabbling
which had been going on for decades finally led to the successive
intervention of the Syrians, the Egyptians, and the Romans.
Judea became part of the Roman province of Syria in 63 B.C.

Needless to elaborate, the Hebrews were unhappy under Roman rule. Their unrest flared into open revolt again in A.D. 66.
Rome stamped out the revolt and destroyed Jerusalem in A.D. 70.
Thus ended the hopes of the Hebrew people for religious and
political freedom—during Biblical times.

ECONOMIC AND SOCIAL BACKGROUND OF
BIBLICAL LITERATURE

The first people to whom the term *Israelites* may be applied—
the people governed by the patriarchs Abraham, Isaac, and Jacob
—were a semi-nomadic tribe who lived chiefly in tents, who
raised herds of sheep and goats, and who moved about as the
need for pastureland or the pressure of hostile neighbors dictated.

With the passage of time in the Promised Land of Canaan
(which they conquered about 1200 B.C.) the Hebrews became
more sedentary, continuing their pastoral economy but devoting
more attention to agriculture. Under Samuel (1060-1020 B.C.)
and in the United Kingdom (1020-922 B.C.) agriculture and trade
flourished. The principal crops included honey, olives, barley,
figs, grapes, apples, onions, garlic, melons, cucumbers, beans,
and peas. The main exports were lumber (especially fir and
cedar), copper, and iron.[4] Fishing became a significant occupation. Palestine's location on the caravan route from the Euphrates

Valley to Egypt led to a brisk commerce with Mesopotamia and Egypt, and trade with neighboring Phoenicia was substantial. Commercial activity made possible the growth of such busy cities as Jerusalem, Damascus, and Samaria. The small trades and crafts and the manufacture of simple articles prospered.

The earliest society had been patriarchal, the father having had almost absolute power over his wife and children. (Some limitations developed prior to the eighth century B.C.) Polygamy had been customary in the patriarchal era, and the practice persisted into the Divided Kingdom (divided in 922 B.C.); but after the eighth century B.C., it became less and less common, so that by the beginning of the Christian era it was comparatively rare, though it was not officially declared illegal for the Hebrews until several centuries later.

Periodically under the judges and kings, recurrent economic and military crises, attributed by the Hebrew prophets to lax morality, induced the people to return to their faith in Yahweh. As each crisis receded, the moral influence of the prophets declined. Conditions of life were hard; when the perils were overcome so that the nation survived, the people attributed their survival to divine intervention.

During the unified monarchy, taxes for the Temple were heavy, forced labor was employed, and foreign artisans were imported to aid in building. Skills and techniques were passed on to successive generations. There is evidence that in the Divided Kingdom, too, there was an advanced material culture—soundly built houses with drains and cisterns, sleeping quarters upstairs, and land set aside at a distance for the cattle. Asses remained the chief means of transporting goods and people. Oxen were used in ploughing and threshing. Brisk trade necessitated the increased use of writing, particularly during the eighth and seventh centuries B.C. The continued leadership of the Temple priests through the centuries has been well established by archaeological findings (the stamped jars and coins identified by E. L. Sukenik as probably belonging to the Hebrews of Judah under Persian rule in the third to fifth centuries B.C. have been regarded as evidence that heavy taxes were paid in order to support the Temple). The Dead Sea Scrolls discovered in recent decades attest to the persisting conflict between material interests and the traditional codes of conduct.

THE RELIGION OF THE EARLY HEBREWS

The orthodox view is that monotheism originated with the early Hebrews, was expounded in the teachings of Moses, and was reinforced and elaborated upon by the later prophets. An evolutionary theory holds that there was a continuous development of the Hebrew religion, perhaps from animism to a belief in one just and merciful God who promised personal immortality.[5]

The Concept of God. Some scholars who reject the orthodox view point out that the earliest Hebrew conceptions of God's nature were strikingly similar to those of other primitive religions and postulate that the Hebrews may have been at first animistic and polytheistic. They assert that the geography of Palestine was favorable to polytheistic ideas—that, prior to the times of the great teachers and judges, the varied landscape and topography and the changeableness of the weather encouraged the animistic belief that a different deity or spirit lived in every mountain stream, every wind, and every thundercloud.* It is a fact that many other tribes who lived in the same general area (for example, the Phoenicians and the Canaanites) were polytheistic.

If the evolutionary view of the Hebrew religion is correct, why did the Hebrews turn early from the idols, the "abominations" of the Egyptians, to the belief in a single God? It has been suggested that they brought monotheism with them from the Arabian Desert, a land with little variety and few changes. Another theory is that observation of the evil consequences of idol-worship (practices such as human sacrifice, for example) induced them to reject the polytheistic beliefs of their neighbors. Their concern with morality, it is said, may have led them to believe in one God as the embodiment of goodness, the source of all

---

* A trace of animism, according to this view, may be preserved in the Hebrews' use of the phrase El Shaddai ("God Almighty" or "The Highest"), found in Genesis 17:1, 28:3, and other passages; this phrase could have referred originally to a mountain deity. See James Muilenburg, "The History of the Religion of Ancient Israel," The Interpreter's Bible, I, 297. There are many Biblical references to the Hebrew worship of (1) bull images (Exodus 32:1-35, I Kings 12:28); and (2) Canaanite baals (nature deities) in "groves in every high hill, and under every green tree . . . And . . . in all the high places" (II Kings 17:10-11). For other specific examples, see Joshua 23:12; Judges 2:13; II Kings 23:12-28; and Jeremiah 2:20, 7:29 and 31, and 17:2.

ethical values, the merciful and just Creator who ruled heaven and earth in accordance with his preconceived plan. The orthodox claim made by both Hebrews and Christians that God directly revealed his nature and his will to chosen spokesmen contrasts sharply, of course, with the various theories ascribing monotheism to the influence of geographical factors and a long historical development.

The Hebrew faith in Yahweh,* rejecting the alien belief in plural gods as the powers that controlled the heavenly spheres, sent the rain, and caused lightning to flame through the clouds, conceived of God as the Supreme Judge of human worth, reward and punishment, and destiny. God was not only the Creator of all things but also the directive cause of historical events. The people had to look, therefore, to God for guidance, justice, and mercy. (For example, in Chapter 18 of Genesis, Abraham pleads with God to spare Sodom if only ten righteous men can be found in that city. Men could appeal to Yahweh, a deity who could be influenced by the sacrificial offering of bullocks, lambs, goats, and doves, as recounted especially in Genesis, Exodus, Leviticus, and Deuteronomy.)

The constant military struggles of the early Hebrews led to the conception of God as a warrior, a conception shared by other primitive cultures (compare Ares of the Greeks and Thor and Woden of the Germanic peoples). Defeats at the hands of their enemies persuaded the Hebrews that Yahweh used the Assyrians and other invaders, just as he used the forces of nature, as a means of punishing his people.

The earliest Hebrews thought of Yahweh as a tribal God who was interested particularly in them, and who had made with them (that is with Abraham) a Covenant to the effect that he would prosper them as his Chosen People if they would worship only him and obey his commandments. The Mosaic God was a deity who could be found in more than one place (e.g., in Egypt or on Mount Sinai) and who set forth a definite religious code

* The name *Yahweh* (or *Yahveh*) is made by supplying vowels to the ancient Hebrew word which in our alphabet is written as *YHVH*, known as the "Tetragrammaton." Its true, original pronunciation is uncertain, inasmuch as ancient Hebrew was written without vowels (a fact discussed below, page 21). The name *Jehovah* has become a popular variant because of its use in the American Standard translation.

of law. He was described as being jealous of other deities, wrathful, and sometimes arbitrary in his gifts and in his afflictions which he brought upon men. Always he was holy and to be revered. During the era of the judges and United Kingdom, the priesthood and Temple organization were established to create respect for (and guide the people in worship of) the one God. Over the centuries the concept was ennobled in eloquent descriptions, with emphasis on the attributes of universality (see Amos and Jonah), justice (see Amos especially), and mercy (see Hosea). The "Unknown Prophet" (author of Isaiah 40–55) suggested the idea of a vicarious sufferer who would atone for the sins of mankind. Persecution by other nations impelled the Hebrews to yearn and pray for a deliverer, a Messiah ("Anointed One") who would overcome their enemies by force and set up a God-fearing empire. Eventually, when further armed resistance against Rome seemed futile, some Hebrews ceased to hope for a temporal, earthly Messiah and placed their faith in a spiritual, heavenly one. It remained for the Christians to teach that Jesus Christ was the incarnation of the Deity, sent to earth as the long-expected Messiah.

The Concept of Immortality. From the earliest times the Hebrews placed comparatively little emphasis on the idea of personal immortality. Their predominant belief was that God rewards people for their good deeds by giving them health, wealth, a long life, and happiness here on earth; and he punishes them here for their evil deeds by means of physical and material adversity. It is noteworthy that the Old Testament story of the Flood differs from the Babylonian Epic of Gilgamesh in that the latter, polytheistic account explains that Utnapishtim (who is comparable to Noah of the Old Testament story) acquired immortality hitherto possessed only by the gods. To be sure, the Old Testament used the word *Sheol* to designate a place or a state beyond the grave, an abode of souls neither especially pleasant for the good souls nor painful for the wicked. Occasional references (as in the Psalms) are made to the possibility of everlasting life: "for there the Lord commanded the blessing, even life for evermore." But the conception of heaven as a reward for the righteous and hell as a punishment for sinners receives its major emphasis in the Apocrypha and the New Testament.

2

The Nature, Origins, and Contents of the Bible

The word *Bible* means "little books." The term is ultimately derived from the Greek *biblos*, "book" (originally "papyrus"); the diminutive of *biblos* was *biblion*, "little book"; the plural *biblia*, or "booklets," passed through Medieval Latin into the Old French *bible* and Middle English *bibul*.

We may regard the Bible as an anthology of ancient Hebrew and early Christian religious literature, as two or three books (Old Testament, Apocrypha, and New Testament), or as a unified, single work of literature. The Bible consists of from 66 to 81 books, according to which of several versions is accepted. The Hebrew Scriptures contain only what Christians call the "Old Testament"; the Catholic Bible contains a number of books which are omitted in most of the modern Protestant Bibles. Written in three languages—Hebrew, Aramaic, and Greek—by scores of authors over hundreds of years, the Christian Bible exhibits many different literary genres and styles.* Yet it has essential unity, based on its point of view, characteristic linguistic tone, and serious dignity; for such reasons, and because of its traditional presentation as one continuous work, we *feel* that the Bible is one book. To some extent, throughout the long period of transmission of the Scriptures, the various compilers, editors,

---

* Nearly all the books of the Bible (exceptions are parts of some of the Prophetic books, Luke, Acts, and certain Epistles) are anonymous; insofar as modern linguistic and textual science can determine, most of the books bear the stamp of revisions throughout the ages. Each of the authors was devoted to his cause; some attributed their work to a great name of the past. Thus we have the Gospel "according to" St. Matthew, with no claim that Matthew wrote it but only that it is in accordance with the teachings of that apostle.

and translators may have brought about a degree of uniformity in the style and language of the particular version accepted by them. In the main, however, unity depends upon a certain "mode of thought" [1]—an earnestness, an intensity, a simplicity, a brevity, and a warmth—which is characteristic of all parts of the Bible and binds them together.

This unity of mode suggests a unity of purpose. For the Old Testament that purpose is to record the Hebrews' continuous quest for God—his nature, his will, and his plans—as a basis for the teaching of divine law and morality. Every mood and every condition of human life—sorrow, joy, loneliness, companionship, love, hate, conspiracy, falsehood, truth, loyalty, heroism, cowardice, war, peace, kindness, brutality, hunger, luxury—all are depicted in simple, direct terms as part of the divine stream of history, teaching the lessons of the past as admonitions, sermons, and guides for all who will listen.

CLASSIFICATION OF THE BIBLE FOR LITERARY STUDY

For purposes of religious instruction the following traditional arrangements of the Scriptures have been widely accepted; for purposes of literary study, a classification based on literary types has been generally adopted.

Traditional Arrangements. For the Hebrews the Holy Scriptures consisted of twenty-four books arranged in three parts: (1) the *Law* (*Torah* in Hebrew), made up of Genesis, Exodus, Leviticus, Numbers, and Deuteronomy; (2) the *Prophets*, consisting of: (*a*) the Earlier Prophets—Joshua, Judges, Samuel, and Kings—and (*b*) the Latter Prophets—Isaiah, Jeremiah, Ezekiel, and (one book) the "Twelve" or "Minor" Prophets; and (3) the *Writings*, made up of Psalms, Proverbs, Job, The Song of Songs, Ruth, Lamentations, Ecclesiastes, Esther, Daniel, Ezra (a combination of what Protestants know as Ezra and Nehemiah), and Chronicles. Terms often used are the *Pentateuch*,* referring to the first five books, Genesis through Deuteronomy; the *Hexateuch*,* the first six books, the Pentateuch plus Joshua;

* The word *Pentateuch* comes from the Greek *penta-* (meaning "five") and *teuchos* meaning "tool" or "book"). *Hexateuch* comes from the Greek *hexa-* (meaning "six") and *teuchos*.

and the "Five Rolls," or *Megilloth*, the five books from the Song of Songs through Esther.

The Roman Catholic Bible is arranged in two parts: the Old Testament and the New Testament. The Old Testament (which includes some of the books placed by Protestants in their Apocrypha) consists of forty-five books: twenty-one "historical," Genesis through Maccabees; seven "doctrinal," Job through Ecclesiasticus; and seventeen "prophetical," Isaiah through Malachi. The New Testament consists of twenty-seven books: five "historical," Matthew through Acts; twenty-one "doctrinal," Romans through Jude; and one "prophetic," Revelation, or the "Apocalypse." (Roman Catholic names of the books and spellings of the names differ in many cases from Protestant ones.)

The King James Version (as well as later Protestant versions) arranges the Bible in three parts: the Old Testament (thirty-nine books); the Apocrypha (fourteen or fifteen books—which, though not included in most modern Protestant editions, have served as useful supplements, or links, to the Old and New Testaments); and the New Testament (twenty-seven books). The arrangement of the Old Testament books differs from that of the Hebrew shown above and follows this grouping: (1) *Law* (Genesis through Deuteronomy); (2) *History* (Joshua through Esther); (3) *Poetry* (Job through the Song of Songs); (4) *Major Prophets* (Isaiah through Daniel); and (5) *Minor Prophets* (Hosea through Malachi). The books of the Apocrypha have been placed at the end of the canonical books of the Old Testament, apparently with no effort being made toward classification. The New Testament is made up of the four *Gospels* (Matthew through John), *Acts*, twenty-one *Epistles* (Romans through Jude), and *Revelation*.

An Approach by Literary Types. Like a modern anthology of English, American, or any other literature, the Bible contains specimens of many different literary types, ranging from simple folklore to artistic lyrics and stories. In its pages we find myths, legends, fables, parables, short stories, essays, lyrics, epistles, sermons, orations, apocalypses, proverbs, history, biography, prophecy, and drama. The compilers made little attempt to arrange the writings according to the genres or according to any estimated dates of composition; consequently many different literary types, written at various times, are scattered throughout the Bible. A single book may contain several genres. Genesis, for example, is made up of myths, legends, folksongs, history, and biography. It is feasible, however, to group the books according to their dominant literary genres. On this basis the Old Testament and Apocryphal books treated here are classified as History and Biography, Prophetic Literature, Lyric Poetry, Dramatic Literature, Short Stories and Tales, Wisdom Literature, and Apocalyptic Literature.

ORIGIN AND EARLY TRANSMISSION OF THE BIBLE

Each of the three main divisions of Biblical literature—the Old Testament, the Apocrypha, and the New Testament—has its own unique history; hence each must be discussed as a separate unit. The chronology of the books in any one division is very difficult—and sometimes impossible—to determine. The historical and biographical books contain legends and songs which must be very ancient as well as others which must have been completed not long after the time of the events related. The prophetic books sometimes bear evidence of having originated in preaching before the Captivity, but of having been edited and annotated after the return to Jerusalem. In the New Testament the Gospel according to St. Mark was probably written before the Gospel according to St. Matthew.

The fascinating story of the writing, collecting, and canonization of the books of the Old Testament covers a period of many hundreds of years, beginning with the early stages of the Hebrew alphabet in the sixteenth and fifteenth centuries B.C.

Linguistic Difficulties for Translators. Except for five scattered passages in Aramaic, the Old Testament was written first in Hebrew. The alphabet of this language was derived from the ancient Phoenician system (North Semitic or Sinaitic). Although vowel sounds were necessarily present in *spoken* Hebrew, for hundreds of years the written alphabet consisted only of consonants. Hebrew practices applied to English would cause the first two lines of the song "America" to read as follows: MCNTRTSFTHSWTLNDFLBRT. The absence of vowels in the written language has caused much confusion among transcribers and has left the meaning of many a passage in obscurity. A given group of consonants with one set of vowels may mean one thing, whereas with another set it may mean something entirely different. For example, the Hebrew letters which correspond to S – PH – R may be read "to count," "to declare," "a scribe," or a "book." [2] Further difficulty in the reading of ancient Hebrew has been caused by the forbidding of ligatures (regarded as desecrations of the holy text) in Scriptural writings, by the similarity of some Hebrew letters, and by the lack of spacing between words and even between prose sentences or lines of poetry. Thus, although the Hebrew scribes often took the utmost pains to transcribe the Scriptures accurately, misunderstandings arose.

The primitive Hebrew language was a member of the Semitic family; it was similar to—and apparently derived from—ancient Chaldean (Babylonian) and Phoenician languages. The numerous invasions, defeats, and periods of captivity suffered by the Hebrews resulted in the mingling of many foreign elements with their primitive speech. This altered language became known as "Aramaic," and by 300 B.C. it had almost entirely supplanted Hebrew as the spoken language of the Hebrews.

In view of the fact that the Old Testament was originally written in Hebrew, it is a surprising fact, that, except for the Pentateuch, most of the book of Isaiah (found in one of the famous Dead Sea [Qumran] scrolls), and brief fragments of other books, no Hebrew manuscript of the Old Testament now available can be assigned to a date earlier than the ninth century A.D. Medieval as well as modern editors and translators have had to rely chiefly on Greek and other versions rather than on Hebrew manuscripts of the Old Testament as their most ancient sources.

Composition, Collection, and Canonization. The belief that the Hebrew alphabet was in existence as early as the sixteenth century B.C. would indicate the possibility of a written literature of that period. It is doubtful, however, that any actual writings have been preserved from such an early date. The oldest fragments of the Old Testament may date as far back as the wanderings in the Wilderness (at some time between 1400 and 1200 B.C.) or even earlier, but as something remembered and transmitted orally before being preserved in written form. It seems almost certain that by the middle of the tenth century a scribe or scribes were writing the history of David's kingdom. The latest of the Old Testament writings (if those of the Apocrypha are excluded)—Ecclesiastes, Daniel, and Esther—were probably written during the second century B.C.

It is not known who first collected into one volume the diverse literary writings that now make up the Old Testament. It is believed that the Law was "canonized" (accepted as divinely inspired and divinely authorized) between 450 and 350 B.C. For the Hebrews in the time of Jesus and the Apostles, the Law was the most authoritative division of the Scriptures. Next in degree of inspiration and authority came the Prophets. It is believed that these eight books (the Twelve Minor Prophets having been lumped together as a single "book") were canonized about 200 B.C. Least in authority, and perhaps for that reason the last to be canonized (in the second century B.C.), were the Writings. The Old Testament also refers to several books no longer extant which may at one time have been regarded by the Hebrews as Holy Scripture. (Note references to "Chronicles of the Kings of Israel" in I Kings 14:19 et seq. and to "Chronicles of the Kings of Judah" in I Kings 14:29 et seq.)

The Hebrew Scriptures (Masoretic Text). There are many reasons for the almost total lack of early Hebrew texts. In the first place, the wars and persecutions which the Hebrews suffered must have destroyed a great deal of their literature. Possibly the three greatest disasters for the Old Testament were the destruction of Jerusalem by Nebuchadrezzar in 586 B.C.; the attempt by Antiochus Epiphanes in 168 B.C. to wipe out all Hebrew culture and religion; and the destruction of Jerusalem by the Romans in A.D. 70. No doubt many ancient Hebrew manuscripts were destroyed deliberately by scribes who wanted to prevent worn-out copies from falling into impious hands or who wanted to prevent what they considered errors from being perpetuated.

From about A.D. 600 to 925, groups of scribes and textual critics known as the "Masoretes" were given the responsibility of preserving and transmitting the traditional Hebrew text of the Scriptures. They carried on their activities in several regions, including Mesopotamia, Babylonia, and Palestine. They derived their name from the Hebrew word *masoreth* (meaning "tradition"), which was applied to the vast number of marginal notes and notes at the ends of the Biblical books. These notes contained, among other matters, variant readings and directions for pronunciation. Perhaps the most extraordinary contribution—and certainly one of the most valuable—was an invention by the Masoretes of a system of vowel sounds and accentual marks, which they inserted into the traditional texts made up of consonants alone. The Masoretes were devoted and painstaking scholars, and it is on their texts that Hebrew Bibles are based today.

Another important Hebrew version of part of the Old Testament was the work of the Samaritans, the inhabitants of the region around the city of Samaria after the Hebrews' return from Exile. Recognizing only the Pentateuch as Holy Scripture, in the fourth century B.C. the Samaritans made their own copies of the first five books of the Old Testament. Since the Samaritans spoke Hebrew, the Samaritan Pentateuch is exceedingly valuable as an independent Hebrew text, preserved by a tradition entirely outside of the Masoretic one.

The Greek Old Testament (The Septuagint). After the conquests of Alexander the Great, the Hellenization of the Mediterranean lands was rapid and rather thorough. The Greek language quickly gained a foothold in Asia Minor and North Africa. By the middle of the third century B.C., there was a distinct need for a Greek translation of the Holy Scriptures because many Egyptian Jews who remained loyal to their ancient faith had adopted the Greek tongue.

The circumstances surrounding the Greek translation have been subject to controversy. An old tradition holds that Ptolemy Philadelphus (who reigned 285-246 B.C.) requested the high priest in Jerusalem to send him a group of scholars who would translate the Law into Greek for his library. The priest obliged and sent Ptolemy seventy-two scholars, who in exactly seventy-two days completed the translation of the Pentateuch. Another version of this story tells that the seventy-two scholars broke up into pairs, that each pair, working separately, translated the whole Law, and that, after the work had been completed, the thirty-six copies were found to be identical! To some scholars it seems more likely that, in contrast to these legends, the Jews in Alexandria were themselves responsible for having the translation made in order to serve those who knew Greek better than Hebrew. The name *Septuagint* (frequently abbreviated as *LXX*), which is applied to this Greek version of the Old Testament, is derived from the Latin word for *seventy,* and it is generally supposed that it refers to the number of translators. Another conjecture is that the name was used for this translation because there were seventy members of the Alexandrian Sanhedrin (Jewish council and tribunal).

Although the facts about the translating are unknown, most scholars agree that the Pentateuch was rendered into Greek in Alexandria about the middle of the third century B.C. The remaining parts of the Old Testament were translated by different scholars at various times during the next century and a half; it is thought that the whole was probably completed about 100 B.C. Naturally enough, the quality of the different books is uneven. Some of the books are quite literally rendered, others freely. Some of the translators took great liberties with the Hebrew text, changing, omitting, or inserting words or phrases as they thought best. It is almost certain that some of the scholars had sources which are not available to us today.

Abandoning in part the traditional Hebrew order and adding the books which now constitute the Protestant Apocrypha, the Septuagint helped establish the order of the books followed in general by most Christian Bibles before the Reformation.

The Greek manuscripts are of two types: uncials and cursives. An *uncial* (from Latin *uncialis,* meaning "an inch high") is written in large, separate letters; a *cursive* is written in a smaller, "running" hand, as the name implies. Most of the uncials, about thirty of which survive, date from the third to the tenth century A.D. The cursives are generally later—from the ninth to the sixteenth century—but some are much older (a few fragments are perhaps from the second century B.C.). More than fifteen hundred cursive manuscripts are known to exist.

The most important uncial manuscripts are the *Codex° Vaticanus* (B), A.D. 300-350; the *Codex Sinaiticus* (S), *c.* A.D. 350; the *Codex Alexandrinus* (A) *c.* A.D. 400-450); and the *Codex Ephraemi* (C), *c.* A.D. 400-500.

The Septuagint was the version of the Old Testament known to the early Christians, who quoted from it to prove that Jesus had fulfilled the old prophecies and was therefore the promised Messiah. So persuasive were their arguments that eventually many of the Hebrews who adhered to Judaism began to consider the

° A *codex* is a book made up of manuscript pages bound together in a way similar to that in use today—as distinguished from a "roll" or "scroll."

Septuagint a Christian Bible and to lose faith in it as a trust-worthy rendering of their ancient Hebrew Scriptures. Conse-quently several "rival" translations appeared in the early Chris-tian centuries.

The great age of our extant copies of the Septuagint and the early dates of its rivals and revisions virtually require all serious students of the Bible to study it.

The Latin Old Testament ("Old Latin" Versions* and the Vulgate). It appears that both Hebrews and Christians felt a need for a Latin version of the Holy Scriptures and that by A.D. 200 the whole of the Old Testament had been translated piece-meal into that language.

Equal in importance to the Septuagint was the Latin transla-tion of the Old Testament made by St. Jerome (Eusebius Hier-onymus, *c.* 340-420), who revised the Old Latin Scriptures on the basis of the Hebrew and Greek texts. He did not attempt a strictly word-for-word translation, but preferred to employ idio-matic language. His free translation, which was very graceful and readable, came to be called the Vulgate, or "People's" version. (A revision of his text was made by the English scholar Alcuin in the eighth century as directed by Charlemagne.)

The Vulgate did not immediately supplant the Old Latin ver-sions; and, indeed, it met with much opposition on the part of conservatives who clung to the earlier and more traditional ver-sions. By the seventh century, however, the Vulgate and the Old Latin versions were used about equally, and the Vulgate there-after steadily gained in popularity. During the remainder of the Middle Ages the latter was *the* version for the Western Christian nations and still is, for the Roman Catholic Church, the authori-tative standard for use in liturgy, pulpit, and theological dis-cussions.

Syriac and Aramaic Versions (Peshitta and Targums). The He-brew, Greek, and Latin versions of the Old Testament are, of course, by far the most important ones. Nevertheless, there are many others—some of great antiquity—which scholars have found to be helpful in their attempts to determine the "original" reading of many passages. Two of the most significant of these ver-sions are the *Peshitta* (or *Peshitto*) and the *Targums.* The Pe-shitta is the Syriac (or East Aramaic) version of the Old Testa-

---

* A term applied to pre-Vulgate versions of the Bible.

ment, which is helpful to Biblical scholars because it is an early, independent translation from the Hebrew (one extant manuscript of part of the Pentateuch dates from the fifth century A.D., and a manuscript of the whole of the Old Testament, from the sixth century). The value of the Peshitta as an independent text is reduced by the fact that some of its revisions were made to agree with Septuagintal readings. The Targums are Aramaic translations of the Hebrew text, plus a large amount of paraphrase and explanatory matter. Originally used in synagogues in Aramaic lands, the Targums were for a long time transmitted orally. The first mention of written Targums belongs to the first century A.D., although it is possible that some were put into writing before the Christian era. Most of the extant Targums are from the fifth century A.D. or later. They are of minor importance in textual criticism, but they throw a considerable amount of light on ancient Hebrew tradition and exegesis.

The Apocrypha. The term *Apocrypha** is now generally employed to designate fourteen or fifteen books which were included in the Septuagint or the Vulgate but which were not considered by the Palestinian Jews to have been genuinely inspired and which were not then extant in the original Hebrew. The Apocryphal books are as follows: Tobit, Judith, The Rest of Esther, The Wisdom of Solomon, Ecclesiasticus (the Wisdom of Jesus, son of Sirach), Baruch (with the Epistle of Jeremiah, sometimes printed as a separate book), The Song of the Three Holy Children, Susanna and the Elders, Bel and the Dragon, I and II Maccabees, I and II Esdras, and The Prayer of Manasses.

The early Christians considered all the books of the Septuagint as more or less canonical. When preparing the Vulgate, St. Jerome returned to the Hebrew text as his guide; he included all the Septuagintal books, but labeled those not in the Hebrew

---

* A plural derived from Greek *apokryphos,* meaning "hidden" or "supplementary" or "spurious." In addition to these books attached to the Old Testament, there are many others (termed *Pseudepigrapha,* meaning "falsely inscribed") which were usually ascribed to well-known Jewish authors. They were written between 200 B.C. and A.D. 200 in Hebrew, Aramaic, or Greek; and they include a variety of genres: legends, psalms, gospels, apocalypses, history, and popular philosophy. See Robert H. Pfeiffer, "The Literature and Religion of the Pseudepigrapha," *The Interpreter's Bible,* I, 421-436.

canon as Apocryphal); and he added three more (also listed as Apocryphal) and placed them after the book of Revelation in the New Testament); these three were The Prayer of Manasses and III and IV Esdras.*

During the Reformation the Protestant churches adopted as canonical only those books which had been in the Hebrew canon. The Roman Catholic Church, on the contrary, accepted as canonical all the books in the Septuagint except III and IV Maccabees, and it rejected St. Jerome's Prayer of Manasses and III and IV Esdras. The Church of England accepted fourteen books of the Protestant Apocrypha for purposes of edification rather than "for the establishment of doctrine." In the Coverdale Bible (1535) and in the King James version (1611) these books were separated from the canonical ones and placed between the Old Testament and the New Testament. From a literary point of view it is regrettable that these books have been omitted from most contemporary Protestant Bibles.

The New Testament. The history of the writing and transmission of the New Testament is far simpler than that of the Old Testament. The languages in which it was first written are less confusing than the ancient Hebrew; the dates of composition, collection, and canonization have been approximated; and the extant manuscripts are closer in time to the dates of their original composition than are those of the Old Testament. Many grammatical constructions and idioms in certain portions (Gospels and Acts) may indicate a possible Aramaic version, but no such

---

* The Protestant Bible divides the single book Ezra of the old Hebrew canon into two books, Ezra and Nehemiah.

The Septuagint Bible made up the book Esdras by reworking the Hebrew book Ezra and adding part of what is now II Chronicles in the Protestant Bible. It also repeated the same Hebrew book Ezra as II Esdras.

The Vulgate Bible added a legend in Josephus to the Septuagintal I Esdras to constitute the book III Esdras. The Vulgate IV Esdras (called II Esdras in the King James Version) is an apocalyptic book; it is called III Esdras when Ezra and Nehemiah are combined in one book. Thus, in the Protestant Apocrypha, I Esdras is approximately the same as the Septuagintal I Esdras, while II Esdras is approximately the same as the Vulgate IV Esdras.

The Roman Catholic (Douay) version includes I and II Esdras as canonical books corresponding, respectively, to the Protestant Ezra and Nehemiah.

version has been discovered, and Biblical scholars now treat the
Greek text as if it were the original. The various epistles and the
book of Revelation were almost certainly written first in Greek.
All the canonical books of the New Testament were probably
written within a century following the death of Jesus—most of
them between A.D. 64 and 105. There are several thousand known
manuscripts of the Greek New Testament. The Latin-speaking
Christians possessed translations from the Greek Scriptures as
early as the second century—perhaps during the first. About fifty
Old Latin manuscripts survive. Much of what has been said
above about the Latin Old Testament is applicable also to the
Latin New Testament.

THE ENGLISH BIBLE BEFORE 1611

There has never been—and there probably never will be—a
really definitive English translation of the Bible, for new translations will be needed as long as archaeological, linguistic, and
historical discoveries continue to throw new light on the Scriptures. This point has been strikingly illustrated during recent
years as the study of the Dead Sea Scrolls has suggested some
new conjectures and interpretations subsequent to publication
(1946, 1952) of the superb Revised Standard Version.

During the past five centuries dozens of English translations
have been made. Some of these, though of great historical and
scholarly significance, are no longer in common use and therefore are of relatively minor concern to the student of the Bible as
literature. Several modern versions have considerable literary
interest and value, however—some because they are eloquent and
poetic, others because they are literal.

The Bible entered England at the end of the sixth century
A.D. In 597 the monk Augustine came to that island as a Christian
missionary, bringing with him from Rome nine books (all in
Latin, of course): a two-volume copy of the Bible, two Psalters,
two copies of the Gospels, and three other religious books.[3]
These were England's first library.

Knowledge of Biblical subject matter was spread orally, and
within less than a century vernacular works on Biblical themes
were appearing. Then came translations in Old and Middle Eng-

lish, leading in the sixteenth century to various Protestant Bibles and an official Roman Catholic Bible.

Old and Middle English Paraphrases and Translations (*c.* 670-1380). Many paraphrases, interlinear glosses, and translations of parts of the Latin Bible appeared between 670 and 1380. The majority of these were intended for use by the clergy, only a few being for popular reading. The Psalms and the Gospels were the favorite books.

Wyclifite Bibles (*c.* 1380-82). Near the end of the fourteenth century John Wyclif (*c.* 1320-84) and his assistants produced *the first complete Bible in English.* It is not known how much of the translation Wyclif himself did, but he·was the inspirational force behind the project; it is believed that Nicholas of Hereford, one of his followers, translated most of the Old Testament. The New Testament was finished about 1380; the Old Testament, about 1382. This "Wyclif-Hereford" version was a translation of the Vulgate. Even in its own day it was not an entirely satisfactory translation; it followed slavishly the word order of St. Jerome's Latin, and the style was often stilted and somewhat crude. A revision, completed before the end of the century and attributed to one John Purvey, attempted successfully to establish a more authentic text and to make the language more up-to-date and idiomatic. The "Lollards," as Wyclif's disciples were called, must have produced astounding numbers of manuscript copies, for more than 170 have survived to the present day.

The Tyndale Bible (*c.* 1525-34). During the third and fourth decades of the sixteenth century William Tyndale (*c.* 1492-1536), using the best available Hebrew, Greek, and Latin texts, produced an English version of the New Testament, of the Old Testament from Genesis through Chronicles, of Jonah, and of parts of the Apocrypha. The English-speaking world is indebted to Tyndale for several contributions: (1) *his New Testament was the first part of the Bible to be printed in English* (1525 or 1526); (2) *he was the first to attempt a genuinely scholarly translation of the Bible from its original languages into English;* and (3) because of its influence on later translators, *his work can be considered a landmark in the development of English prose style.* (His revised New Testament of 1534 has been the basis for subsequent versions down to our own times.)

The Versions of George Joye (1530–c. 1535). George Joye, at one time an associate of Tyndale, gave us the first printed English versions of the Psalms (1530, revised 1534), Isaiah (1531), Jeremiah and Lamentations (1534), and perhaps Proverbs and Ecclesiastes (c. 1535). Although much of his translation was very free and some of his diction infelicitous, his work appreciably influenced later translations.

The Coverdale Bible (1535). In 1535 Miles Coverdale (1488?–1569) produced *the first complete Bible printed in English*. More an editor than an original translator, Coverdale made no attempt to find the earliest and most "authentic" texts; but he did gather the best sources with which he himself could deal competently, and he tried to harmonize them. The English-speaking world owes him a debt of gratitude for (1) numerous beautiful and felicitous phrases, copied and preserved in later translations, and (2) the first printed version of the English Apocrypha as a whole and a large portion of the Old Testament—Esther, Job, and all the prophets from Ezekiel through Malachi.

The Matthew Bible (1537). A version of the Scriptures now known as the "Matthew Bible" appeared in 1537. Its title-page describes it as a new translation by one Thomas Matthew; actually it is a compilation (chiefly of Tyndale and Coverdale texts), and the compiler is believed to have been John Rogers, a Protestant who for political reasons wished to keep his name secret. Its only important contribution was the printing of the hitherto-unpublished translation of the so-called "historical" books (Joshua through II Chronicles) attributed to Tyndale.

The Taverner Bible (1539). In 1539 Richard Taverner revised the Matthew Bible, making a considerable number of verbal changes based on his expert knowledge of Greek. This version was of relatively small importance, but occasionally it hit upon a fortunate phrase preserved in later Bibles.

The Great Bible (1539-41). As late as 1539 no Bible had been royally authorized in England. Now, Thomas Cromwell, Henry VIII's most influential minister, and Thomas Cranmer, Archbishop of Canterbury, desired an English translation which the whole nation would find acceptable. Cromwell chose Coverdale to supervise the project. The first edition came from the press in 1539. The format of the first printing was a large folio; hence the name "the Great Bible" was given to the version. A second printing appeared in the following year. These two issues of the first edition are sometimes called "Cromwell's Bible." To the second through the fifth editions (1540-41) was added a long preface by Archbishop Cranmer. All these editions are referred to as "Cranmer's Bible."

Although Coverdale made some use of Hebrew, Latin, and Greek texts, this version was essentially a revision of the Matthew Bible supplemented by portions of the Old Testament (e.g., Ezekiel through Malachi) and of the Apocrypha based on Coverdale's 1535 version.

An injunction by Cromwell and subsequent injunctions by Henry VIII firmly established the Great Bible over a long period as *the* Bible for English-speaking people. The Psalter for the Anglican Book of Common Prayer was adopted from the Great Bible and still remains in use with little alteration.

The Geneva Bible (1557, 1560). Mary Tudor's persecution of Protestants caused many to flee to the Continent. Some, along with other political and religious refugees from all over Europe, sought haven in Geneva, Switzerland. One group, including John Calvin, John Knox, Miles Coverdale, and Theodore Beza (the foremost Biblical scholar of the time) undertook a new English translation of the Bible. In 1557 they published at Geneva their version of the New Testament; the whole Bible, exclusive of the Apocrypha, appeared three years later.

The Geneva Bible was a thorough revision based on the Great Bible version of the Old Testament and on a 1552 edition of Tyndale's New Testament. The translators (or revisers) also used various Greek and Latin texts.

The Geneva Bible introduced many innovations. It was the first English Bible: (1) to be printed in roman instead of black-letter type; (2) to divide the text into verses;* (3) to use italic print for words which were not in the original languages but which the translators felt needed to be added for the sake of clarity. It was printed in quarto form, and so because of its relatively small size and its legibility it was far more convenient than the black-letter folio of the Great Bible. It contained a preface by Calvin and marginal notes of distinctly Calvinistic

* For the division of the Bible into chapters, we are indebted to the *Sacrorum Bibliorum Concordantiae* of Cardinal Hugo of Saneto Caro (*c.* 1200-1263).

and Puritan bias. Furthermore, it provided tables, maps, wood-cuts, chapter summaries, running titles, and (after 1579) a Calvinistic catechism.[4]

The translation itself was the best that had been made up to that time. In the first place, the scholarship which produced it was more thorough than that behind any previous edition. The translators aimed at such a literal rendering that they felt it necessary to apologize (in the preface) for the preservation of the "Ebrewe phrases" that might sound harsh to readers familiar with other versions. It is true that this striving for accuracy sometimes made the diction bare and unpoetic, but most of it was lofty and forceful, and its simplicity appealed to the average reader. Innumerable passages were taken over word for word by the King James translators.

Despite its dedication to Queen Elizabeth, the Geneva Bible never became the official or authorized version for the English Church; the Calvinistic notes probably prevented its adoption. But it became so popular that at least 140 editions were published between 1560 and 1644, and before 1611 (date of publication of the King James Bible) it was probably read by more people than any other English version. Although it has been called "the Bible of Shakespeare, of John Bunyan, of Cromwell's army, of the Puritan pilgrims, and of King James himself," [5] there is some doubt about which version of the Bible Shakespeare and Bunyan used.

The Bishops' Bible (1568). Royal and ecclesiastical disapproval of the Calvinistic tendencies of the Geneva Bible led to the decision that another English version was needed. In 1566 Matthew Parker, Archbishop of Canterbury, was chosen as editor-in-chief. He divided the actual task of revision and annotation among a group of bishops and other church scholars. Some of these did little more than copy out the text of the Great Bible; some tried to blend the Geneva and the Great Bible texts; still others made sweeping changes of their own. The result was a Bible sadly lacking in uniformity. The book of Psalms was so bad that in the fourth and all later editions (except one of 1585) the version found in the Great Bible was substituted.

Inferior though it was, the Bishops' Bible, by order of the Archbishop, supplanted the Great Bible—at least in church services. Only one edition of the latter was published (1569) after Parker's Bible appeared. Outside the Church the Bishops' Bible was never so popular as the Geneva Bible, but the demand was sufficiently great to warrant the publication of twenty editions, the last appearing in 1606.

In only a few instances did the King James Version follow the Bishops' Bible.

The Rheims-Douay Bible (1582-1609). Just as the Protestants fled from England during the reign of Queen Mary, so the Catholics exiled themselves to escape persecution by Queen Elizabeth. Many Catholic exiles settled at Douai in Flanders, some of them moving later to Rheims. A group of them, under the leadership of Gregory Martin, undertook to produce an English version of the Bible which would be acceptable to Romanists. The New Testament was published at Rheims in 1582 and hence is known as the "Rheims New Testament"; subsequently it became part of the so-called "Douay Bible." It was not till 1609-10 that the Old Testament translation was published at Douai.

The title page stated that the translation was made from the "authentical Latin"—that is, from the Vulgate—and that editions in Greek and "other" languages were consulted.

The Douai translators, fearing that they might change the sense of the "divinely inspired" Vulgate version, tried to translate the Latin as literally as possible and therefore did not achieve the eloquence later to be found in the freer and more idiomatic King James Version; it should be remembered, however, that for scholarly purposes, there is still a good deal of value in literal translations.

The Rheims-Douay Bible is significant (1) because it is the basis of modern Roman Catholic English Bibles (see p. 37, below) and (2) because it exerted an appreciable influence on the diction of the King James Version.[6]

MODERN VERSIONS OF THE ENGLISH BIBLE

There are several versions of the Bible now in use in the churches and the homes of English-speaking people all over the world. Each has its own particular merits and shortcomings; all are worthy of the respect and attention of students of literature.

Some adhere rather closely to certain traditions; others are more willing to accept and incorporate the conclusions of the "higher criticism" and of modern science. Some are fairly literal renderings of ancient manuscripts; others are comparatively free translations. Some are valued for their eloquence, others for their simplicity and clarity. Some retain the centuries-old tradition of printing all the Bible as prose and observing merely the chapter-and-verse conventions within each book; others attempt to appeal to the modern reader by dividing prose passages into logical paragraphs and by printing poetry *as* poetry—that is, by preserving the integrity of each line of verse and beginning each line with a capital letter. The table on pages 38-39 may prove useful for comparison of seven versions most widely used today.

The King James Bible (1611). When James I acceded to the throne in 1603, there were three Bibles in use in England: the Bishops' Bible, which was used in most churches; the Great Bible, which was still used in some rural churches; and the Geneva Bible, which was found in many homes. None of these was entirely satisfactory. The Bishops' Bible was an uneven production which had never pleased either scholars or the people in general; the Great Bible was cumbersome and hard to read; and the Geneva Bible smacked of Puritanism.

Aware of the widespread use of all three versions, King James felt that one official version would not only help bind his nation together and lessen theological disputes, but also be a credit to his regime. In 1604 he appointed fifty-four * learned men to make a new translation. Apparently they were selected solely on their merits as Biblical scholars and not on the basis of their religious leanings, for some were Anglican churchmen, some were Puritans, and some were laymen. They were divided into six groups—two each at Oxford, Cambridge, and Westminster. Each group revised a specific portion of the Scriptures; their revision was finally edited by a committee of six. The new version was completed in 1610 and published in 1611.

The first King James Bible was a folio volume, printed in black-letter type; roman type was used for words supplied by the

* The extant list contains only the names of the forty-seven men who actually served.

revisers but not in the original Hebrew, Aramaic, or Greek.* The Apocrypha was placed between the two Testaments. Included were a preface, a table of contents, an almanac, various tables, and (in some copies) a map of Canaan and a genealogical chart. At the beginning of each chapter there was a summary of its contents.

This version was as accurate a translation as early seventeenth-century scholarship could achieve. The scholars appointed by the king made a conscientious effort to avail themselves of the most trustworthy texts and commentaries—"Chaldee, Hebrewe, Syrian, Greeke . . . , Latin, Spanish, French, Italian . . . [and] Dutch." Apparently they made use, too, of all the previously printed English versions. Except in interpolated chapter synopses, they tried not to go counter to their sources or beyond them. If they were obliged for the sake of clarity to supply English words, they indicated this typographically (by roman type, as mentioned above). It must be remembered, however, that compared with twentieth-century scholars who have access to numerous manuscript sources and photostats and who know more about ancient history, ancient linguistics, and ancient prosody, the King James translators were at a great disadvantage.

They were not only conscientious scholars but also excellent literary stylists. They were fortunate in that the English language during Jacobean times was perhaps closer to the Hebrew and Greek than it has been since. The translators did an almost miraculous job of choosing effective wording, whether derived from an earlier English version or originated by the King James scholars themselves.[7] They deliberately used various synonyms for the translation of a single Hebrew or Greek word for the sake of variety and richness. An amazing merit of the 1611 Bible is the uniformity of diction and style. Its homogeneity and evenness make it impossible for a reader without inside information to ascertain where one scholar or company of scholars began or left off. The genius with which they made use of their materials has been the subject of many articles and whole books. Perhaps it is sufficient to say here that—despite the passage of centuries

* Modern editions (1) are printed in roman type, with the revisers' interpolations in italics, and (2) have been modernized in spelling and given minor revisions.

and the publication of such modern Bibles as the Smith-Good-speed translation and the Revised Standard Version—the King James Bible, judged merely as a piece of literature, is still considered by many to be the finest English version of the Scriptures.*

For the modern student the principal shortcomings of the King James Bible are (1) occasional inaccuracy of translation, (2) obscurity resulting from the use of words which are now archaic or obsolete, and (3) failure to distinguish typographically between poetry and prose.[8] Anyone who wishes to understand the King James Version thoroughly needs to read a modern-speech translation concurrently and to consult a commentary.

Modern Roman Catholic Bibles. In 1750 and again in 1763 Bishop Richard Challoner of London and Francis Blyth—both converts to Catholicism—made a major revision of the Rheims-Douay Old Testament. (Challoner completed several revisions of the Rheims-Douay New Testament, the last in 1772). Influenced considerably by the King James Bible, Challoner greatly improved the syntax and diction of the 1609 Catholic version, especially by weeding out many archaisms and Latinistic constructions. The Challoner text (though subsequently revised several times) remained "the standard English Catholic Bible."[9] A modern Catholic translation has been prepared by The Episcopal Committee of the Confraternity of Christian Doctrine. The New Testament appeared in 1941 and portions of the Old Testament in 1952, 1955, and 1961; some of the remaining books of the Old Testament are still in preparation.

There are two other notable Catholic versions of the twentieth century: (1) the Westminster Bible, edited by Cuthbert Lattey and Joseph Keating, an independent translation from the Hebrew and Greek, published piecemeal between 1913 and 1935 and in a single-volume edition in 1948; (2) the Knox Bible, translated by Ronald A. Knox, not a revision of the Challoner text,

---

* This Outline will use the King James Version as a basis for discussion and for all references and quotations unless some other version is specified.

Although called the "Authorized Version," the King James Bible was never officially "authorized" by either king or Parliament. The king's appointment of the fifty-four scholars was the only authorization that took place.

COMPARISON OF MODERN BIBLES

Characteristics	King James	Modern Douay (1950)	English Revised and American Standard
Tradition Followed	Follows Tyndale tradition. Borrows from most of the other 16th-century Bibles.	Faithful to Roman Catholic tradition. Follows Douay version of 1750, which is a revision of the Rheims-Douay Bible of 1582-1609.	Faithful to English and American Protestant tradition. Uses King James Version as basis, but adopts many conclusions of "higher criticism" and of science.
Literalness of Translation	Fairly free translation.	Literal, conservative translation of Vulgate.	Idiomatic, but very literal translation.
Style and Diction	Eloquent, colorful, fluent. Some of Jacobean diction now obsolete.	Latinistic, but limited modernization of diction.	Simple, and clear. Some of diction is modernized, but many archaic forms retained. English Revised Version employs British locutions; American Standard, American locutions.
Mechanics, Spelling, and Punctuation	Uses traditional chapter-and-verse divisions only.	Psalms (Confraternity text) indicates poetry typographically; other books use only chapter-and-verse divisions, with no attempt at paragraphing and no distinction between prose and verse.	Chapter-and-verse markings retained, but prose is divided into paragraphs. Some (but not all) poetry indicated typographically.

COMPARISON OF MODERN BIBLES (CONT.)

Moffatt	Hebrew (1917)	Smith-Goodspeed	Revised Standard
Abandons King James tradition.	Adheres to Masoretic tradition.	Abandons most church traditions; utilizes all available data from science and "higher criticism."	Follows King James tradition, but makes many changes on basis of 20th-century discoveries in archaeology, linguistics, etc.
Exceptionally free translation—sometimes almost a paraphrase.	Fairly free translation of Masoretic text.	Fairly free.	Idiomatic but literal translation.
Simple, conversational. Modernized diction; uses *thou, thy,* etc., only for Deity.	Eloquent, fluent. Adopts many of King James readings, but modernizes some of diction. Retains *thou* forms.	Aims at simplicity and current American usage. Modernizes verb endings, uses *thou* forms only for Deity.	Retains some of King James eloquence, but simplifies and modernizes the diction. Modernizes verb endings; uses *thou* forms only for Deity.
Chapter-and-verse markings retained. Modernizes spelling, punctuation, and mechanics. Prose divided into paragraphs. Poetry indicated typographically.	Retains chapter-and-verse markings. Indicates poetry typographically. Divides prose into paragraphs.	Places chapter-and-verse markings in margin. Indicates poetry typographically. Divides prose into paragraphs.	Retains chapter-and-verse markings. Indicates poetry typographically. Divides prose into paragraphs. Places variant or rejected passages in footnotes.

but a *new* translation of the Vulgate, with cognizance being taken of Hebrew and Greek sources (the New Testament appeared in 1944, part of the Old Testament in 1948, and the remainder in 1950).

The Revised Version and the American Standard Version (1881-1901). The King James Bible was so generally acceptable that no Protestant ecclesiastical body made any official attempt to bring about a major revision till late in the nineteenth century. By that time many archaeological and linguistic discoveries and many changes in the English language since 1611 warranted a new revision. In 1870, at the invitation of the Convocation of the Anglican Church, fifty-two British scholars undertook the task. The New Testament was published in 1881, the Old and New Testament in one volume in 1885, and the Apocrypha separately in 1895. This was called the Revised Version or the English Revised Version.

Although the revisers adopted many conclusions of contemporary scientists and of the "higher critics," they were faithful to English Protestant tradition, and they endeavored to alter the King James text *only* when "faithfulness" to the best obtainable source material so dictated. They modernized punctuation and mechanics; they relegated chapter-and-verse numerals to the margins; they distinguished some (but not all) of the poetical passages from prose typographically; and they indicated the logical divisions of prose passages by paragraphing. They tried to give idiomatic expression to a literal rendering of their sources. They aimed rather at accuracy, simplicity, and clarity than at eloquence and magnificence. Unlike the King James translators, they strove for consistency in the translation of each Hebrew and Greek word. They modernized some of the Jacobean diction of the King James Version, but retained such archaisms as the *-eth* and *-edst* forms of verbs (*thirsteth, walkedst*) and the "familiar" second-person-singular pronouns *thee, thou, thy, thine.*

A group of thirty American Biblical scholars was invited to co-operate with the British revisers. It was agreed that the American company would send its suggestions to the British committee before final decisions were made, and the English revisers were to adopt whatever suggestions they thought wise and to include all others in an appendix. The American group agreed not to give their support to the publication of any other edition for fourteen years after the appearance of the English Revised Version.

The inclusion of many antiquated words (such as *holpen* for *helped*) and a number of others which passed currency in Great Britain but not in the United States (such as *corn* for *grain*) induced the American company to bring out its own edition in 1901. This edition contained an appendix listing the readings of the English Revised Version which the American scholars had rejected.* The title page of the American volume was the same as that for the British except that there was added: "Newly Edited by the American Revision Committee. A.D. 1901. Standard Edition." Hence it has come to be called the "American Standard Version."

Moffatt's Translation (1913, 1924). James Moffatt published a modern-speech translation of the New Testament in 1913 and of the Old Testament in 1924; both Testaments were published together in one volume in 1926. Believing the Hebrew text to be "often desperately corrupt," he undertook to correct it by (1) amending phrases which he found "broken or defective," (2) shifting "phrases . . . , verses, and sometimes . . . entire sections," and (3) inserting words or phrases he regarded as necessary.[10] This version is not merely a revision but a completely new translation—a translation so free and in such modern, colloquial language that I. M. Price has called it "often a paraphrase rather than a translation" and "Moffatt's running commentary on the whole Bible." [11] It uses the *thou* forms of the pronoun only in reference to the Deity; it abandons the archaic verb forms; it indicates poetic passages typographically; and it divides prose into logical paragraphs—retaining, however, the traditional chapter-and-verse numerals. Though an exceptionally free translation, it is an interesting and enlightening version.

The Hebrew Scriptures (1917). A number of times during the last two centuries, Jewish scholars have revised their English translation of the Holy Scriptures.[12] The most noteworthy version is one published in 1917 by the Jewish Publication Society of America. The revisers spent some twenty-five years consulting not only the Masoretic text, on which the revision is based, but

---

* Many critics have considered one change made by the Americans to be especially undesirable: the rendering of the Hebrew *YHVH* as "Jehovah" instead of "the Lord."

also many other significant ancient versions (Septuagint, Vulgate, Targums, Peshitta, and others) and all existing English Bibles.[13] In style and diction it is similar to the King James Version; it employs the archaic verb endings and "familiar" pronominal forms. It distinguishes typographically between poetry and prose. This version of the Hebrew Scriptures was reprinted, with minor revisions, in 1955. (A new translation of the Pentateuch, introducing modern interpretations of the original Hebrew was published by the Jewish Publication Society in 1963.)

The Smith-Goodspeed Translation, The "Chicago Bible" (1923-39). A valuable and attractive translation of the Bible was made during the third and fourth decades of this century. In 1923 E. J. Goodspeed brought out his version of the New Testament. Four years later J. M. P. Smith, A. R. Gordon, T. J. Meek, and Leroy Waterman published their translation of the Old Testament. In 1931 the Old Testament of Smith *et al.* and the New Testament of Goodspeed were combined in a single volume, entitled *The Bible—An American Translation.* In 1938 Goodspeed translated and published the Apocrypha, and in 1939 this was included with the two Testaments in *The Complete Bible: An American Translation.* This and the 1931 edition are often called the "Chicago Bible."

This was a fairly free translation which modernized and Americanized the diction. The term "the Lord" was used in place of "Jehovah" (which was used in the American Standard Version); the forms *thou, thee,* etc., were used only in reference to the Deity; and special typographical means were used to distinguish verse from prose.

The Revised Standard Version (1946-57). A period of forty-five years elapsed between the appearance of the American Standard Version and that of the next "authorized" version of the Bible. During that time many ancient papyri in the Greek dialect *Koiné* had been discovered, and much progress had been made in understanding Biblical Greek. Furthermore, the modern-speech versions (such as the Smith-Goodspeed) and the free translations (such as that of Moffatt) had called much popular attention to the infelicities in the diction of the Revised and the American Standard versions.

In 1929 the International Council of Religious Education, representing forty Protestant denominations in the United States and

Canada, set in motion the machinery for the preparation of a new revision. Thirty-two scholars participated. The New Testament was finished first and published separately in 1946. The Old Testament was completed in 1951, and both Testaments were published in a single volume in 1952. The Revised Standard Version of the Apocrypha was published in 1957.

Using the American Standard Version as their point of departure, the revisers consulted all the best obtainable sources. The diction was brought up to date. The -eth and -edst forms of the verbs were abandoned; and *thou, thee, thy,* and *thine* were used only to refer to God. *Jehovah* was dropped as the name for the Deity—or, as the revisers expressed it, "the committee agreed immediately and unanimously to 'return unto the Lord.'" [14] Archaic words and idioms were modernized. For example, where the King James Bible says that Joseph "was minded to put her [Mary] away privily," the Revised Standard Version says that he "resolved to divorce her quietly."

Virtually all Protestant scholars agree that this Bible is the most nearly accurate translation ever made. Although some readers have objected to its changing of the wording (and often the sense) of many a time-honored passage, the high degree of accuracy in the Revised Standard rendering commends itself to modern scholarship. Furthermore, this version clarifies many passages which no other English version has ever made clear. Though inferior to the King James Bible in beauty of expression and magnificence of language, the Revised Standard Version is invaluable as a much more accurate rendering of the Scriptures.

Although the traditional chapter-and-verse divisions are retained, prose passages are divided into paragraphs as determined by the sense of the passage. Quotation marks appear wherever modern usage dictates. Footnotes (citing parallel passages, giving variant readings, or calling attention to some emendation or to some uncertainty of translation) are placed at the bottom of the page. The summary of each chapter, found in the King James Version, is omitted, but a very brief indication of the contents of each page is found at the top of the page. A typographical distinction is made between poetry and prose.

In 1966 a Catholic edition of the Revised Standard Version, prepared by the Catholic Biblical Association of Great Britain, was published. It includes some notes for Catholic readers but is essentially the same as the Protestant edition and is regarded as a landmark in the ecumenical movement.

The New English Bible (1961, 1970). In 1947 the Church of Scotland, the Church of England, and various Free Churches of England organized a committee to arrange for a new translation of the Bible in the light of all the known facts concerning the linguistic and historical development of Biblical literature. Three groups of translators (one group each for the Old Testament, the Apocrypha, and the New Testament) collaborated in the work; a fourth group provided guidance concerning literary style and linguistic problems. The principal aim was that of reproducing clearly the meaning and general effect of the Biblical passages by means of modern, accurate, and dignified expression. The translation of the New Testament, completed and approved in 1960, was published in 1961 jointly by the Cambridge University Press and the Oxford University Press. The translations of the Old Testament and the Apocrypha were published in 1970. The modern tone of the text aroused some controversy. Favorable comment emphasized the simplicity and clarity of the translation; unfavorable comment deplored the loss of power and the lack of authoritative tone.

Part Two
History and Biography

The scope of Biblical history is very broad. The historical and biographical books of the Old Testament trace the history of the Hebrew people (with some gaps) from the creation of the world down through the rebuilding of Jerusalem after the return from the Babylonian Exile (*c.* 400 B.C.). Then after an interval of slightly more than two centuries, the story is resumed in the Apocryphal I and II Maccabees, which tell about the Hebrew rebellion (*c.* 167-134 B.C.) against Antiochus Epiphanes and his successors. Finally, the biographical and historical books of the New Testament relate the life of Jesus Christ and the history of the early church to about A.D. 65.

The various authors of this comprehensive history drew on many different sources. For information about the earliest centuries (before *c.* 1000 B.C.), the historiographers had to rely almost entirely on oral tradition—myths,* legends, accounts of famous battles, scraps of folksongs, and the like—all handed down by

* A *myth* is a traditional story about a god or demigod or about the origin of the world or of people and things on it; to the non-orthodox scholar, the myth has no factual basis. A *legend* is a tale about some national, racial, or tribal hero or event; generally it contains some basis in fact, but the events related are ordinarily exaggerated or falsely ascribed to the persons involved; often it is difficult to distinguish between the historical and the fictional elements in a legend. Both myths and legends fall under the general heading of *folklore*, which includes, in addition, folksongs, oracles, and folk riddles. The usual characteristics of folklore are anonymity, spontaneity, objectivity, evidence of communal interest, imagination, irony, and humor. (Summarized from Laura H. Wild, *A Literary Guide to the Bible.* New York: Harper and Brothers, 1922, pp. 22-32.)

45

word of mouth, perhaps for many generations. The oldest *written* records on which the Biblical historians depended were probably codes of laws, such as the original Mosaic form of the Ten Commandments. Near the beginning of the tenth century B.C., it is believed, a priest began writing down an account of current happenings at the court of King David, many of which the priest himself had witnessed; this practice apparently continued intermittently for several centuries. So..ie later works consisted of personal memoirs, such as those of Nehemiah. Considered all together, the historical and biographical books of the Bible show a fairly continuous evolution in the direction of accuracy and authenticity—an evolution from those books which depended upon tradition and legend, through those which relied upon law codes and court records, to those which to a large extent were made up of diaries and transcriptions of eyewitness accounts.

The student of the Bible should remember that the conception of history as a scientifically accurate record of events is a relatively modern idea. It simply never occurred to some of the ancient Jewish historians that it was incumbent upon them to investigate the reliability of their sources, to weed out all information that might be biased, and to distinguish between hearsay evidence and verifiable fact. Their primary concern was to present each religious truth as they saw it (often as miraculous truth governed by divine intervention) and to bring that truth home to the reader by any literary means that came to hand. They thought and wrote emotionally and figuratively. Hence some of their writings may contain more of *poetic* truth than statistical or historical evidence.

Most Biblical scholars today believe, for example, that Ruth and Esther are fictional narratives, each with a distinct purpose of its own. Some commentators have suggested that the accounts of Creation in Genesis are mythological and that Adam and Eve symbolize mankind and womankind but were never intended to be regarded as a particular man and a particular woman. A number of critics have held that the "tall tales" about Samson belong to the realm of legend rather than to the realm of history. Many scholars believe that some of the stories about such patriarchs as Reuben and Judah should be interpreted as referring not to the patriarchs themselves but to the *tribes* of which they were the progenitors. And, finally, nearly all students of the Bible recognize that the dates, the vital statistics, and the chronology of events as given in the Old Testament and the Apocrypha are often inconsistent from the modern point of view—or at least are often based on methods of calculating time which were probably quite different from our own.

Despite the presence of much nonhistorical matter, there is, of course, a great deal of real history to be found in the Bible. In fact, written records of neighboring lands, such as Egypt, Assyria, Greece, and Rome, and archaeological discoveries made in Palestine itself corroborate many of the accounts given by Biblical historians.

The Founding of the Hebrew Nation

The Hexateuch: Genesis through Joshua

A very ancient tradition, going back perhaps as far as the fifth century B.C.,[1] ascribed the composition of the first five Biblical books (the Pentateuch) to Moses; and a somewhat later tradition claimed the hero Joshua to be the author of the book which bears his name. Modern scholars believe that the Mosaic passages, having been transmitted as oral tradition, were repeatedly reinterpreted and supplemented until the composite work (the six books of the Hexateuch) was complete in its final form.

THE FIVE DOCUMENTS

Repetitions, inconsistencies, chronological difficulties, and differences in style within the long narrative indicate that the compilers of the Hexateuch were relying on more than one source.[2] Intensive scholarly investigation has led to the identification of five principal documents: J, E, D, H, P.

The J Document.* At some time between 950 and 850 B.C.[3] a scribe (or scribes) steeped in the tradition of the southern tribes (Judah and Benjamin) wrote a history of the Hebrews covering the period from Creation down to the last years of the reign of King David. This document emphasized (1) the peculiar relationship between God and the Israelites, his "Chosen People";

---

* So called because the document uses the Hebrew letters YHVH (the "Tetragrammaton") as the name of the Deity; German scholars used the letter J to represent the Hebrew letter yodh, the first of the four Hebrew letters. Some English renderings of the Tetragrammaton are Yahweh, Yahveh, and Jehovah (American Standard Version).

(2) the legends and traditions of the southern tribes; and (3) the importance of Hebron, David's first capital.[4] "J" (as both the document and its author are called) has a primitive and anthropomorphic conception of God, and he stresses the importance of sacrificial offerings. He is an excellent storyteller; his narratives move dramatically and swiftly, and they abound in graphic and concrete details. His material may be found in Genesis, Exodus, Leviticus, Numbers, Joshua, Judges, and (probably) I and II Samuel. Some specimens of his writing are The Story of Creation (as given in Gen. 2:4-26); The Tower of Babel Story (Gen. 11:1-9); and the Story of Abraham, Sarah, and Lot (Gen. 18–19).[5]

The E Document.* About 700 B.C.,[6] soon after the Assyrians had overwhelmed the Northern Kingdom (Israel), an author now designated "E" reworked the J Document and included a new set of traditions—those followed by a group from the north, whose center of worship was probably Shechem. E shows less anthropomorphism and more didacticism than J, and his history is more systematic, logical, refined, and elaborate than that of J. Material from the E Document may be found in Genesis, Exodus, Numbers, and Joshua, and perhaps in Judges, I and II Samuel, and I and II Kings. Some examples of E narrative are The Sacrifice of Isaac (Gen. 22:1-19), Moses in the Bulrushes (Ex. 2:1-10), and Moses and Jethro (Ex. 18).[7]

The D Document.† In 621 B.C., during the reign of Josiah, king of Judah, a book of law was found in the Temple at Jerusalem (II Kings 22:8). It is now believed that this book was partially or perhaps wholly identical with our book of Deuteronomy.[8] Its date has been placed at some time between 722 and 621 B.C. Its contents consist of rules for religious practices, and its emphasis is on the purification of worship by recognizing the Temple at Jerusalem as the only sanctuary of God. "D" (also known as "the Deuteronomist") has a lofty style. It is believed that he wrote not only all (or most) of Deuteronomy but also about half of Joshua.

The H Document.†† About 570 B.C. an unidentified scribe or priest compiled some rules for ethical and ceremonial guidance.

---

* So called because the author uses the word *Elohim* for the Deity.
† So called because it furnished the "Deuteronomic Code."
†† So called because it provides us with the "Holiness Code."

This document of rules, now known as the "Holiness Code," is approximately identical with Leviticus 17—26.

The P Document.* About 500 B.C., after the return from the Babylonian Exile, the priests at Jerusalem felt the need to consolidate and systematize Jewish religious law and history, to provide a unified constitution or manifesto for the restored Hebrew nation. They felt obligated to preserve the sacred material of the J, E, D, and H documents, but they rewrote some of it and added new portions of their own. They avoided anthropomorphisms and softened some passages they regarded as too harsh or otherwise objectionable. Their emphasis was on ritual and on instruction in the letter of the Law. They aimed at preciseness and accuracy, and they zealously recorded dates, measurements, catalogues, and genealogies. The style of the P Document is dry, formal, prosaic, and methodical, full of mannerisms and stereotyped phrases. There are, however, some lofty and magnificent passages—for example, the Story of Creation as found in the first chapter of Genesis. Material from this document appears in Genesis, Exodus, Leviticus, Numbers, and Joshua.[9]

About 350 B.C., or perhaps slightly earlier, the entire material of five documents was re-edited and put into approximately the form in which we have it today. Such was the development of the Hexateuch, "a work of such range and power as to seem to most people the supreme and characteristic creation of the Hebrew genius." [10]

GENESIS †

"In the beginning God created the heaven and the earth." Writers of classical Greek literature might have expressed this initial idea of Genesis as follows: "In the beginning there was only chaos, whence came Mother Earth, Love, and Night." Or one of the authors of a collection of great Germanic literature might have expressed the same idea this way: "Once there was only a bottomless pit, a world of mist, and a world of light." What a difference between those two sentences and the opening sentence of the Bible! The first four words of Genesis strike the keynote of the whole Bible: "In the beginning *God*. . . ." There-

---

* So called because it is the work of priests.

† The word *Genesis* is of Greek derivation and means "beginning."

after the priestly authors dramatically unroll the process of Creation: of light, of heaven, of the earth with its grass and herbs
and trees, of the seas, of the sun and the moon and stars, of
birds and fish and animals, and finally of man, the most wonderful of God's creatures. Light was created prior to the formation of the sun, moon, and stars. God created all in six days but
rested on the seventh, instituting the Sabbath. Simplicity and
brevity intensify the drama and impact of the story. The reader
feels that elaboration or explanation (attempted in some translations) inevitably weakens the force of the original.

Thus the book of Genesis starts with the origin of the universe; it continues the story to a point roughly estimated to be
about 1600 B.C.[11] The book falls logically into two parts: (1) accounts pertaining to the era from Creation to the advent of Abraham (1:1–11:9); and (2) stories of the patriarchs Abraham,
Isaac, Jacob, and Joseph (11:10–50:26).

The Mythological Cycle (1:1–11:9). A Biblical myth is an account of material phenomena to explain their divine origins and
development. In this sense, to the non-orthodox scholar the first
eleven chapters of Genesis are chiefly mythological. This portion
of the book answers the questions that primitive man everywhere
has always asked: Where did the earth and the planets come
from? How did man get here, what is his nature, and why does
he have so many troubles? How did different races and different
languages originate? In answering these questions, these eleven
chapters are concerned with mankind in general rather than with
only the Hebrews. Not till the introduction of Abraham at the
end of Chapter 11 does Genesis become specifically an account
of the Jewish people.

THE TWO ACCOUNTS OF CREATION (1:1–2:3 and 2:4-26). Two
distinct accounts of Creation are given in Genesis. The first (1:1
–2:3), from the P Document, is a very orderly story: on each of
the first six days God creates a different class of things; then on
the seventh he rests. As for the human race, we are told very
simply that "God created man in his own image, in the image of
God created he him; male and female created he them." The
author marvels at God's power and rejoices over the whole process: "And God saw that it was good." The second story (2:4-26),
from the J Document, is less elaborate (considered by some more
anthropomorphic) than the preceding one: there is no division

of the work into days, and of the creation of man we are told merely that the "Lord God formed man of the dust of the ground, and breathed into his nostrils the breath of life; and man became a living soul." It is to this second document, however, that we owe the story of the Garden of Eden (2:8-15), the name "Adam," and the account of the creation of Eve from Adam's rib. Monogamy is represented as God's law of marriage.

THE FALL OF MAN (Ch. 3). Adam has been forbidden to eat the fruit of only one tree in Eden, the Tree of Knowledge; if he eats its fruit, he shall "surely die." The serpent tempts Eve with the fruit, assuring her that she not only will continue to live but also will grow wiser, so that she will be "as gods, knowing good and evil." Eve eats some of the fruit and gives some to Adam. God declares the penalties to be imposed for this disobedience: for Eve, the pain of child-bearing and subservience to her husband; for Adam, a life of hard labor ending in death. Then God drives Adam and Eve from Eden back to the western land of their origin where they must till the soil in hardship to obtain sustenance. (The text [3:22] states another reason for the expulsion, namely, God's fear that Adam might eat the fruit of the Tree of Life and become divinely immortal.)

THE FIRST MURDER (4:1-15). The story of the first murder possibly is meant to illustrate a conflict between the two ancient occupations of farming and sheepherding. Cain and Abel, the sons of Adam and Eve, are respectively a farmer and a keeper of sheep. The sacrificial offering of the sinful Cain is rejected by God, whereas that of the good Abel is accepted. In jealous anger Cain waylays Abel in the field and slays him. Here the author gives a fine psychological portrait of the guilty Cain: "And the Lord said unto Cain, 'Where is Abel thy brother?' And he said, 'I know not: Am I my brother's keeper?'" Then the Lord states the penalty for the murder: the earth no longer responds to Cain's efforts to cultivate it, and he will live in exile as a permanent "vagabond in the earth." Sin follows the family history: thus, one of Cain's descendants practices polygamy contrary to lawful precedents (4:19).

STORIES ABOUT NOAH (Chs. 6–9). After some genealogies* of the generations from Adam to Noah come two stories about the

* One of the most famous of the people mentioned in the genealogies is Methuselah (5:21-22, 25-27), who is said to have lived 969 years. Popular

latter. The first, the famous story of the Flood, closely resembles
a Babylonian story, and there are more or less parallel accounts
in the mythologies of many races. Briefly summarized, the narrative in Genesis is as follows: When God perceives that mankind has become wicked, he decides to destroy all men except
the righteous Noah and his family. Obeying God's instructions,
Noah builds an ark and takes into it his family (including the
wives of his three sons) and a male and a female of each species
of created animals. Every other living thing is destroyed by rains
which last "forty * days and forty nights." At length a dove proves
that the flood is subsiding by finding and bringing back to the
ark a live olive twig. God sends a rainbow † as a sign of his
promise never to punish mankind with such a flood again. Noah's
three sons became the fathers of all mankind.

The second tale about Noah (9:20-27) was probably told to
justify the Hebrews' enslavement of the Canaanites: Ham, one
of Noah's sons and progenitor of the Canaanites, discovers his
father drunk and "uncovered within his tent." He tells his two
brothers, Shem and Japheth, about the spectacle; but they mod-
estly refuse to view their father's nakedness, and, walking back-
ward with averted gaze, they cover him up. On awakening, Noah
curses Ham and condemns him and his descendants to be servants to the other two sons and their descendants. The existence
of this tale explains why the medieval mystery plays and Marc
Connelly's *Green Pastures* depict Noah as a bit too fond of the
bottle.

In the medieval play *The Deluge* the story is embellished
with gaiety as Mrs. Noah is pictured as refusing to board the

---

tradition holds that he lived longer than anybody else ever has. The chron-
ology given in Chapters 5–7 shows that Methuselah died in the year of
Noah's Flood. Hence some scholars have concluded from this portion of
Genesis that Methuselah was drowned in the Flood.

* "Forty" is a round number often used in the Bible to denote a considerable quantity. The Israelites wander forty years in the wilderness (Nu.
14:33 and 32:13), Eli judges Israel forty years (I Sam. 4:18), David and
Solomon reign forty years each (I Kings 2:11 and 11:42), and so on.

† It has been suggested that the rainbow symbolized God's bow from
which he shot the arrows of lightning. Hence the appearance of the rainbow
in the sky represents a laying aside of God's weapon of wrath against mankind. See Cuthbert A. Simpson, exegesis to Genesis, *The Interpreter's
Bible*, I, 551.

ark and has to be pushed into it. Noah complains about the stubborness of all women. Another medieval play, the Wakefield *Noah,* depicts a similar situation in which Noah and his wife quarrel and exchange hefty blows. In general, both medieval and modern plays on Biblical themes are mere stories in contrast to the vivid tales in the Old Testament which are related as historical events controlled by God for his inexorable purpose. Therefore the Biblical language is brief, simple, direct, and sober, with little or no embellishment.

THE TOWER OF BABEL (11:1-9). In the course of time, men again become proud and excessively ambitious. Their pride leads them to build the Tower of Babel, which is to be so high that its top will reach heaven. Foreseeing the lengths to which their vanity and ambition might drive them, God causes the men (who are "of one language and of one speech") to speak different languages and scatters them over the face of the earth.

Legends of Four Hebrew Patriarchs. The second division of Genesis consists of biographical stories of the four earliest Hebrew patriarchs.

ABRAHAM (12:1–25:8).* Abraham (originally called Abram †), a descendant of Shem, is so devout and God-fearing, so righteous and trustworthy, that God selects him to be the progenitor of his "Chosen People." Abraham's birthplace was Ur of the Chaldees, whence his family had taken him to live in Haran. Now directing him to leave Haran and go to Canaan, the Lord promises to make of Abraham's descendants "a great nation" and a blessing to all other nations. This promise (12:2-3) is the beginning of the "Covenant" between God and the Hebrews which is to play a very significant role in the religious life of the people. The Covenant is repeated in 15:1-21 and again in 17:1-8. Although there is nowhere in Genesis a description of Abraham's obligations under the Covenant, there is an implication (17:9 ff.) that God will keep his promise to the Chosen People only so long as they worship him, keep his commandments, and live

* Because the stories of Abraham, Isaac, Jacob, and Joseph naturally overlap, so must the chapter-and-verse divisions given here. The birth of Abraham is announced in Gen. 11:26.

† Names had great significance. To know the name of something implied authority and power over it. God changed Abram's name to Abraham and with it changed his destiny.

righteous lives. (See reference to the Chosen People in Deut.
7:6: ". . . God hath chosen thee . . . above all people that are
upon the face of the earth.")

Obeying God's order, Abraham moves to Canaan, taking with
him his wife Sarah (originally named Sarai) and his nephew
Lot and the latter's wife. Unable to obtain enough food in
Canaan, the migrants go to Egypt where Abraham passes off
Sarah as his sister (she was his half-sister)* to avoid being
killed by the Egyptians on her account. (They would have murdered the husband of a woman they coveted.) Pharaoh takes
Sarah into his house and gives Abraham gifts but later discovers
the truth and expels the migrants from Egypt.

Returning to Canaan, the two families find that there is insuffi-
cient grazing land in a single area to support them. Abraham,
knowing that the families must separate, magnanimously gives
Lot first choice of the region in which to settle. Lot chooses the
plain of Jordan, and settles down in Sodom, while Abraham establishes his household on the plain of Mamre in the Hebron
area—a place later to become famous as David's first capital.

After dwelling in Canaan for ten years, Abraham still has had
no offspring. (It was customary at this time for a barren wife
to provide her husband with a slave as a concubine who never,
however, attained the legal status of a wife. Eventually, bigamy
came into frequent practice, and then the rights of offspring became matters of controversy.) Sarah persuades him to take as a
second wife Hagar, her Egyptian maid, who becomes pregnant.
A family quarrel ensues: Hagar is contemptuous of Sarah's bar-
renness, and Sarah retaliates by mistreating her. Hagar flees to
the wilderness, where a son, Ishmael, is born. (This episode
could be interpreted as an explanation for the enmity between
the Israelites and the Ishmaelites, Bedouins living in the deserts
south of Palestine.)

Next is a story which is the first of a series of Biblical narratives concerning childless women to whom the Lord grants the
gift of bearing a child.† God tells Abraham that Sarah is going
to bear him a son. Both Abraham and his wife laugh in disbelief

---

* This story of passing off his wife as his sister appears three times in
Genesis (12:13; 20:2; 26:7).

† Compare the conceptions of Samson (Judges 13:2-7), of Samuel (I
Sam. 1:4-23), and of John the Baptist (Luke 1:5-24).

at the prospect, for Sarah is ninety years old, while her husband says he is a hundred (17:17).° Despite their old age, however, Sarah conceives and gives birth to Isaac.

Meanwhile, Sodom and its neighbor city Gomorrah have become so wicked that God decides to destroy them. Abraham, trying to save Sodom, scolds God for injustice to the good people there, but the Lord rejects his protest because not even ten righteous men could be found in the city. Righteous Lot and his family are told to flee from Sodom. As her punishment for disobeying God's injunction that during their flight they must not watch the destruction of the cities (by "brimstone and fire"), Lot's wife is turned into a pillar of salt (19:26).

Another account tells that Lot's two daughters make their father drunk, cohabit with him, and bear him two sons, who are to become the ancestors of the Moabites and the Ammonites; thus the historian explains the origins of two of the traditional enemies of the Israelites.

In obedience to God's command, when Isaac is eight days old Abraham has him circumcised as a sign of the Covenant between God and Abraham's descendants. In this way Abraham institutes the important Jewish tradition of circumcision.[12]

Upon the death of Sarah (Chapter 23), Abraham buys a plot of ground near Hebron in which to bury her body.† He later remarries and has sons by his second wife and his concubines; his favorite son is Isaac, to whom he leaves all his possessions when he dies at the "good old age" of 175.

ISAAC (21:1—22:13, 24:1-67, and 35:28-29). Concerning the character of Isaac, the second of the Jewish patriarchs, the Bible has little to say. He seems to be a nondescript figure who is presented only in relation to his father and his sons.

A highly dramatic story, one of the most profoundly moving in all literature, is told concerning the young Isaac. To test Abraham's loyalty and faith, God commands him to slay the boy and to make of his body a sacrificial offering. "Take now thy son, thine only son Isaac, whom thou lovest, . . . and offer him . . .

° According to Genesis 17:24, he was ninety-nine.
† Centuries later, after the return from the Babylonian Exile, this purchase was to furnish legalistic grounds for the Israelites' claim to this portion of Canaan, then occupied by the Edomites. (Simpson, exegesis, *The Interpreter's Bible*, I, 647.)

for a burnt offering. . . ." The devout old man prepares to slaughter his only son, on whom rests his sole hope for the future of the family; the boy helps in the preparation, ignorant of his father's intentions. When Isaac turns to ask: "Behold the fire and the wood: but where is the lamb for a burnt offering?" Abraham replies: "My son, God will provide himself a lamb for a burnt offering." Such faith and obedience are rewarded: as the father takes the knife to kill his son, an angel stops him. Then Abraham sees a ram caught in a thicket by his horns; he sacrifices the ram as a burnt offering instead of his son. God renews the promise to multiply Abraham's descendants and make them victorious "because thou hast obeyed my voice"—a fitting conclusion to a story filled with dramatic challenge, suspense, and deep emotion. (Note, however, that throughout the history of the Hebrew people human sacrifice was rejected as being contrary to their religion; even the sacrifice of animals was often condemned insofar as it became a substitute for obedience to God's laws.) It is useful to contrast the medieval Brome play *Abraham and Isaac* with this Biblical account. The play exaggerates the child's emotions ("I pray you, father, change your face, and kill me not with your knife") and ends with a moralizing epilogue. Despite the high literary quality of medieval and modern literature using a Biblical theme, how much more eloquent and dramatic is the simple, straightforward Old Testament story which carries its own convincing moral lesson!

Isaac grows to manhood, and his father seeks a suitable wife for him. The discovery and winning of Rebekah is a beautiful pastoral idyl (Chapter 24).

JACOB (ISRAEL) (25:19–35:29). The biography of the third of the patriarchs is a saga of greed, envy, and shrewd treachery.

Soon after Rebekah becomes pregnant, she feels two children struggling in her womb (apparently against each other). Considering this an omen, she asks God what it means, and he tells her that she is to give birth to twins who will be the forefathers of two rival nations. (This incident serves as an explanation of the origin of the traditional enmity between the Hebrews, the descendants of Jacob, and the Edomites, the descendants of Esau.) At the moment the twins are born, the animosity continues, for Jacob is holding on to the foot of Esau, the firstborn. When they reach manhood, twice Jacob practices his wiles on his elder brother. First, he catches Esau in a weak moment, when Esau comes in from the field faint with hunger. Jacob refuses him food except in exchange for his birthright—that is, for Esau's rightful place as heir to the headship of the family. Esau concedes and thus sells his birthright for a "mess of pottage." Then, second, abetted by his mother, Jacob conspires to cheat Esau of his father's blessing. Now, Isaac is partial to Esau, the hairy, masculine huntsman, who brings him savory venison; Rebekah, on the other hand, prefers Jacob, the smooth-skinned "plain man, dwelling in tents." When Isaac (now blind with age) sends Esau out to hunt game and tells him to prepare it in his customary way, Rebekah disguises Jacob by dressing him in Esau's clothes and by putting hairy goatskins on his hands and neck so that he will feel like Esau; she also prepares savory meat to be served to Isaac. Jacob lies about his identity as he approaches his father; Isaac feels the hairy hands, smells the clothes, eats the meat, and is convinced that Jacob is Esau. He blesses Jacob and makes him lord over his brothers. The moment of Esau's return is a dramatic one. When he perceives that he has been cheated, he cries "with a great and exceeding bitter cry" (27:34). Isaac blesses him, too, but cannot revoke the decrees making Jacob head of the clan.

In order to escape Esau's murderous wrath, Jacob flees to Haran and becomes the servant of his uncle Laban, Rebekah's brother. En route he sees in a dream a vision of a ladder reaching to heaven, on which angels are ascending and descending. God appears at the top of the ladder and renews the promises he has made to Abraham and Isaac; Jacob vows faithfulness to God (27:41–28:22).

Jacob falls in love with Laban's pretty young daughter Rachel. Her father agrees to the match provided Jacob will labor for him for seven years. At the end of the time Laban proves as untrustworthy and as guileful as his sister Rebekah. He requires Jacob to marry Leah, the unattractive, "weak-eyed" older sister of Rachel and to labor seven more years before he can marry his beloved. At the end of the fourteen years Laban again proves dishonest by trying to cheat Jacob of his sheep, but this time Jacob outwits the uncle and departs for his native region with Leah, Rachel, and much wealth (Chs. 29–31).

By this point Jacob has shown pretty well what his characteristics and abilities are. His most obvious trait is craftiness, derived, no doubt, from his mother.* In addition to craftiness, Jacob is endowed with tremendous strength and hardihood: he uses a rock as a pillow (Gen. 28:11), he single-handedly rolls a great rock from a well (29:10), and he wrestles successfully with a supernatural being (32:24-30) later referred to as God himself ("I have seen God face to face, and my life is preserved"). God changes Jacob's name to Israel (32:28-30), which means "contender with God." Jacob is also patient (witness the fourteen years of labor for Rachel), and he is capable of great parental love (see below the accounts of his affection for Joseph and Benjamin). His best characteristic is his unswerving faith in God (see, for example, 28:16, 31:5-16, and 32:9-12).

Fearing now that Esau may still seek revenge for his former injuries, Jacob sends him a series of presents. Esau forgives him, the two are reconciled, and Jacob settles down to rear a large family and to accumulate great riches (32:1—33:15).

Jacob begets twelve sons and one daughter: (1) Leah bears Reuben, Simeon, Levi, Judah, Issachar, Zebulun, and the daughter, Dinah; (2) Rachel bears Joseph and Benjamin; (3) Bilhah, Rachel's maidservant, bears Dan and Naphtali; and (4) Zilpah, Leah's maidservant, bears Gad and Asher. The sons are of prime importance in Jewish history. Ten of them (Levi and Joseph excepted) lend their names to ten of the well-known "tribes of Israel." (Levi's descendants, though called a tribe, are set aside as a priestly group, and Joseph's two sons, Ephraim and Manasseh, become the progenitors of two "half-tribes.") The suffix -ite is attached to the name of the head of each tribe to indicate a descendant; for example, a Danite is a descendant of Dan, a Benjamite is a descendant of Benjamin, and so on.

JOSEPH (Chs. 37—50). Many commentators have remarked that the story of Joseph is one of the most skillfully told narratives in the Bible. To an anthropologist and a student of folklore, the exciting plot resembles that of the universally popular tale of Cinderella, with Joseph as the mistreated protagonist, the elder

---

* This trait seems to be admired by the author of this portion of Genesis and by some other Biblical authors; see, for example the tales about Ehud, Jael, and Gideon in Judges 3 and 5—7. Many later writers of Biblical books, however, deplore anything that smacks of trickery and deceit; see especially Jer. 5:2, Amos 8:5, Mark 7:22, and Romans 1:29.

brothers corresponding to the cruel stepmother and stepsisters, and Pharaoh playing the part of the fairy godmother. Of course, to the orthodox scholar, the theme of the Joseph story seems to be much more serious and elevated than that of Cinderella, for the Biblical tale illustrates how God sometimes works in obscure and mysterious ways to preserve his Chosen People; it also accounts for the Israelites' presence in Egypt about 1600 B.C.

In many respects Joseph is the most attractive of the four patriarchs. Since he was the first son of Jacob's beloved wife Rachel (ten others being sons of Leah, whom Jacob did not love, or of the servants), Jacob loved him best of all his twelve sons. As an adult Joseph is so chaste that he refuses to be seduced by his master's wife; he is so astute an administrator that Pharaoh places him in charge of all the food supplies in Egypt; and he is of so tender and forgiving a nature that he holds no grudge against his brothers for selling him into slavery.

The ten oldest sons of Jacob, resentful of the partiality which their father shows to Joseph and also of Joseph's dreams exalting him above his brothers, decide to kill the boy: "Behold, this dreamer cometh. Come now . . . let us slay him. . . ." But Reuben persuades the others to throw Joseph into a pit instead, intending to rescue him later; then Judah suggests selling the boy to a caravan of merchants en route to Egypt. This they do (without Reuben's knowledge), then dip Joseph's coat, or long-sleeved robe (given to him by his father), in the blood of an animal and bring it home to Jacob, telling him that Joseph has been killed by a wild animal.

The merchants sell Joseph to Potiphar, captain of Pharaoh's guard. Potiphar's wife tries to seduce Joseph. When he remains loyal to the captain and rejects her advances, she tells Potiphar that Joseph has tried to seduce her. To substantiate her accusation, she shows him a garment which Joseph has left in her grasp when he fled from the house. "The Hebrew servant . . . came in unto me to mock me: And it came to pass, as I lifted up my voice and cried, that he left his garment with me, and fled out" (39:17-18). Joseph is thrown into prison, but even there he prospers: he wins the favor of the keeper, who puts him in charge of all the other prisoners. Pharaoh's head butler and baker are also in prison and have strange dreams which Joseph correctly interprets. Eventually Pharaoh frees the butler but hangs the baker, as predicted by Joseph. Later the monarch himself has two dreams which his magicians are unable to interpret: one, that seven fat cows were devoured by seven lean ones, and another, that seven plump ears of grain were eaten by seven blighted ones. Joseph interprets the dreams of Pharaoh to mean that there will be seven years of prosperity followed by seven years of famine. He advises Pharaoh to store up great supplies of food during the "fat" years. Impressed by Joseph's abilities, Pharaoh makes him overseer of all Egypt (41:40-44).

The dreams come true, and only Egypt has food during the "lean" years. Driven by famine in Canaan, Joseph's ten older brothers come to Egypt to buy grain. Joseph knows who they are and is filled with love for them. They, however, do not recognize this exalted official as their brother. He sells them grain, but tells them not to come back for more without bringing with them their youngest brother, Benjamin, who has replaced Joseph as Jacob's favorite son. When a second trip to Egypt is necessary, the brothers bring Benjamin with them, much against their father's wishes. Again Joseph sells them grain, but this time he has his own silver cup put into Benjamin's bag. Then he sends his servants to accuse the brothers of stealing the cup. When it is discovered in Benjamin's bag, Judah implores Joseph to let him become Joseph's servant (as a penalty) in Benjamin's stead. Overcome by emotion, Joseph breaks into tears, reveals his identity, and is reconciled with his brothers. Jacob is brought from Canaan to spend the remainder of his days with all his sons in Egypt.

Especially memorable are the passages relating the following events: (1) Reuben's discovery that Joseph is not in the pit (37:29-30); (2) Jacob's sorrow over Joseph's reported death (37:34-35); (3) the brothers' humbling themselves before Joseph in Egypt and his various schemes to confuse and try them (42:6-34); (4) the attempts by Judah to protect Benjamin (44:22 and 44:32-34); and (5) the scene of revelation and reconciliation (45:1-15).

Jacob (now known as Israel) and his family settle in the fertile Egyptian land of Goshen. The Egyptians are compelled by famine to sell their lands to Joseph, as Pharaoh's agent. He makes slaves of them, introducing universal slavery, and establishes a 20 per cent levy on production. But Jacob's family prosper. In a famous passage Jacob blesses his twelve sons and the two sons of Joseph, namely, Ephraim and Manasseh * (48:10—49:27). The book closes with the deaths respectively of Jacob and of Joseph. At a future date (as recorded in Exodus 13:19) the Israelites show their reverence for the memory of Joseph by carrying his remains with them on their journey from Egypt to Canaan.

EXODUS

The word *Exodus*, a Greek derivative, means "the going out." As applied to the second book of the Hexateuch, it refers to the epic passage of the children of Israel from Egypt to Canaan—a passage regarded by many scholars as a historical fact. This book covers the period from the death of Joseph in Egypt to the building and dedication of the Tabernacle in the wilderness. It has three main divisions: the period of bondage in Egypt (1:1—15:21), the journey to Mount Sinai (15:22—19:25), and events at Mount Sinai (Chs. 20—40). The first two divisions are chiefly narrative, and, dominated as they are by the towering figure of Moses, they are literarily almost equal to the book of Genesis. The last section contains some excellent narrative and descriptive passages, but it is made up largely of laws and rules, which (though of great religious, ethical, and cultural significance) are of secondary importance as literature.

Bondage in Egypt and Escape from Bondage (1:1—15:21). "Now there arose up a new king over Egypt, which knew not Joseph." This sentence (which has become proverbial) marks a drastic change in the fortunes of the Israelites. After more than four hundred years (Ex. 12:40), the descendants of Jacob have become a multitude: "and the land was filled with them." The new Pharaoh [13] so fears their power that he orders not only the extremely harsh enslavement of the Hebrews but also the drowning of each newborn Hebrew male.

THE BIRTH OF MOSES (2:1-10). One of the women of the tribe of Levi saves her baby by putting him into a basket made of bulrushes, setting it afloat among the reeds at the edge of the river, and instructing her daughter Miriam to watch the basket from a distance.[14] The child is discovered by Pharaoh's daughter,

* Their mother was an Egyptian woman (Asenath) whom Pharaoh gave Joseph as his wife.

who takes pity on him and rescues him, even though she recognizes that he is a Hebrew. Miriam now comes forward and
offers to find a nurse for the baby. When the princess accepts
the offer, Miriam cleverly brings the baby's mother, whom
Pharaoh's daughter pays to nurse him. Later Pharaoh's daughter
adopts the boy and names him Moses, "because," she says, "I
drew him out of the water." [15] Nothing else is told of the childhood of Moses.

MOSES' EXILE AND HIS CALLING BY GOD (2:11–4:28). The
adult Moses is one of the most commanding and inspirational figures in the Old Testament. Writing about him six or eight centuries after his death, the Deuteronomist says: "And there arose
not a prophet since in Israel like unto Moses, whom the Lord
knew face to face" (Deut. 34:10). From the point of view of
the orthodox scholar, this intimacy with God accounts in large
measure for Moses' great power. "He was, in Spinoza's words, a
'God-intoxicated' man and through that intoxication confirmed,
one might better say created, in the Hebrew race that religious
faith which was to endure after their life as a nation had died
and to which we owe the religion of Christianity." [16] Moses is a
superb combination of humility and boldness. He is humble, as
is shown in his doubting his own ability (he is "slow of speech")
to lead the Israelites out of bondage (Ex. 4:10); yet he is bold
enough to upbraid God himself for giving him the burden of
leading them. Two other traits of his are often seen together:
quickness of temper and a "passionate sense of justice." Both of
these are observable in his slaying of the Egyptian who is beat-
ing a Hebrew (Ex. 2:11-12) and his driving away of the shepherds who are mistreating Jethro's daughters (Ex. 2:16-17).
Another characteristic that deserves mention is his patient perse-
verance, as seen in his dogged leading of the children of Israel
through wilderness for forty years, despite their complaining
and backsliding.

The first incident told about Moses as a man is the killing of
an Egyptian. Moses flees to the land of Midian to escape punishment. There he marries Zipporah, the daughter of Jethro, a Midianite priest.* Moses remains in Midian "forty"years (according

* The Midianites (later to become enemies of the Hebrews) were a semi-
nomadic people who lived southeast of Canaan.

to later chronology). Then the old king of Egypt dies; but his successor is equally oppressive to the Israelites, and the latter renew their cries to God for deliverance. God answers their prayers by choosing Moses as their deliverer. In a most impressive miraculous scene (3:2-6), Moses sees a fire in a bush in the wilderness, but the fire does not destroy the bush—"and, behold, the bush burned with fire, and the bush was not consumed." God tells Moses that he has chosen him to lead the Israelites out of Egypt into Canaan, "a land flowing with milk and honey." God promises to "smite Egypt with all my wonders" to force the Egyptians to let the Hebrews go. Moses objects that the people will not believe him; God answers his reluctance by enabling him to do miracles: Moses' rod turns into a serpent and his hand is smitten with leprosy; then both are restored. Again Moses objects that he is no speaker and therefore cannot sway the people with oratory; God promises that Aaron,* Moses' brother, who is a good orator, will be his spokesman. Moses obeys and returns to Egypt.

THE PLAGUES AND THE ESCAPE (4:29—15:21). Here is a dramatic story filled with suspense, conflict, and progressive action, including miracles, leading to the climax of victory. Moses and Aaron go up to Pharaoh and petition him to let the Hebrews go to the wilderness, but he haughtily refuses and says that the two petitioners are interfering with the Hebrews' labor. Moses threatens him with a plague—turning the water of the Egyptians to blood, and the plague is actually inflicted. Pharaoh's magicians duplicate the feat, and therefore the king remains obstinate. Then Moses calls down, one after another, eight more plagues: of frogs, gnats, flies, cattle-sickness, boils, hail, locusts, and darkness. Each time Egypt suffers from a plague, Pharaoh promises to let the children of Israel go, but becomes obdurate after the plague is removed. Now the Lord has reached the end of his patience with the Egyptians. He tells Moses to instruct each He-

* The Biblical historian's probable motive for mentioning the appointment of Aaron the Levite is to emphasize the divine ordination of the priesthood of Israel. "The passage seems to reflect strained relations between priest and prophet here represented by Moses in the writer's own day [700-450 B.C.?]." (J. Coert Rylaarsdam, exegesis to Exodus, *The Interpreter's Bible,* I, 879.

brew family to mark its doorposts and lintels with the blood of
a lamb, because he is going to smite the first-born of every family
in Egypt, "both man and beast," except those whose houses are
so marked; these he will "pass over." The Lord gives a number
of detailed instructions, such as the eating of unleavened bread
for seven days. (Thus are explained the origins of both the Jewish festival of the Passover and the rite of Unleavened Bread.[17])
All happens as the Lord has promised, and great is the grief in
the land of Egypt, "for there was not a house where there was
not one dead." At last, Pharaoh allows the Israelites to depart
and take their flocks and herds with them. Six hundred thousand
men—in addition to the women and children—set out for Canaan.

God then hardens Pharaoh's heart so that Pharaoh regrets his
decision to free the Hebrews and sends all his chariots and horse-
men in pursuit. As the Hebrews, guided by a pillar of cloud by
day and a pillar of fire by night (signs of the presence of God °),
reach the Red Sea, God performs a glorious miracle to save them.
He causes an east wind to blow all night and divide the waters
so that there is a passageway of dry land through the sea. This
enables the Hebrews to reach the shore, but in the morning when
the Egyptians drive their chariots along the same passageway
through the sea, God lets the waters come together again and
drown them all.

Then Moses and the people sing their triumphant song (15:1-
18), the opening words of which are perhaps the oldest piece of
literature in the Bible.[18] It is an exultant lyric, and the opening is:

> I will sing unto the Lord, for he hath triumphed gloriously:
> The horse and his rider hath he thrown into the sea.

Contrast such terse, dramatic language with the medieval Caedmonian poem *Exodus* (*c.* A.D. 675), which pictures Moses as a
Teutonic warrior as well as a lawgiver and relates how a heroic
God intervened to assist the despondent Hebrews: "The waves
mounted . . . blood-stained the flood . . . the fated men fell. . . ."

° Some scholars have sought to explain these phenomena by suggesting
that Mount Sinai, toward which the Israelites were traveling, was a volcano and that the pillars of cloud and fire were the visible signs of an
eruption. See J. Edgar Park, exposition to Exodus, *The Interpreter's Bible*,
I, 931.

The medieval writers felt obliged to adapt, explain, and spell out the moral that the Egyptian armies were beaten because they "fought against God."

The Journey in the Wilderness to Sinai (15:22—19:25). After their escape the Israelites begin a "forty-year" period (commencing about 1200 B.C.) of wandering across deserts and wastelands. The first phase, the journey to Mount Sinai, is filled with hardships. Time after time they regret that they ever left the "fleshpots of Egypt," and they accuse Moses of leading them into the wilderness only to let them die there. Their first trial comes soon after they have crossed the Red Sea; they are thirsty, and they try the waters of Marah but find them bitter; Moses sweetens the waters by throwing a tree into them. Then the wanderers fear that they will starve to death, but God sends them initially a flock of quail and then a steady supply of manna, "the bread which the Lord hath given you to eat." Again they lack water, and Moses produces it by striking a rock in Horeb. Finally, they are attacked by the Amalekites.* The Hebrews find that they are victorious as long as Moses holds up his hands; Aaron and Hur, therefore, stand on each side of him and hold his hands up until the battle is won.

After a reunion with his wife, two sons, and father-in-law, Moses leads his people on to the foot of Mount Sinai (or Horeb).[19] There follows the highly dramatic story (accompanied by an eruptive volcano, thunder and lightning, and clouds from which issues the voice of God) that tells how the Lord summons Moses to the top of Mount Sinai and there proclaims the Ten Commandments and various ordinances (all written down by Moses) as well as two subsequent "tables of stone, written with the finger of God" (31:18).

Moses and the Giving of the Law (Chs. 20—40). Therefore the last twenty-one chapters of Exodus contain not only the Ten Commandments but also the numerous other laws and rules. Some of the latter pertain to matters of universal interest, such as perjury, slander, charitableness, and legal justice. Others are of somewhat narrower interest, inasmuch as they deal with ceremonies, sacrifices, holy garments, the building of the Tabernacle,

---

* The Amalekites, who lived just north of Kadesh, were a tribe related to the Edomites. The reference here helps to account for Israel's long feud with them. See Rylaarsdam, exegesis, *The Interpreter's Bible*, I, 959-960.

and the like. Though of great value to the student of history and religion, these laws are of lesser interest to the student of litera- ture. It should be noted in passing, however, that despite ap- proval of slavery and cruel punishment (e.g., "thou shalt not suffer a witch to live"), these Hebrew laws are generally con- ceded to be more humanitarian than the laws of most other peoples of the same period. They require, for example, hospi- tality to strangers, kindness to widows and orphans, respect for the aged, and charity for the poor. One particular law has often been misinterpreted: "eye for eye, tooth for tooth," etc. (21:23- 25), is a *limit* to which legally inflicted punishment can go—not an invitation of vengeance.[20] One other interesting law (28:30) requires the placing of the Urim and Thummin (oracles) in the breastplate of Aaron when he goes "before the Lord" in the Temple; these oracles were the Hebrew equivalent of pagan oracles and might be consulted upon practical issues.[21]

The Ten Commandments, of course, are the most significant laws given in the book; they and the narrative passages of this portion of Exodus require some comment here.

THE TEN COMMANDMENTS (20:1-17). The Ten Command- ments form a code of laws for a pastoral and agricultural people; some analogous laws have been found in the codes of the an- cient Egyptians and Babylonians. The age of the Ten Command- ments is uncertain. Most scholars now believe that, though based on a shorter version attributed to Moses, some of them are of far later date and that in their later form they were inserted into the J or the E Document.[22] They outline two kinds of obliga- tions: duties to God and duties to other men.[23] They may be briefly summarized as follows:

(1) Thou shalt have no gods except the Lord.

(2) Thou shalt not make or worship idols.

(3) Thou shalt not take the name of God in vain.*

---

* This commandment had special significance for the Hebrews, who used many devices in the Old Testament to avoid pronouncing the divine name. The use of God's name for ordinary matters implied lack of respect for his transcendence. In fact, they believed that somehow God's name expressed his character or power (see Rylaarsdam, exegesis, *The Interpreter's Bible*, I, 983). Belief in the efficacy of a proper name was held not only by the Hebrews but by people all over the world; proper names were widely used in invoking or exorcising various deities, spirits, devils, fairies, and the like.

(4) Thou shalt keep the Sabbath day holy.

(5) Thou shalt honor thy parents.*

(6) Thou shalt not kill.

(7) Thou shalt not commit adultery.

(8) Thou shalt not steal.

(9) Thou shalt not bear false witness (that is, commit perjury in court).

(10) Thou shalt not covet.

ESTABLISHMENT OF THE PRIESTHOOD: EPISODE OF THE MOLTEN CALF (28:1–32:35). Moses establishes a hereditary priesthood by appointing Aaron and his sons to be priests (28:1). Somewhat later (32:28-29) he consecrates the other Levites as priests (Aaron, it should be noted, is a descendant of Levi; see 2:1).

While Moses is on Mount Sinai "forty days and forty nights" receiving from God the Ten Commandments and the so-called Code of the Covenant (Chapters 20–23), the Israelites break the Second Commandment. Wearied of waiting for their leader, they ask Aaron to make gods for them—palpable and visible gods. Aaron agrees and makes a golden calf † by melting down the earrings of the people. Informed by God of what has happened, Moses comes down from the mountain. So furious is he when he sees the people dancing about the golden calf that he breaks the stone tablets containing God's commandments—"written with the finger of God"! Furthermore, he burns the calf "in the fire," grinds it into powder, mixes the powder with water, and makes the people drink the mixture. He orders the slaying of three thousand men: "slay every man his brother and every man

---

The use may be seen in the old Germanic fairy tale about Rumpelstilzchen (who vanishes forever when he discovers that the queen has learned his strange name) and in Shakespeare's *Hamlet*, where the titular character employs various appellations to make his father's ghost communicate with him:

> "I'll call thee Hamlet,
> King, father, Royal Dane; O answer me . . ."

* Perhaps this commandment was included because of the nomadic custom of abandoning aged and dependent parents.

† Calf-worship was a form of nature mysticism practiced in Canaan. Scholars believe that this story was not attached to the Moses cycle till after the eighth century B.C., when the people of the Kingdom of Israel were worshiping two golden calves, originally set up by Jeroboam I (see I Kings 12:28 and Rylaarsdam, exegesis, *The Interpreter's Bible*, I, 1063-1064).

his companion, and every man his neighbor." God sends a
plague upon the people as additional punishment for making the
golden calf (32:35).

Conclusion (Chs. 34—40). After Moses has prayed two inter-
cessory prayers in behalf of the people (32:11-13 and 32:30-35),
God relents and agrees to send an angel who will lead them to
the Promised Land of Canaan. He reminds Moses of the Covenant made with Abraham: that God will prosper the Hebrews
and make them a mighty and "chosen" people if they will worship him and obey his commandments. God "writes" the Ten
Commandments again for Moses (34:1). When the great lawgiver returns to his people, the skin of his face shines because
he has been talking with God (34:29).* Now an ark is built to
house the Ten Commandments (virtually identified with the
Covenant [24]), and the ark is placed inside an elaborately constructed but portable tabernacle.[25] The Ark of the Covenant is
hereafter the holiest and most zealously guarded of the Israelites'
religious paraphernalia.

The book ends with an awe-inspiring account of God's presence: "And Moses was not able to enter into the tent of the congregation, because the cloud abode thereon, and the glory of the
Lord filled the tabernacle" (40:35). The children of Israel continue their journey only when the cloud is raised from the tabernacle. "For the cloud of the Lord was upon the tabernacle by
day, and fire was on it by night, in the sight of all the house of
Israel, throughout all their journeys" (40:38).

LEVITICUS

The word *Leviticus*, borrowed from the Septuagint, denotes
"a book for the Levites." One should remember that Moses and
Aaron were of the tribe of Levi (Ex. 2:1-2), that Moses consecrated all the Levites "to the service of the Lord" (Ex. 32:28-29),
and that Moses ordained Aaron and his descendants to be priests
(Ex. 28:1). In the early centuries, before the Babylonian Exile,
the Levites (as distinguished from the Aaronites) perhaps performed some priestly functions: but between 586 B.C. and the

---

* Compare Christ's Transfiguration (Matt. 17:1-8). For the word *shone*
(Ex. 34:29) the Vulgate used the translation "horned," whence the origin
of the tradition that Moses had horns, as he is often represented in Renaissance paintings and in Michelangelo's famous piece of sculpture. See Park,
exposition, *The Interpreter's Bible*, I, 1081.

end of Temple worship in A.D. 70 they "were the lower personnel of the sanctuary—assistants, gate-keepers, musicians, and the like —while the priests, through the ordination of Aaron and his sons, held final authority in matters of ritual." [26] Leviticus, however, was apparently a handbook not merely—or even principally— for the subordinate Levites, but for *all* the personnel who served within the Temple. Compiled more than seven centuries after the death of Moses, its purpose "seems to have been to project back into early times the highly developed ritual of the temple and to connect it with an early shrine, the tabernacle or trysting tent." [27] "It may be compared to those convenient casebooks which are composed for the benefit of students of the law. The volume itself will have a date, but its contents will be drawn from the legislation and judicial decisions of many generations." [28]

Most lawbooks make dull reading for the average person, and Leviticus is no exception. Its contents, however, are of considerable value to the student of religion, ethics, sociology, and Jewish history.[29]

The book may be divided into four sections: (1) Chapters 1—10, laws concerning sacrifices of animals (e.g., bulls, goats, sheep, or birds) and the consecration of the priesthood; (2) Chapters 11—16, laws concerning "cleanness," * purification (man being sinful and only God being holy), and atonement (Yom Kippur being the day reserved for fasting, special sacrifices, and penance); (3) Chapters 17—26, the Holiness Code,† which is the oldest section of Leviticus and is not so much concerned with priestly activities in the Temple as with holy feasts, social behavior, sexual behavior, and the observance of sabbatical and jubilee years (25:1-55); and (4) Chapter 27, laws concerning vows and tithes.

NUMBERS

The title of the fourth book of the Bible refers to the two "numberings" or censuses of the Israelites which are related in

* "Clean" and "unclean" are terms which have a special meaning in Jewish law. Many of the laws concerning cleanliness originated in the practice of hygiene, but "unclean" came to be applied to any "departure from prescribed practice" (Roy B. Chamberlin and Herman Feldman [eds.], *The Dartmouth Bible* [Boston: Houghton Mifflin Co., 2nd ed., 1961], p. 119).

† See below, p. 78, for a chart of the four codes found in the Pentateuch.

the book. The Hebrew title for the book, "In the Wilderness," is
more accurate than the one found in the King James Bible. Only
five chapters (1–4 and 26) are devoted to the taking of the
census. Most of the other chapters tell about the thirty-nine
years of wandering in the wilderness. Numbers begins where Exodus leaves off (at the departure of the Hebrews from Mount
Sinai) and continues the narrative of migration till Israel has
reached the outskirts of Moab. The first thirty-eight years of the
journey are rather sketchily covered in the first nineteen chapters, whereas the account of the events of the final year of wandering fills seventeen chapters.

Though of greater literary interest than Leviticus, the book of
Numbers contains much material which the average reader will
willingly skip. For instance, Chapters 5, 6, 15, 18, and 19 record
more rules and laws—laws concerning leprosy, adultery, jealousy,
and trespassing, and rules pertaining to priestly and Levitical
duties.

Only one of these chapters requires comment here. All of
Chapter 6 is concerned with the preparation and consecration of
a *Nazarite*. The word itself denotes one who is set apart or especially dedicatéd; here it is applied to one who has undertaken
to keep three vows for a specified period. These vows are (1) to
abstain from all alcoholic beverages—even from grapes, grape
seeds, and skins, (2) to leave the head unshaven, and (3) to
avoid touching or coming near a corpse. As we shall see later
(in the discussion of the book of Judges), Samson the Nazarite
kept the second of these vows but not the other two. Though
not mentioned again in the Pentateuch, the Nazarites were numerous in later periods of Jewish history and are mentioned in
Amos 2:11-12 and in I Maccabees 3:49.[30]

At the end of this section on the consecration of a Nazarite,
the Lord dictates to Moses "the most beautiful benediction in
the Scriptures":[31]

> The Lord bless thee, and keep thee:
> The Lord make his face shine upon thee, and be gracious
>   unto thee:
> The Lord lift up his countenance upon thee, and give thee
>   peace. (6:24-26)

The narrative portions of the book are told with the same
vigor and enthusiasm that we see in Genesis and Exodus. Most

of the narratives are short—accounts of mere incidents—but taken all together, they make up a memorable though episodic history of almost forty years of passage through a wasteland, a passage altogether so painful and discouraging that the people repeatedly "murmur" against their leaders and almost lose faith in God. Only the stalwart leadership of Moses is able to stifle rebellion and persuade the people to persevere till they can reach the Promised Land.

The book falls into three logical divisions: (1) preparations to leave Mount Sinai (1:1—10:10); (2) the wandering in the wilderness (10:11—19:22); and (3) the events of the last year before reaching Canaan (20:1—36:13).[32]

Preparations for the Journey (1:1—10:10). God commands Moses to take a census of the twelve tribes. The total number of the people "from twenty years old and upward, all that were able to go to war" is 603,550. The Levites, the women, and the children are not counted in this number. After offerings by all the princes (tribal leaders), the people are ready to set out on their journey.

Wandering in the Wilderness (10:11—19:22). The story of the sojourn in the wilderness is principally one of grumbling and dissatisfaction on the part of the people. They continually find fault with Moses and are even ungrateful for the Lord's providence. This period of wandering is of immense significance to Hebrew tradition. It is referred to countless times by later Biblical historians, by the Psalmists, and by the prophets. Sometimes (as in Hosea 11:1-5) it is regarded as a sort of childhood of the nation, a training period, an age of innocence. Nearly always it is pointed out as an era when God was especially protective and provident.

QUAILS AND PLAGUE (11:1-33). Although manna still falls every night, the people yearn for the meat and the fish, the cucumbers and the melons, the onions and the garlic to which they have been accustomed in Egypt. They complain so loudly that Moses takes the problem to God. Angry at their complaints, God promises to send them enough meat to last a whole month—so much that it will come out of their nostrils! A wind blows to the people a great multitude of quails, which fall and cover the earth. When the people eat, a terrible plague smites them so that many die.

SEDITION OF MIRIAM AND AARON (12:1-15). Even the brother and the sister of Moses become disaffected and resent their brother's authority. "Hath the Lord indeed spoken only by Moses? hath he not spoken also by us?" Again the Lord is displeased. This time he afflicts Miriam with leprosy. Then Aaron repents, while Moses prays to God that Miriam may be cured; after seven days of the punishment she is made well again.

RECONNAISSANCE OF CANAAN (13:1—14:35). Next Moses sends out twelve spies, one from each tribe, to reconnoiter the Promised Land of Canaan. On their return, ten of the spies report that the land is indeed flowing with milk and honey, but that it is inhabited by men of great stature and even by giants, "the sons of Anak," in whose sight the Israelites would be as mere grasshoppers. Caleb and Joshua, the other two spies, dissent from the majority report and urge invasion of the land. Agreeing with the ten spies, the people again murmur and weep and wish that they had died in Egypt; once more the Lord becomes angry and, in spite of Moses' entreaties, decrees that the murmurers shall never enter the Promised Land.

The Last Year of the Journey (Chs. 20—36). As the years roll slowly on, little progress toward Canaan is made by the still-murmuring Hebrews. Miriam dies in Kadesh and is buried there (20:1). Aaron dies upon Mount Hor and is succeeded by his son Eleazar (20:22-29); even Moses loses his right to enter the Promised Land.

STRIKING OF THE ROCK (20:2-13).* In a period of serious drought the people again wish that they had died earlier. Moses and Aaron ask God for water and are told to *speak to* a particular rock and that it will give enough water for the people and their animals. Moses, who has formerly interceded for the people, now loses his patience: "Hear now, ye rebels; must we fetch you water out of this rock?" And instead of speaking to the

---

* One should remember that this is the second rock-striking episode told of Moses (the other is in Ex. 17:1-7). Biblical scholars feel reasonably sure that the compilers of the Hexateuch used different sources containing two versions of the same event and for one reason or another did not conflate the two accounts. One Rabbinical explanation of the second striking is that the rock which Moses struck according to Exodus followed the Israelites in their journey across the wilderness—an explanation accepted by Paul, who augments the ancient tradition by identifying the rock with Christ (I Cor. 10:4).

rock, he strikes it with his rod. Water gushes forth in great plenty. God says that Moses and Aaron will be punished for their disobedience by not being allowed to enter Canaan.*

THE FIERY SERPENTS (21:4-9). The people are incurably rebellious. When they murmur again, God sends a plague of fiery serpents upon them. Again Moses intercedes for the people, and the Lord tells him to make a brass serpent and put it on a pole; anybody bitten by one of the live snakes may be cured by looking at Moses' brazen one.

BALAAM AND HIS ASS (Chs. 22—24). Indubitably the finest literary gem in the book of Numbers is the story of Balaam. Apprised of the victories which the Israelites have won over the Amorites, Balak, king of the Moabites, fears this multitude which has come out of Egypt. Desiring to lay a curse upon the Israelites, he sends for the prophet Balaam, "a transitional figure between the primitive soothsayer and the type of moral prophet, unique among the Hebrews."[33] Now, Balaam is a worshiper of the Lord, and he asks the Lord for guidance in the matter. God at first refuses but later agrees to allow Balaam to go to Balak. When Balaam sets out on his ass, God sends an angel to block the way. Only the ass, however, can see the angel with "his sword drawn in his hand." When Balaam repeatedly urges the animal forward, it turns first aside, then crushes its master's foot against a wall, and finally falls down. Balaam strikes the ass with his staff, whereupon God allows the beast to speak: "What have I done unto thee, that thou hast smitten me these three times?" At last Balaam's eyes are opened; he sees the angel, realizes that the Israelites have God on their side, begs God's forgiveness, and is allowed to proceed on his journey to meet Balak. When the king asks the prophet to curse the Israelites, Balaam refuses and delivers four poetic oracles of great literary excellence (23:7-10, 23:18-24, 24:3-9, and 24:15-24). In these he praises the Israelites as God's Chosen People and predicts their future greatness as a nation.

We learn eventually (31:8) that Balaam is slain in battle as the Hebrews advance victoriously against the Moabites and the Midianites.

* The cause of God's punishment of Moses and Aaron is a matter of dispute. Numbers 20:12 says that the offense is "unbelief," but 20:24 says that it is "rebellion."

THE SECOND CENSUS (Ch. 26). Encamped on the plains of Moab, the Hebrew people are again counted. Although the various plagues and also God's decision not to allow any of those who left Egypt (except Caleb and Joshua) to enter the Promised Land tend to limit the Hebrew migrants to Canaan, the number of fighting men available there reaches the substantial total of 601,730.

THE END OF THE JOURNEY (Chs. 27–36). As they stand beside the river Jordan, the descendants of Israel reach important decisions. The tribes of Reuben and Gad choose to remain on the east bank of the Jordan. Forty-eight cities are given to the Levites; six of these are set aside as places of refuge for those who have unintentionally committed homicide.° Joshua is appointed successor to Moses.

DEUTERONOMY

The name of the fifth book of the Hexateuch is of Greek origin and means "second law." It refers to the repetition by Moses of the religious and ethical code which he enjoins the people to obey.

The nucleus of the book of Deuteronomy (Chs. 5–26 and 28) is believed to be identical with the book of law discovered in the Temple at Jerusalem in 621 B.C., during the reign of Josiah.† It seems likely that all but a few chapters (added by later editors) were the work of a priest or prophet of the kingdom of Judah and that he wrote the book during the reign of Manasseh, the predecessor of Amon and Josiah. This author is known as "the Deuteronomist."

Manasseh had been a wicked king. He had let the Temple in Jerusalem fall into disrepair, he had turned to the worship of other gods than the Lord, and he had even burned his own son as a sacrificial offering (see II Kings 21). The Deuteronomist was eager to restore the people of Judah to the religious practices traditionally believed to have been handed down by Moses.

° The brutal customs of the time are reflected in the accounts of how the Hebrews conquer the Midianites, burn their cities, kill all the men (31:7) and capture the women and children. Moses objects to sparing the women; he orders the killing of all mature women and male children, but allows the girls to be kept as slaves.

† See the discussion of the D Document on p. 50.

He emphasized God's goodness and love and the necessity of worshiping him and him alone.

"The author must have been a man of strong feeling, abundant imagination, and a disciplined mind, for he has transformed law into literature and made legal statutes flame with spiritual passion. . . . In this book we have something unique: law flaming with personality, the spirit of the law speaking in the cadences of great music, statutes luminous with spiritual passion. Law has become literature, the literature of power." [34]

Deuteronomy is essentially a restatement of the Mosaic law. But there is a considerable difference between this lawgiving and most of the juridic writings in the Old Testament: Deuteronomy is addressed not to the priests, the kings, or the judges, but to the laity. Instead of being concerned principally with ceremonies and rituals, it treats many matters of daily conduct: the religious education of children (6:20-25); sacrifices (12:5-14); food (12:15-28 and 14:3-21); tithes (14:22-29); the relief of poverty (15:4-11); the treatment of slaves and servants (15:12-18); the observance of festivals (16:1-17); lying witnesses (19:16-19); the inheritance of first-born sons of two wives (21:15); the punishment of a rebellious son by stoning him to death (21:18-21); sexual purity (22:13-30); divorces (24:1-4); loans and pledges (24:10-13); humanity to culprits—the famous limiting of a flogging to forty stripes lest "thy brother should seem vile unto thee" (25:1-3); proper treatment of animals at work (25:4); and many others. (As noted above, the oft-quoted law of revenge, "life shall go for life, eye for eye, tooth for tooth . . ." [19:21] was not strictly enforced but was interpreted as a plea for equitable, proportionate justice as in requiring adequate, but not excessive, compensation for serious injury.) It is the spiritual satisfaction derived from the keeping of such laws that enables Psalmists to exult with such outbursts as "O how love I thy law! it is my meditation all the day" (Psalms 119:97) and "Thy word is a lamp unto my feet, and a light unto my path" (Psalms 119:105). And it was Christ's violation of some of these laws that made the Pharisees hostile to Christianity.

The book of Deuteronomy consists chiefly of three addresses and two poems, all attributed to Moses. Bits of narrative are interspersed among these five main divisions, and the book ends with an account of the death of Moses.

The First Address (1:1—4:40). In his first speech Moses gives a brief review of all that has happened to the Israelites since their departure from Horeb (Mount Sinai). He stresses the fact that God has kept his half of the Covenant and urges the Israelites to keep theirs by obeying God's laws.

The Second Address (Chs. 5—26). This address makes up the bulk of the book. Here are repeated the Ten Commandments (5:6-21) and other laws, known as the "Covenant Code" (Chs. 12—28). "The emphasis is on justice and righteousness as it applies to both the private and the collective life of the people of Israel." [35] In this address there is a prediction (18:15-22) that God will send to Israel a prophet into whose mouth God will

---

THE FOUR CODES OF THE PENTATEUCH [36]

Four principal collections of legislation appear in the Pentateuch. Some of the individual laws may have originated as early as the days of Moses; the collection or codification, however, was much later.

1. *The Covenant Code* (Ex. 20—23) is regarded as the oldest body of Hebrew law, and it reflects an agricultural society. Its name is derived from the Covenant between God and the Israelites, the promise of God to prosper them provided they kept these laws. This code may be dated between 900 and 650 B.C.

2. *The Deuteronomic Code* (Deut. 12—28) reflects a more humanitarian spirit and a nobler concept of God than does the Covenant Code. Here God is universal and more loving, and he expects man to be merciful and generous. This code insists, too, on centralization of worship, especially in Jerusalem. The code is generally dated 621 B.C.

3. *The Holiness Code* (Lev. 17—26) emphasizes ritual, but lays some stress, too, on personal and social ethics. Some scholars consider the code post-Exilic (that is, later than 536 B.C.); others think it originated about a century before that date.

4. *The Priestly Code* (scattered through Exodus, Leviticus, and Numbers) emphasizes ceremonialism, cult, and ritual as deemed especially significant by the priests and scribes in Jerusalem after the Hebrews' return from the Babylonian Captivity. Most scholars date these priestly laws about 400 B.C.

put his commandments. It seems likely that the Deuteronomist is here justifying the important role of the prophets of the eighth and seventh centuries; and this passage may have had a great deal to do with the growth of the Messianic hope of the Hebrews.

The Third Address (29:1–31:6). In short speeches (Chapters 27, 28) * Moses lists the blessings which will be bestowed on the people if they obey God's law and also the dire consequences if they disobey. Again he reminds them of the Covenant and tells them that their future is in their own hands: they have the freedom to choose whether or not they will earn the blessings which God has promised. "Choice is a perilous gift. Morality is a matter of choice. Without morality life is not attainable and the result is death." [37] "See, I have set before thee this day life and good, and death and evil" (30:15).

The Last Song of Moses (32:1-43). After delivering his final warning to the people, Moses bursts into song, glorifying God and praising his justice and his goodness:

> He is the Rock, his work is perfect:
> For all his ways are judgment:
> A God of truth and without iniquity,
> Just and right is he. (32:4)

The song reviews how God has brought Israel safely through many tribulations:

> He found him [Israel] in a desert land,
> And in the waste howling wilderness;
> He led him about,
> He instructed him,
> He kept him as the apple of his eye. (32:10)

But Israel has provoked God to anger by worshiping strange deities and sacrificing to devils. God therefore has punished Israel by allowing other nations to mistreat it. Now it has repented of its sins, and God will avenge the suffering of his Chosen People. (This portion suggests that The Last Song of Moses is of Exilic or post-Exilic origin.)

---

* Chapter 27, believed to be an interpolation by some Exilic or post-Exilic editor, is a disjointed chapter consisting of (1) exhortations and precepts put into the mouth of Moses and (2) a series of curses upon those who disobey certain laws.

The Blessing of Moses (Ch. 33). This poem is reminiscent of
Jacob's blessing (Gen. 49:2-27); but, unlike the other poem, it
"idealizes its subjects" [38] instead of detailing the characteristics
of each tribe. It barely mentions Judah and Reuben, or Dan and
Naphtali, and it fails to mention Simeon at all. The tribe of Levi
and the two tribes descended from Joseph (Ephraim and Manasseh) receive the most attention. Though literarily inferior to The
Last Song of Moses, the Blessing is, nevertheless, a noble and
majestic poem. It contains many such striking figures as these:

> And the Lord shall cover him [Benjamin] all the day long,
> And he shall dwell between his shoulders. (33:12)

> His [Joseph's] glory is like the firstling of his bullock,
> And his horns are like the horns of unicorns:
> With them he shall push the people together
> To the ends of the earth. (33:17)

And finally these immortal lines:

> The eternal God is thy refuge,
> And underneath are the everlasting arms . . . (33:27)

The Death of Moses (Ch. 34). The Pentateuch closes appropriately with the death of its greatest figure, the faithful and in-
domitable lawgiver, who has now led the wayward children of
Israel to the boundary between Moab and Canaan. His work is
finished. Alone he walks to the top of Mount Nebo. From there
God shows him the Promised Land, which he has been forbidden
to enter. So Moses, the Lord's servant, dies in the land of Moab.

JOSHUA

The last book of the Hexateuch is named for its leading character; the Hebrew proper name means "the Lord saves."

The book of Joshua is an idealized and "schematized" [39] history of the Israelites' conquest and division of Canaan. It covers
a period of about twenty-five years, beginning at a point shortly
after the death of Moses. This history gives the impression that
virtually all the tribes were united under the command of Joshua,
that the conquest was steadily progressive, and that except for
a few spots Canaan was conquered by the end of the twenty-five-
year period. This impression is contradicted by the account of
the same period contained in the first chapter of Judges. The

book of Joshua seems to be a neat but somewhat misleading rearrangement by the Deuteronomist and the priestly editors of
events which took place over more than a century. Archaeological
excavations indicate that there *was* a series of battles and de-
structions of cities in Palestine at the end of the thirteenth century B.C. and later.

The book is not altogether a pleasant one. It is too bloody and
full of merciless destruction to appeal to modern taste. Its titular
hero has the virtues of courage, singleness of purpose, persever-
ance, and obedience to God; but he is cruel and revengeful, and
he lacks the grandeur and the vision of Moses. The God of
Joshua is depicted as "a God of war, revenge, and bloodshed,
who hates the enemies of Israel with merciless and bitter hatred.
. . . This is primitive religion at its worst." [40]

The purpose of the book is twofold: first, to demonstrate how
God has kept his promise to his Chosen People as long as they
obeyed his commandments; and second, to make Joshua appear
a hero and a worthy successor to Moses.

The book has three main parts: (1) the conquest of Canaan
(Chs. 1—12); (2) division of the conquered territory (Chs. 13—
22); and (3) Joshua's farewell address and his death (Chs. 23—
24).

The Conquest of Canaan (Chs. 1—12). The first twelve chapters
tell of Israel's crossing of the Jordan River (the waters are miraculously dammed so that the people cross the river on dry ground)
and of the subduing of most of western Palestine about 1200 B.C.
Although the account contains much bloodshed and cruelty, it
is an orderly and spirited tale told with great enthusiasm. Several episodes deserve special notice.

RAHAB AND THE SPIES (2:1-22 and 6:22-25). The important
city of Jericho lies athwart the intended route of the Israelites;
it must be captured if the campaign is to succeed. Having been
a spy himself, Joshua knows the value of espionage and so sends
two men into Jericho to "view the land." They find lodging at
the house of Rahab, a harlot, who tells them that the inhabitants of Jericho are faint with terror at the approach of Israel.
She says that the Israelites' earlier victories have convinced her
that their God is indeed the God of heaven and earth. Therefore
she turns traitor to her own people and hides the spies when a
searching party sent by the king of Jericho comes to find them.

After exacting a promise that she and her family will be protected when the city falls, she lets the spies down over the wall of the city by means of a "scarlet cord"; this cord is to mark her house when Israel enters Jericho. Later, when the city does fall to the conquerors, Rahab and all her kindred are spared, and she is allowed to live out her days in her native land.

THE FALL OF JERICHO (Ch. 6). As the Hebrews' army approaches Jericho, the city shuts itself up within its walls and prepares to withstand a siege. In obedience to the directions of the Lord, Joshua proceeds in the following manner: a great procession marches around the city once every day for six days. First comes the main body of the soldiers—"mighty men of valor"; next are seven priests, who blow continually on trumpets of rams' horns; after these come some more priests bearing the Ark of the Covenant; finally, a rear guard follows the Ark. On the seventh day the procession marches around Jericho seven times, the priests blowing the trumpets all the while. Then Joshua says to the people: "Shout; for the Lord hath given you the city!" And the people shout with a great shout, and the walls fall down flat, so that the people go up into the city, every man straight before him, and they take the city. Except for Rahab and her kinsmen, every living thing in the city is destroyed, "both man and woman, young and old, and ox, and sheep, and ass, with the edge of the sword." * Joshua pronounces a curse against anyone who should ever rebuild the city.

THE SIN OF ACHAN (Ch. 7). After Jericho the next obstacle in the path of Israel is the small city of Ai. Joshua sends an expeditionary force of three thousand to take the city; but they are repulsed and some of them are slain. When Joshua cries out to God in grief and despair, God tells him that the defeat is punishment for a sin committed by some Israelite. Investigation reveals that Achan has appropriated for his own use a garment, some silver, and some gold—all from the spoils of Jericho.

* Archaeological excavations have demonstrated that the walls of Jericho did fall. Scholars have suggested that one may suppose, "without minimizing the divine guidance of events," that the physical cause of the collapse of the walls was an earthquake. See John Bright, exegesis to Joshua, *The Interpreter's Bible*, II, 581-582. The account in Joshua is an excellent illustration of how Old Testament historians could incorporate into their narratives such actual facts as the mysterious ruins of a city—whether their purpose was to substantiate the legends or merely to account for the facts.

Joshua orders Achan and all his family and possessions, including the stolen spoils, to be brought into the valley of Achor. There the culprit and his family are stoned and their bodies burned. "So the Lord turned from the fierceness of his anger."

THE DESTRUCTION OF AI (8:1-29). Now Joshua employs a stratagem to overcome Ai. He sends his main force of thirty thousand to lie in ambush on the west of the city. Next he leads an attack from the north. When the defenders of Ai come out in a mass, the Israelites on the north retreat, and their enemies pursue them. Then the soldiers in ambush rush in, capture the city, and burn it. Twelve thousand of its inhabitants are killed. The king, who has been taken captive, is hanged. The "cattle and spoil" of the city are appropriated by the Israelites.

THE WILES OF THE GIBEONITES (Ch. 9). Fearing the might and the cruelty of Joshua's men, the inhabitants of Gibeon send to Joshua envoys who (by displaying to him worn-out shoes and clothes, patched wineskins, and moldy bread) pretend that they have come from a distant land. Joshua makes a peace pact with them. When he discovers that they are in reality close neighbors, he decrees that thenceforth the Gibeonites must be the servants of the Israelites—"hewers of wood and drawers of water."

THE BATTLE OF GIBEON (10:1-27). Five kings of the Amorites now join forces to oppose Joshua. They attack him at Gibeon, but the Lord comes to the aid of his people. The Israelites begin to gain the upper hand, yet Joshua fears that daylight will fail before his victory is complete. Therefore he prays to the Lord and speaks the famous words:

> Sun, stand thou still upon Gibeon;
> And thou, Moon, in the valley of Ajalon. (10:12)

The Lord answers his prayers, and the sun and the moon remain motionless till the enemies of Israel are routed. To add to the Amorites' troubles, God sends great hailstones, which kill more men than do the Israelites. The five kings flee and hide in a cave. When Joshua is told of their hiding place, he orders the mouth of the cave to be closed with great stones; and he commands his men to pursue the Amorites so that they cannot re-enter their city. After the great slaughter is ended, the five kings are brought from the cave; they are killed and their bodies are hanged for display.

THE END OF THE CAMPAIGN (10:28–12:24). Joshua's men fight many other battles, two of the most famous being those at the waters of Merom and at Hazor. All enemies are defeated, even the giant race of Anakim to whom (Num. 13:33) the Israelites are "as grasshoppers." Altogether, thirty-one kings and their armies are vanquished (including those at Jericho). Although large areas (such as the land of the Philistines in the southwest) remain unconquered, Joshua decides that it is time to divide the country among the tribes that have crossed the Jordan.

The Division of Canaan (Chs. 13–22). The ten chapters devoted to the assigning of land to each tribe repeat much of the material found in Exodus and Deuteronomy, and they contain much methodical listing of cities, rivers, and families. This is the sort of writing which was especially dear to the priestly authors, but which the modern student of literature is inclined to skip.

Joshua's Farewell Address and His Death (Chs. 23–24). Joshua is now "old and stricken in age." Like Moses, he calls all the Israelites together to hear his final exhortations. He points out the great blessings which the Lord has showered upon them. He urges them "to do all that is written in the book of the law of Moses." Fearing that they might be tempted to worship the gods of the Canaanites, he warns his people that the Lord "is an holy God; he is a jealous God; he will not forgive your transgressions nor your sins." The people promise to serve the Lord and obey his voice.

Joshua dies and is buried on Mount Ephraim.

Rise and Fall of the Monarchy

(From Judges to the Exile)

After the death of Joshua, as the need for a strong central government in Israel became clear, the monarchy was established under Saul. The history of the Hebrew people from the period before Saul until the time of the Exile in 586 B.C. is related in Judges, I and II Samuel, and I and II Kings.

JUDGES: TREND TOWARD NATIONAL UNITY AND SECULAR GOVERNMENT

This book derives its name from the title given to the leaders of various groups of Israelites before the establishment of the monarchy under Saul. Although called "judges," these dignitaries usually served at one and the same time as military and religious leaders and as civil magistrates.

It is believed that the composition of the book of Judges went through the following stages: [1] (1) Between 1200 and 900 B.C. historical stories and legends developed, many of them in the form of narrative poems. (2) These were transmitted orally for a few centuries, and then they were converted into prose tales, possibly by the authors of the J and E documents.[*] (3) At some time during the eighth or the seventh century B.C., an unidentified editor (possibly the one who conflated the J and E documents) combined the separate tales into a continuous narrative. (4) The Deuteronomist [†] re-edited most of the material now making up Judges 2:6—16:31, probably about 621 B.C. (5) In the latter part

[*] See above, pp. 49-51, the discussion of the growth of the Hexateuch.

[†] See above, pp. 50 and 76-80, the discussion of the D Document and the book of Deuteronomy.

of the sixth century B.C., after the Exile, some unknown editor added the introduction (1:1—2:5), the "appendixes" (17:1—21:25), and possibly 3:31 and 9:1-57.

The book of Joshua leaves the impression that by the time of the death of the titular hero, the Hebrew tribes had pretty well subdued most of Canaan and had organized themselves into a united nation under one leader. The book of Judges, on the contrary, gives a picture of the tribes frequently squabbling with each other and continually fighting against their non-Hebrew neighbors. Biblical scholars are inclined to believe that Judges gives the more accurate account.

The book is not, however, an entirely reliable history. Much of its material belongs to the realm of folklore: the chronology is confused; and many of the tales are colored by the editors' desire to point a moral.

The three main parts of the book are: (1) the introduction (1:1—2:5); (2) a cycle of stories about the lives and the times of the twelve (or thirteen if "King" Abimelech is counted) judges who presided over some of the Israelites after the death of Joshua (2:6—16:31), and (3) the two appendixes, concerned respectively with the migration of the Danites (17—18) and the offense of Gibeah (19—21).

Post-Exilic Introduction to the Book (1:1—2:5). The first portion of the book of Judges is an attempt by the post-Exilic editor to furnish a transition between the book of Joshua and the Deuteronomist's tales of the twelve judges. It tells of several conquests in the land of Canaan, some of which have already been related in the book of Joshua.

Tales about the Judges (2:6—16:31). The longest and by far the most significant portion of the book deals with the adventures of the judges themselves. This section uses a review of the funeral of Joshua to emphasize the fact that a new era began soon after the death of that hero. Next, the cycle of stories about the judges is set into a sort of didactic framework: each story is made to illustrate the Deuteronomist's favorite thesis: that God is just and will punish his people when they sin against him, but is merciful and will send aid when they are obedient or repent and beg for deliverance. Every story is introduced by an almost stereotyped formula: "And the children of Israel did evil in the sight of the Lord. . . . And the anger of the Lord was hot against Israel, and

he delivered them into the hands of spoilers that spoiled them. . . .
But when the children of Israel cried unto the Lord, the Lord
raised up a deliverer . . ."[2] In each case the deliverer is one of
the judges.

These judges and the passages which tell of their exploits are
designated in the following table:

   (1) Othniel (1:11-13; 3:7-11).
   (2) Ehud (3:12-30).
   (3) Shamgar (3:31).
   (4) Deborah (4-5).
   (5) Gideon (6:1—8:32).
   (6) (Perhaps) Abimelech (8:33—9:57).
   (7) Tola (10:1-2).
   (8) Jair (10:3-5).
   (9) Jephthah (10:6—12:7).
 (10) Ibzan (12:8-10).
 (11) Elon (12:11-12).
 (12) Abdon (12:13-15).
 (13) Samson (13—16).

Of this number, Shamgar, Tola, Jair, Ibzan, Elon, and Abdon are
sometimes known as the "minor" judges. Abimelech is called a
"king," (9:6); some commentators, however, include him in the
list of judges.

OTHNIEL (1:11-13; 3:7-11). Othniel, the first of the twelve
judges, is renowned for his military expoits (he captures Debir,
receiving Caleb's daughter for his wife as a reward, and later
rescues the Israelites from a neighboring king).

EHUD THE TYRANNICIDE (3:12-30). Once when the people do
evil, they are forced by God to serve Eglon, King of Moab, for
eighteen years. Then Ehud, chosen to deliver Israel's tribute to
Eglon, conceals a two-edged dagger beneath his clothes and deceives Eglon by pretending that he has a secret which nobody
but the king must hear. Ehud says: "I have a message from God
unto thee." Now, "Eglon was a very fat man. . . . And Ehud put
forth his left hand, and took the dagger from his right thigh, and
thrust it into his belly; and the haft also went in after the blade;
and the fat closed upon the blade, so that he could not draw the
dagger out of his belly; and the dirt came out." After so daring a
feat, Ehud rallies the Israelites and leads them in a victorious
battle against Moab.

DEBORAH THE PROPHETESS (Chs. 4–5). Far more renowned than Ehud is Deborah, prophetess and judge, whose religious fervor and "flaming patriotism" [3] inspire the soldier Barak to lead Israel's army against the Canaanitish host under the command of Sisera. Now the Israelites have been cruelly oppressed by Canaan for twenty years. Deborah convinces Barak that the Lord will give his people victory over Sisera on Mount Tabor, by the river Kishon, where Sisera's "nine hundred chariots of iron" will be ineffective. A battle takes place, and Deborah's prophecy is fulfilled: all of Sisera's men are killed, and Sisera himself finds refuge in the tent of a Hebrew woman named Jael, who pretends friendship but kills him while he sleeps.

These events, related in unadorned prose in Chapter 4, become the subject of a brilliant victory song in Chapter 5, known as the "Song of Deborah and Barak." *

There is no other poem in Hebrew literature, whether early or late, which displays such seemingly unconscious and spontaneous literary art. The intense patriotic and religious passion of its writer flames in every line, sweeping on and up to the dramatic climax. It is throughout both an ancient *Te Deum* in praise of the God of Israel and a superb account of a mighty contest in which not only kings fought, but the stars of heaven and a river in its divinely swollen course. . . . Nothing is finer in the annals of war of any literature than this, nor has it been excelled in imagination or in expression by any of the later war poems of Israel.[4]

Exclusive of a brief introduction and a final curse, the poem may be divided into three main parts. The first part (5:4-11) describes the terrifying approach of God himself toward the battlefield: the earth trembles and the mountains melt. Then there is a picture of the villages and highways, which have long been left desolate for fear of the Canaanites. The second section (5:12-18) opens with a plea to Deborah and Barak to arise, sing, and lead on to victory. Next comes a series of praises for those tribes which respond to Barak's appeal for mobilization—Ephraim, Benjamin, Machir (Manasseh), Issachar, and Naphthali. The author voices his (or her) contempt for the cowardly tribes of Gilead (Gad), Reuben, Asher, and Dan, who have refused

* It is believed that this song is (with the possible exception of part of the Song of Moses and the People [Exodus 15:1]) the oldest part of the Bible, to be dated 1150-1100 B.C.

to join in the battle. The third and most ecstatic part of the ode
(5:19-31) begins with a litotes full of grim and exultant humor: *

> The kings came and fought;
> Then fought the kings of Canaan,
> In Taanach by the waters of Megiddo;
> They took no gain of money.

The Israelites are aided by the natural forces:

> They fought from heaven.
> The stars in their courses fought against Sisera.
> The river of Kishon swept them away,
> That ancient river, the river Kishon.

The climax of the whole story is the slaying of Sisera. Wearied
beyond endurance and fearful for his life, he asks Jael for shelter and protection. She calms his fears by bringing him better
refreshment than he requests:

> He asked water, and she gave him milk;
> She brought forth butter in a lordly dish.

When he falls asleep, she seizes a nail (or tent peg) and with a
hammer drives it through both his temples. The poetess gloats
over the scene which she imagines must be taking place at Sisera's home:

> The mother of Sisera looked out at a window,
> And cried through the lattice,
> "Why is his chariot so long in coming?
> Why tarry the wheels of his chariots?"

The ladies in waiting assure Sisera's mother that her son is only
gathering up the spoils of battle.

Without offering any transition, the poetess then ends the ode
abruptly:

> So let all Thine enemies perish, O Lord:
> But let them that love him be as the sun
> When he goeth forth in his might.

GIDEON THE SHREWD (6:1—8:32). The tale of Gideon is an exciting and melodramatic tale. About 1100 B.C. the Midianites,
Amalekites, and other "children of the east" were continually

---

* Compare the many litotes in *Beowulf*.

making predatory raids on Israelite settlements. The number of these predators was so great that the historian likens them to swarms of grasshoppers or locusts. The Hebrews are now confronted with a new "secret weapon" *—the camel (this attack by the Midianites has been called the first camel raid in recorded history [5]). Once again, as in the days of Deborah, normal agricultural activity among the Israelites is almost at a standstill. The Lord calls upon Gideon, the youngest son of a poor farmer, to deliver his people. Gideon begins his work for the Lord by destroying his father's altar to Baal and the grove beside it (6:25-27). He has misgivings about his abilities as a soldier, but when the Lord promises him aid and reassures him by giving him three miraculous signs, Gideon agrees to undertake the mission. Thirty-two thousand men flock to his standards, but only ten thousand remain when he sends home all who admit to being afraid. The number is still far too great, for the Lord wants the Israelites to know that it is the divine might and not the power of the people which will overcome Midian. The number is therefore reduced by a test: the men are all led to the water and told to drink. All who throw themselves on their knees to drink are judged insufficiently vigilant and alert; the three hundred who drink from their hands are chosen.

Now Gideon plans a surprise attack by night. He gives each man a torch (concealed in a pitcher) and a trumpet. This group then surrounds the Midianite camp. In the dead of night at a signal from Gideon, all three hundred wave the torches on high, break the pitchers (to sound like the clashing of armor), blow on the trumpets, and cry out: "The sword of the Lord, and of Gideon!" Believing themselves surrounded by a mighty army, the Midianites flee in panic, and the Lord sets "every man's sword against his fellow." The rout is complete. The next day the Ephraimites aid in "mopping up." Never again are the Israelites molested by the robbers of Midian.

The picture of Gideon is a rather attractive one. To be sure, he is cruel and sometimes vengeful: he captures and executes the two princes and the two kings of the Midianites, and he punishes the elders of Succoth (for their refusal to feed his

* The Hebrews are continually having to fight against superior weapons (for example, the iron chariots of the Canaanites as recorded in Judges 4:13).

army) by tearing their flesh with thorns and briers. But he is a humble servant of God, not at all ambitious or eager for personal glory; witness his refusal to be made king (8:22-23). Furthermore, he is a shrewd general, and he is very human in his early fear of the Midianites, his requiring of miraculous signs from God, his yearning for the earrings of the slain foe, and his self-indulgence during his latter years (he has seventy sons by "many wives" and also an illegitimate son, Abimelech).

"KING" ABIMELECH (8:33–9:57). Son of Gideon and a concubine from the city of Shechem, the cruel and treacherous Abimelech murders all his legitimate half-brothers except Jotham who escapes death by going into hiding. Then he is made king by the men of Shechem. Somewhat later his subjects revolt and are ruthlessly destroyed. While besieging an enemy city, Abimelech himself is grievously wounded by a woman who fractures his skull with a piece of millstone; he orders one of his soldiers to slay him so that posterity will not say that he was killed by a woman.

Of greater literary interest than the story of Abimelech itself is the famous Fable of Jotham (9:7-21), one of the rare instances of this type of folklore in the Bible.* When Abimelech is made king, Jotham (from a safe distance—"on the top of Mount Gerizim") tells how the bramble accepted the position as king of trees after the olive tree, the fig tree, and the vine all had refused the offer of the crown. The bramble then warned the trees that if they were disloyal, he, the bramble, would destroy them all with fire. Jotham is, of course, pointing out to the Shechemites that they have chosen a wicked and dangerous sovereign, and he prophesies that Abimelech and his subjects will destroy each other.

JEPHTHAH THE RASH (10:6–12:7). The piteous tale of Jephthah and his daughter has always been a favorite with modern readers. It contains several elements which appear in the traditional literature of many nations: (1) "the rise to power of a banished hero";[6] (2) the rash vow, especially a vow to sacrifice some-

* The Bible contains many parables but few fables. Both of these genres are short tales which illustrate some truth or moral principle. The fable, however, is in a lighter vein and on a lower ethical plane than the parable and unlike the parable usually contains some impossible phenomenon, such as the talking of animals, whereas the parable contains no such phenomenon. Another instance of the fable in the Bible is that of the body and its members (I Cor. 12:14-26).

thing; and (3) the lament of a maiden for her virginity (that is, a maiden's lament over the fact that she is about to die before she has experienced marriage and motherhood).*

Jephthah, of humble birth (he is the son of a harlot), is driven from his native land (Gilead) into the land of Tob. When oppressed by the Ammonites, the Gileadites recall Jephthah and make him their leader. He vows to God that if he is victorious, he will sacrifice as a burnt offering whoever comes first out of his house to meet him on his return. He subdues the Ammonites, and his only daughter (whose name is never mentioned) comes out to greet him "with timbrels and with dances." Deep is his grief, but after an interval of two months (during which time she dwells in the mountains and bemoans her virginity), he carries out his vow. Each year thereafter the women of Gilead spend four days lamenting the daughter of Jephthah.

SAMSON THE MIGHTY (Chs. 13–16). It is generally agreed that the stories of Samson constitute the literary masterpiece of the book of Judges. Their central figure is not only a typical legendary strong man but also a tragic hero.

The accounts of Samson's exploits have several earmarks of folklore—exaggeration, practical joking, posing of riddles, and broad, boisterous humor. Killing a thousand Philistines with the jawbone of an ass, catching three hundred foxes and tying torches to their tails in order to burn his enemies' grain fields, pulling down a temple with his bare hands—such feats compare with the mighty deeds of Hercules in Greek legends, of Thor in Norse mythology, and of Paul Bunyan in American loggers' yarns.

If great physical strength and a penchant for practical joking were the only characteristics of Samson, then he would not be especially heroic; but his is the story of a devout and valorous man, who, chosen by God to deliver the Israelites from the Philistines, suffers ignominy and death at the hands of the cruel enemy. Consequently his downfall has inspired the creation of many noble works of art, notably Milton's *Samson Agonistes*, Handel's *Samson*, and Saint-Saëns' *Samson and Delilah*.

This is Samson's story as told in the book of Judges:

An angel appears unto the wife of one Manoah and tells her that she is going to conceive and bear a son,† who will deliver

---

* Compare Iphigenia's lament in Euripides' *Iphigenia at Aulis* and Antigone's lament in Sophocles' *Antigone*.

† See note, p. 56, above.

The Great Sea

Tyre

Accho

ASHER

NAPHTALI

Sea of
Chinnereth

BASHAN

Dor

MT CARMEL

ZEBULUN

ISSACHAR

Meqiddo

MANASSEH

MANASSEH

Jordan

Joppa

EPHRAIM

Shiloh

Bethel

River

GAD

AMMON

DAN

Jericho

BENJAMIN

Ashdod

Jerusalem

Bethlehem

Ashkelon

PHILISTINES

JUDAH

Gaza

Hebron

Salt Sea

REUBEN

SIMEON

N

Beer-sheba

MOAB

PALESTINE
THE PERIOD
OF THE JUDGES

SCALE OF MILES

5   30

KNOWN BOUNDARIES

PROBABLE BOUNDARIES

SEIR

EDOM

From *A Handbook for Know Your Bible Study Groups,* © 1959 by Abingdon Press. By permission of the publisher.

the Israelites from the Philistines, the current scourge of God's people. The angel warns her against ever shaving the boy's hair. In due time Samson is born, grows into manhood, and soon manifests prodigious strength.

His first feat is the slaying of a lion with his bare hands. This he accomplishes en route to visit an unnamed Philistine woman. On his return he notices a swarm of bees and some honey in the carcass of the lion. This suggests to Samson a riddle, which he later poses to thirty Philistine men: "Out of the eater came forth meat, and out of the strong came forth sweetness." He wagers a "change of garments" with each that none of them can solve the riddle. His sweetheart wheedles the answer from him and divulges it to her countrymen. And wrathful Samson smites "thirty men of them" (other Philistines) and uses their clothing to pay off his wager.

Samson's "wife," as the Philistine woman is now called, is given by her father to another man. It is at this time that Samson's fox-escapade destroys the fields of the Philistines, who retaliate by burning at the stake Samson's wife and her father. Samson takes revenge, first by slaughtering many of the Philistines. When the Philistines attack the men of Judah, however, he allows the latter to bind him and deliver him to the Philistines. Then he breaks his bonds, seizes the jawbone of an ass, and with it kills a thousand Philistines. Thereafter, he judges Israel in peace for twenty years.

A subsequent adventure takes place in Gaza, where Samson has fallen in love with Delilah, another Philistine woman. Bribed by her fellow countrymen to find the secret of Samson's great strength, Delilah uses her feminine wiles on the Hebrew hero. Thrice he gives her false answers, and thrice he breaks the bonds she puts on him. Then he foolishly tells her the truth—that the secret of his might lies in his unshaven hair. As soon as he falls asleep, the treacherous Delilah shaves his head and calls the Philistines, who put out Samson's eyes, bind him in fetters, and throw him into prison. Later, when his hair has grown long again, the Philistines add to the degradation of the fallen hero by forcing him to play the fool. They require him to amuse a great crowd gathered for a festival in honor of their god Dagon. When he is led into the temple, Samson prays to the Lord for strength so that he may avenge himself. God answers his prayer:

Samson leans with all his might upon the middle pillars support-
ing the temple, and pushes them down, so that the temple falls
and kills three thousand Philistines as well as Samson himself.
Samson's brothers recover the body of the hero and bury it.

Post-Exilic Appendixes to the Book (Chs. 17—21). At the end
of the book of Judges are added two narratives which are un-
related to the exploits of the judges but which tell about the
same period in history.[7]

MIGRATION OF THE DANITES (Chs. 17—18). This is an account
of how the tribe of Dan (which up to this time has found no
place in which to settle) conquers the Sidonian city of Laish,
renames it "Dan," and then makes an ephod * to be worshiped.
Perhaps the strangest thing about the tale is that the author nowhere condemns the Danites for idol-worship, but is content to
remark: "In those days there was no king in Israel, but every
man did that which was right in his own eyes."

THE OFFENSE OF GIBEAH (Chs. 19—21). This is a brutal story
of revenge. The concubine of a certain Levite of Mount Ephraim
is raped to death by a group of Benjamites in the city of Gibeah.
The Levite cuts the body of the dead woman into twelve pieces
and sends each one to a different part of Canaan in order to
shock the various tribes into helping him seek vengeance. The
Israelites of other tribes gather "together as one man"—perhaps
an indication of increasing national unity.[8] First they ask that
the offending group from Gibeah be put to death. When this is
refused, they wage war against the Benjamites and kill all but
six hundred whom they later provide with wives from Jabesh-
gilead and Shiloh.

I AND II SAMUEL AND I KINGS 1—2: GROWTH OF MONARCHY TEMPERED BY THEOCRACY

The four books which in the English Bible are called I and II
Samuel and I and II Kings were once a single continuous narrative. The Hebrew text, lacking vowels, required the use of only

---

* The word *ephod* is apparently used to denote two different articles at
different times. Sometimes (as in Ex. 28:6-12) it is a garment, especially
one worn by a priest; at other times it is a box, an ark, or a tentlike structure, used as an instrument of divination. For a discussion of the problem,
see George B. Caird, introduction to I and II Samuel, *The Interpreter's
Bible*, II, 872-874.

two scrolls; in the Jewish Scriptures these were known, respectively, as the book of Samuel and the book of Kings. The Greek text (the Septuagint) filled four scrolls; the artificial division into four parts has been continued in English versions. Our name for the first two books is misleading, for only eight of the forty-five chapters are primarily concerned with Samuel; he dies before any of the events in II Samuel take place. The first two chapters of I Kings belong logically with the "David cycle" found in the books of Samuel.

I and II Samuel are drawn principally from two sources: [9] (a) The "early" source was probably written about the middle of the tenth century B.C. There is little doubt that the author of this document was a priest, a contemporary of David, and an eyewitness of many of the events which he records. Many commentators are convinced that this author was Abiathar, the priest and close friend of David who was discarded by Solomon (see I Kings 2:26). A modern Biblical scholar, Alice Parmelee, claims that he, not Herodotus, deserves the title "the father of history":

As far as we know, this volume, written by a Hebrew priest around 1000 B.C., is the oldest book of history in the world. With no models to follow, Abiathar, or whoever the author was, created the art of history writing.[10]

(b) The "late" source is of uncertain date; some parts seem to have been written early (c. 900 B.C.), and others much later, perhaps as late as 700 B.C. The authors' names and identities are unknown. According to some Biblical scholars, it was probably during the seventh century B.C. that these two sources were conflated with many discrepancies, repetitions, and contradictions. About 550 B.C. some reviser, following the Deuteronomic traditions, re-edited the whole narrative. This was the last major revision of the books, but there were several significant later interpolations, some believed to be as late as the fifth century B.C.[11]

The two books of Samuel, plus the opening two chapters of I Kings, depict the transition of the Hebrew nation from a loose confederation of tribes under the semi-theocratic government of the judges into a unified monarchy. This transition extended over slightly more than half a century (c. 1030–c. 973 B.C.). Another important development during the period was the rise of prophets, lay leaders who in later centuries were destined to figure prominently in the religious and political affairs of the Jewish people.

Samuel is perhaps the finest narrative book in the Bible. The style of the book is simple; the narrative, easy, unified, and progressive, incident following incident as in a well-connected story. The details are always sufficient to make the pictures and incidents vivid, distinct, and realistic, yet they are never dry or cumbersome. But the chief glory of the book is its masterly characterization. Here are real men and women, heroic enough to have a godlike vision of truth and righteous behavior, yet they are true citizens of the earth where there is nothing absolutely perfect.[12]

The books of Samuel consist principally of the biographies of Samuel himself, of Saul, and of David. These stories overlap each other, for each of the three main characters becomes involved in the lives of the other two. In order to present three unified cycles, some reorganization of Biblical material is necessary.

Samuel the Kingmaker [13] (I Sam. 1—8 and 9—25, *passim*). Like the judges of earlier generations, Samuel appears at a time of national emergency. The last of the judges and one of the first of the prophets, he is at the same time a priest, a soothsayer, a spokesman for God, and a political leader. In the two latter roles he is a prototype of such great prophets as Elijah and Isaiah.

BIRTH AND CHILDHOOD (I Sam. 1—3). The story opens with an account of the quasi-miraculous conception of Samuel by Hannah.* This unhappy woman, one of the two wives of Elkanah, cries to the Lord "in bitterness of soul" because she is barren, and she promises the Lord that if he will give her a son, she will dedicate him to God "all the days of his life." Eli, the priest of the temple at Shiloh, who has watched her weeping and praying silently, accuses her of drunkenness; she, of course, denies the charge. The Lord grants her petition, and in due time Hannah triumphantly presents the baby Samuel to Eli. Then follows Hannah's famous song of praise (I Sam. 2:1-10).†

Hannah leaves Samuel with Eli in the temple at Shiloh; there the old priest brings him up in the service of the Lord. The historian gives an appealing picture of Hannah's coming once a year to offer a sacrifice and to bring a little coat for her son.

---

* See note, p. 56.
† Comparable to Mary's Magnificat (Luke 1:46-55).

When Eli has grown very old, he is saddened by the fact that his two sons, apparently in succession for the judgeship, have fallen into evil ways. In contrast with these sons, Samuel has continued to grow "in favour both with the Lord, and also with men." One day Samuel receives a special summons from the Lord. While sleeping, the young boy hears a voice calling his name. Thinking it to be Eli's, he runs to the priest; but Eli denies having called him and tells him to go back to sleep. The call comes again, and again Eli tells Samuel to return to his bed. When the voice calls the third time, the priest tells the lad that it is God who is calling and that the next time he must answer: "Speak, Lord; for thy servant heareth." A fourth time God calls, and now he foretells to Samuel the destruction of the sons of Eli for their iniquity. Samuel soon afterward is recognized as a seer and a prophet of the Lord.

ADMINISTRATION (I Sam. 4–8). When the Philistines wage a victorious battle against the Israelites, thousands of the men of Israel (including the two sons of Eli) are slain, and the Ark of the Covenant is captured. On hearing of the disaster, Eli, now ninety-eight years old, falls dead. Samuel succeeds him as judge of Israel.

The capture of the Ark, though a major disaster to Israel, brings misfortune to the Philistines. First, they set the Ark in the temple of their god Dagon, but on the following morning the statue of Dagon is found fallen and broken. The Ark is moved from Ashdod to Gath and then to Ekron, and the inhabitants of these cities are smitten with a plague of emerods (tumors). In terror the Philistines abandon the Ark in Bethshemesh, and it is reclaimed by the Israelites, who repent their sins and completely subdue the enemy. Samuel thereafter judges Israel—apparently in peace and prosperity—for many years.

When he has grown old, he turns the government over to his sons Joel and Abiah. But these sons are corrupt, and they so "pervert judgment" that the elders of Israel clamor for a monarch: "Make us a king to judge us like all the nations." Samuel feels that the people have rejected God as their king. He prays to the Lord but is instructed to give in to the popular demand and to find a king of Israel; he is to warn the people, however, of the evils of kingship. (The warning which Samuel accordingly delivers [I Sam. 8:11-18] is probably a reflection of the opinions of the Biblical historian, writing in retrospect.)

RETIREMENT AND FURTHER PROPHETIC ACTIVITIES (I Sam. 9—25, *passim*). The remainder of Samuel's deeds belong more properly to the cycles of tales about Saul and David and therefore require only the briefest mention here. The old prophet anoints Saul to be king of Israel, but later on, reconsidering matters, turns against him and anoints David (instead of any of Saul's sons) as future successor to the throne. Thus, despite the establishment of a monarchy, Samuel continues to exercise a powerful influence on the political affairs of Israel all the days of his life. He dies during the reign of Saul (I Sam. 25:1).

The Tragedy of Saul[14] (I Sam. 9—31, *passim*). The sad story of the first king of Israel is, as Mary Ellen Chase points out, like a Greek tragedy. On the whole a good man, Saul has a "tragic flaw," which, along with outside circumstances, brings about his downfall.

The son of a prosperous farmer of the tribe of Benjamin, he is described as "a choice young man, and a goodly . . . from his shoulders and upward he was higher than any of the people" * (I Sam. 9:2). He evidently has a forceful and attractive personality, for he succeeds in uniting the people and in maintaining their loyalty throughout his reign. But he is subject to fits of melancholia. He is the prey of his "complex and passionate nature" which holds "within itself the seeds of despondency and madness." [15]

Israel's debt to Saul is considerable, for in addition to unifying the tribes, he wins important victories over nearly all the nation's enemies, including the Philistines, and he establishes a base on the east bank of the Jordan.

ANOINTING AND EARLY VICTORIES (I Sam. 9:1—10:27, 11:1-15, and 14:47-52). On a mission to find his father's lost asses, Saul seeks the advice of the seer Samuel ("he that is now called a Prophet was before time called a Seer"). The Lord tells Samuel that this tall and handsome youth is the one chosen to become king. Samuel anoints Saul with oil and announces to him God's

---

* Extraordinary stature is a characteristic of the traditional "tragic hero." One should compare the various descriptions of Tamerlane and also the ancient Greek custom of increasing the height of tragic heroes by the use of the cothurnus (thick-soled shoe).

will that he be the ruler of Israel. Saul is overwhelmed and later
hides when Samuel tries to present him to a throng of people
summoned to convene at Mizpah. The convention chooses him
by lot, however, and all the people shout: "God save the king!"

The new king's first official act is to defeat the Ammonites who
are besieging Jabesh-gilead. Subsequently he leads his army victoriously against the Moabites, the Ammonites, the Edomites,
the kings of Zobah, and the Amalekites. He repulses the Philistines, too, but is unable to put an end to their raids on his land.

SHORTCOMINGS AND REJECTION (I Sam. 10:8, 13:8-14, and 15:
1-35). Modern commentators are inclined to regard the Philistines' slaying of Saul and his sons and David's accession to the
throne of Israel as historical events which require no explanation. The Deuteronomic historian, however, evidently feels that
Saul's failure to found a dynasty does need to be accounted for,
especially since God directed Samuel to anoint Saul, thereby enabling him to become the potential progenitor of a dynasty.[16]
The historian's usual explanation of a calamity is that it is a
punishment inflicted by God for wrongdoing. So Saul is charged
with being guilty of two things: usurpation of priestly functions
and failure to obey divine commands. Therefore Samuel, acting
as God's agent, rejects Saul twice.

The first rejection precedes a great battle against the Philistines. An important item in the preparations for the conflict is the
offering of a sacrifice to God. The aged Samuel promises to be
present to officiate, but fails to appear at the appointed time.
Saul himself presides at the offering. On arrival, Samuel denounces Saul for usurping the priestly duties; he proclaims that
the kingdom shall be taken away from Saul and given to another. In spite of the rebuke, Saul and his son Jonathan win a
great victory over the Philistines.

Now Samuel sends Saul to destroy the Amalekites. He instructs the king to kill every living thing—"man and woman, in-
fant and suckling, ox and sheep, camel and ass." Again Saul is
victorious, but his soldiers bring back alive some sheep and
oxen to sacrifice to the Lord, and Saul spares the life of Agag,
the captive king of Amalek. In great wrath once more, Samuel
asks: "Hath the Lord as great delight in burnt offerings and
sacrifices, as in obeying the voice of the Lord? Behold, to obey
is better than sacrifice, and to hearken than the fat of rams."

For the second time, Samuel announces that the Lord has rejected Saul as king of Israel. In deep sorrow and repentance, Saul humbly promises to obey the Lord and to worship him. Samuel then hacks Agag to pieces with a sword.

DECLINE (I Sam. 16:14-23 and 18—27, *passim*). Having rejected Saul, Samuel anoints David to be the successor to the throne. As the spirit of the Lord descends upon David, it departs from Saul, and "an evil spirit from the Lord" troubles him. Renounced by Samuel and even by God, well might Saul be depressed. He calls for a musician to play for him and relieve his melancholy. Ironically (or perhaps providentially), it is David who is summoned. Immediately Saul learns to love him and soon makes him his armor-bearer. Thereafter whenever the fit of melancholy falls, David plays on the harp, and the evil spirit leaves Saul.

According to another story,* Saul's melancholia is principally the result of his jealousy over David's success as a soldier. To reward David for killing the giant Goliath and for defeating the Philistines, Saul makes him a high officer in the army. But when the women sing: "Saul hath slain his thousands, and David his ten thousands," Saul's jealousy knows no bounds. Twice he hurls a javelin at David, who each time eludes the weapon. Again Saul sends messengers to kill David in his sleep, but Michal (Saul's own daughter, who has been given to David in marriage) enables her husband to escape.

In the meantime, David has formed a close friendship with Jonathan, Saul's son, who tries to convince his father that David has done no wrong; but Saul will not listen, and David has to flee for his life. He finds refuge at one place and then another; Saul pursues him wherever he goes. David has an opportunity to kill Saul, but only cuts off a piece of the sleeping king's robe and later shows it to him from a distance. Saul is overwhelmed with remorse: "Is this thy voice, my son David?" He weeps and says to David: "Thou art more righteous than I: for thou hast rewarded me good, whereas I have rewarded thee evil." Unfortunately the remorse is short-lived, and the pursuit recommences. Again David has a chance to kill Saul, but declines to raise his hand against the Lord's anointed. At length David escapes to

---

* Obviously from a different source, for in this second account, David is introduced as an unknown; see I Sam. 17:55-58.

the land of the Philistines, where he is befriended by the king of Gath.

DEATH (I Sam. 28 and 31 and II Sam. 1:1-16). Saul feels that his son Jonathan and his daughter Michal have turned against him; he knows that his former friend David has joined the enemy Philistines, and he suffers because the Lord has forsaken him (Samuel, incidentally, has died during the course of Saul's pursuit of David). Saul presents a pitiable figure as he surveys the multitudes of Philistines arrayed against him at Gilboa. He is afraid and his heart trembles. He seeks the aid of the Lord, but the Lord does not answer him. There is bitter irony in Saul's next move. He has formerly banished all soothsayers and sorcerers from his kingdom, but now he seeks the aid of one of those he has banished. He employs the witch of Endor to call up the spirit of Samuel. That spirit asks: "Why hast thou disquieted me, to bring me up?" Saul answers: "I am sore distressed; for the Philistines make war against me, and God is departed from me, and answereth me no more, neither by prophets, nor by dreams; therefore I have called thee, that thou mayest make known unto me what I shall do." The spirit holds out no hope: the Philistines will win the battle, Saul and his sons will be killed, and David will take over the kingdom.

In a spirit of desperation comparable to that of Macbeth meeting the hosts of Macduff at Dunsinane, Saul joins in the battle against the Philistines. The tale is briefly told by the historian. The men of Israel flee from the enemy. Many of the Israelites are slain, including Saul's sons Jonathan, Abinadab, and Melchishua. Saul himself falls upon his own sword; his body is captured by the enemy, but is later retrieved by the Israelites, burned, and the bones buried at Jabesh.

A different account of Saul's death (apparently intended by the Biblical historian to be understood as a mere story) is given in the first chapter of II Samuel. Here an Amalekite comes to David and says that he himself slew Saul at Saul's request. David has the Amalekite killed for slaying the Lord's anointed.

David, Founder of the Royal Line (I Sam. 16—30, *passim* and II Sam.—I Kings 2). David was incomparably the greatest of the Hebrew kings. An able military leader and an astute administrator of public affairs, he extended the boundaries of the country to their greatest limit (including areas in Transjordan to the east and to Tyre in the north), inspired the fear and respect of foreign neighbors, established the national capital at Jerusalem, filled the coffers of the royal treasury, and founded a dynasty which was to rule for more than four hundred years. It is not surprising that the reign of David is traditionally regarded as the most glorious era in Jewish history or that it was the Davidic line from which, during centuries of oppression, the Hebrews expected a Messiah.

The Biblical historian devotes about half of I Samuel and virtually all of II Samuel to the stories of David's public achievements and private affairs.

ANOINTMENT AND RISE TO FAME (I Sam. 16:1—18:16). After rejecting Saul, the Lord directs Samuel to go to Bethlehem and there to anoint one of the sons of Jesse (which of the sons God does not designate) as future king. The historian gives an exciting account: Samuel says that he fears to go lest Saul kill him; the Lord tells him to pretend that he is going merely to offer a sacrifice. The elders of Bethlehem tremble at Samuel's unexpected appearance in their town, and they ask him: "Comest thou peaceably?" He assures them that his mission is peaceful and invites them to a sacrifice. He sends a special invitation to Jesse and his sons. The people sense the significance of the situation, and as the eldest of Jesse's sons comes forth, they whisper: "Surely the Lord's anointed is before him." One by one, seven stalwart sons are presented to the old seer. When Samuel asks whether these are all of Jesse's children, Jesse answers that only the youngest remains and that he is keeping the sheep. Samuel says, "Send and fetch him." This one is David, and when he appears—"ruddy, and withal of a beautiful countenance, and goodly to look to"—the Lord says, "Arise, anoint him: for this is he." Samuel anoints him, and thenceforth the spirit of the Lord dwells upon David.

The next appearance of David (I Sam. 16:14-23, discussed above) is as Saul's musician and armor-bearer.

The historian now evidently draws upon another source of information, for a conflicting story is told of David's introduction to the court of Saul. The Israelites are once again at war with the Philistines, who are led by Goliath, a mighty champion nearly ten feet high. This giant mocks the people of Israel and challenges them to produce somebody suitable to meet him in single combat. David (who is now described as keeper of his father's sheep) is sent on an errand to deliver food to his brothers in Saul's army. Hearing of Goliath's insults to God's people, David offers to fight the giant. Saul calls for David and equips him with armor, but David finds it too heavy, lays it aside, and goes into combat armed only with a slingshot and five pebbles. Goliath is outraged that such a stripling should be sent against him, and he curses David by his pagan gods. David replies: "I come to thee in the name of the Lord of hosts, the God of the armies of Israel, whom thou has defied." Then he slings a stone, which sinks into his opponent's forehead. David cuts off Goliath's head with the giant's own sword.* The Philistines flee, and the Israelites pursue them and gain a great victory.

This is the point where David launches his career as a popular hero and so begins to arouse Saul's jealousy.

DAVID AND JONATHAN (I Sam. 18:1-4, 19:1-7, 20:1-42, 23:16-18; II Sam. 1:17-27, 4:4, and 9:1-13). In the meantime, David has formed a close friendship with Saul's son Jonathan. The historian says that Jonathan's soul is "knit with the soul of David" and that Jonathan loves him "as his own soul." Jonathan gives David his robe and other garments, "even to his sword, and to his bow, and to his girdle." When Saul tries to kill David, Jonathan warns his friend to hide and then attempts to convince Saul that David is innocent of any offense. He espouses David's cause with such warmth that Saul is provoked to anger. Saul calls Jonathan the "son of a perverse rebellious woman" and tries vainly to kill him with a javelin. Jonathan hastens to David's hiding place and advises him to flee. After they have bidden each other a tearful farewell, David departs into exile. Only once more do they see each other, and then for just a short time while David is hiding in the wilderness.

The deaths of Jonathan and Saul inspire one of the finest

---

* These stories of the youthful David show several folk elements: (1) the parade of the seven elder sons first and the presentation of the youngest only upon request; (2) discrepancy in the traditions about the killing of Goliath (in II Sam. 21:19 his slaying is attributed to one Elhanan); (3) the use of a special sword for beheading a monster; compare Beowulf's decapitation of the corpse of Grendel; and (4) the offer of riches and a king's daughter (Merab, I Sam. 17:25) to whoever will overcome a monster. The lack of any further reference to David's use of a slingshot in warfare is noteworthy.

poems in the Bible—the only one except for a brief elegy over
Absalom (according to the noted literary scholar Mary Ellen
Chase[17]) that may be attributed unquestionably to David. It
is a dirge laden with deep personal sorrow:

> The beauty of Israel is slain upon thy high places.
> How are the mighty fallen! . . .
> Saul and Jonathan were lovely and pleasant in their lives,
> And in their death they were not divided.
> They were swifter than eagles,
> They were stronger than lions. . . .
> How are the mighty fallen in the midst of the battle!
> O Jonathan, thou wast slain in thine high places.
> I am distressed for thee, my brother Jonathan:
> Very pleasant hast thou been unto me:
> Thy love to me was wonderful,
> Passing the love of woman. (II Sam. 1:19-26)

A sequel to this story reveals the enduring quality of David's
affection for Jonathan. After David has become well established
as king of Israel, Mephibosheth, the lame * son of Jonathan, is
brought before him. Now, it was customary for an Oriental ruler
to wipe out all the descendants of a former ruler in order to prevent their attempting to gain the throne for themselves (compare Abimelech's slaughter of his half-brothers, related in Judges
9:5). David does the unexpected: when he discovers the identity
of Mephibosheth, instead of killing him, he graciously takes him
into the king's household, so that Mephibosheth thereafter eats
at David's own table.

PUBLIC ACHIEVEMENTS (II Sam. 2—8 and 10). Soon after Saul
is killed in battle, God directs David to return to his native land.
A delegation from the tribe of Judah meets him and proclaims
him king; he sets up his capital at Hebron. The other tribes,
however, adhere to Ishbosheth, one of Saul's sons. Civil war follows, Ishbosheth is slain, and David is accepted by all the tribes
as their king (II Sam. 5:1).

One of his first acts as king of a united Israel is to conquer the
fortified city of Jerusalem (or Zion), held by the Jebusites; this
he makes his new capital (II Sam. 5:6-9). He brings here the

---

* Mephibosheth is lame because his nurse dropped him when he was
five years old. The implication is that David adopts him not out of pity for
his lameness but out of affection for Jonathan.

Ark of the Covenant and plans to build a temple for the Ark to stay in, but is told by the Lord that the task will be accomplished by David's son. God promises, however, to make David's royal lineage and his kingdom prosper forever.

In the court at Jerusalem are several interesting people who are to play significant roles in the drama of David's public and domestic life: Joab, the commander of the army—treacherous, ruthless, and vengeful; Nathan, a bold and upright prophet, who fears the Lord more than he does David; and Abiathar, a learned and observant priest (and possibly the royal historian).

Surrounded by these and many other devoted followers, David begins a reign which, though destined to be long and glorious, is marred by foreign wars and internal rebellions. At different times David defeats the Moabites, the Syrians, the Edomites, and the Ammonites.

DAVID AND MICHAL (I Sam. 18:17-27, 19:11-17, 25:44; II Sam. 3:13-16, 6:16-23). David has many wives and many children, and some of these bring him great sorrow. One of the most pathetic domestic stories is concerned with Michal, his first wife. Soon after Saul has grown jealous of David's popularity, Saul learns that his own daughter Michal loves David. Perceiving a way in which he may be able to destroy his rival, Saul agrees to the match provided that David will give him as a "marriage gift" * a hundred foreskins of the Philistines. David accepts the proposal, kills not one hundred but two hundred Philistines, presents their foreskins to Saul, and marries Michal. In his jealous hatred, Saul sends some henchmen to kill David, apparently before the marriage is consummated.[18] Michal learns of the approach of the assassins, deceives them by placing a dummy in David's bed, and enables David to escape by letting him down through a window. While David is in exile, Saul gives Michal to Phalti (or Phaltiel or Paltiel), to whom she transfers her love and with whom she lives for several years. During this period David acquires several wives and concubines. When he becomes king, he takes Michal away from Phalti, who is heartbroken over having to give her up: he goes "with her along weeping behind her. . . ." Michal is later said to despise David

---

* In ancient Hebrew society it was customary for the groom to present a gift to the bride's father. See Caird, exegesis to I and II Samuel, *The Interpreter's Bible*, II, 984.

"in her heart" when she sees him, clad only in a priest's apron, "leaping and dancing" to celebrate the coming of the Ark to Jerusalem. She greets him with the sarcastic gibe: "How glorious was the king of Israel today, who uncovered himself today in the eyes of the handmaids of his servants, as one of the vain fellows shamelessly uncovereth himself!" David punishes her by refusing thenceforth to cohabit with her. Thus the matter ends unhappily for all involved.

DAVID AND BATHSHEBA (II Sam. 11—12). David is guilty of a most reprehensible act as the result of his passion for a woman:

One year during the season "when kings go forth to battle," * David himself stays in Jerusalem but sends his army, under Joab, to fight the Ammonites. While on the roof of his palace, he looks down into a neighboring courtyard and sees a woman bathing, and the woman is "very beautiful to look upon." He ascertains that she is Bathsheba, the wife of Uriah the Hittite. Ignoring the fact that she belongs to another man, David has her brought to his palace and makes her his mistress. When she later reveals to him that she is going to bear a child, he gives orders that Uriah be put into the "hottest" part of the battlefront and that the other soldiers "retire" from him, "that he may be smitten, and die." All happens as David has planned: Uriah is killed, and David marries Bathsheba.

Retribution follows this act of injustice. Believing that the Lord is not only the God of the Covenant and the Hebrew God of battle but also a Deity interested in righteous behavior, the historian tells us that David's deed has so displeased the Lord that the Lord sends the prophet Nathan to rebuke David. Nathan tells David a story about a rich man and a poor man. The former had "exceeding many flocks and herds," but "the poor man had nothing, save one little ewe lamb, which he had bought and nourished up: and it grew up together with him, and with his children; it did eat of his own meat, and drank of his own cup, and lay in his bosom, and was unto him as a daughter." When entertaining a traveler, the rich man spared his own flock, killed the poor man's ewe lamb, and served it. On hearing this tale of injustice, David is angry and vows to have the rich man restore the

* Biblical scholars are in disagreement as to whether ancient Oriental kings "went to battle" in the springtime when the weather was propitious, or whether they went in the fall when all crops had been harvested.

lamb fourfold. Then comes the most dramatic part of the story. Nathan unflinchingly says: "Thou art the man." He goes on to tell David that God is displeased over the murder of Uriah and the seizure of Bathsheba. David is humbly penitent: "I have sinned against the Lord." The Lord forgives him but punishes him by causing Bathsheba's son to die. Soon, however, Bathsheba conceives again and bears another son, Solomon.

DAVID AND ABSALOM (II Sam. 13–19). Some of David's other children bring great sorrow to their father. Amnon conceives a violent passion for his half-sister Tamar, a virgin. He pretends illness and asks that Tamar bring food to him. As soon as he and she are alone, he ravishes her. When Absalom, Tamar's full brother, hears of the outrage, he plots vengeance against Amnon. For two years he awaits a favorable opportunity. At last he invites all of David's sons to a sheepshearing. Amnon attends, and when he is "merry with wine," Absalom's servants kill him. Absalom himself flees into Syria. David is grief-stricken over the death of Amnon, but apparently mourns even more over the absence of his son Absalom (13:38-39).

After Absalom has remained in exile three years, David sends Joab to bring him back to Jerusalem; but David refuses to see his son for two more years. Absalom summons Joab to come to him, hoping that he can persuade the trusted general to intercede for him; but Joab will not come. Absalom spitefully sets fire to Joab's barley field. At length Joab does persuade David to see Absalom, and apparently father and son are reconciled.

Absalom, however, is bitter and disaffected, ambitious and revengeful. Knowing that neither primogeniture nor hereditary succession to the kingship has been established in the new kingdom, he decides to employ his own methods for usurping the throne. He acquires "chariots and horses, and fifty men to run before him" (the ancient equivalent of Hitler's "storm troopers"), makes rash promises to every malcontent, disparages his father's abilities, and soon steals "the hearts of the men of Israel" (15:6). When he feels that he has a sufficiently large following, he goes to Hebron (under the pretext of fulfilling a religious vow), and from this former capital of Judah he sends out messengers all over the country to announce: "Absalom reigneth in Hebron." The conspiracy thrives. Many men, including Ahithophel, one of David's trusted counselors, join Absalom.

Fearing military disaster and perhaps seeking a more strategic military position,[19] David flees from Jerusalem, taking with him his family, the priests Zadok and Abiathar, the Levites, and the Ark of the Covenant. Then he decides to have Zadok and Abiathar carry the Ark back to the city; these two and Hushai, another faithful supporter, are to remain in Jerusalem as his spies and informants. Absalom triumphantly moves into the capital.

David's band continues its flight and crosses the Jordan into the land of Gilead. Ahithophel advises Absalom to let him pursue David with twelve thousand men. Hushai, pretending to be a deserter from David's camp, disagrees with Ahithophel and advises Absalom to gather a great host from all over Israel and to lead the host himself. When Absalom follows the advice of Hushai, Ahithophel hangs himself.

Befriended by some of the Gileadites and Ammonites, David makes a stand at the wood of Ephraim and prepares to fight against the rebel army. Before the battle he warns his men not to harm his traitorous son: "Deal gently for my sake with the young man, even with Absalom." The fighting now begins, and the rebels are ignominiously defeated. In the course of the battle Absalom himself is riding on a mule. As he passes under an oak, his head is caught in a fork of the tree, the mule runs from under him, and he is left hanging helpless. When the news of this event reaches Joab, he hurries to the spot, and, in spite of David's injunction to spare the young man, hurls three darts into Absalom's heart. Then he buries the body in a pit.

When David hears of his son's death, his grief is crushing. The lament that he utters is one of the most heart-rending cries in all literature: "O my son Absalom, my son, my son Absalom! would God I had died for thee, O Absalom, my son, my son!"

Soon thereafter David and all his band return to Jerusalem. Joab is apparently forgiven for disobedience and allowed to remain in an influential position. David pardons many of those who refused to follow him—including the lame Mephibosheth; and he rewards the Gileadites and others who have supported him. The rebellion is at an end.

DAVID'S DECLINING YEARS AND DEATH (II Sam. 20—24; I Kings 1—2). As David approaches old age, there are several occurrences which prevent his reign from being tranquil: a revolt of the northern tribes (II Sam. 20), a three-year famine (II Sam.

21:1-14), a three-year plague (II Sam. 24), and four more battles against the Philistines (II Sam. 22—23). A census at this time records 1,300,000 men of military age—a dubious population figure (II Sam. 24:1-9).

In the account of one of the battles against the Philistines, the historian records an incident which adds to the attractiveness of David's character. The aging king voices a longing for some of the water from the well beside the gate of Bethlehem, now held by the Philistines. At the risk of their lives David's three mightiest men break through the enemy lines, procure some of the water, and bring it back to David. Deeply touched, David will not drink, but pours the water out, saying, "Be it far from me, O Lord, that I should do this: is not this the blood of the men that went in jeopardy of their lives?"

When David reaches extreme old age, he is adjudged by political and religious experts to be senile and unfit to rule. He is willing to abdicate (I Kings 1:48), but when the choice of a successor must be made, his advisers split into two factions. One faction (including Joab and Abiathar) supports Adonijah, the eldest surviving son; succession by primogeniture, however, has not yet been established as a custom in Israel. The other faction supports Bathsheba's son Solomon. When Bathsheba hears that Adonijah has attracted a large following and has had himself proclaimed king, she and Nathan go to David and remind him of an old promise [20] to make Solomon his successor. David orders Nathan to anoint Solomon, messengers to blow trumpets, and the people to shout: "God save king Solomon!" When Adonijah hears the uproar, he flees to the Temple and begs Solomon's mercy. Temporarily Solomon allows him to depart in peace.

David charges his son Solomon to obey God's commandments. After a reign of "forty" years, David dies and is buried in Jerusalem.

Adonijah pleads with Bathsheba until she agrees to request Solomon to give him Abishag as his wife (Abishag is a young woman who has been appointed to sleep with David and so keep him warm in his old age). Solomon construes the request as a sign of royal pretensions on Adonijah's part (inasmuch as it was an ancient Semitic custom for a new king to take over his predecessor's women),[21] and he has Adonijah executed. He also orders the banishment of Abiathar; and, obeying an injunc-

tion formerly laid upon him by David, he decrees the execution
of Joab (who is guilty of the murder of two military leaders
under David's protection).

Thus Solomon establishes his kingdom.

I KINGS 3—22 AND II KINGS: TRIUMPH AND DOWNFALL OF MONARCHY TEMPERED BY THEOCRACY

Like the two books of Samuel, I and II Kings originally formed
one continuous Hebrew scroll, and the division into "books" was
made in the Septuagint. The books derive their name from the
fact that they deal with the reigns of the kings of Israel and
Judah from the days of David to the Exile.

The writing and revising of I and II Kings was a long process,
perhaps extending over nearly eight centuries.[22] The principal
steps seem to have been as follows:

A short while before the death of King Josiah of Judah (609
B.C.), some writer whose name is unknown composed the major
portion of I and II Kings (I Kings 2:1-12, 3—22 and II Kings
1:1—23:25a). He drew on the following no-longer-extant sources:
(1) the Acts of Solomon (mentioned in I Kings 11:41), probably written in the tenth century B.C.; (2) the Book of the Chronicles of the Kings of Israel (mentioned in I Kings 14:19 and in
sixteen other places), finished about 725 B.C.; (3) the Book of the
Chronicles of the Kings of Judah (mentioned in I Kings 14:29
and in fourteen other places), finished about 590 B.C.; and (4)
tales of the Southern Kingdom, by the prophet Isaiah, written
about 715-700 B.C.

At some time between 610 and 538 B.C. two successive editors
of strong Deuteronomic tendencies revised the manuscript, adding the conclusion (II Kings 23:25b—25:30) and interpolating
many passages of northern origin, especially those relating to
Ahab, Elijah, and Elisha.

There is evidence that various post-Exilic editors continued to
revise the books of Kings—perhaps as late as the middle of the
second century B.C. At some unknown date the passages which
now form I Kings 1 and 2 were severed from the manuscript of
II Samuel and made to serve as an introduction to the reign of
Solomon.

The purpose of the original compiler (probably in 610 B.C.)
was to prove the necessity of obeying the Deuteronomic law. He

illustrated this principle by demonstrating how "good" kings (that is, those who fulfilled the law), like Josiah, were successful and prosperous, whereas the "wicked" ones, like Ahab, brought disaster upon themselves and their country. Thus the narrative in the two books of Kings is not a history in the sense of a full and careful record of the important events that took place in Palestine during the period covered. "Rather it is an attempt to present in systematic order the development of certain attitudes toward race and religious ideals that finally led to the great disaster [the Babylonian captivity]." [23]

The author's method is clear and consistent. First he tells of the reign of Solomon. Then, after the division of the country into the kingdoms of Israel and Judah, he tries to deal contemporaneously with the events of both kingdoms; that is, he begins with the accession of one king, tells about the events in his reign, and then goes on to the history of the other kingdom during the same period. For each king of Judah he gives the date of accession (in "terms of the year of the reigning king of Israel" [24]), the age of the king at the time of his accession, the name of the queen mother, and a summary of the king's attitude toward the Deuteronomic law. For each king of Israel he gives the date of accession (in terms of the year of the reigning king of Judah), the name of his capital, the length of his reign, and his opinion of the king's ethical and religious nature. This framework is readily adaptable to the author's didactic purpose.

Although I and II Kings make up "a religious philosophy of history rather than a history proper, yet as always with the Jewish writers the ideas are conveyed through such vivid pictures of concrete personalities that the latter have for us a value in themselves over and above the principles they are designed to illustrate." [25]

The two books of Kings exhibit the Jewish nation at its peak of fame and prosperity under Solomon, its division into two kingdoms, its moral and spiritual decay (a decay arrested from time to time by the efforts of prophets and "good" kings), its growing fear of invasion by Assyria and Babylonia, and, finally, its complete subjugation by those foreign powers. During this period of about four centuries, the role of the prophets—those lay spokesmen for God—increased in importance, so that sometimes they wielded great political influence and vied with the official ecclesiastical groups for the religious and ethical leadership of the people. At all times, religion, not mere political organization, united the Hebrew people, even when they were physically divided into separate kingdoms. The laws, rights, and duties of the kings were set forth as only one portion, not the main portion, of the religious tradition.

The "Golden Age" of Solomon (I Kings 3—11). In the description by the Biblical historian, the reign of Solomon (c. 960—c. 922 B.C.) was the "Golden Age" of Israel—an era of peace and prosperity, when the people were "eating and drinking, and making merry" (I Kings 4:20) and when they "dwelt safely, every man under his vine and under his fig tree" (I Kings 4:25). The boundaries of the kingdom stretched from the Euphrates to the land of the Philistines and on to the borders of Egypt (I Kings 4:21). Modern historians, however, suspect that the era was one of false prosperity, that Solomon's lavish expenditures brought the nation to the verge of bankruptcy, and that his conscription of labor and the levying of high taxes (as well as his later tolerance of foreign gods) caused much popular unrest, ending in the division of the kingdom at Solomon's death. They point out that, except in the capital, most of the kingdom did not enjoy great prosperity most of the time. Towns at a distance from Jerusalem had a poor, peasant economy (in contrast to Solomon's wealth and imported luxuries) without extremes of utter poverty and great riches. Prior to the eighth century, debtors and the poor had to be protected, reducing somewhat the disparity between rich and poor. On the other hand, defaulting debtors might have to become slaves. (But religious tradition made it a capital crime to kidnap an Israelite in order to sell him into slavery.)

SOLOMON'S WISDOM AND RICHES (I Kings 3—4 and 9:10—10:29). According to the Biblical author, the greatest glories of the epoch are the splendor of the court and the wisdom of the sovereign: "King Solomon exceeded all the kings of the earth for riches and for wisdom" (I Kings 10:23). His wisdom is a special gift of God. Soon after Solomon ascends the throne, the Lord appears to him in a dream and asks what gift he would like to have. Already wise, Solomon answers, "Give therefore thy servant an understanding heart to judge thy people, that I may discern between good and bad; for who is able to judge this thy so great a people?" Because he has requested wisdom rather than long life or wealth, God promises to give him not only wisdom but also riches and honor.

The first manifestation of Solomon's great probity is his famous decision concerning the disputed child: each of two harlots claims to be the mother of a little boy. When Solomon offers to split the child into two pieces, one of them agrees but the other quickly relinquishes her claim. Solomon gives the boy to the latter.

"And Solomon's wisdom excelled the wisdom of all the children of the east country, and all the wisdom of Egypt. For he was wiser than all men. . . . And he spake three thousand proverbs: and his songs were a thousand and five." * 26

As for his opulence, he has forty thousand stalls of horses, fourteen hundred chariots, a throne made of ivory overlaid with gold, golden drinking vessels, and golden shields. He makes "silver to be in Jerusalem as stones, and cedars made he to be as the sycamore trees that are in the vale, for abundance." In other words, gold is so plentiful that silver is considered of little value. (Modern archaeological discoveries indicate, however, that copper mining was probably one of the main sources of Solomon's wealth. Control over copper districts intensified conflict between Israel and Edom.) He imports cedars from Lebanon, gold from Ophir, linen from Egypt, and ivory, apes, and peacocks from Tarsus. The point stressed by the historian is that Solomon's commerce extends to three continents: Asia, Africa, and Europe.

An effective climax to the summary of Solomon's splendor and wisdom is given in the famous account of the visit of the queen of Sheba.† Having heard much of his renown, this woman travels to Jerusalem to learn whether the tales she has heard have been accurate. Rich herself, she is not likely to be impressed by any ordinary display of wealth, but when she sees the house of Solomon (he has built his magnificent temple prior to her visit), the food on his table, the apparel of his attendants, and all the other

---

* This quotation helps to explain why the books of Proverbs and The Song of Songs have been traditionally attributed to Solomon. (There is no real evidence that he wrote either.)

† Sheba is a region in southwestern Arabia.

luxury with which he is surrounded, there is "no more spirit in her." She is equally astounded by his wisdom: there is no question which she can ask that he cannot answer.

Her summary of her admiration is eloquent: "It was a true report that I heard in mine own land of thy acts and of thy wisdom. Howbeit I believed not the words, until I came, and mine eyes had seen it: and, behold, the half was not told me: thy wisdom and prosperity exceedeth the fame which I heard."

THE BUILDING OF THE TEMPLE (I Kings 5—9). To the devout Hebrew historian, the building of the Temple at Jerusalem is an event of supreme importance. The Temple will centralize the worship of the Lord in one spot and will do away with the worship in local shrines—the "high places."

Now the Lord has promised David that his son would build the Temple. Solomon happily undertakes the task. He engages the services of Hiram, king of Tyre, who agrees to furnish the wood. Solomon conscripts an army of more than 180,000 workmen—stone-cutters, wood choppers, and burden bearers. After seven years of labor the Temple is finished. It is a large and elaborate structure, made chiefly of stone, cedar, and cypress, decorated with carvings of cherubim, of palm trees, and of flowers, covered with gold. (The plan and methods of building are believed to have been Phoenician, and similar walls with three rows of stone and cedar beams have been excavated in Syria). Solomon celebrates the completion of the Temple with a great festival, a sacrificial offering (of 22,000 oxen and 120,000 sheep), and a long prayer of dedication and blessing.

SOLOMON'S APOSTASY AND DEATH (I Kings 11). Although he is said to be incomparably wise and although he is a devout worshiper of the Lord, Solomon is guilty of great and foolish transgressions: he allows his wives to "turn away his heart after other gods." He has seven hundred wives and three hundred concubines. Many of these are foreigners, who persuade him to build altars and burn incense and offer sacrifices to such deities as Ashtoreth of the Sidonians, Milcom and Molech of the Ammonites, and Chemosh of the Moabites. The Lord tells Solomon that as a punishment the kingdom will be divided and most of it given to another line of kings. God punishes him further by inciting the kings of Edom and Syria to rebel against him. After reigning "forty" years, Solomon dies and is succeeded by his son Rehoboam.

The Divided Kingdom (I Kings 12–22). When the people convene to proclaim Rehoboam king, they petition him to lighten the burdens of taxation and forced labor which his father Solomon had placed on them. His wise old counselors warn him to do as the people request, but Rehoboam is induced to maintain and even to increase oppressive taxes by his rash young friends, who advise him to say to the people: "My little finger shall be thicker than my father's loins. And now whereas my father did lade you with a heavy yoke, I will add to your yoke: my father hath chastised you with whips, but I will chastise you with scorpions." °

In the meantime, Jeroboam, an exiled henchman of Solomon's who had once been in charge of the forced labor, has returned from Egypt. Now the ten northern tribes revolt against Rehoboam and choose Jeroboam as their king. The latter sets up his capital at Shechem; his kingdom is called "Israel." The tribes of Benjamin and Judah remain faithful to Rehoboam; his realm is known henceforth as "Judah."

POLITICAL EVENTS. The political history of both kingdoms (as told in I and II Kings) is presented in tabular form (pp. 117-120) and consequently requires only a brief summary here.

The kingdom of Judah continues under the Davidic dynasty during its entire existence as a nation, except for one brief interval (the reign of Athaliah, 842-837 B.C.). Twice it wages war against its sister kingdom Israel; and twice it allies itself with Israel against Syria. Edom gains its independence from Judah. In the eighth century B.C. under Ahaz and Hezekiah, the Southern Kingdom appeases Assyria by paying tribute. In the early years of the sixth century Judah becomes entangled in alliances with Egypt and thereby provokes Nebuchadrezzar of Babylon to overrun the country, to take many captives, and to burn Jerusalem (586 B.C.).

The history of the Northern Kingdom is more turbulent than that of Judah. During its existence of two hundred years, nineteen monarchs of nine different dynasties rule the land. Seven kings are assassinated. The capital is moved from Shechem to

---

° A "scorpion" probably referred to a scourge made of leather and spikes.

SOVEREIGNS OF THE SOUTHERN KINGDOM (JUDAH)

1. *Rehoboam* (922-915),[27] son of Solomon.* A "bad" king. I Kings 12 and 14:21-31.

2. *Abijam* (915-913). A "bad" king. I Kings 15:1-8.

3. *Asa* (913-873). A "good" king—destroys idols, forbids worship in local shrines, restores Temple treasures; wages war against Baasha, king of Israel. I Kings 15:9-24.

4. *Jehoshaphat* (873-849). On the whole a "good" king, but insufficiently zealous in prohibiting worship in local shrines. Joins King Ahab of Israel in ill-fated war against Syria. I Kings 22.

5. *Jehoram* (*Joram*) (849-842). A "bad" king—marries Athaliah, daughter of Ahab and Jezebel of Israel, and allows his kingdom to worship the gods of his in-laws. During his reign Edom successfully revolts against Judah. II Kings 8:16-24.

6. *Ahaziah* (842). A "bad" king—walks "in the way of the house of Ahab." He joins Israel in a war against Syria. He is killed in battle by Jehu. II Kings 8:25-29, 9:16-28.

7. *Athaliah* (842-837), daughter of Ahab and Jezebel, seizes throne on death of her son Ahaziah. A "bad" queen—kills most of "seed royal" of the Davidic line and tries to substitute Baal-worship for worship of the Lord. II Kings 11.

8. *Joash* (*Jehoash*) (837-800), grandson of Ahaziah and Athaliah, is restored to throne when Athaliah is deposed. A "good" king—repairs Temple in Jerusalem, but gives Temple treasures to king of Syria and fails to prohibit worship in local shrines. II Kings 12.

9. *Amaziah* (800-783). A "good" king, but one who still permits worship in "high places." II Kings 14:1-20.

10. *Azariah* (*Uzziah*) (783-742). A "good" king, but one who still does not abolish worship in local shrines. II Kings 14:21-22; 15:1-7.

11. *Jotham* (750-735). A "good" king, but one who still permits worship in local shrines. II Kings 15:32-38.

12. *Ahaz* (735-715). A "bad" king—worships at local shrines and burns his son as a sacrificial offering. Enlists aid of

---

* Except for Athaliah and Joash, each of the kings through Jehoahaz inherits the throne from his father.

SOVEREIGNS OF THE SOUTHERN KINGDOM (JUDAH)
(*Continued*)

Tiglath-pileser, king of Assyria, against the kings of Israel and Syria. Pays tribute to Assyria. II Kings 16.

13. *Hezekiah* (715-687). A "good" king—abolishes local shrines, defeats Philistines, and keeps Assyrians out of Judah. Associated with the prophet Isaiah. II Kings 18—20.

14. *Manasseh* (687-642). A "bad" king—worships Baal, practices magic, and sacrifices his son as a burnt offering. II Kings 21:1-18.

15. *Amon* (642-640). A "bad" king. II Kings 21:19-26.

16. *Josiah* (640-609). A very "good" king—repairs the Temple and brings about the great Deuteronomic reformation upon the discovery of the Book of Law in the Temple (621 B.C.). He destroys all the pagan shrines and altars, and he reinstitutes the observance of the old Jewish customs and festivals, such as the Passover. II Kings 22:1—23:30.

17. *Jehoahaz* (609). A "bad" king. Rules only three months (he is deposed by the king of Egypt). II Kings 23:31-34.

18. *Jehoiakim* (*Eliakim*) (609-598), son of Josiah, placed on throne by king of Egypt when Jehoahaz is dethroned. A "bad" king. He first pays tribute to Egypt, but then becomes vassal of Nebuchadrezzar of Babylon. He next rebels against Nebuchadrezzar and so provokes a war which is destined to have most disastrous consequences. II Kings 23:34—24:5.

19. *Jehoiachin* (598), son of Jehoiakim. A "bad" king. He continues the war against Babylon. Jerusalem falls (597), and many Hebrews (including Jehoiachin) are carried as exiles into Babylon. Later (561) Jehoiachin is freed from prison and given some privileges. II Kings 24:6-16, 25:27-30.

20. *Zedekiah* (*Mattaniah*) (598-586), uncle of Jehoiachin, placed on throne when Jehoiachin is deposed. A "bad" king. Like his predecessors, he rebels against Nebuchadrezzar, who again captures Jerusalem and burns it. Zedekiah's sons are killed, his eyes are put out, and a governor is appointed to rule the land. II Kings 24:17—25:22.

SOVEREIGNS OF THE NORTHERN KINGDOM (ISRAEL)

1. *Jeroboam I* (922-901), first ruler of the Northern Kingdom, chosen by the ten northern tribes as ruler when they revolt against Rehoboam of the southern tribes. A "bad" king—sets up golden calves for worship in Dan and Bethel and appoints priesthood not descended from Levi. Makes Shechem his capital. I Kings 12:12—14:20.

2. *Nadab* (901-900), son of Jeroboam I. A "bad" king. I Kings 14:20, 15:25-31.

3. *Baasha* (900-877), assassinates Nadab, establishes second dynasty. A "bad" king—idolatrous. Sets up capital at Tirzah. I Kings 15:27—16:7.

4. *Elah* (877-876), son of Baasha. A "bad" king. I Kings 16:8-10.

5. *Zimri* (876), an army officer, assassinates Elah, establishes the third "dynasty," which lasts only seven days. A "bad" king—idolatrous. I Kings 16:9-20.

6. *Omri* (876-869), commander of Elah's army, defeats and deposes Zimri, establishes fourth dynasty. A "bad," idolatrous king, but a strong one. He builds Samaria and makes it his capital. I Kings 16:16-28.

7. *Ahab* (869-850), son of Omri. A notoriously "bad" king—worships Baal. Husband of Sidonian princess Jezebel. He is the opponent of the prophet Elijah. Appropriates Naboth's vineyard. I Kings 16:29—22:40.

8. *Ahaziah* (850-849), son of Ahab. A "bad" king. Tries vainly to kill Elijah. I Kings 22:40, II Kings 1:1-18.

9. *Joram (Jehoram)* (849-842), son of Ahab. A "bad" king. He wages war successfully against Moab, unsuccessfully against Syria. Sometimes opponent of Elisha. II Kings 1:17—9:26.

10. *Jehu* (842-815), officer in the Israelitish army, anointed by Elisha, kills Joram and Jezebel and mounts throne, thus establishing the fifth dynasty. The first "good" king of Israel—destroys images and temples of Baal; but he does allow continuance of worship of golden calves set up by Jeroboam I. II Kings 9—10.

11. *Jehoahaz* (815-801), son of Jehu. A "bad" king. II Kings 13:1-9.

SOVEREIGNS OF THE NORTHERN KINGDOM (ISRAEL)
(*Continued*)

12. *Joash* (*Jehoash*) (801-786), son of Jehoahaz. A "bad" king. He wages war against Judah and sacks Jerusalem. II Kings 13:9—14:16.

13. *Jeroboam II* (786-746), son of Joash. A "bad" king, but Israel enjoys great prosperity during his reign. II Kings 14:23-29.

14. *Zachariah* (746-745), son of Jeroboam II. A "bad" king. II Kings 15:8-12.

15. *Shallum* (745), a conspirator, assassinates Zachariah and assumes throne, thus establishing the sixth dynasty, which lasts only a month. A "bad" king. II Kings 15:13-15.

16. *Menahem* (745-738), another conspirator, kills Shallum, takes throne, and sets up the seventh dynasty. A "bad" king. Pays tribute to Assyria to prevent ravaging of Israel. II Kings 15:14-22.

17. *Pekahiah* (738-736), son of Menahem. A "bad" king. II Kings 15:22-26.

18. *Pekah* (737-732), son of an army officer, assassinates Pekahiah and mounts throne, thus establishing the eighth dynasty. A "bad" king. During this reign the Assyrians under Tiglath-Pileser conquer part of Israel and take many captives into Assyria. II Kings 15:27-31.

19. *Hoshea* (732-724), a pro-Assyrian candidate for the crown, assassinates Pekah and takes the throne, thus establishing the ninth dynasty. A "bad" king. He conspires with Egypt against Assyria, which now overruns Israel and takes the inhabitants captive. Thus the Northern Kingdom comes to an end (722 B.C.). II Kings 17.

Tirzah and then to Samaria. In the first half of the ninth century a bond between Israel and Sidon is formed by the marriage of King Ahab to the Sidonian princess Jezebel. In addition to the two wars against Judah, Israel fights Moab and Syria. For a few years the Northern Kingdom staves off the Assyrian avalanche by paying tribute. About 734 B.C. Assyria conquers part of Israel and takes some captives. When King Hoshea makes an alliance with Egypt, the Assyrians complete the conquest of Israel and lead many more Israelites into exile (722 B.C.).

RELIGIOUS CONDITIONS. To the authors of the books of Kings, the religious conditions of the two kingdoms are fully as important as—and in large measure control—the political events.

In the Southern Kingdom the center of Yahweh-worship is, of course, the Temple in Jerusalem.* Worship at local shrines, such as groves and "high places," is, in the eyes of the Deuteronomic editors, an abominable practice, and the designation of each king of Judah as either "good" or "bad" depends primarily on whether he prohibits or condones such practice. Although Solomon and some of his successors are said to have worshiped idols and non-Hebrew deities, such worship is less widespread in the Southern Kingdom than in the Northern. Lacking a central temple, the people of the Northern Kingdom worship at various shrines of Yahweh, and furthermore, they are rather easily persuaded to shift their allegiance from Yahweh to foreign deities. The worship of false gods and the prevalence of social injustice and of personal immorality help occasion the rise of prophets, who, often in opposition to the royally appointed priests, exhort the people to return to the true God and to ethical behavior. Before the end of the eighth century the prophets interpret the threat of an Assyrian invasion as God's warning that he will use some alien power as an instrument to punish his Chosen People unless they reform. They refuse to reform, and hence—according to Biblical historians as well as the prophets—God subjects the people of both kingdoms to exile.

Jeroboam, Prototype of a "Wicked" King (I Kings 12—14). As soon as he establishes his capital in Shechem, Jeroboam sets up two golden calves as objects of worship, representative of Yahweh "as the God of physical forces." [28] Worship at these two shrines is considered by the Deuteronomic compilers to be apostasy to the Lord. Matters are made worse by Jeroboam's appointment of a priesthood not derived from the house of Levi. Despite the protests of an unnamed "man of God" and despite the withering of his own hand (sent by God as a punishment for his apostasy), Jeroboam persists in his evil ways. The historian is particularly bitter about Jeroboam's wickedness and seems to feel that this king is in large measure responsible for Israel's future apostasy;

* Emphasis by the priests on Temple worship in Jerusalem after the return from Babylon helps to explain why the Southern Kingdom takes pre-eminence over the Northern in post-Exilic writings.

time after time the books of Kings use such phrases as "walking in the way of Jeroboam and in his sin which he did, to make Israel to sin." [29]

Ahab, Israel's Most "Wicked" King (I Kings 16:29—22:40). According to the author of I Kings 16, Ahab, the son of the strong king Omri, does more to provoke the Lord to anger than had all the kings of Israel who formerly reigned. Not only does he follow the idolatrous ways of Jeroboam, but also he marries the Sidonian (Phoenician) princess Jezebel,* who persuades him to worship Baal † and to build altars to him. Repeatedly Ahab is warned by the prophet Elijah to mend his ways and to worship God, but the king obstinately refuses to obey.

Ahab leads his country in two wars against Syria (Ch. 20). For a long time, apparently, Ahab has been a vassal of Ben-hadad, the Syrian king. Now Ben-hadad besieges Samaria, Ahab's capital, reduces its garrison to a desperate state, and demands its complete capitulation, including the surrender of the silver, the gold, and the wives and the children of Ahab. Ahab agrees; but when Ben-hadad insultingly orders him to allow Syrian servants to search his house and take anything they please, Ahab (after a conference with his subjects) decides to resist. A small body of Israelites takes the overconfident Syrians completely by surprise, throws them into a panic, and then, with the aid of several thou-

---

* There is an unproven theory that Psalm 45 was originally written to celebrate the marriage of Ahab and Jezebel. If the theory is correct, then perhaps the contemporary court Psalmist did not agree with the Deuteronomic historian that Ahab was a wicked king. It is interesting to note that the author of I Kings 20:1-34 is more favorable to Ahab than is the historian responsible for the other passages which concern this king. These differences of opinion are a good reminder that the Bible is a complicated collection of writings by different authors in different ages. See Norman H. Snaith, exegesis to II Kings, *The Interpreter's Bible,* III, 166.

Some commentators call Jezebel a Tyrian princess rather than a Sidonian. Both Tyre and Sidon were cities in Phoenicia.

† The Hebrew word *baal* (plural, *baals* or *baalim*) means "lord" or "master." The baalim were local nature deities of the Canaanites. The singular *Baal* is used by the compilers of I Kings to refer to Melkart, the chief male deity of the Phoenicians. In Israel under Ahab and Jezebel, there was some fusion of Canaanite baalism and the Tyrian cult of Melkart. See D. C. Simpson, commentary on I and II Kings, *The Abingdon Bible Commentary,* ed. by Frederick Carl Eiselen, Edwin Lewis, and David G. Downey (Nashville, Tenn.: Abingdon-Cokesbury Press, 1929) p. 426.

CYPRUS

The Great Sea

PHOENICIA

Mt. LEBANON

A R A M (SYRIA)

Sidon

Damascus

Tyre

Megiddo

R. Jordan

KINGDOM

Samaria

Joppa

Bethel

PHILISTIA

Jerusalem

KINGDOM OF ISRAEL

Tekoa

Gaza

Dead Sea

AMMON

KINGDOM
OF
JUDAH

MOAB

EDOM

(ARABIAN DESERT)

N

SCALE OF MILES

0   10   60

DIVIDED KINGDOM
(ca. 860 B.C.)

From *A Handbook for Know Your Bible Study Groups,* © 1959 by Abingdon Press. By permission of the publisher.

sand more Israelites, wins a crushing victory. The Syrians claim
that they have been defeated because the Israelites' God is a
deity of the hills and not of the plains; therefore they muster another army and meet Ahab's men again, this time on level ground.
Because the Syrians have belittled his power, the Lord punishes
them by allowing the Israelites to defeat them again—so decisively that Israel frees itself of vassalage. Ben-hadad himself is
captured but is mercifully set free by Ahab. In a passage (I Kings
20:35-43) written by an author inimical to Ahab, a prophet
predicts disaster for this king for making peace with the Syrians
instead of destroying them utterly.

After three years of friendly relations with Syria, Ahab decides
to seize some disputed territory held by the Syrians (I Kings
22:1). He and Jehoshaphat, the king of Judah, form an alliance
and begin preparing for war. As is his custom, Ahab invites four
hundred prophets—"men of God," not prophets of Baal—to ask
whether he should attack the Syrian forces; all these prophets
encourage him to proceed with the invasion, and one, named
Zedekiah, even exhibits some iron horns to symbolize how Syria
will be gored. There is, however, another prophet, Micaiah, who
has not been consulted because he has a reputation for foretelling evil.* When Jehoshaphat insists on hearing what Micaiah has
to say about the matter, that prophet lies at first and predicts
success for Israel, because he is afraid that he will be punished
if he again foretells disaster † Ahab, however, apparently senses
that Micaiah is lying and therefore urges him to tell the truth.
Thereupon the prophet predicts disaster for the expedition and
death for Ahab; furthermore, he reveals why the four hundred
prophets have predicted falsely: when God was seeking a way to
bring about Ahab's downfall, one of his spirits volunteered to be
a "lying spirit" in the mouths of the four hundred, and God accepted the offer. (Thus the Biblical author intimates that God
sometimes uses devious means to motivate human conduct.)

* The failure to invite to a gathering someone of ill omen is perhaps a
folk element which has crept into the Biblical story. Compare the slights to
(1) the wicked witch in the story of the Sleeping Beauty and (2) the
goddess Eris (Discord) in the Greek myth about the marriage of Peleus
and Thetis.

† Compare Calchas' reluctance to tell Agamemnon the cause of the
plague on the Greeks at the opening of the *Iliad*.

When Zedekiah hears Micaiah's oracles, he angrily strikes his rival on the cheek and asks: "Which way went the Spirit of the Lord from me to speak unto thee?" Micaiah replies that Zedekiah will receive the answer to that question when hiding (presumably from the Syrians) in his inner chamber.

Believing the predictions of the four hundred prophets, Ahab throws the lone dissenter Micaiah into prison and continues with preparations for the battle. But perhaps he has been shaken by Micaiah's prophecy, for he disguises himself as a common soldier. Despite this precaution, he is killed by a random arrow. His blood flows into his chariot, which is later washed in a pool of Samaria. Some dogs lick up this blood in the pool, and thus is fulfilled an old prophecy made by Elijah (see below, p. 129).

Jezebel, Prototype of a "Wicked Woman" (I Kings 16:31, 18:4, 19:1-3, 21:5-25; II Kings 9:30-37). Although relatively few verses of the Bible are concerned with Jezebel, the wife of Ahab, so great is her reputation for evil that her name has become a common noun, a synonym for a "wicked woman." Not only does she reintroduce Baal-worship into Israel, but she "stirs up" her husband to act with all the despotism and cruelty of the average Oriental monarch of the era. Furthermore, she banishes the prophets of the Lord and replaces them with 450 prophets of Baal and 400 prophets of the groves (local shrines). After Elijah discredits and destroys her prophets (I Kings 18:17-40), she sends him a message of the most violent hatred: "So let the gods do to me, and more also, if I make not thy life as the life of one of them by to-morrow about this time." She is unable, however, to carry out her threat because Elijah escapes into Judah. One of her worst crimes is the instigation of the cold-blooded murder of Naboth; for this Elijah prophesies that the "dogs shall eat Jezebel by the wall of Jezreel" (I Kings 21:23).

When the conspirator Jehu kills her son, King Joram,* Jezebel knows that her death, too, is imminent. She takes great pains to beautify herself, painting her face and adorning her head.[30] As Jehu enters the gates of Jezreel, she mocks him from her window, comparing him with Zimri, who had gained the throne for seven days by murdering his master. Jehu persuades Jezebel's servants to throw her out the window; then his horses trample her to death. Somewhat later he remembers that she is a king's

* See below, p. 126.

daughter and therefore deserves a decent burial, but when his servants return to inter her body, they find only her skull, her feet, and the palms of her hands; all else has been devoured by the ferocious dogs which roam the streets of Jezreel. Thus is fulfilled Elijah's prophecy of Jezebel's fate.

Jehu's Conspiracy (II Kings 9–10). During the reign of Joram (Jehoram), who is one of Ahab's sons, the prophet Elisha * stirs up a revolution which is destined to put an end to the "wicked" dynasty of Omri (the father of Ahab). While Israel is at war with Syria, Elisha sends a disciple to anoint Jehu, a captain in the Israelitish army, as king of Israel. Jehu wastes no time in implementing his nomination. He drives furiously † to Jezreel, where Joram, who is recuperating from a battle wound, drives in a chariot to meet him. "Is it peace, Jehu?" Joram asks hopefully. Jehu replies that there can be no peace while the land is so full of idolatry. Joram flees, but Jehu pursues him, kills him, and (as an act of retributive justice) throws his body into Naboth's vineyard.†† The people proclaim Jehu king.

The new sovereign promptly proceeds to obliterate the house of Ahab. At his direction the elders of Samaria and Jezreel kill all seventy of Ahab's surviving sons and send their heads to him. Next he lures all the prophets of Baal into their temple, where he has them slain; he breaks and burns the sacred pillars and converts the temple into a latrine. Thus he wipes out the worship of Baal in Israel. The Lord rewards him by promising that his descendants "unto the fourth generation" will rule the kingdom. But Jehu allows the people to continue to worship the two golden calves which Jeroboam set up in Bethel and Dan and to which the people offered sacrifices as if to gods; therefore he is punished by having to fight continually against the Syrians, who harass the land and take all of Israel east of the Jordan.

The Elijah Cycle (I Kings 17–19, 21; II Kings 1:1-17). The prophet Elijah plays so important a role in the drama of Israel that it has been necessary to mention him frequently in the foregoing accounts. Comparable to Samuel as God's agent for select-

---

* See below, pp. 130-132, the discussion of the cycle of stories about Elisha.

† The furious driving of Jehu has become proverbial, and the common noun *jehu* denotes (in slang) a reckless or fast driver.

†† See below, p. 129.

ing and rejecting kings, Elijah's political influence in his own day
was considerable. He was, furthermore, a forerunner of Amos
as a stern and vociferous critic of the paganism and the social injustice rampant in the Northern Kingdom. He left so deep an impression on the Hebrew people that a large number of traditions
grew up about his name: Malachi, for instance, prophesied that
it would be Elijah who would announce the coming of the Messiah (Mal. 4:5); in New Testament times the priests and Levites
of Jerusalem were anxious to learn whether Elijah had been re-
incarnated in John the Baptist (John 1:21); Elijah appeared with
Moses at the Transfiguration of Christ (Matt. 17:3, Mark 9:4,
Luke 9:30); and even today some Orthodox Jews set a chair for
him at the rite of circumcision and leave a door "ajar for his
entrance at Passover." [31]

The Elijah cycle is based on a series of tales from the Northern
Kingdom, written perhaps as early as 800 B.C. The cycle bears
evidence of an oral transmission over a rather long period: it relates several events which may be considered legendary (such as
the ravens' feeding of Elijah), and it reflects the popular admiration for the heroic prophet who dared to stand up for God in
defiance of the rulers of Israel. In I and II Kings the stories about
Elijah are told with great enthusiasm. Full of vivid pictorial details and dramatic crises, they are "among the most brilliant and
charming in Hebrew literature and their author an accomplished
teller of tales." [32]

PROPHECY OF DROUGHT (I Kings 17). The abruptness with
which the historian introduces Elijah helps to convey an impression of the "suddenness" [33] and unpredictability of the intrepid
old prophet: "And Elijah the Tishbite, who was of the inhabitants
of Gilead, said unto Ahab, As the Lord God of Israel liveth, before whom I stand, there shall not be dew nor rain these years,
but according to my word." To escape Ahab's anger, Elijah flees
to an uninhabited region, where ravens bring him food and
where he drinks from a brook. When the brook dries up, he goes
into a city and seeks food and drink from a poor widow, whose
plea of poverty is piteous: "As the Lord thy God liveth, I have
not a cake, but an handful of meal in a barrel, and a little oil in
a cruse: and, behold, I am gathering two sticks, that I may go in
and dress it for me and my son, that we may eat it, and die"
(I Kings 17:12). Elijah promises her aid if she will feed him. She

consents, and he miraculously causes her meal barrel and oil cruse never to become empty thereafter, "until the day that the Lord sendeth rain upon the earth." He performs another miracle in reviving her dead son.

THE CONTEST AT MOUNT CARMEL (I Kings 18). In the third year of the drought and famine, in obedience to God's command Elijah goes back to see Ahab in Samaria. As soon as the king beholds him, he accuses the prophet: "Art thou he that troubleth Israel?" Fearlessly Elijah replies, "I have not troubled Israel; but thou, and thy father's house, in that ye have forsaken the commandments of the Lord, and thou hast followed Baalim." Then he orders Ahab to assemble at Mount Carmel all the people of Israel, the 450 prophets of Baal, and the 400 prophets of the groves. When they have all gathered, Elijah confronts the people with a disturbing question: "How long halt ye between two opinions? If the Lord be God, follow him: but if Baal, then follow him." The people are unable to answer a word.

Next Elijah challenges the pagan prophets to a contest. The prophets are to prepare one sacrifice and Elijah to prepare another. Each side will then call on its deity to send fire to consume its sacrifice. The prophets accept the challenge. They pray to Baal "from morning even until noon," but nothing happens to the bullock which they have cut up on their altar. Elijah mocks them: "Cry aloud: for he is a god; either he is talking, or he is pursuing, or he is in a journey, or peradventure he sleepeth, and must be awaked." The prophets leap on their altar, cry aloud, and even cut themselves with knives, but still there is no answer. Now Elijah prepares his altar. Fire falls upon the sacrificial offering and consumes not only the bullock but also the altar itself and even the stones and the dust. The people are converted and fall on their faces and cry out: "The Lord, he is the God!" At Elijah's direction they slay all the prophets of Baal. Finally Elijah says that the drought is at an end, he and Ahab go to Jezreel, and soon rain falls plentifully on Israel.

SECOND EXILE AND THE ANOINTING OF ELISHA (I Kings 19). Fleeing again (this time to escape the wrath of Jezebel), Elijah goes to a wilderness in southern Judah. There he prays for his own death. An angel brings him bread and water. A very memorable scene follows. The Lord tells him to go up on a mountain and to stand there before the Lord. "And, behold, the Lord passed by, and a great and strong wind rent the mountains, and brake in pieces the rocks before the Lord; but the Lord was not in the wind: and after the wind an earthquake; but the Lord was not in the earthquake: And after the earthquake a fire; but the Lord was not in the fire: and after the fire a still small voice." This is the voice of the Lord. It tells him to go back north and to anoint Hazael to be king of Syria, Jehu to be king of Israel, and Elisha to be Elijah's own successor as a prophet. Elijah obeys the "still small voice" and sets out. En route he encounters Elisha and casts his mantle upon him as a token of discipleship.

NABOTH'S VINEYARD (I Kings 21). In the town of Jezreel near Samaria a man named Naboth owns an excellent vineyard, which Ahab covets. He offers Naboth either another vineyard or money, but Naboth (who regards the property as a family heritage which cannot rightfully be sold) refuses each offer. Perceiving her husband's disappointment, Jezebel tells Ahab that she will procure the vineyard for him and sends two false witnesses to Jezreel to proclaim that Naboth has blasphemed God and the king and incite the people to stone him to death. As soon as Ahab hears that Naboth is dead, he takes possession of the coveted vineyard. Then the Lord sends Elijah to say to Ahab: "Thus saith the Lord, In the place where dogs licked the blood of Naboth shall dogs lick thy blood, even thine." In despair, Ahab cries out to Elijah: "Hast thou found me, O mine enemy?" Elijah foretells that all Ahab's male descendants will be slain and that dogs will eat the body of Jezebel by the wall of Jezreel.

RELATIONS WITH AHAZIAH (II Kings 1:1-15). Upon the death of Ahab, the king's son Ahaziah ascends the throne of Israel. Like his father and his mother, Ahaziah is an idolater and a worshiper of Baal. After ruling only two years, he is injured by a fall. He sends messengers to inquire of Baal-zebub, the god of Ekron, whether he will recover. Deploring the king's consulting of a foreign god instead of Yahweh, Elijah intercepts the messengers and sends them back to Ahaziah. Three times the king dispatches soldiers to arrest the prophet, who twice calls down heavenly fire upon the soldiers (the third time the leader of the soldiers begs Elijah for mercy) and then visits the king and prophesies his early death. Ahaziah dies soon after that.

THE ASCENSION OF ELIJAH (II Kings 2:1-15). Several years later, Elijah knows that it is time for him to depart this world.

Together he and Elisha walk to the banks of the Jordan River. Elijah parts the waters by striking them with his mantle,* and the two prophets cross to the other side. Elijah asks his companion what boon he would like to be granted; Elisha replies with the famous words: "I pray thee, let a double portion of thy spirit be upon me." Soon they behold a chariot of fire and horses of fire, and a whirlwind carries Elijah up into heaven. His mantle symbolically falls on Elisha, who parts the Jordan again with the garment and sadly returns to Jericho.

The Elisha Cycle (II Kings 2–9, 13:14-21). As a prophet, Elisha is somewhat less impressive and less admirable than Elijah. Whereas the latter seems to be interested primarily in religion and righteous conduct and to be remote and aloof, appearing suddenly at moments of crisis, Elisha is greatly concerned with political matters, and he is ubiquitous—always on hand to participate in whatever is going on. Although he is zealous in helping those who serve the Lord, Elisha is sometimes cruel and bloodthirsty; witness his instigation of Jehu's plot against the whole family of Ahab.

Furthermore, the Elisha cycle has less literary merit than the stories about Elijah; it is less organically unified and "more filled with the miraculous and the legendary." [34]

SEVEN MIRACLES OF ASSISTANCE (II Kings 2:19-22; 3:11-20; 4:1-44; and 6:1-7). As Elijah's successor, Elisha immediately begins to perform miracles, usually to help people in distress.

Four of these marvels are concerned with providing or purifying food or drink. One of his first acts is to aid the men of Jericho, whose water supply is bad and whose land is barren; Elisha "heals" the water by casting salt into it. On another occasion the combined armies of Israel, Edom, and Judah, which are waging war against Moab, find that their water supply is exhausted. Elisha orders the Israelites to dig many ditches; these he causes to fill up with water. In Gilgal he purifies some poison pottage by throwing meal into it. And at another time he causes twenty loaves of barley and a sack of corn to increase so as to be sufficient to feed a hundred men.

The similarity of two of Elisha's miracles to deeds performed by Elijah suggests that these later stories are in reality "doub-

---

* Compare Moses' parting of the Red Sea (Ex. 14:21) and Joshua's dividing of the waters of the Jordan (Jos. 3:15-16).

lets," or borrowings from the earlier cycle—a suggestion which gains weight when one considers how nearly alike the names of the prophets are. In the first of these two tales about Elisha, he miraculously increases a poor widow's supply of oil. In the second, he raises a young boy from the dead.

A seventh miracle of assistance is making an iron axe head (which has fallen into the Jordan) rise and float.

CURSING THE CHILDREN (II Kings 2:23-25). Once as Elisha is leaving Jericho, some children rudely make fun of him, shouting: "Go up, thou bald head; go up, thou bald head." Elisha curses them in the name of the Lord, and two she-bears come out of the forest and tear forty-two of the children. This story, shocking to modern readers, is probably told to inculcate respect for prophets.

NAAMAN'S LEPROSY (II Kings 5). The most skillfully told of all the stories about Elisha is that concerning Naaman, commander of the Syrian army, who has leprosy. Naaman's little maidservant, an Israelitish captive, grieves over her master's illness and tells him that a prophet in Samaria could cure him. Naaman goes to Samaria, bearing with him many valuable presents—gold, silver, and ten festal garments. First he calls upon the king and asks to be cured. Joram rends his own clothes and asks in despair: "Am I God, to kill and to make alive, that his man doth send unto me to recover a man of his leprosy?" When Elisha hears about the king's predicament, he sends for Naaman and tells him to wash himself seven times in the river Jordan. Naaman is angry that the cure should be so simple and asks: "Are not Abana and Pharpar, rivers of Damascus, better than all the waters of Israel?" His servants persuade him, however, to try the prophet's prescription. The malady disappears—his flesh becomes clean "like unto the flesh of a little child." The miracle convinces him that the Lord is the only God. Filled with gratitude, he urges Elisha to accept the gifts which he has brought from Syria, but Elisha refuses them. Then Naaman asks two more favors: first, that he be allowed to carry back to Syria some Israelitish earth on which to worship the Lord—apparently because he feels that Yahweh cannot be worshiped except on such soil; [35] and second, that he be forgiven in the future for accompanying his master into the temple of the god Rimmon and appearing to worship the false deity. Elisha grants his requests: "Go in peace."

After Naaman's departure, Gehazi, the servant of Elisha, yearns for some of the dazzling gifts which his master has refused. He overtakes Naaman and says that Elisha has reconsidered and would like a talent of silver and two changes of garments. Naaman insists that he take two talents with the garments, and Gehazi accepts. When Gehazi returns, Elisha asks where he has been. The servant lies: "Thy servant went no whither." Then Elisha rebukes him for lying and for being avaricious, and as a punishment causes him to be smitten with Naaman's leprosy. This is a moral tale showing the evils of greed. The smiting of Gehazi with the very leprosy of Naaman is a typical folk element—the "punishment fits the crime."

THE CONFOUNDING OF THE SYRIANS (II Kings 6–7). The Syrians and the Israelites are at war with each other once again. Ben-hadad of Syria suspects the presence of spies in his army, because all his maneuvers seem to be known beforehand by the Israelites. When told that Elisha can divine his secret counsels and report them to the king of Israel, Ben-hadad sends a great host to capture the prophet. Elisha's servant becomes terrified, but Elisha "opens his eyes" and enables him to see the encircling mountains full of heaven-sent horses and chariots of fire. Then the prophet causes blindness to fall on all Ben-hadad's men, and he leads them to Samaria, pretending that he is taking them where they can capture Elisha. In Samaria he restores their sight and causes King Joram to let them go peacefully back to Syria.

After a brief truce, war begins again, and the Syrians besiege Samaria so that terrible famine comes to the city. The Israelites are reduced to eating asses' heads, doves' dung, and even their own children. Accused of causing the disaster, Elisha prophesies that the famine will be ended immediately. The Lord makes the Syrian army hear a noise like the roaring of a great host of horses and chariots. Believing themselves to be under attack by the Egyptians and the Hittites, the Syrians flee in panic, leaving their food and equipment behind them. The Samarians rush out to seize the abandoned supplies, and the famine is ended.

Athaliah's Usurpation of the Throne of Judah (II Kings 11:1-21). In the Southern Kingdom, Athaliah, the daughter of Ahab and Jezebel, hearing that her son Ahaziah is dead, assumes the throne and tries to wipe out all the descendants of King David in order to strengthen her own position as sovereign. She succeeds in killing all the "seed royal" of the house of Judah except the one-year-old Joash (Jehoash), the son of Ahaziah. This child is saved by Jehosheba, the sister of Ahaziah, who at first hides him in her own bedchamber; then she and Jehoiada * the priest hide the lad in the Temple for six years. At the propitious moment Jehoiada gathers a considerable group of soldiers, shows Joash to them, and persuades them to swear allegiance to him. The priest anoints and crowns the young prince, and the people clap their hands and shout: "God save the king." When Athaliah hears the trumpets blowing and the people rejoicing, she tears her clothes † and cries: "Treason! Treason!" But Jehoiada's men seize her and kill her with the sword. Thereafter the people destroy the temple, altars, and images of Baal and slay Baal's priest.

Hezekiah, a Virtuous but Foolish King (II Kings 18—20). Events of great importance take place in the Southern Kingdom during the reign of Hezekiah, the son of Ahaz.

REFORM (II Kings 18:1-12). King Hezekiah is very different from his sinful and idolatrous father. Not only does he worship the Lord, but he removes the high places, breaks the images, cuts down the groves, and even destroys the brazen serpent supposedly handed down from Moses—a serpent to which the people are accustomed to burn incense. For these reforms God gives Hezekiah victory over the Philistines and (for a while) freedom from the Assyrians.

THE DESTRUCTION OF SENNACHERIB (II Kings 18:13—19:37). Sennacherib, the king of Assyria, captures many fortified cities of Judah, and Hezekiah himself sends tribute—treasures from his own house and from the house of the Lord. Then Sennacherib accuses Hezekiah of trying to enlist the aid of the king of Egypt, whom the Assyrian scoffingly refers to as a "bruised reed." Sennacherib demands more tribute. Next we are introduced to the prophet Isaiah, who is violently opposed to an alliance with Egypt and who delivers God's messages to Hezekiah. The king of Judah seeks Isaiah's advice about increasing the

---

* The book of II Chronicles (22:11), followed by Racine in *Athaliah*, makes Jehosheba the wife of Jehoiada.

† The tearing of one's clothes was an impressive gesture indicative of distress. Jacob, for example, rends his garments when he is told that Joseph has been killed by a wild beast (Gen. 37:34).

tribute to Sennacherib. In a famous "taunt song" delivered to Hezekiah by Isaiah, God promises to defeat the blasphemous Assyrians (II Kings 19:21-28) and to save Jerusalem for the time being. That night a terrible plague ("the angel of the Lord") smites Sennacherib's men and kills 185,000: ". . . and when they arose early in the morning, behold, they were all dead corpses." Sennacherib returns to Nineveh and is murdered by his own sons soon thereafter.

FOLLY (II Kings 20:12-19). By this time Babylon has become a great power in the Orient. Baladin, the king of Babylon, sends his son with letters and a gift for Hezekiah. Most unwisely, the king of Judah shows the young man all his treasures—"the silver, and the gold, and the spices, and the precious ointment, and all the house of his armour, and all that was found in his treasures: there was nothing in his house, nor in all his dominion, that Hezekiah shewed them not." When Isaiah hears about this foolish act of vanity, he makes a dire prediction: "Behold, the days come, that all that is in thine house, and that which thy fathers have laid up in store unto this day, shall be carried into Babylon: nothing shall be left, saith the Lord." Hezekiah seems undisturbed by this prophecy, so long as he will have peace in his day.

Josiah and Deuteronomic Reform in the Southern Kingdom (II Kings 22:1–23:30).[36] After the reigns of the "wicked" kings Manasseh and Amon, the "good" king Josiah succeeds to the throne of Judah. He does that which is right in the sight of the Lord and walks in all the ways of David, turning not aside to the right hand or to the left. He also repairs the Temple.

By far the most important event during his reign is the high priest Hilkiah's discovery of the lawbook in the Temple.* When Josiah reads this book and considers how its laws have been ignored by the people of Judah, he is so alarmed that he rends his clothes and commands Hilkiah and others: "Go ye, enquire of the Lord for me, and for the people, and for all Judah, concerning the words of this book that is found: for great is the wrath of the Lord that is kindled against us, because our fathers have not hearkened unto the words of this book, to do according unto all that which is written concerning us." He assembles

---

* See above, p. 50, for the discussion of the D Document, believed to be based on this book discovered by Hilkiah.

all the people to hear the lawbook read. Then follows the great Deuteronomic reformation (621 B.C.). Once again all the pagan shrines, altars, and images over the entire kingdom are destroyed, and their priests are either killed or suppressed. Wizards and magicians are "put away." Of great importance is the reinstitution of the observance of the Passover. The historian gives Josiah the highest accolade: "And like unto him was there no king before him, that turned to the Lord with all his heart, and with all his soul, and with all his might, according to all the law of Moses; neither after him arose there any like him."

Josiah meets an untimely end (c. 609 or 608 B.C.) in an expedition against an Egyptian king who is leading a raid on Assyria.

End of Monarchy and National Independence (II Kings 23:31 —25:30). The history of the reigns of the last four kings of Judah is made up of accounts of one catastrophe after another. During Josiah's reign a prophetess has foretold that after Josiah's time the Lord will punish the people of Judah for their sins. Punishment now threatens in the form of military invasion—by Babylon from the north and by Egypt from the south.

Jehoahaz, the son of Josiah, is taken captive by Pharaoh of Egypt, who dethrones him and places Eliakim, another of Josiah's sons, on the throne. At first Eliakim (whose name Pharaoh changes to Jehoiakim) pays tribute regularly. But then he becomes a vassal of Nebuchadrezzar, king of Babylon. After three years he rebels against Babylon, and so Nebuchadrezzar makes war against him. The Babylonians are joined by bands of Syrians, Moabites, and Ammonites, the ancient foes of the Jewish people. "Surely," says the historian, "at the commandment of the Lord came this upon Judah, to remove them out of his sight, for the sins of Manasseh, according to all that he did."

While the war is still going on, Jehoiakim (who has ruled eleven years) dies and is succeeded by his son Jehoiachin. This king also does evil in the sight of the Lord. In the eighth year (597 B.C.) of his reign, therefore, the Lord allows Nebuchadrezzar to take Jerusalem and to send ten thousand inhabitants of the country (including Jehoiachin) to Babylon as captives.

Nebuchadrezzar gives the Hebrews one more chance. He makes Mattaniah, Josiah's son, king of Judah and changes his name to Zedekiah. Zedekiah, however, is sinful, and the Lord causes him to rebel unsuccessfully against Nebuchadrezzar. Now

Nebuchadrezzar's patience is exhausted; he besieges Jerusalem and burns it to the ground, including the Lord's Temple. After killing Zedekiah's two sons in the presence of their father, Nebuchadrezzar puts out Zedekiah's eyes and appoints Gedaliah, a Hebrew, governor of the land. Seven months later the people revolt, kill the governor, and flee to Egypt. Thus the kingdom of Judah comes to an end.

A note of hope is preserved in a sort of postscript. The historian mentions that in the thirty-seventh year of Jehoiachin's captivity, Evil-merodach, the new king of Babylon, frees the Jewish monarch from prison, allows him to eat at the king's own table, and gives him an annuity for the remainder of his life.

5

Establishment of a Church State
after the Exile

I and II Chronicles, Ezra, Nehemiah, and I Esdras

After the fall of Jerusalem to the Babylonians in 586 B.C., the "desolation of Judah was practically complete." [1] The Temple was burned, and the walls of the capital city were flattened. An estimated 27,000 Hebrews were deported; a few others escaped into Egypt. Apparently only a handful of small farmers and herdsmen remained in what had once been the Southern Kingdom.

The ten tribes of the kingdom of Israel who had been led into exile by the Assyrians in 721 B.C. had become "lost"; that is, they had been scattered over Asia Minor and had ceased to exist as a racial unit. But the two Southern tribes, Benjamin and Judah, refused to be absorbed by their captors and struggled valiantly (by payment of tribute to Assyria when necessary to save the tribes) to preserve their worship of Yahweh, the strongest bond which held them together. Nebuchadrezzar, king of Babylonia, destroyed Jerusalem and exiled the people of Judah in 586 B.C. In exile (586-536 B.C.) they originated worship in the synagogue, a practice which has been followed ever since that time by Jews living outside of Palestine; and they continued their writing of law, history, and prophecy.

It appears that Nebuchadrezzar treated the Hebrews with some degree of leniency but that his successors, Nabunaid and Belshazzar, were rather oppressive. At any rate, the exiles welcomed Cyrus of Persia as a deliverer when he conquered Babylon in 539 B.C.; he issued an edict permitting them to return to their own country. A band of Jews, led by one Sheshbazzar, made plans to take advantage of Cyrus' offer, but little seems to have been accomplished till about 520-516 B.C., when another group, under Zerubbabel, a descendant of Jehoiachin, returned to Jerusalem, built a makeshift Temple, and recommenced the ancient ceremonies of worship.

History is silent concerning the Jews in Palestine for the following seventy-two years. Then in 444 B.C. the Persian king (probably Artaxerxes II) authorized Nehemiah to rebuild the walls of Jerusalem. Early in the fourth century B.C. the priest Ezra brought about 1,800 Hebrews back to the city and effected some religious reforms.

The Jews were granted a large degree of autonomy as long as they remained under Persian rule.

I AND II CHRONICLES: A RE-EVALUATION
OF ANCIENT JEWISH HISTORY

In the original Hebrew, I and II Chronicles were a single book. The Hebrew name for this book was *Dibhre Hayyamin*, meaning "annals." [2] The compilers of the Septuagint divided this work into two books and gave them the title *Paraleopomena*, meaning "things omitted" (that is, things left out of the books of Samuel and Kings). St. Jerome used the word *Chronicon* (an approximation of the Hebrew title), from which the English name of the books is derived.

For a long time there has been—and there still is—much scholarly disagreement about the authorship and the date of the two books of Chronicles. [3] Some scholars assert categorically that Ezra was the author and that he wrote the books about 380-350 B.C. Other commentators have vigorously maintained that the books were written much later, perhaps as late as 250 B.C., and that the identity of the author is unknown. The majority opinion appears to be that I and II Chronicles, Ezra, and Nehemiah were all written by the same person (but not Ezra), probably a Levite, and that the books of Chronicles were composed between 332 and 250 B.C. The author is called "the Chronicler."

The books of Chronicles are not history in the present-day sense of the term or even in the sense that Samuel and Kings are history. The Chronicler had no intention of writing an authentic and systematic record of events; *that* had already been done adequately in the Hexateuch, Judges, Samuel, and Kings.

Instead, the author intended to present so selective and so idealized a narrative that his contemporaries would not mistake it for real history but would plainly recognize the sermonic purposes for which it was written.

In order to understand the sermonic thesis, one needs to recall the status of the Jewish people. Although their dream of national glory had been shattered, some of them had returned from exile and had re-established the worship of Yahweh in Jerusalem. By the middle of the fourth century B.C., however, the priests had apparently become indolent in their duties and the people apathetic in their worship. Against these tendencies the Chronicler took his stand. His purposes were to recall the priests and Levites to a more zealous performance of their official functions, to inspire in the people a greater devotion to God, and to stress the importance of Temple worship in Jerusalem according to the ancient book of laws.

His method is to idealize the "good old days," the glorious times of David and Solomon, and then to demonstrate the evils which befell the kingdoms when the later kings and the people ceased to worship God and obey his commandments. David is emphasized as a religious leader rather than a great political and military figure, and he is given credit for establishing the entire system of Temple worship and for introducing music into the religious ceremonies. The stories in I and II Samuel which are detrimental to his character (notably the Bathsheba episode) are omitted. Since the Chronicler is primarily interested in Temple worship, he restricts his narrative almost entirely to the events in Jerusalem and the kingdom of Judah.

Both books of Chronicles have usually been considered less distinguished literature than Samuel and Kings. In the first place, they are repetitions of parts of those earlier books of history and have little real information to add. In the second place, they omit many of the "human interest" stories found in the older books, such as the charming account of Samuel's birth and childhood and the stories about Elijah. In the third place, the books of Chronicles contain many inaccuracies, exaggerations, and inconsistencies; for example, Jehoshaphat is said to have 1,160,000 soldiers in Jerusalem. The chief literary value of the books lies in the Chronicler's ability to share his own earnest devotion with his readers and in his addition of a few idyllic and lyrical passages which do not appear in Samuel or Kings.

Genealogical Survey of History from Adam to David (I Chr. 1–9).[4] The first nine chapters of I Chronicles trace the ancestry of the Israelites and their relatives. Chapter 1 takes us from Adam through the sons of Esau. Chapters 2–9 are devoted to the genealogies of the twelve tribes of Israel, including the "half-tribes" of Manasseh and Ephraim. Special attention is given to the Levites and to the tribe of Judah, from which tribe the Davidic line is descended. The purpose of compiling these genealogies was to establish "the rights of the several Levitical families in post-exilic Jerusalem to fulfill their various functions . . . [and to support] the claim of other important families in the Jewish community to count themselves truly as children of Abraham, heirs of the divine promise."[5]

The Reign of David (I Chr. 10–29). Nearly all the material in the last twenty chapters of I Chronicles is taken from I and II Samuel and I Kings. The Chronicler begins with the death of Saul and ends with the death of David. In order to carry out his religio-ethical aims, he omits or changes many passages and adds a few of his own.

The most significant deletions are those concerning the conception, birth, and childhood of Samuel; the reign of Saul; David's slaying of Goliath; David's affair with Bathsheba; and Absalom's rebellion.

The principal additions made by the Chronicler are as follows: (1) attributing Saul's death to his consulting of the witch of Endor (10:13-14); (2) gathering of the armies at Hebron to proclaim David king of all Israel (12:23-40); (3) Hiram of Tyre's aid to David (14:1); (4) David's psalm of thanksgiving for the bringing of the Ark to Jerusalem (16:7-36); (5) David's contributions to the Temple (22:14-16 and 28:14-19);* (6) assignment of the Levites, singers, and other attendants in the Temple (23:2–27:34); (7) David's pattern for the Temple (28:11-13); and finally (8) David's last prayer (29:10-19).

The Reign of Solomon and the Subsequent History of Judah (II Chr.). The second book of Chronicles covers the reign of Solomon and the history of the kingdom of Judah from the reign

---

* Note that God forbade David to build the Temple "because thou has shed much blood upon the earth," and reserved that high privilege for David's peaceable son, Solomon, for whom God "will give peace and quietness unto Israel in his days." The Temple was to be the visible sign of God's presence, the symbol of Jerusalem as the holy city, and the center of the Hebrew faith.

of Rehoboam to the edict of Cyrus which permitted the Israelites to go back to Palestine. Thus the book repeats much of
I and II Kings. But it ignores the history of the kingdom of Israel except when the affairs of that kingdom are closely related
to those of Judah.

As in the case of I Chronicles, the author changes his sources
to suit his purposes. He whitewashes the character of Solomon,
saying nothing about his being led into idolatry by his multitude
of wives. He expands many passages which emphasize the work
of the prophets and their messages from God. For example, in I
Kings the account of the invasion of Palestine by Shishak is covered in four verses (14:25-28), whereas the Chronicler goes into
great detail about the invasion, the prophet Shemaiah's pronouncements to Rehoboam, and that king's repentance—a total of
twelve verses (II Chr. 12:1-12). He stresses more the reigns of
four good kings of Judah—Asa, Jehoshaphat, Hezekiah, and
Josiah. He inserts two passages which enhance the prestige of
the Levites (20:19-21 and 31:2-19). He mentions by name the
prophet Jeremiah and tells of his predictions (36:21-22). And
finally, the Chronicler adds the passage telling of the Persian
conquest of Babylon and freeing of the exiles (36:20-23): "Thus
saith Cyrus king of Persia. All the kingdoms of the earth hath the
lord God of heaven given me; and he hath charged me to build
him an house in Jerusalem, which is in Judah. Who is there
among you of all his people? The Lord his God be with him,
and let him go up."

EZRA AND NEHEMIAH: THE CHRONICLER'S ACCOUNT OF THE REBUILDING OF JERUSALEM

In the ancient Jewish canon the books of Ezra and Nehemiah
formed a single work, entitled simply "Ezra." The division into
two parts was probably made in the Vulgate. The book of Ezra
derives its name from its main character, the priest who led religious reform in Jerusalem about 397 B.C. The book of Nehemiah
is named for its main character, the cupbearer of King Artaxerxes I or II.

One of the few matters concerning the books of Ezra and Nehemiah on which virtually all scholars agree is the fact that they
were written (or compiled) by the man responsible for the preparation of I and II Chronicles, the man known as "the Chron-

icler." In all four books he shows a fondness for lists, catalogues, and genealogies; an unusual interest in Temple procedures and the functions of the Levites; and what would seem today a lack of concern for chronological and historical accuracy. In the book of Ezra he skips without warning a period of several decades (after Ezra 6:22), and he shifts back and forth from first to third person, as if he is simply copying his sources verbatim. Some of the inaccuracies are attributable to the facts that the two books were probably written more than a century after the events described and that the events had occurred in a very unsettled period that left few reliable records.

For the book Ezra, the Chronicler *undoubtedly* used some official reports written in Aramaic * concerning the persecution of the Jews (Ezra 4:8–6:18 and 7:12-26); and he *probably* utilized (1) a memoir written by the priest Ezra,† (2) official Temple records, genealogies, and lists of names, and (3) oral traditions. The chief evidence in favor of his use of an account by Ezra himself is the fact that part of the narrative concerning that priest is written in the first person, whereas most of the book is in the third person.[6]

It should be noted here that the literary form known as the "epistle" (which was later to form a significant portion of the New Testament) makes its first appearance in the Holy Scriptures in Ezra. Four letters are included in the book: 4:11-16, 4:17-22, 5:7-17, and 7:12-26.

The principal source for the book of Nehemiah is a personal memoir written by Nehemiah himself (*c.* 432 B.C.). This memoir probably comprises Neh. 1:1–7:4, 11:1-2, 12:27-43, and 13:4-31,[7] sections which, taken together constitute a vital and intimate narrative revelatory of the personality and the religious devotion of its author. They are written in the first person.

---

* Aramaic is the language which resulted from the mingling of foreign elements with primitive Hebrew, especially during the Exile. By 300 B.C. Aramaic had almost entirely supplanted primitive Hebrew as the spoken language.

† Considering the Chronicler's tendency to idealize and invent, some reputable scholars have doubted the very existence of Ezra as a historical character and have believed him to be a figment of the Chronicler's imagination —an embodiment of priestly virtues as conceived by an ardent Levite. If Ezra never really existed, then it follows that the above-mentioned memoir by Ezra is spurious. This rather extreme view is not widely held today.

There is little doubt that a later copyist or redactor has disarranged the Ezra-Nehemiah narrative as written by the Chronicler, so that now it is decidely chaotic. Parts of the Ezra narrative have been pulled out of the original account and transferred
to Nehemiah.

In order to rearrange the passages correctly, we should have
to solve another very difficult problem: did the man Ezra precede
the man Nehemiah in point of time, or did he follow him? Ezra
6—9 says that the priest Ezra went to Jerusalem in the seventh
year of the reign of Artaxerxes, and Neh. 2:1-5 says that in the
twentieth year of Artaxerxes' reign Nehemiah requested permission to rebuild Jerusalem. Therefore many scholars have concluded that, since Artaxerxes I ruled 465-424 B.C., Ezra's reforms
began in 458 and Nehemiah's journey to Jerusalem took place in
445 or 444. Other scholars, however, have argued rather convincingly that the activities of Nehemiah necessarily preceded
Ezra's reforms; they point out, for example, that Nehemiah has to
rebuild the wall of the city (Neh. 1:3) and that Ezra thanks
God for the wall (Ezra 9:9); and that Nehemiah regrets that
the number of Jews in Jerusalem is small (Neh. 7:4 and 11:1-2),
whereas Ezra speaks of "a great congregation" (Ezra 10:1).[8]
Therefore, these scholars believe, Ezra's monarch was Artaxerxes
II, who reigned 404-358 B.C.; Ezra, then, would have gone to
Jerusalem in 398 or 397 B.C. instead of in 458. It is pretty well
established that Nehemiah's labors of reconstruction began in
444 B.C.

If Nehemiah's rebuilding of the city wall preceded Ezra's reforms, the material should be arranged as follows: Ezra 1—6,
Neh. 1:1—7:4, Neh. 11-13, Ezra 7-8, Neh. 8, Ezra 9-10, and Neh.
7:5-73.[9] This arrangement seems the most logical one and for the
purposes of the present Outline will be assumed.

Zerubbabel and the Temple (Ezra 1—6). The book of Ezra
opens with a repetition of Cyrus' decree found at the end of
II Chronicles. According to the Chronicler, Zerubbabel (or
Sheshbazzar [10]) now gathers together a large number of Hebrews
from the tribes of Benjamin and Judah and sets out for Jerusalem. They are allowed to take with them great quantities of the
sacred vessels which Nebuchadrezzar had carried to Babylon.
They set up a sacrificial altar, revive the observance of the Feast
of Tabernacles (or Booths), and lay the foundations of a new
Temple (536 B.C.).

Next the author records the beginning of the historic enmity between the Judeans and the Samaritans,* an enmity which lasted well past the time of Christ. The Samaritans, as worshipers of Yahweh, ask to be allowed to help in the building of the Temple. Zerubbabel refuses their aid, with the haughty remark that the Samaritans and the Jerusalem Jews have nothing in common. Thereafter the Samaritans successfully harass the restorers of the Temple till the second year of the reign of Darius I (520 B.C.).† Apparently it is these Samaritans, these "adversaries of Judah and Benjamin," who persuade Tatnai (Tattenai), the Persian governor of the province, to write to Darius about authority to rebuild the Temple. King Darius finds the old decree of Cyrus and issues a new one to the effect that the restorers are not to be hindered in their efforts. Four years later (516 B.C.) the Temple is completed and dedicated with great rejoicing.

Nehemiah's Petition (Neh. 1:1–2:8). About three generations after the reconstruction of the Temple, Nehemiah, the cupbearer of Artaxerxes I, records in his memoir the piteous condition of Jerusalem as reported to him in Susa (Shushan), the Persian capital, by some Hebrews who have just returned from Palestine: "The remnant that are left of the captivity there in the province are in great affliction and reproach; the wall of Jerusalem also is broken down, and the gates thereof are burned with fire." Nehemiah is so sorrowful that he sits down and weeps and for several days mourns and fasts and prays. Noticing his sad countenance, Artaxerxes asks the cause. "Then I was very sore afraid, and said unto the king, Let the king live for ever: why should not my countenance be sad, when the city, the place of my fathers' sepulchres, lieth waste, and the gates thereof are consumed with fire?" Artaxerxes inquires what he wants to do about

---

* The term *Samaritan* was applied not only to the inhabitants of the city of Samaria but also to all those who, after the fall of the kingdom of Israel, dwelt in the region around the Northern capital. For two reasons the Judean Hebrews looked with scorn upon the Samaritans: first, they considered the Samaritans to be "collaborationists" with the Assyrians and Babylonians; and second, they believed that the Samaritans had polluted the pure Hebrew blood by intermarriage with foreigners, a practice against which both Nehemiah and Ezra exhorted.

† Verses 5-23 of Ch. 4 are probably the Chronicler's addition to the narrative found in his sources. These verses refer to a later period (the reigns of Ahasuerus [Xerxes I], 486-465, and Artaxerxes I, 464-424) and tell about enemies who interrupted the building of the *walls*, not the Temple.

it. Again Nehemiah is afraid, but, after uttering a prayer to God, he begs to be allowed to go to Jerusalem and rebuild it. The king is gracious and, not in the least displeased, asks simply how long Nehemiah will be gone. He gives his cupbearer letters of recommendation and authority, and Nehemiah sets out.

Rebuilding of the Wall (Neh. 2:9—7:4). He arrives safely in the city, but his troubles are only beginning. His efforts are continually opposed by "foreigners," especially Sanballat the Horonite,* Tobiah the Ammonite, and Geshem the Arab. They accuse him of plotting to rebel against Artaxerxes and of wanting to make himself king. Nehemiah perseveres in spite of their accusations, and work on the wall begins. Sanballat and the others ridicule their efforts: "What do these feeble Jews? . . . will they revive the stones out of the heaps of the rubbish which are burned? . . . Even that which they build, if a fox go up, he shall even break down their stone wall." Five times Sanballat tries to lure Nehemiah away from the city so that he may harm or kill him, but Nehemiah will not be tricked. He steadfastly answers: . . . "I am doing a great work, so that I cannot come down: why should the work cease, whilst I leave it, and come down to you?" (Neh. 6:3). The enemies even threaten to make armed attacks on the builders of the wall, so that some of Nehemiah's men have to stop construction and stand guard. Every workman labors on the wall with one hand and carries a weapon in the other.

Nor are these the only difficulties which Nehemiah has to overcome. There is dissatisfaction among his own group. Many of them are suffering from economic distress. High taxes and famines have forced some to borrow from their more affluent Jewish brethren, who have been exacting exorbitant interest, foreclosing mortgages on property, and even enslaving the sons and daughters of those unable to pay their debts. Nehemiah rebukes the creditors, and work on rebuilding the wall continues.

After only fifty-two days the wall is completed and solemnly dedicated. Nehemiah sets appropriate guards about it and appoints priests and Levites to their various duties in the city.

Nehemiah's Reforms (Neh. 13). The former cupbearer's troubles are not yet over; he still has to solve many real problems—politi-

---

* Sanballat was apparently associated with the hostile Samaritans (see Neh. 4:2). A "Horonite" was an inhabitant of Beth-horon, a city of Ephraim.

cal, economic, religious, and social. While he is away on a visit
to Susa, his priest Eliashib desecrates the Temple by allowing
the pagan and alien Tobiah, Sanballat's crony, to live in a chamber of the building. Upon returning from Persia, Nehemiah casts
Tobiah out and cleanses the Temple. Next, the Levites neglect
their duties for the legitimate reason that they have not been
paid their promised portions. Nehemiah conciliates them by collecting tithes and paying the overdue salaries. Then he discovers that the people are failing to keep the Sabbath day holy:
they are allowing buying and selling to be carried on upon that
day; he quickly puts a stop to this. Finally, one of Nehemiah's
most serious problems is his people's intermarriage with foreigners—Ashdodites,* Ammonites, and Moabites. He is forced
to use drastic measures: "And I contended with them, and cursed
them, and smote certain of them, and plucked off their hair, and
made them swear by God: Ye shall not give your daughters
unto their sons, nor take their daughters for your sons, or for
yourselves." These measures must have had some effect, for
Nehemiah says that he has cleansed the Israelites from "strangers" (foreigners). The problem, however, is solved only temporarily; a few decades later Ezra is faced with it again.

Nehemiah ends his memoir with the characteristic prayer:
"Remember me, O my God, for good" (Neh. 13:31).

Ezra's Reforms (Ezra 7—8; Neh. 8, Ezra 9—10; and Neh. 7:5-73).
The second part of the book of Ezra opens with the introduction
of Ezra himself, plus a tracing of his ancestry back to Aaron,
the brother of Moses. (This genealogy is probably included to
assure the reader that Ezra is of genuine priestly stock; the
reader is also told that Ezra is a scribe learned in the law of
Moses.) Ezra requests Artaxerxes to allow him to go to Jerusalem to teach Moses' law to the children of Israel there. Then
follows a letter (in Aramaic) from Artaxerxes which not only
grants Ezra's request but also allows him to take up a collection
from the people in Babylon and to draw on the Persian treasury
in each of the provinces through which he passes. Finally, the
letter authorizes Ezra to appoint magistrates and to enforce laws.

Writing in the first person, Ezra bursts into an exuberant praise
of God for putting such things into King Artaxerxes' heart.

* Ashdod was formerly a Philistine territory, and its people worshiped the
god Dagon.

After proclaiming a fast, Ezra prepares to set out for Palestine. Here (still in the first person) he inserts a very interesting and very human comment. He says that he is making the journey without the protection of soldiers because he has told the king that God will be his protector; therefore he would have been ashamed to ask for a military convoy. Ezra and several companions make the journey in safety, deliver their treasures to the keepers of the Temple, and offer sacrifices to the Lord.

Now (Neh. 8:2) the people assemble. Ezra opens the book of Moses' law and reads to them.* The people weep, for they perceive how flagrantly they have been disobeying that law. Ezra comforts them.

Next, Ezra is greatly perturbed upon discovering that the Israelites of Jerusalem have been intermarrying with foreigners—Canaanites, Hittites, Perizzites, Jebusites, Ammonites, Moabites, Egyptians, and Amorites. Ezra tears his clothes, pulls out the hair of his head and beard, and sits down "astonied." The reasons for his grief are, first, that he does not want the Hebrew blood defiled, and second—and more important—that he fears the foreigners will lead the people of Israel away from the true God, as they had done in the days of Solomon and Ahab. Again he assembles the people and in their presence offers a prayer of confession to God. The people, too, confess their sins, promise to put away all alien spouses and their children, and never more to intermarry. A solemn feast of repentance is proclaimed, and after another prayer by the leader of the Levites, the people sign a covenant to abjure marriage with foreigners, to pay tithes, and to obey the law of the Lord.

Thus the account of Ezra's reforms ends on a happy note.

I ESDRAS: A SECOND POST-EXILIC ACCOUNT OF JEWISH HISTORY FROM JOSIAH TO THE REBUILDING OF JERUSALEM

The word *Esdras* is the Greek form of *Ezra*. In Protestant Bibles the book is known as "I Esdras" and is part of the Apocrypha; in the Vulgate it is a noncanonical book called "III Esdras" (see p. 28). (I and II Esdras in Catholic Bibles are, respectively, Ezra and Nehemiah in Protestant Scriptures.)

---

* An interesting linguistic fact is here preserved. The people no longer understand pure Hebrew, and Ezra has to use interpreters to explain his reading to the people. See Neh. 8:7-8.

Modern scholars believe that I Esdras is a fragment of a Greek translation (*c.* 150 B.C.) of the work of the Chronicler—Chronicles and Ezra-Nehemiah—a translation older than the canonical version preserved in the Septuagint. The translator responsible for I Esdras was probably an Alexandrian Jew.[11]

This Apocryphal book is a freer and more idiomatic translation of the Chronicler's narrative than the Vulgate one. It covers the period from the last days of Josiah to Ezra's reading of the law to the people of Jerusalem.

Significant Departures from the Ezra-Nehemiah Account. There are two significant differences between the account of the rebuilding of Jerusalem as given in I Esdras and that given in the books of Ezra and Nehemiah. In the first place, I Esdras 2 says that Artaxerxes orders the rebuilding of Jerusalem and its Temple to cease, because the Samaritans have written him a letter warning that the Jews are planning a rebellion; this account says that the work of reconstruction ceased till the second year of the reign of Darius.* In the second place, I Esdras makes no mention at all of Nehemiah.

The Contest of the Three Guardsmen (3–4). An interesting addition to the old story of Zerubbabel has some of the characteristics of a folk tale, a medieval *débat,* and even a Platonic dialogue.[12] Zerubbabel (Zorobabel) is one of the three bodyguards of King Darius.† These young men suggest a contest to be held before the king. Each of them is to nominate the strongest thing in the world and then to defend his nomination; the king and his noblemen are to be the judges of the wisdom of the three speeches and to choose the winner. The three bodyguards also suggest that the winner be given an appropriate prize. Darius approves the contest.

The first guardsman says that *wine* is the strongest of all things, because it can make a man sinful, happy, belligerent, or self-confident. The second guardsman argues that the *king* is the strongest, for he can impose his will on all others. But Zerubbabel wins, first, by demonstrating in great detail that *woman* is able to bend any man (even a king) to her will, and, second, by pointing out that *truth* is stronger even than woman, because it endures forever, is approved by all, and is an attribute of God.

* Contrast the account found in Ezra 5:3–6:22.
† In the book of Ezra, Zerubbabel is a subject of Cyrus, not of Darius.

The court, of course, cheers the speech of Zerubbabel and adjudges him the wisest, and his wisdom finds favor in the sight of Darius. Instead of choosing gold or other riches, Zerubbabel asks that Darius permit him to take back to Jerusalem the vessels which have been carried away by Nebuchadrezzar and to rebuild the Temple. Darius kisses him and grants his request.

Thus does I Esdras provide an explanation for Darius' kindness to the Jews.

6

The Maccabean Revolt

I and II Maccabees

There is no Biblical record of the events which took place in Palestine between the time of Ezra's reforms (c. 397 B.C.) and the early part of the second century B.C. During that long period, however, many things happened which affected the future of the Hebrews. In 331 B.C. the Persian empire fell before the onslaughts of Alexander the Great, who had conquered Palestine in 332 B.C., and he soon took over the rule of all Persian-held territories. When Alexander died in 323 B.C., his empire was divided among four of his generals. The eastern, or Syrian, section became the portion of Seleucus and his descendants, known as the Seleucids. The southern, or Egyptian, area (which included Palestine) fell to Ptolemy * and his descendants; under these monarchs the Hebrews enjoyed a mild and tolerant rule similar to that which they had enjoyed under the Persians; they had virtually complete religious freedom and a considerable degree of autonomy. Then in 198 B.C., Antiochus III, the Seleucid king of Syria, defeated the Egyptians near Mount Hermon and made Palestine part of his kingdom. The policy of the Seleucids, very different from that of the Ptolemies, was to impose Greek customs, language, and religion upon all the people in their dominions. Abhorrent as this policy was to many of the Hebrews, there was no open rebellion until Antiochus IV (Epiphanes) in 168 B.C. erected an altar to the Greek god Zeus in the Temple at Jerusalem. The uprising which ensued in 167 B.C.—led by Judas Maccabeus and other members of his family—continued more than thirty years

---

* Ptolemy II (Philadelphus), who ruled c. 285-c. 246 B.C. is traditionally reputed to have sponsored the preparation of the Septuagint.

and at last succeeded in giving the Jewish people a large measure of political and religious freedom and a dynasty of Hebrew
rulers for almost a century.

The following table [1] outlines the most significant events of
the Maccabean period:

198 B.C.	Antiochus III, the Seleucid king of Syria, defeats Egypt, annexes Palestine, and tries to Hellenize the Hebrews.
175 B.C.	Antiochus IV (Epiphanes) accedes to throne, continues Hellenization of Palestine. "Collaborationist" Hebrews build gymnasium for Greek type of athletics in Jerusalem.
171 B.C.	Antiochus IV sacks Temple in Jerusalem.
168 B.C.	Antiochus IV perpetrates many atrocities against the Hebrews in Jerusalem. In 167 B.C. the priest Mattathias, of the Hasmon family,* leads some Hebrews in revolt. Several battles follow.
166 B.C.	Mattathias dies and is succeeded as military leader by his son Judas Maccabeus, who wins several victories over the Syrians.
165 B.C.	Judas purifies Temple, inaugurates Hebrew festival of Hanukkah.
161 B.C.	Judas defeats Syrians under General Nicanor, inaugurates Jewish festival of Nicanor's Day. Judas makes mutual-assistance pact with Rome.
160 B.C.	Judas slain in battle, succeeded as military leader of Hebrews by his brother Jonathan. War continues two more years.
158-153 B.C.	Peace with the Syrians.
142 B.C.	Jonathan slain by enemy, is succeeded by his brother Simon, who continues war, defeats Syrians, wins virtual independence for the Jews. Peace for seven years.
134 B.C.	War resumed. Simon slain by his own son-in-law; succeeded as priest-king by his son John Hyrcanus.
134-104 B.C.	Reign of John Hyrcanus, marked by peace and prosperity. Rise of Pharisees and Sadducees.
104-63 B.C.	Period of internal unrest and civil wars.
63 B.C.	Pompey the Great called in to settle dispute over throne, establishes Roman control over Palestine; Hasmoneans are puppet-kings.

* Mattathias' descendants are known as the Hasmonaeans, as well as Maccabees.

40 B.C.   Herod the Great appointed King of Judea, replacing
                 the Hasmonaean dynasty.

The Maccabean period witnessed the rise of two religio-politi-
cal parties which were later to be of great importance: the Sadducees and the Pharisees. Though not even mentioned in the
canonical books of the Old Testament, in the New Testament
they are treated as long-established and influential sects.

The Sadducees were "the aristocratic supporters of the Maccabean dynasty, the wealthy minority from which the priesthood
was recruited."[2] Generally they rejected belief in personal immortality and looked with distrust upon anything miraculous or
apocalyptic. "Educated, worldly and more than tinged with
Hellenism, they wished to confine their religion to what was
literally 'written in the law of Moses' and rejected the traditional rules and ceremonies, taught by the Pharisees, not literally
supported by Biblical authority."[3]

Opposed to the Sadducees were the Pharisees, usually identified with the Hasidim (or Assideans). In I Maccabees 2:42 the
Hasidim are described as mighty warriors. In later times the
Pharisees were recognized as a pious group of teachers who
stressed not only the Mosaic law but also the traditional priestly
or rabbinical interpretations of that law which had been handed
down since the time of Ezra. The term *Pharisee* (an Aramaic word
meaning "the separated") was first applied to a member of this
group about 110 to 105 B.C. and apparently referred to "their
meticulous care in avoiding anything ceremonially unclean."[4] By
the time of Christ the rabbinical interpretations of the law had
become excessively numerous and complicated, and Christ on
some occasions attacked the Pharisees, apparently because he felt
that many of them were more interested in the letter of the Law
than in its spirit or in genuine goodness. Although *Pharisaism*
is today almost synonymous with hypocritical self-righteousness,
in the first century A.D. and earlier, to be a Pharisee was an honor.
St. Paul was trained as one (see Acts 23:6), and some scholars
have claimed that Christ himself was brought up as one.

It was in Maccabean times, too, that belief in personal immortality came to be widespread. In most Old Testament books
written before the second century B.C., little is said about the
afterlife. Sheol, it is true, is frequently mentioned, but it is always

a shadowy underground place where, upon dying, men are "gath-ered" to their people; it is a region neither of punishment for the wicked nor of reward for the righteous.* So far as is known, the eighth-century prophet Isaiah was the first Biblical writer to mention bodily resurrection (Isa. 26:19). Many generations, how-ever, were to pass before belief in the "resurrection of the body and the life everlasting"—one of the central tenets of Christianity—became an important part of Hebrew doctrine. The best pre-Christian statement of this belief appears in II Maccabees (see p. 353).

It is worth noting here that the epistle, which had already appeared as a literary type in the book of Ezra (see above, p. 136), plays an important role in the two books of Maccabees. Six letters appear in I Maccabees (8:23-27, 31:32; 10:18-20, 52-54; 13:36-40; and 15:2-9) and two in II Maccabees (1:1-9 and 1:10—2:18).

The two books of Maccabees are named for Judas Maccabeus, one of the great Hebrew military heroes whose deeds are nar-rated in these books. The word *Maccabeus* probably means "hammer" or "hammerer."[5]

I MACCABEES: HISTORY OF THE REVOLT
FROM 168 TO 135 B.C.

The name of the author of I Maccabees is unknown. Some scholars believe him to have been a Sadducee, but evidence that he was is inconclusive.[6] The book was first written in Hebrew at some time between 135 and 63 B.C., probably shortly after 100 B.C.[7]

All commentators agree that the book is, in the main, a trust-worthy historical narrative. It is especially accurate and valuable as a record of dates; each event is dated according to the year of the reign of the Seleucids, who began their rule in late 312 or early 311 B.C.[8] Although strongly partisan in favor of the Macca-bees, the author gives an almost completely unprejudiced report, telling the failures as well as the successes of his protagonists. He has little or nothing to say about miracles or supernatural hap-penings. His style is plain, rapid, and straightforward; he gives few details about the battles he records.

Although he does not have so didactic an intent as either the author of Kings or the "Chronicler," it may be said that his his-

* See, for example, Gen. 25:8, 35:29, 49:29, and Deut. 32:50.

tory illustrates the thesis that the faithful and courageous will gain success and glory.[9]

After a brief introduction summarizing the period from Alexander's conquest of Persia down to Antiochus III's defeat of Egypt, the author launches into his main task of telling about Antiochus Epiphanes' attempts to wipe out the Judaistic religion, the resultant rebellion, and the establishment of the Maccabean (or Hasmonaean) dynasty, which was to last till 40 B.C. The book covers the period 168-135 B.C. In addition to the main narrative thread, which is concerned with the Jewish resistance to Syrian oppression, the book contains many records of international politics, intrigues, treaties, abrogations of treaties, and treachery; these records are too numerous and too confusing (without extensive explanatory notes) to be treated here, but they are of great value to students of ancient Oriental history.

The Atrocities of Antiochus Epiphanes (Ch. 1). After a victorious expedition against Egypt, in 168 B.C. Antiochus Epiphanes decides to enforce upon Jerusalem his policy of Hellenization. He robs the Temple of its golden altar, its candlestick, and its gold and silver vessels. Somewhat later he sends to the city his tribute collector, who kills many of the people, takes many others captive, sets fire to the buildings, and pulls down the houses and the walls. Next Antiochus builds a great citadel in Jerusalem and puts into it a garrison of Syrian soldiers. Worst of all, as far as the faithful worshipers of Yahweh are concerned, he sends a decree over his whole kingdom that everybody is to follow the Greek religion. He burns copies of the Mosaic law and forbids the offering of sacrifices to any but Greek gods, the circumcision of children, and the observance of the Sabbath and festival days. Antiochus' men hang circumcised infants about their mothers' necks and then kill these mothers. Perhaps the last straw is the building of an altar to Zeus in Yahweh's own Temple and the sacrificing there of swine, an abomination to devout Jews. The historian sadly admits that many Jews give in to Antiochus' demands and embrace the pagan religion which he advocates; but many others eschew the pagan ceremonies, choosing to die rather than to profane the holy covenant.

Mattathias (Ch. 2). One of those who refuse to obey the orders of the king is the priest Mattathias. He and his five sons—Joannan, Simon, Judas, Eleazar, and Jonathan—move away from Jerusalem; they mourn for the city and its people, and they continue to worship the true God.* When Mattathias sees a Hebrew offering a sacrifice on a heathen altar, he slays the man forthwith. He also kills the king's commissioner, pulls down the altar, and then flees with his sons to the mountains. Other faithful Hebrews join them.

A sad but interesting story is told concerning a thousand of the most pious refugees who refuse to offer resistance to the Syrians on the Sabbath and so are slaughtered. Mattathias and his immediate friends, however, decide that self-defense is justifiable, even on the Sabbath.

Eventually Mattathias and his group are strong enough to carry on guerrilla warfare against the Syrians. They destroy many heathen altars and forcibly circumcise many Hebrew children.

When Mattathias feels that his life is drawing to a close, he appoints Judas Maccabeus, the mightiest of his sons, to be military commander.

Judas Maccabeus (3–9:22). Judas now assumes leadership of the rebels in their struggle for religious freedom. He is a superb leader, as a poem (3:2-9) indicates: "In his acts . . . like a lion, and like a lion's whelp, roaring for his prey." In addition to being a shrewd and valiant soldier, he is also an eloquent orator. Before each battle he exhorts his men to remember how God has helped the Hebrews in times past, and he assures them that God will still be their protector. With fasting and prayer they prepare for battle, placing their trust in God.

The Syrians now oppose the Hebrews in force. Despite overwhelming odds, Judas and his men defeat Antiochus' armies in several major battles. During the course of one of these encounters, the Syrians employ elephants against Judas' men—the first military use of elephants in recorded history (6:30). Judas' brother Eleazar, believing the Syrian king to be upon one particular elephant, valiantly attacks the beast and kills it by striking it on the underside. The elephant falls upon Eleazar and kills him.

After a number of decisive victories, Judas is able to march into Jerusalem, cleanse the Temple, and build a new altar. For eight days the Hebrew people offer sacrifices to God and cele-

* Three of these sons—Simon, Judas, and Jonathan—are to play important roles in the history of the period.

brate the dedication of the new altar "with mirth and gladness."
Thus Judas inaugurates the great festival known as Hanukkah
(or Chanukah), which is still observed today (4:36-59).

Soon after the death of Antiochus Epiphanes (c. 164 B.C.),
Judas makes peace with the Syrians and succeeds in winning
religious freedom for his people—the main objective for which he
has been striving (6:60).

Three years later war breaks out again, and once more Judas
is victorious. He defeats the Syrian general Nicanor and celebrates his victory by inaugurating the festival known as Nicanor's
Day, observed annually for more than two centuries (7:49).[10]

Next Judas makes a mutual-assistance pact with Rome (Ch. 8).
This is of great significance, for it is the Hebrews' first official
dealing with the great new empire of the West (161 B.C.).

The following year Judas is slain in battle (9:1-27).

Jonathan Apphus (9:28—12). Judas Maccabeus is succeeded by
his brother Jonathan as military leader of the Jews. With the aid
of Simon, another son of Mattathias, Jonathan rallies the Jewish
forces and defeats the Syrians. After a two-year peace the Syrians
try another battle but are once more defeated (158 B.C.). Now
they agree to a covenant with the Hebrews, and the latter enjoy
a five-year period of peace (9:70-73). Jonathan is appointed by
the Syrian ruler to be high priest of Israel; this appointment is a
very important event, inasmuch as the priesthood thenceforth
becomes hereditary. Thus is established the line of priest-kings
which is to rule the Israelites till 40 B.C.

During the period of Jonathan's leadership of the Jews, Syria
suffers from much internal political intrigue and civil war. Once
when Jonathan sides with one Syrian faction, another lures him
into a Syrian city with a declaration of friendship, treacherously
takes Jonathan prisoner, and slays all his men (142 B.C.).

Simon Thassi (Chs. 13—16). Now it is Simon's turn to exhort
the Hebrews to oppose the tyranny which threatens them. He
gathers an army and marches against the enemy faction of the
Syrians; the leader of the faction tries to deceive him by promising to free Jonathan on condition that Simon will send him two
hundred talents of silver plus Jonathan's two sons. Simon is not
deceived, but sends the sons and the silver lest the Hebrew
people accuse him of not trying to save Jonathan. The Syrians
kill Jonathan anyhow and retreat.

Judea enjoys peace for about seven years. Simon strengthens his position by building fortresses all over the land and putting garrisons into them. He also forms an alliance with the Syrian king, who confirms his appointment as high priest and who releases the Israelites from the payment of all taxes and tributes. Thus Simon succeeds in winning for his people virtually complete political independence (142 B.C.).

In 134 B.C. the Syrians begin once more to persecute the Hebrews and to slay them, so that the followers of Simon have to defend themselves again. Simon being very old, his two sons, Judas and John, lead the people against the Syrians and win a victory. Simon and his sons Mattathias and Judas are treacherously slain by Simon's own son-in-law. John (surnamed Hyrcanus) succeeds his father as priest-king (134 B.C.).

Thus ends the history of the Jews insofar as it is to be found in the Apocrypha.

II MACCABEES: A PHARISAIC VIEW OF THE REVOLT FROM C. 176 TO 161 B.C.

The second book of Maccabees is not, as one might expect, a sequel to I Maccabees. Instead it is a retelling of approximately the first seven chapters of that history, and it covers a period of about fifteen years as opposed to the thirty-three years of I Maccabees.

This anonymous book is believed to have been written in Greek by a pious Alexandrian Hebrew of strong Pharisaic tendencies. It purports to be a condensation of a five-volume work by one Jason of Cyrene. Whereas the author of I Maccabees may have showed Sadducean leanings, the author of II Maccabees emphasizes the belief in immortality, miracles, the supernatural, and the apocalyptic. The date of composition is uncertain. Scholars have suggested various times, ranging from 125 B.C. to about a century later.[11]

As a record of events, it is far less trustworthy than I Maccabees. It "reads more like religious pleading than history or literature. . . ."[12] Its aim is to teach religious truths as conceived by the Pharisees of the second (or first) century B.C.

The style of II Maccabees is more rhetorical, more florid, less rapid, and less concise than that of I Maccabees.

The book opens with two prefatory letters (1:1-9 and 1:10—2:18)—both written by the Hebrews in Judea and addressed to the Hebrews in Egypt and both telling of some of the hardships suffered by the Judean Hebrews. Chapters 3—5 give an account of how the Maccabean revolt broke out; chapters 6—7 give more details about the persecution of the Hebrews; and chapters 8—15 cover the revolt up to Nicanor's Day.

The details of some incidents—especially of miracles—and some theological doctrines as covered in II Maccabees are worthy of special notice.

The Vision of Heliodorus (Ch. 3). Apparently during the reign of Antiochus III,° Onias, priest of the Temple in Jerusalem, becomes involved in an argument with Simon, governor of the Temple, over the matter of "disorder in the city." Spitefully Simon informs the king that the treasury of the Temple holds "infinite sums of money." The king sends his treasurer, Heliodorus, to Jerusalem to fetch the money. When he arrives, Onias informs him that Simon has exaggerated—that the Temple has only four hundred talents of silver and two hundred talents of gold. Furthermore, Onias says, that is laid by for the relief of widows and fatherless children. Regardless, Heliodorus prepares to take money. Onias is nearly prostrate with grief: "Then whoso had looked the high priest in the face, it would have wounded his heart; for his countenance and the changing of his colour declared the inward agony of his mind." The people join him in demonstrations of grief, and Onias begs God to save the treasury. As Heliodorus and his men come to take the money, God causes a miracle. A terrible warrior, clad in gold armor and seated upon a horse, appears before Heliodorus. The horse smites Heliodorus with its forefeet, so that the man is "compassed with great darkeness" and has to be borne off on a litter. Lest the king think that his treasurer has simply been attacked by the Jews, Onias prays God to spare Heliodorus' life. The prayer is granted, and Heliodorus offers thanks and a sacrifice to the Lord. When he returns to the king, he tells that monarch that "he that dwelleth in

---

° The historian is vague about this date, but a later reference (4:1-10) to the death of "the king" and the accession of Antiochus Epiphanes leads one to believe that the events related in Chapter 3 occurred during the reign of Antiochus III.

heaven hath his eye on that place and defendeth it, and he beateth and destroyeth them that come to hurt it."

Onias and Jason (4:1—5:27). Onias has a wicked brother Jason, who is a Greek sympathizer. Jason. "labors underhand" to supplant Onias as high priest; he promises Antiochus Epiphanes three hundred sixty talents of silver, plus a revenue of eighty more, if the king will appoint him high priest in Onias' stead. He also offers Antiochus a hundred fifty talents for a license to build a gymnasium "for training up of youth in the fashions of the heathen." The king accepts Jason's money, and Jason undertakes a thorough Hellenization of his fellow Hebrews. Two years later, however, Jason is superseded as high priest by Menelaus, who promises the king five hundred sixty talents of silver; Jason is forced to flee to the land of the Ammonites. Menelaus is even worse than Jason, "bringing nothing worthy the high priesthood, but having the fury of a cruel tyrant and the rage of a savage beast." He robs the Temple treasury to pay his debt to the king. Now, hearing the rumor that Antiochus has been killed in battle in Egypt, Jason raises some troops and attacks Menelaus. The report of Antiochus' death proving false, Menelaus flees to the king for protection. Antiochus returns from Egypt, reinstates Menelaus, and punishes Jerusalem by raiding the Temple and slaughtering the people. This is the raid which leads to the Maccabean rebellion.

The Courage of Eleazar the Scribe (Ch. 6). During the course of Antiochus' persecution of Jerusalem, one Eleazar, an aged scribe, is ordered by the king's men to eat some swine's flesh. He is forced to put some of the pork into his mouth but, "choosing rather to die gloriously than to live stained with such an abomination," spits it out. Then those "in charge of the wicked feast," taking pity on the old man, tell him that he may bring his own meat and *pretend* that he is eating flesh of the swine. After thinking over the proposal, he declines and wills them "straightway to send him to the grave," for, he says, "many young persons might think that Eleazar, being fourscore years old and ten, were now gone to a strange religion; and so they through mine hypocrisy and desire to live a little time and a moment longer, should be deceived by me, and I get a stain on mine old age and make it abominable." Thereupon he is flogged to death, but he leaves "his

death for an example of a noble courage and a memorial of virtue, not only unto young men but unto all his nation."

The Massacre of the Seven Brothers (Ch. 7). Now seven young
men and their mother are ordered to eat swine's flesh; when they
refuse, they are "tormented with scourges and whips." Resolutely
one of them tells their tormentors that they had rather die than
transgress the laws of their fathers. This reply so enrages the
king that he orders pans and caldrons to be heated, and he commands his men to seize the brother who has spoken so bravely,
to cut out his tongue, to cut off the "utmost" parts of his body,
and to fry him in a pan while the remainder of his family watches.
One by one each brother is tortured in this manner, but each one
exhorts the others not to weaken, and each dies professing faith
in God and a belief that he will be raised up "unto everlasting
life." The mother, too, is equally brave and equally resolute. She
is massacred last of the eight.

**Judas' Prayer and Offering for the Souls of the Dead (12:36-
45).** Judas Maccabeus prepares to bury some of his soldiers who
have been slain in battle. He and his men discover under the
coats of the slain "things consecrated to the idols of the Jamnites,
which is forbidden the Jews by law." Then, says the historian,
every man attributes the death of each of these soldiers to the
sinful dependence on heathen talismans; and Judas' men pray
God that their deceased fellows' sins "might wholly be put out of
remembrance." Furthermore Judas takes up an offering and sends
it to Jerusalem "to offer a sin offering, doing therein very well and
honestly, in that he was mindful of the resurrection: for if he had
not hoped that they that were slain should have risen again, it
had been superfluous and vain to pray for the dead."

This passage is of special significance for two reasons. In the
first place, belief in the resurrection of the dead (a tenet that is
fundamental among Christians) is a Pharisaic belief, as was mentioned above; the Sadducees did not adhere to this doctrine. In
the second place, the passage is partially responsible for the
Protestant rejection of II Maccabees as a canonical book. Most
Protestant sects strongly disapprove of prayers for the dead and
of offering money to redeem a soul from punishment in the afterlife.

Judas' Vision of Onias (15:1-16). Directly before the great
battle against Nicanor's army, Judas Maccabeus delivers a rous-

ing oration to his men. In the course of his exhortations, he tells them that he has just had a dream, in which there appeared the figure of the dead Onias, holding up his hands and praying for the whole body of the Hebrew people.

This done, in like manner there appeared a man with gray hairs, and exceeding glorious, who was of a wonderful and excellent majesty. Then Onias answered, saying, "This is a lover of the brethren, who prayeth much for the people, and for the holy city, to wit, Jeremias the prophet of God." Whereupon Jeremias holding forth his right hand gave to Judas a sword of gold, and in giving it spake thus, "Take this holy sword, a gift from God, with which thou shalt wound the adversaries."

After Judas' speech the men are filled with confidence.

Then Nicanor and they that were with him came forward with trumpets and songs. But Judas and his company encountered the enemies with invocation and prayer. So that fighting with their hands, and praying unto God with their hearts, they slew no less than thirty and five thousand men; for through the appearance of God they were greatly cheered.

Nicanor is one of the slain, and Judas has Nicanor's head severed from his body. He cuts out the tongue and has his men "give it by pieces to the fowls," and he hangs the head on a tower as a "manifest sign unto all of the help of the Lord." Then Judas inaugurates the great festival of Nicanor's Day.

At this point the author concludes his tale with an engaging passage—a passage which is eminently appropriate for the ending of the history of the Jews before the time of Christ:

And here will I make an end. And if I have done well, and as is fitting the story, it is that which I desired: but if slenderly and meanly, it is that which I could attain to. For as it is hurtful to drink wine or water alone; and as wine mingled with water is pleasant, and delighteth the taste; even so speech finely framed delighteth the ears of them that read the story. And here shall be an end.

Part Three
Prophetic Literature

Some of the prophetic writings of the Old Testament are among the finest manifestations of the Hebrew genius. The loftiness of their ethical teachings and the nobility of their conceptions of God make them invaluable as religious documents, and the beauty and the forcefulness of their language assure them of a high rank in the realm of world literature.

Any introduction to the study of the prophetic books of the Bible must try to supply the answers to several questions: What *is* a prophet? How did prophetism arise, and in what ways was it transformed? Which Biblical books should be labeled "prophetic literature"? What are the literary characteristics of these books? And, finally, into what chronological categories do these books fall?

It would be a serious mistake to regard the Old Testament prophet as primarily a predictor of future events. Although the Bible applies the term to such unlike persons as Moses, Balaam, and Hosea, they all have one function in common—to deliver some divinely revealed message. In the Biblical sense, then, *a prophet is a spokesman for God.*

Some of the prophetic messages have been preserved in separate books which bear their authors' names; these authors are known as the "literary" prophets. They are to be distinguished from their predecessors, the "prophet-counsellors,"[1] great leaders like Elijah and Elisha, who played prominent roles in the political and spiritual life of the people, but who, so far as we know, wrote nothing and whose words and deeds are recorded only in the "historical" books of the Bible.

Two currents flowed together to form the stream of Hebrew prophetism as seen in the works of the literary prophets (the principal concern of this section). One current is "ecstatic" prophetism. At least as early as the eleventh century B.C. there were bands or guilds of men who, by their behavior, have earned the epithet "ecstatic": they leapt, danced, sang, fell into trances, and engaged in divination.* Some bands, such as the one to which Saul attached himself (I Sam. 10:5-10), wandered about the countryside, often in the vicinity of some religious shrine; others, such as Ahab's four hundred "lying prophets" (I Kings 22:6-12), were retained by monarchs for consultation.

The second current is the succession of bold, uncompromising figures who dared to speak out against social injustice, oppression, and paganism—often in the face of opposition by king and priest.† Moses defied Pharaoh, Samuel pointed out to the priest Eli the wickedness of his sons, Nathan reproached David for his treatment of Uriah, and Elijah denounced Ahab and Jezebel for their idolatry and injustice.[2]

The confluence of this second tradition with ecstatic prophetism produced the great literary prophets of the eighth and later centuries. They show more kinship with the Nathan-Elijah strain than with the ecstatics, but their religious fervor, their mystical visions, and their hearing God "speak"—all these show the persistence of the ecstatic element.[3]

Considered as types of literature, the Earlier, or Former, Prophets of the Jewish canon‡ are really history rather than prophecy and have been discussed as such; Lamentations is a series of lyrics; and Daniel and Jonah are prose narratives. Setting aside these books, then, we shall deal with the remaining fifteen prophetic literature: Amos, Hosea, Isaiah, Micah, Zephaniah, Na-

* Similar practices may be observed among the Phoenician prophets of "Baal" (I Kings 18:25-29), the devotees of the Greek god Dionysus, the Moslem dervishes, and even some modern evangelical sects. Compare also the "talking in tongues" of the early Christians (see, for example, Acts 2:1-6) and the voices heard by Joan of Arc.

† It should be noted, however, that in many cases the prophets co-operated with the monarchy and the priesthood. Samuel, of course, was the "king-maker" and was a priest himself; Nathan served David's house for many years; Ezekiel was a priest; and Isaiah was an adviser to at least two kings of Judah. See George Sprau, *Literature in the Bible* (New York: Macmillan Co., 1932), pp. 103-106.

‡ See pp. 19-20 for an account of the classification of the Prophetic books.

hum, Habakkuk, Jeremiah, Ezekiel, Haggai, Zechariah, Obadiah, Malachi, Joel, and the Apocryphal book of Baruch.

Most scholars believe that *all* the prophetic books are compilations. It seems likely that in many cases the original core of the book was a series of short, ecstatic oracles and that later (sometimes *centuries* later) these utterances were expanded and so arranged as to form more or less unified and coherent treatises. In some instances, as in the case of Isaiah,[4] much of the editing probably was performed by the prophet himself; in other instances, as in the case of Jeremiah,[5] only a small percentage of the finished book is attributable to the titular author.

The authors (and editors) vary widely in historical background, point of view, tone, and literary ability—from Amos, who fulminates, to Hosea, who gently persuades; from the melancholy and pessimistic Jeremiah to the rhapsodic and confident Unknown Prophet, author of Second Isaiah.* But nearly all of them are inspired with a passion for righteousness and agree in depicting a universal, consistent, and just God who rewards men and nations when they obey his moral law and who punishes them when they sin against it. Some of the books are written entirely in prose, others chiefly in poetic form; some have great literary merit, others are relatively undistinguished.

The fifteen books of prophecy to be considered here may be divided into four groups: (1) those addressed to the Kingdom of Israel before its fall in 721 B.C.; (2) those addressed to the Kingdom of Judah prior to the destruction of Jerusalem in 586 B.C.; (3) those written in the period of Judah's Exile (586–538 B.C.); and (4) those written after the return to Jerusalem.

* It is commonly agreed that the book which in both Jewish and Christian Bibles is called "Isaiah" is in reality the work of at least three prophets, widely separated in time. Chapters 1–39 will therefore be treated as one unit (I Isaiah) and Chapter 40–55 as another (II Isaiah), and Chapters 56–66 as still another (III Isaiah).

Eighth-Century Prophets
Amos, Hosea, Isaiah, and Micah

From the political and economic points of view, the reign of Jeroboam II (*c*. 786-746 B.C.) was the most glorious period in the history of the Northern Kingdom (Israel). The military successes of Assyria had compelled Syria to withdraw some of the forces she had been using against Israel, with the result that Jeroboam's armies were able to win sweeping victories, recover all the territory formerly taken from the Israelites by the Syrians, and even to capture Damascus itself (II Kings 14:23-29). Commerce throve, and the country as a whole became prosperous. The wealth, however, was gathered into the hands of a few, and the majority of the people suffered from poverty and oppression. As for religion, most of the "upper class" congratulated themselves on being the favorite worshipers of so powerful and so generous a Deity. They held many celebrations in his honor, and they performed many sacrificial rites; but they often neglected to obey his commandments regulating their personal and social behavior. Furthermore, some elements of the Canaanite fertility cults, accompanied by sexual immorality (e.g., "sacred prostitution") had crept into Yahweh worship. It was into a milieu of luxury, greed, corruption, bribery, licentiousness, and religious complacency that Amos and Hosea, the earliest known literary prophets, came to deliver their respective messages.

These messages attempted not only to jolt the people out of immorality, but also to present them with a new, more sublime concept of the Deity—a God free of the old anthropomorphisms and capriciousness; a God not merely of the Chosen Hebrews, but one who controlled the whole world and who could use the Assyrians or anybody else as his instruments of punishment; a just

and merciful God who required that his people also practice justice and mercy.

While the Northern Kingdom was thriving but growing ever
more dissolute under Jeroboam II, the Southern Kingdom was
enjoying a similar period of prosperity under King Azariah (Uzziah) (c. 783-742 B.C.). Her fortunes deteriorated, however,
under Azariah's successors Jotham (c. 750-735 B.C.), Ahaz (c.
735-715 B.C.), and Hezekiah (c. 715-687 B.C.). In 734 B.C. Syria
and Israel invaded Judah, and King Ahaz, ignoring the advice
of his counselor Isaiah, called on the Assyrians for aid; the military result was that the Syro-Israelitish allies were defeated, but
the practical outcome was that Judah henceforth for many decades was forced to pay tribute to Assyria. Understandably, the
payment of this tribute was decidely irksome, and it seems that
sometimes the Judeans fell into arrears. About 711 B.C. Assyria
sent a punitive force into Judah, either because Hezekiah was
withholding tribute or because he was engaging in intrigues with
Egypt against Assyria. Ten years later Hezekiah's alliances with
Babylonia and Egypt were the occasion for Sennacherib's famous raid on Jerusalem (see pp. 133-134); the city was saved
when a terrible disaster decimated the Assyrian army, but Hezekiah was forced to surrender and to pay a large indemnity.
Thereafter for three generations Judah apparently made no attempt to throw off the Assyrian yoke.

Isaiah and Micah, the eighth-century B.C. prophets of Judah,
agreed with Amos and Hosea that Assyria was the "rod" of God's
anger (Isa. 10:5).

AMOS: PROPHET OF RIGHTEOUSNESS
AND DIVINE JUSTICE

The earliest of the literary prophets was Amos. The superscription and a biographical (or autobiographical) passage in his
book (1:1 and 7:10-15) tell us that he was a herdsman and a
dresser of sycamore figs and that his home was in or near the
small town of Tekoa, about twelve miles south of Jerusalem. Although a citizen of the Southern Kingdom, he evidently made
frequent excursions into the Northern one (perhaps to market
his wool), for he was thoroughly familiar with the social, economic, and religious conditions there; and at least one of his prophetic attacks was made at Bethel, a large religious center in the

Northern Kingdom near the border between Israel and Judah. This attack so infuriated Amaziah, the priest of the local sanctuary, that he sent a messenger to report it to King Jeroboam II in Samaria; and he ordered the stern and courageous herdsman to go back home and to confine his prophesying to Judah.

It is not surprising that the message of the prophet upset Amaziah and his henchmen; it was unexpected and decidedly drastic. Amos announced to them that Yahweh himself had revealed his wrath against Israel for its corruption, its social injustice, and the hypocrisy of its rituals and sacrificial offerings, unaccompanied by righteous behavior. Therefore Yahweh, the God of justice, was going to destroy the sinful kingdom.

Amos' style, well suited to such a message, is austere but oratorically effective. Its characteristics are rapidity, balance, fluidity, and regularity. The prophet adds much color and vividness to his warnings by numerous picturesque references to rural scenes—the roar of the lion, the basket of summer fruit, the mildew in the orchard, the bird caught in a snare, the grasshopper devastating a field, and the corn being sifted in a sieve.[6]

Amos issued his warnings about 750 B.C., near the end of Jeroboam's reign. It is unknown whether he himself wrote down any of his own words; perhaps that task fell to some of his devoted followers. Many interpolations were made by later editors—some of the passages apparently having been added after the fall of Israel (721 B.C.).

The structure of the book is relatively simple. Four main parts are readily discernible: (1) Oracles of Indictment (Chs. 1–2); (2) Three Sermons (Chs. 3–6); (3) Five "Visions of Judgment" (7:1–9:8a); and (4) Epilogue (9:8b-15).

Oracles of Indictment (Chs. 1–2). The oldest of the books of prophecy opens with an account of an incident that may have happened during a festival held at Bethel or another trade center of Israel. The streets are crowded with people who have come to participate in the ceremonies and to sell their various wares. Perhaps a few smile condescendingly at the rustic attire of a shepherd from "down South" who has come to offer his wool for sale. They are puzzled, however, by the sternness of his countenance, so out of keeping with their own holiday mood; and they listen when he stops at a street corner and begins to speak in a loud voice. With the adroitness and eloquence of an ac-

complished orator, Amos first tells them something that they like
to hear: the Lord is angry with the Syrians for their ruthless
slaughter of the Gileadites (see II Kings 10:32-33); his voice will
roar from Zion so that the top of Mount Carmel will wither; he
will destroy Damascus (the Syrian capital), devastate the land,
and send the people into exile. No doubt the revelers cheer this
prediction, for they have formerly suffered grievously at the
hands of the Syrians. Next the shepherd-prophet tells of God's
wrath against one after another of Israel's neighbors—most of
them traditional enemies of the Hebrews: the Philistines (1:6-8),
the Tyrians (1:9-10), the Edomites (1:11-12), the Ammonites
(1:13-15), and the Moabites (2:1-3); all will be destroyed for
their military aggressions. The merrymakers, we may imagine,
shout approval at each succeeding announcement. But then,
without warning,* Amos hurls a hornet's nest into the midst of
his audience: Israel, too, will be obliterated for her sins (2:6-16)!
Her people have sold the innocent to satisfy their own greed, oppressed the poor, and wallowed in sexual immorality, even in
God's Temple. Despite God's special interest in his Chosen People (2:9-12), they have repeatedly transgressed and they must be
punished.

> Therefore the flight shall perish from the swift,
> And the strong shall not strengthen his force,
> Neither shall the mighty deliver himself:
> Neither shall he stand that handleth the bow;
> And he that is swift of foot shall not deliver himself:
> Neither shall he that rideth the horse deliver himself.
> And he that is courageous among the mighty
> Shall flee away naked in that day, saith the Lord. (2:14-16)

Three Sermons on Israel's Wickedness and Her Doom (Chs.
3—6). The second section of the book of Amos is a series of three
sermons elaborating upon the themes of the first two chapters. Although these sermons are presented as if they were a continuation
of Chapters 1—2, they may in fact be later compilations of Amos'
oracles, drawn perhaps from oral tradition of listeners' notes and
edited by the prophet's followers.

---

* The oracle against Judah (2:4-5) is believed to be a later interpolation.
See Hughell E. W. Fosbroke, exegesis to Amos, *The Interpreter's Bible*, VI,
784-786.

Amos proclaims that he is speaking under divine compulsion:

> The lion hath roared,
> Who will not fear?
> The Lord hath spoken,
> Who can but prophesy? (3:8)

God has passed judgment, Amos continues, on the degenerate and luxurious life of the rich, especially those in Jeroboam's capital city, Samaria, who tread upon the poor and accept bribes to condemn the innocent. Where such injustice and oppression prevail, God is outraged by "holy" rituals and sacrifices:

> I hate, I despise your feast days,
> And I will not smell in your solemn assemblies.
> Though ye offer me burnt offerings and your meat offerings,
> I will not accept them:
> Neither will I regard the peace offerings of your fat beasts.
> Take thou away from me the noise of thy songs;
> For I will not hear the melody of thy viols.
> But let judgment run down as waters,
> And righteousness as a mighty stream. (5:21-24)

The Lord has repeatedly warned the Israelites (5:21-24) with plagues and famines and assaults by hostile armies; but they have refused to repent. Therefore he is going to send an adversary who will conquer the land, despoil the palaces, demolish the sanctuaries at Bethel, Gilgal, and Beersheba, and carry the people into exile "beyond Damascus."

As if in answer to the question, "Will anybody escape?" Amos answers (in 3:12) with wrathful sarcasm that the Lord may perhaps save a few, much as a shepherd might recover two legs or a piece of an ear of a sheep from the mouth of a lion.

Five Visions of Judgment (7:1—9:8a). The third section of the book consists chiefly of accounts of five visions which Amos has seen, plus some autobiographical narrative. Most of this section is written in the first person and is believed by many scholars to have been written down by Amos himself or dictated by him to some scribe.[7]

The first two visions which Amos sees are symbolic of God's future destruction of the Israelites. One vision is of a great "brood" of locusts which when it matures will swoop down and devour all vegetation in the late spring, the most crucial period for Palestinian crops. The other vision is of a devastating fire. In both cases Amos pleads with the Lord to spare Israel ("Jacob") and seems momentarily to have some success.

In the third vision, Amos sees God holding a plumbline—an instrument for testing Israel, to see whether it "measures up" to his standard of righteousness. Finding that the nation falls far short, the Lord is determined not to "pass by" it again—that is, not to overlook the people's iniquities but to judge them. He has made up his mind to lay waste the "high places" and the sanctuaries and to "rise against the house of Jeroboam with the sword" (7:9).

In the fourth vision, Amos is shown a "basket of summer fruit," symbolic of the Israelites "ripe for destruction,"[8] because they have oppressed the poor and needy. Soon their dead bodies will be found everywhere; earthquakes and darkness will come upon the land; the songs in the Temple will change into lamentations and the feasts into mourning.[*]

In the fifth vision, Amos beholds God himself standing on an altar and ordering the total destruction of the sanctuary so that it will fall upon the congregation. Those who survive will be slain with the sword—not one will escape. God will search out even those who try to dig their way into Sheol or climb into heaven. He will pursue them into the land of their exile and there set his "eyes upon them for evil, not for good" (9:4). He considers them as any of the other peoples—the Ethiopians, the Philistines, or the Syrians—whom he also rules and judges.

> Behold, the eyes of the Lord God are upon the sinful kingdom,
> And I will destroy it from off the face of the earth. (9:8a)

The Hopeful Epilogue (9:8b-15). It is believed that some years after Amos wrote his dire prophecies, an unknown author, feeling that the message was too drastic, attached an epilogue which offers a ray of hope: some individuals will survive and will return from exile to rebuild the cities and replant the vineyards. Eventually the ancient glories of the Davidic kingdom will be restored. The people will enjoy prosperity and will never again be removed from the land which God has given them.

---

[*] Here (7:10-17) the portrayal of the visions is interrupted by an account of Amaziah's charge of conspiracy (see p. 169) and Amos' uncompromising reply. The source of this third-person narrative is not known. It may have been placed in its present position for dramatic effect.

HOSEA: PROPHET OF DIVINE LOVE AND MERCY

As Amos had predicted, Israel's prosperity under Jeroboam II came to an end. After the death of that monarch (*c*. 746 B.C.), the country entered a period of political upheaval; six kings ruled in about fifteen years. Invasion from Assyria under Tiglath-pileser III became ever more imminent; Syria, Israel's neighbor on the northeast, was overrun in 732 B.C. Meanwhile, the evils against which Amos had preached continued, and another prophet, Hosea, felt compelled to add his voice of warning.

The exact dates of Hosea's ministry are unknown. Part of the book which bears his name seems to have been written in the last years of Jeroboam's reign; other sections appear to be much later—perhaps as late as 722 B.C., the year before the fall of Samaria.

The messages of Amos and Hosea are similar in many respects, but there are several noteworthy differences. Both prophets censure Israel for her corruption, social injustice, and immorality, and both warn that Assyria will be used as God's instrument of retribution. Hosea differs from Amos, however, in tone, in his conception of God, and in his hope for redemption.

Hosea adds an important new element to the Hebrew conception of Yahweh. Whereas Amos conceives of him pre-eminently as a stern God of justice, Hosea depicts him as a God of love and mercy, eager to forgive his people if they repent. Hosea interprets the Covenant as an agreement of love, such as might exist between a man and his wife; that the wife has not kept her part of the bargain brings much sorrow both to God and the prophet.

Amos holds out little or no hope for Israel. He says that the people have persisted in their sins and that therefore the country will be utterly destroyed; it is too late even for repentance.* Hosea, on the contrary, teaches that God will forgive the contrite and will gladly renew his Covenant with them.

In keeping with his milder message, Hosea's style is more graceful, more lyrical, and less rugged than that of Amos. Except for Chapters 1 and 3 and part of Chapter 2, the book is in poetic form. Unfortunately, the text of Hosea is among the most chaotic of all in the Old Testament; despite conjectural emendations, some passages remain rather incoherent.

* The passages which prophesy the restoration of Israel are generally regarded as a late interpolation.

The two principal divisions of the book are as follows: Chapters 1—3, a symbolic demonstration of the forgiving nature of God, and Chapters 4—14, a warning to the Israelites, combined with a promise of redemption.

The Redemption of Gomer: An Allegory (Chs. 1—3). Hosea compels the attention of his readers by beginning with a striking story. In obedience to God's command, he says, he married Gomer, an immoral woman or one of immoral inclinations. After bearing three children, she deserts Hosea and becomes a prostitute. Nevertheless, Hosea buys her back as a common slave and makes her his wife again—because he loves her and has compassion on her.*

The parallel between Hosea's relationship with Gomer and that of God with Israel is obvious. God has loved the Israelites as his Chosen People, but they have been unfaithful to him; they have gone chasing after pagan deities and lusts of the flesh. Now Hosea makes his chief point: if he, a mere man, can show such love and forgiveness to his wayward wife as to take her back into his home and heart, how much greater must be God's love and mercy for his erring children. Even as Hosea rescues Gomer from her wretched predicament, so will God redeem the Israelites if they repent.

The Redemption of Israel: A Plea (Chs. 4—14). The major portion of the book is an exposition of the Israelites' infidelity to God, coupled with a promise of forgiveness and restitution if they will "return unto the Lord." All of the people, and especially the Ephraimites,† have been guilty of idolatry (4:12-13 and 8:4-6), harlotry and adultery (4:13-14), murder and robbery (6:7-9), intrigue and subversion (7:3-7). The corrupt priesthood has led the people astray (4:6-15), nor can they rely on their incompetent kings or on foreign alliances (7:8—8:10). God will punish them by exiling them to Assyria, and nettles and thorns will cover the possessions that they leave behind (9:1-6).

---

* There has been much scholarly dispute over whether the story about Hosea and Gomer is genuine autobiography or a symbolic story. There is also disagreement over whether Gomer engaged in prostitution *before* or *after* her marriage to Hosea. For discussions of these two points, see John Mauchline, introduction to Hosea, *The Interpreter's Bible,* VI, 560-561.

† Ephraim was the most important of the ten Northern tribes, and references to the Ephraimites may be considered as applying to all the people of the Northern Kingdom.

In earlier days God has nurtured the Israelites lovingly and tenderly (11:1, 3-4). Now they have deserted him, and he must punish them severely (11:2, 5-7). But he still loves them, and he will not deal with them wrathfully. He is filled with compassion for them:

> For I am God, and not man;
> The Holy One in the midst of thee. (11:9)

He will bring them back from Assyria and redeem them from the grave and death:

> O death, I will be thy plagues;
> O grave, I will be thy destruction.* (13:14)

When his people repent and renew their allegiance to him, then he will "heal their backsliding" and "love them freely" (14:4).

> I will be as dew unto Israel:
> He shall grow as the lily,
> And cast forth his roots as Lebanon.
> His branches shall spread,
> And his beauty shall be as the olive tree,
> And his smell as Lebanon.
> They that dwell under his shadow shall return;
> They shall revive as the corn,
> And grow as the vine:
> The scent thereof shall be as the wine of Lebanon. (14:5-7)

ISAIAH: PROPHET OF HOLINESS (ISA. 1—39)

Little is known of Isaiah's family or his early life, but some scholars have conjectured that he was a member of the Jerusalem aristocracy. The book tells us (1:1) that his ministry extended during the reigns of four kings of Judah (beginning with Azariah). He was the trusted counselor of Jotham and Hezekiah, but it appears that when Ahaz rejected Isaiah's advice about seeking Assyrian aid against Syria and Israel, the prophet withdrew from court life till the accession of Hezekiah (see p. 133).[9] Tradition holds that soon after the wicked Manasseh came to the throne (c. 687 B.C.), Isaiah suffered martyrdom by being sawed in two.[10]

---

* These lines seem to be the source of Paul's famous cry of triumph in I Cor. 15:55.

As a statesman, Isaiah was an isolationist, opposed to all "entangling alliances." We have already noted (see p. 175) his opposition to Ahaz' enlisting the help of Assyria; he foresaw that such an alliance would make Judah a tributary nation. Later, however, he opposed with equal vigor Judah's plan to default on its payment of tribute to Assyria and to ally itself with Egypt. From first to last his policy of neutralism was based on religious conviction that Judah should rely for protection not on any earthly power but on God. However, Isaiah did *not* believe that God would shield Judah from invasion; like Amos and Hosea, he warned that God would use the Assyrians as a scourge of the sinful Judeans.*

For the modern reader the religious messages of Isaiah are of far greater significance than his political ones. He made three significant contributions to the development of Hebrew theology: (1) emphasis on the *holiness* of God; (2) belief in a "saving remnant" through whom the race and the worship of Yahweh would be preserved; and (3) prediction of the coming of a Messiah who would usher in a "new golden age."[11]

Isaiah's style is one of the loftiest in the Old Testament. Its most outstanding quality, according to Professor John R. Macarthur, is its sublimity, "which ranks with that of Aeschylus and Milton."[12] His lively imagination provides him with a wealth of apt and unforgettable figures of speech. He expresses an extraordinarily wide range of emotions: anger at injustice (1:21-25), scorn of arrogance and pride (3:16-26), awe before the holiness of God (6:1-5), exuberance over the goodness and the glory of the future Messianic age (12:2-6). Other features of his style are verbal splendor, construction of neatly rounded rhetorical periods, and stateliness of rhythm.[13] The effectiveness of Isaiah's diction and imagery is attested by the large number of passages from the book which, through the King James translation, have become familiar in our language: "though your sins be as scarlet" (1:18), "beat their swords into ploughshares, and their spears into pruninghooks" (2:4),[14] the "Prince of Peace" (9:6), and "a little child shall lead them" (11:6).[15] A substantial portion

---

* The political activities of Isaiah have already been mentioned in the discussion of II Kings (above) and therefore will not be dealt with in detail here. The portions of Isaiah which record these activities are 1:1—8:18, 28-32, and 36-39.

of the text of Handel's *Messiah* oratorio is taken verbatim from this source.

As this book now stands, the arrangement of Isaiah's oracles is often chaotic. The following summary will attempt, by a regrouping of certain passages, to provide the most understandable order.

The book consists principally of several collections of the prophet's oracles, plus numerous editorial interpolations of varying length. Although the Isaian authorship of some passages is in dispute, most scholars agree that the following sections are by later hands than the prophet's: 11:10—14:23 (probably pre-Exilic, that is, before 587 B.C.),[16] 24—27 and 33—35 (post-Exilic), and 36—39, a historical appendix which closely resembles (and is probably largely derived from) II Kings 18:13—20:20.[17]

Isaiah's "Call": A Vision of God's Holiness (Ch. 6). Isaiah gives us the most graphic account of a prophet's experience of being "called" by God to be his spokesman.* One day while he is in the Temple, he "sees" God sitting upon a throne, "high and lifted up." The Deity's flowing garments fill the Temple. He is attended by a band of seraphim, angelic creatures with six wings each and with the faces, hands, and voices of men.[18] As they cover their faces and feet with their wings, they sing:

> Holy, holy, holy, is the Lord of hosts:
> The whole earth is full of his glory. (6:3)

The Temple trembles and is filled with "smoke."† Overcome by a sense of his own human unworthiness in contrast with the ineffable holiness of the Deity in whose presence he stands, he cries out:

Woe is me! for I am undone; because I am a man of unclean lips . . . : for mine eyes have seen the King, the Lord of hosts. (6:5)

A seraph seizes a burning coal from the altar and purifies Isaiah by touching his lips with the coal: "Thine iniquity is taken away, and thy sin purged." Then the Lord asks for a messenger, and Isaiah replies, "Here am I; send me." The Lord directs him to prophesy to the people, but predicts that they will continue in

---

* Compare the account of the sudden conversion of the Apostle Paul (Acts 9:3-9).

† Comparable to the "cloud" of glory that filled the tabernacle built by Moses' followers (Ex. 40:34). See R. B. Y. Scott, exegesis to Isaiah 1—39, *The Interpreter's Bible*, V, 209.

their evil ways till the land is made desolate by invasion. However, "a tenth" will survive.

Isaiah's emphasis on God's holiness* is one of the most important of his contributions to the Hebrew-Christian conception of the Deity. Holiness, it is true, had been considered an attribute of God since the beginning of Yahweh-worship, but it is Isaiah's insistence that has imprinted it so indelibly upon our consciousness and identified it with God's sovereign righteousness.

The People's Rebellion and Future Punishment (1—5, 9:8—10:22, 14:28—23:18). In obedience to God's command, Isaiah goes forth to try to reform the people. He begins by pointing out to the inhabitants of Judah their tragic condition because they have rebelled against the Holy One of Israel who directs all history according to his plan. This "sinful nation" must be punished.

THE PEOPLE'S INIQUITIES (1:19-23, 2:6-22, 3:16—4:1, 32:9-14). Isaiah exposes in the Southern Kingdom essentially the same sins that Amos had found rife in Israel: injustice, murder, bribery in the law courts, neglect of the poor and the widows and orphans, idolatry, self-indulgence, and vanity. In an especially memorable passage he depicts the haughty and luxury-loving women of Jerusalem, walking with "stretched forth necks and wanton eyes," mincing on "tinkling" feet, and displaying their necklaces, bracelets, anklets, scarves, bonnets, rings, brooches, headbands, earrings, nose jewels, mantles, turbans, and veils (3:16-23).

EMPTINESS OF THEIR RITUALS (1:10-17). Again like Amos, Isaiah denounces the people for the hypocrisy of their sacrifices and holy rites—meaningless and unacceptable to God when unaccompanied by ethical behavior:

> Bring no more vain oblations;
> Incense is an abomination unto me . . .
> And when ye spread forth your hands,
> I will hide mine eyes from you:
> Yea, when ye make your prayers, I will not hear:
> Your hands are full of blood. (1:13, 15)

---

* The Hebrew word comes from the word for *separation* and suggests "otherness" and mysterious power—that is, inviolable perfection as distinct from any type of goodness which human beings can realize. (See George A. Buttrick [ed.], *The Interpreter's Dictionary of the Bible* [Nashville, Tenn.: Abingdon Press, 1962], II, 616-623.)

WHY WILL THEY NOT LEARN? (1:5-9, 18; 5:24-30; 9:8—10:4).
Why will Judah not learn from experience? She has been chastised for her sins numberless times; she is like a rebellious servant
who has been beaten from head to foot till he is a mass of
"wounds, and bruises, and putrifying sores"; yet she continues to
revolt. She has watched the judgment which has fallen on the
Northern Kingdom at the hands of the Syrians and the Philistines
(c. 737 B.C.).* Such warnings should be sufficient, but Judah is
stubborn and complacent. Believing that the Lord will continue
to withhold punishment, she says to herself: "Though your sins
be as scarlet, they shall be as white as snow; though they be red
like crimson, they shall be as wool" (1:18). But the nation is deluding herself; she must make a choice now—either to repent and
be forgiven, or to continue in her iniquities and suffer the consequences.[19]

THE CHASTISEMENT TO COME (5:1-24a, 10:5-19, 14:24—23:18).
These passages are especially significant in their revelation of
Isaiah's view of Yahweh as a universal God and the God of history—a Deity who holds all time in his hand and who uses the
nations according to his own purposes.[20]

In the "Song of the Vineyard" (5:1-24a), the prophet uses a
parable to bring home to the Jews their crisis: Whereas they
have formerly been like a fine vineyard, planted and lovingly
tended by God, now their unrighteousness has persuaded him to
destroy the vineyard; its walls and hedges will be torn down, and
it will become a wasteland.

Assyria will become the rod of God's anger (10:5), the instrument of his punishment. Eventually, however, Assyria will become intoxicated with her own successes and will herself be punished for her pride and arrogance (14:25).

The impiety of other nations, too, will cause their downfall. Israel (10:17-19), Babylon (13, 21:1-10), Philistia (14:29-32),
Moab (15:1—16:14), Egypt (19:1-17), Edom (21:11-12), the
Arabian tribes Dedan and Kedar (21:13-17), the Phoenician cities Tyre and Sidon (23:1-14)—all will be judged.

The "Saving Remnant" (10:20-27). In a short passage Isaiah
kindles a ray of hope for the Jews—and at the same time elabo-

* It is believed that the passages concerning Israel's calamities described
events which had already taken place following a war with Syria. See Scott,
exegesis, *The Interpreter's Bible*, V, 234-235.

rates a doctrine which is later to be of the utmost importance for both Jews and Christians: the doctrine of the "Saving Remnant." The Lord will vent his anger against Judah, the prophet says, but after "a very little while" his anger will cease; the Lord will not utterly destroy his Chosen People, but will preserve a few repentant ones, who will return "unto the mighty God."

The Messiah and the Messianic Age (2:2-5, 9:1-7, 11—12, 25:6-8, 29:15-24). Isaiah is the earliest Biblical book to state clearly the belief in the coming of a "Messiah,"* a savior who would deliver the Hebrews from their oppressors and bring in a Golden Age of righteousness and peace.

The prophet's words have been given a number of different interpretations. The ancient Hebrews believed (and some modern Jews still believe) that Isaiah was foretelling the advent of a temporal as well as spiritual leader who would subdue their political enemies and set up his own rule based on justice and on the worship of Yahweh. The traditional Christian interpretation is that Isaiah was predicting the coming of Christ. Some scholars today suggest that the Messiah passages were written to celebrate the coronation of Hezekiah, a king who, Isaiah hoped, would be far wiser and more righteous than his predecessor Ahaz.[21]

Here is what Isaiah *says*: From the Saving Remnant will come a new ruler, descended from King David, a scion from the "rod of Jesse."† He will break the yoke of the oppressor and burn the implements of warfare:

> For unto us a child is born,
> Unto us a son is given:
> And the government shall be upon his shoulder:
> And his name shall be called Wonderful Counsellor,‡
>   The mighty God,
> The Everlasting Father, the Prince of peace. (9:6)

* *Messiah* means "the Anointed One." See Scott, exegesis, *The Interpreter's Bible*, V, 231.

† Jesse was the father of David.

‡ There should be no comma (as in the King James Version) between *Wonderful* and *Counsellor*, which two words form a unit. See Scott, exegesis, *The Interpreter's Bible*, V, 233.

The Spirit of the Lord will rest upon him, and he will be filled with wisdom and understanding. He will be the righteous judge and ruler of many nations. Thus will begin a new age of universal peace and love in the spirit and worship of God:

> The wolf also shall dwell with the lamb,
> And the leopard shall lie down with the kid;
> And the calf and the young lion and the fatling together;
> And a little child shall lead them. (11:6)

MICAH: "CHAMPION OF THE PEASANTRY"[22]

Amos, Hosea, and Isaiah all denounced the exploitation of the poor, but they seem to have been most concerned with the great urban centers, such as Jerusalem and Samaria. The fiery prophet Micah, on the other hand, called special attention to the mistreatment of the small farmers and day laborers in the rural regions.

Little is known of Micah's activities. He lived in Mareshah, a village in southwestern Judah near the Philistine border. Apparently he delivered his prophetic messages in Jerusalem. The superscription of his book states that his ministry was carried on during the reigns of Jotham, Ahaz, and Hezekiah (c. 750–687 B.C.); internal evidence of the prophecies themselves, however, indicates that his activity was confined to the years 714–700 and perhaps to the two periods of crisis brought on by the Assyrian raids in 711 and 701.[23]

Most scholars agree that Micah wrote nearly all of chapters 1–3 and 6:1–7:4. Concerning the other portions there is much disagreement; many commentators consider them post-Exilic.[24]

Although Micah has neither the poetic sublimity of Isaiah nor the oratorical skill of Amos, he is a forceful writer. His style is bold and eloquent. His indignation explodes in impassioned metaphors as he describes the mistreatment of the poor, and his exposition of God's ethical mandates achieves classic simplicity.

The Doom of Jerusalem (Chs. 1—3 and 6:9-16). Micah predicts the utter destruction of Jerusalem. God has observed the transgressions of the inhabitants and is now coming down himself as a witness against them. When he approaches, the moun-

tains will melt under him like wax before a fire, and the valleys
will be cleft. He will punish the princes and the rulers,

> Who hate the good and love the evil;
> Who pluck off [the people's] skin from off them,
> And their flesh from off their bones;
> Who also eat the flesh of my people,
> And flay their skin from off them;
> And they break their bones,
> And chop them in pieces as for the pot,
> And as flesh within the caldron. (3:2-3)

The landowners and powerful men lie awake at night devising
new schemes for exploiting the poor (2:1); they covet the poor
man's fields and take them away by violence; they pull the robes
off innocent travelers; and they throw widows and children out
of their homes (by foreclosing the mortgages). Even the prophets
and the priests have become greedy (3:5, 11).

To punish these evildoers, God will bring the Assyrians to
demolish Jerusalem in the same fashion that they have already
laid waste to Samaria; the city will be "plowed up as a field"
and become only a pile of ruins. Then the people of Judah will
be carried into exile (1:5, 16; 3:12).

The Essence of True Religion (6:1-8). In a short but famous
passage Micah gives us "the simplest and most compelling summary of the entire prophetic teaching . . . which some regard
as the essence of all religion itself."[25] In "a cosmically constituted
court"[26] God brings suit against the Hebrews. He himself is the
prosecuting attorney, and the hills, mountains, and foundations
of the earth are summoned to serve as the jury. As evidence of
his goodness to his people, he recounts how he has brought them
out of Egypt and aided them against various foes. Dramatically
he asks what he has done to cause the defendant to be so wicked:

> O my people, what have I done unto thee?
> And wherein have I wearied thee?
> Testify against me. (6:3)

Apparently humbled and penitent, the people ask how they
can atone for their iniquities. Shall they present sacrificial offerings of calves and rams? rivers of oil? their own children?*

---

* For references to the ancient custom of human sacrifice, see II Kings 16:3,
17:17, and 21:6.

The magnificently simple answer may well serve as a universal rule of all religious and ethical conduct, for it is a prestatement, in different words, of Jesus' two "greatest commandments" (to love God and to love one's neighbor*):

> He hath showed thee, O man, what is good;
> And what doth the Lord require of thee,
> But to do justly, and to love mercy,
> And to walk humbly with thy God? (6:8)

* Mark 12:29-31 and Matt. 22:36-40.

8

Judah's Pre-Exilic Prophets
of the Seventh and Sixth Centuries

Zephaniah, Nahum, Habakkuk, and Jeremiah

For almost a century and a half after the fall of Israel, the Kingdom of Judah managed to survive as a nation by paying tribute
to her Assyrian overlords. Assyria reached the zenith of her
power in the middle of the seventh century. Then she was weakened by invasions of the northern barbarians, the Scythians and
Cimmerians; far more serious was the threat from the rising
Babylonian (Chaldean) Empire to the southeast. In 626 B.C.
Babylonia won her independence from Assyria; in 612 B.C. the
Babylonians together with the Medes captured the Assyrian
capital Nineveh; and in 605 B.C. Babylonia decisively defeated
the Egyptian armies at Carchemish. Henceforth for more than
five decades Babylonia was mistress of the vast territories formerly held by the Assyrians. Egypt adopted the policy of inciting
the small nations of Asia Minor to revolt against the Chaldean
colossus, frequently promising them aid but seldom supplying
any. Abetted by Egypt, Judah withheld tribute from Babylonia
in 597 B.C.; King Nebuchadrezzar responded by besieging and
capturing Jerusalem and deporting many leading citizens, including the young king Jehoiachin. Further Jewish intrigues with
Egypt caused Nebuchadrezzar to lose what remained of his patience; in 586 B.C. the Babylonians destroyed Jerusalem, including the Temple, and led many thousands of Judeans into captivity in Babylonia.

Such was the turbulent and tragic political background against
which Zephaniah, Nahum, Habakkuk, and Jeremiah carried on
their ministry. As in the preceding century, the prophets of

Judah interpreted the military and political disasters as God's punishment of his wayward people. Despite the warnings of Isaiah and Micah and despite the fact that Judah had witnessed the fall of her sister-nation Israel, the Judeans persisted in their sinfulness. After the death of the "good" King Hezekiah, they were led in their wickedness by two especially "bad" monarchs, Manasseh (687–642 B.C.) and Amon (642–640 B.C.), on whose idolatry the Biblical historians and prophets laid much of the blame for Judah's subsequent misfortunes. Under the "good" King Josiah (640–609 B.C.), there was a drastic reversal of religious policy; the famous "Deuteronomic reforms" of 621 B.C. (see p. 134) persuaded a large number of the people to return to the worship of Yahweh and to obey his laws. However, beneficial though these reforms were in some respects, the Deuteronomists' emphasis upon Yahweh's Covenant with the Hebrew nation, upon Temple worship, and upon the meticulous observance of the letter of the Law caused many devout and well-meaning Judeans to lose sight of what the eighth-century prophets had taught about the universality of God and the superiority of justice and mercy to ritualism.

Jeremiah and his three contemporary prophets present a variety of attitudes towards the events and the conditions of their troublous epoch. Each prophet has a distinctive message for his people.

ZEPHANIAH: PROPHET OF GOD'S DAY OF WRATH

After the death of Isaiah (c. 692 B.C.), no prophet arose during the wicked reigns of Manasseh and Amon to call the people back to God; at least, no record of any has been preserved. It was well along in the reign of Josiah that another courageous figure dared to interpret the signs of the times and issue a warning. That man was Zephaniah, apparently a distant cousin of King Josiah and the great-great-grandson of King Hezekiah.[1]

The occasion for the writing of Zephaniah's short book of prophecy may have been the threat of a Scythian invasion of Judah about 625 B.C., but this is uncertain.[2]

Zephaniah does not belong to the first rank of the Old Testament prophets. He has neither the soaring imagination of Isaiah and Ezekiel nor the tenderness and sympathy for humanity of Hosea and Jeremiah. He is not, however, an inconsiderable figure as the reawakener of Judah's conscience in his time and as a prophet of God's judgment in history.

Borrowing from Amos and Isaiah, Zephaniah delivered a message of unrelieved pessimism.* His book is one of "continuous denunciation"[3] of the sins of the Judeans and their neighbors, combined with an admonition that the time of punishment is at hand:

> The great day of the Lord is near,
> It is near, and hasteth greatly
> Even the voice of the day of the Lord:
> The mighty man shall cry there bitterly.
> That day is a day of wrath,
> A day of trouble and distress,
> A day of wasteness and desolation,
> A day of darkness and gloominess,
> A day of clouds and thick darkness,
> A day of the trumpet and alarm
> Against the fenced cities,
> And against the high towers. (1:14-16)

This is the most well-known passage in the book, and it is believed to be the basis for the rather terrifying thirteenth-century hymn *Dies Irae* (attributed to Thomas of Celano)[4] which forms part of the Roman Catholic Requiem Mass.

NAHUM: PROPHET OF GOD'S JUDGMENT ON THE ASSYRIANS

In 612 B.C. the city of Nineveh, capital of the Assyrian Empire, was captured by a coalition of Chaldeans and Medes. This event was hailed with wild joy by the peoples who had been subjected to the cruel oppression of the Assyrians for more than a century. The short Biblical book of Nahum is an exuberant paean on this victory.

Nothing is known of the author except that he was an inhabitant of the now unidentifiable city of Elkosh. Whether the book was written before or after the fall of Nineveh is a matter of dispute. It is entirely possible that Nahum foresaw the fall of the hated capital and wrote his victory song *ante eventum*. At

---

* The last twelve verses, which hold out promise and comfort to the Hebrews and which foretell the conversion of all peoples, are believed to be a post-Exilic interpolation.

any rate, the year 612 B.C. may be accepted as the approximate date of composition.

Some commentators have been reluctant to call the poem a book of prophecy. Certainly it bears little resemblance to the books of Amos, Hosea, Isaiah, Micah, and Jeremiah. It contains no condemnations of the Hebrews for their wrongdoings, nor does it urge them to live uprightly or to worship God. It does not contribute to the development of the Hebrew concept of the Deity as a universally just and loving God; on the contrary, its characterization of Yahweh is a retrogression to the conception of a vengeful god of war, interested primarily in the Israelites.

Why, then, *was* the book included in the sacred canon? A careful reading of the book will supply the answer: it is a condemnation of militarism and cruel despotism in general—*sic semper tyrannis*. Furthermore, it is Yahweh, the God of the Hebrews, who has brought about the destruction of the Assyrians; to him belong the glory and the gratitude.

Regardless of its ethical and religious values, the poem is a superb piece of war poetry which ranks with Deborah's Song (see p. 88) as one of the great victory paeans of world literature. It is packed with intense emotion; its language is vigorous and concise; and its imagery is extraordinarily concrete and vivid.

The poet gives us a brief summary of the crimes of Assyria. She has been like a lion, tearing prey in pieces (2:11-12); Nineveh has been a bloody city, "full of lies and robbery" (3:1), a harlot guilty of a multitude of fornications, "the mistress of witchcrafts, that selleth nations through her whoredoms, and families through her witchcrafts" (3:4).

At last Yahweh has called a halt to these crimes:

> Behold, I am against thee, saith the Lord of hosts,
> And I will burn her chariots in the smoke,
> And the sword shall devour thy young lions:
> And I will cut off thy prey from the earth,
> And the voice of thy messengers shall no more be heard. (2:13)

Now we are privileged to witness, step by step, the fall of Nineveh: the manning of the ramparts and the furious attack by the Chaldeans:

> The noise of a whip, and the noise of the rattling of wheels,
> And of the prancing horses, and of the jumping chariots.

> The horseman lifteth up both the bright sword and the
>   glittering spear:
> And there is a multitude of slain,
> And a great number of carcasses;
> And there is none end of their corpses;
> They stumble upon their corpses ... (3:2-3)

We watch as the queen and the other women flee from the city;
we see the gathering of the spoils and the smouldering of the
ruins after the battle. The poem ends on a calmly exultant note:

> Thy shepherds slumber, O king of Assyria:
> Thy nobles shall dwell in the dust:
> Thy people is scattered upon the mountains,
> And no man gathereth them.
> There is no healing of thy bruise;
> Thy wound is grievous:
> All that hear the bruit of thee shall clap hands over thee:
> For upon whom hath not thy wickedness passed continually?
>   (3:18-19)

HABAKKUK: PROPHET OF FAITH

The book of Habakkuk, like that of Nahum, was intended to
provide encouragement in a time of trouble rather than corrective warning in a time of prosperity. It might be described more
accurately as a series of philosophical reflections and a psalm
than as a book of prophecy.

There is little scholarly agreement about the authorship and
the date (or dates) of composition.[5] *Habakkuk* may be only
a nickname, and nothing is known of the man to whom it is
given except that he probably lived near the end of the seventh
century. He may have written only ten verses of the book
(1:6-11 and 14-17). It is likely that the remaining portions
were written by several hands at various times between 500 and
200 B.C. Most commentators agree that Chapter 3 was the work
of a single author and that he was *not* the author of any other
portion of the book.

In both theme and philosophical conclusion, Habakkuk resembles the book of Job. Chapters 1 and 2 discuss the ever-
recurrent problem of why the good suffer and the wicked
prosper; Chapter 3 is a psalm asserting faith in God and his
purposes.

The multiple authorship has produced several styles. Some passages are tense, forceful, and dramatic; others are personal and lyrical; still others (especially Chapter 3) are elevated, dignified, and magnificent.

The Chaldean Scourge (Ch. 1). How long (the prophet asks) will God allow the "bitter and hasty nation," the violent and cruel Chaldeans, to prevail? Is God not everlasting and just? Why, after observing the treachery of the Chaldeans and their devouring of the people more righteous than they—why does God withhold his hand?

"The Just Shall Live by Faith" (Ch. 2). In the second chapter, God responds to the prophet's queries, but does not answer them directly. Man, he says, will in time understand God's plans; in the meanwhile, "the just shall live by faith."*

Then follows a series of "taunt-songs," in which various "woes" are predicted for oppressors who are guilty of cruelty, covetousness, rapacity, bloodshed, and drunken orgies. One woe invoked upon idolators, ends with a verse that has become familiar in worship services.

> Woe unto him that saith to the wood, Awake:
> To the dumb stone, Arise, it shall teach!
> Behold, it is laid over with gold and silver,
> And there is no breath at all in the midst of it.
> But the Lord is in his holy temple:
> Let all the earth keep silence before him. (2:19-20)

A Psalm of Thanksgiving and Trust (Ch. 3). Feeling, perhaps, that the writings attributed to Habakkuk (especially what is now Chapter 1) were too skeptical and bitter, some editor borrowed a hymn from a collection of psalms and ascribed it to Habakkuk. This hymn is an impressive prayer of praise, thanksgiving, and trust. Just as God's vengeance against his enemies has been terrible in the past, so will it be in the future. Like Job, the psalmist will remain faithful through all adversities:

> The mountains saw thee, and they trembled:
> The overflowing of the water passed by:
> The deep uttered his voice,
> And lifted up his hands on high.

* Compare Isa. 5:8-22. Quoted by Paul in Romans 1:17 and Galatians 3:11.

The sun and moon stood still in their habitation:
At the light of thine arrows they went,
And at the shining of thy glittering spear. . . .
Yet I will rejoice in the Lord,
I will joy in the God of my salvation.
The Lord God is my strength,
And he will make my feet like hinds' feet,
And he will make me to walk upon mine high places.

(3:10-11, 18-19)

JEREMIAH: PROPHET OF INDIVIDUAL WORSHIP

The age-old reputation of Jeremiah as a prophet of gloom is an inadequate reflection of the qualities and the accomplishments of a great man. It is true that he was pessimistic about the fortunes of the Hebrews and that he foretold calamities to befall them; but the same may be said of Amos, Isaiah, and Micah; and like these earlier prophets, Jeremiah made great contributions to the development of Hebrew theology.

The prophet was the scion of a priestly family (1:1), but never became a priest himself. He was born and reared at Anathoth, a village two miles northeast of Jerusalem.[6] His traditionally accepted birthdate is 650 B.C., but some scholars believe that he was not born until 627.[7] At some unknown date he moved to Jerusalem. There he carried on his prophetic activities during the reigns of Josiah (640–609 B.C.), Jehoahaz (Shallum) (609 B.C.), Jehoiakim (Eliakim) (609–598 B.C.), Jehoiachin (Coniah) (598 B.C.), and Zedekiah (Mattaniah) (598–586 B.C.).* When Jerusalem fell to the Babylonians in 586 B.C., Jeremiah stayed on as adviser to Gedaliah, the Jewish governor appointed by Nebuchadrezzar. Then upon the assassination of Gedaliah, the prophet was forced to accompany the group of Jews who fled into Egypt. There he lived for perhaps fifteen or sixteen more years, still urging his fellow countrymen to remain faithful to Yahweh. Tradition holds he was stoned to death by some members of this group.

Jeremiah took an active interest in the political affairs of Judah. After the great Babylonian victory at Carchemish (605 B.C.), he saw clearly that Judean opposition to the new world power would be futile; he viewed Babylon as an instrument used

* See 1:3.

by God to punish Judah for her sin; and he consistently tried to persuade his nation that her only chance for survival lay in submission, which would be followed by eventual restoration. Such advice led both the people and the monarchs to consider him a traitor. On one occasion he was beaten and placed in stocks for predicting the destruction of Jerusalem (20:1-6); another time he was thrown into prison for prophesying that the Hebrews would be delivered into Nebuchadrezzar's hand (37:16-21); and the pro-Egypt party almost succeeded in putting him to death for continuing to implore King Zedekiah to surrender to Babylon (38:1-13). Even after his abduction into Egypt, he prophesied that Nebuchadrezzar would also invade and conquer that country (43:8-13).

Scarcely more popular than his political views were his religious tenets, which antagonized king, priest, and populace. He vigorously attacked Josiah's Deuteronomic reforms, because he felt that they placed too much emphasis on ritualism at the expense of true morality. His principal theological teachings, which seemed revolutionary to most of his contemporaries, were as follows: (1) Yahweh is a universal Deity who can be worshiped as well in Babylon as in the Temple at Jerusalem; he is not merely the tribal God of the Hebrews but the God of all peoples who directs history according to his purpose. Though shocking to the priests and the smug citizens of Jerusalem, these doctrines were of inestimable value to the exiles in Babylonia and contributed greatly to the preservation of Yahweh-worship among the Jews of the Dispersion. "Jeremiah has been called 'the spiritual founder of the Synagogue' and the 'preserver of Judaism.' "[8] (2) God is more interested in the righteousness of each person than in a national religion centering on the Temple. The old Covenant with Israel has been found ineffective; now God will establish a new Covenant written upon the hearts of the people. Each one will have to answer for himself. Jeremiah lays great stress upon the spiritual communion between the individual and God, whom he depicts as a kind shepherd and an understanding father.

A unique and valuable feature of Jeremiah's book is the glimpse it gives us of the processes of prophetic authorship. Chapter 36 tells us that Jeremiah dictated a scroll of oracles to Baruch, his secretary. The scroll was read to groups of people

in the Temple and in the royal palace (the winter of 605 b.c.).[9]
The oracles were principally a record of Jeremiah's prophecies
against Israel, Judah, and other nations. King Jehoiakim was so
angry that he cut up the scroll and burned it; he also ordered
the arrest of Jeremiah and Baruch, but they escaped and remained in hiding. At God's command the prophet dictated his
oracles to Baruch again. This second scroll may be considered
the "first edition" of our own book of Jeremiah; it contained a
large portion of the present Chapters 1–6 and 8–9. After the fall
of Jerusalem some scribe—probably Baruch—added most of the
material in Chapters 10–23, consisting chiefly of more oracles
by the prophet. The first twenty-three chapters are written mostly
in the first person.

Chapters 26–43 form an interesting biography of Jeremiah
and were probably written (in the third person) by Baruch;
Chapters 46–51 are believed to be a collection of oracles of various post-Exilic authors; and Chapter 52 is a narrative appendix,
derived almost verbatim from II Kings 24:18–25:30. The remaining portions of the book (Chapters 7, 24–25, and 44–45)
are believed to be interpolations by some Deuteronomic editor.

Part of the book is in poetry, part in prose. The diction and
syntax are usually simple. There are fewer striking figures of
speech than in Isaiah; the metaphors in Jeremiah are generally
drawn from everyday life, especially rural life. The book is distinguished by the personality of the prophet—his sincerity, sensi-
tivity, and emotional power.

Jeremiah is the second longest book in the Bible, surpassed
only by the book of Psalms. It is also one of the most chaotic
books. The oracular and narrative passages are not arranged
either chronologically or topically, and little attempt is made to
provide transition from one topic to another. There is much repetition and duplication. In the interest of clarity, this Outline will
omit a number of passages (including the interpolated oracles
against foreign nations [Chapters 46–51] and most of the historical and biographical ones which have been summarized
briefly above) and will regroup many others.

The Sins of the People and the Call to Repentance (2:1—4:4;
5:1-13, 26:31; 6:9-21; 7:1-31; 8:4-11; 10:1-16; 11:1-17; 23:9-40;
and 25:1-7). Jeremiah was well acquainted with the sayings
of the eighth-century prophets; he was especially indebted to

Hosea. Like them, he enumerates the sins of his countrymen: idolatry, greed, oppression of the poor and helpless, injustice, perjury, stealing, corruption among the priests and the prophets, sexual immorality, and even murder; and he calls on the people to repent.

He borrows fom Hosea the comparison of the Hebrews to a faithless wife; she has deserted her husband (Yahweh) and played the harlot (with false Canaanitish deities) in every "high place" and under every green tree. In spite of God's love for his people and his oft-repeated warnings to them, they have been continually unfaithful to him ever since he brought them from Egypt in the days of Moses. This idolatry seems to cause Jeremiah greater grief than any other sin of the people; he calls attention to it in at least five passages (2:1–4:4, 5:7-24, 10: 1-16, 11:1-17, and 23:9-40).*

Like Amos and Micah, Jeremiah chides the people for thinking that they can escape judgment for their iniquities by burning incense and sacrificing burnt offerings. After committing all their sins, they rush to the Temple and say: "The temple of the Lord, The temple of the Lord, The temple of the Lord. . . . We are delivered . . ." (7:4, 10). Such people have made the Lord's house a "den of robbers" (7:11).†

Time after time he pleads with the people to repent and to abandon their evil ways, but he has little hope that they will heed his entreaties.

Predictions of Siege, Exile, and Death. Because the "backsliding children" have "forgotten the Lord their God," the prophet foretells dire consequences.

TWO ADMONITORY VISIONS (1:11-16). Jeremiah says that the Lord has shown him two visions which should serve as warnings

---

* Most of these rebukes were probably delivered during the reigns of Jehoiakim and Zedekiah, under whom the Deuteronomic reforms of Josiah were discarded.

† Jesus quoted this phrase when he cleansed the Temple. See Matt. 2:13, Mark 11:17, and Luke 19:46. In Jeremiah's attack, it should be noticed, the emphasis is upon the Temple as a place of refuge (a robbers' den or cave), not a place where cheating or other dishonest deeds take place. (James Philip Hyatt, exegesis to Jeremiah, *The Interpreter's Bible*, V, 872.) Jeremiah's "Temple sermon" was a result of his perception that the Deuteronomic reformers had overemphasized ritual and Temple worship to the neglect of other portions of God's Law—those portions dealing with moral and social behavior.

to the Jews. In the first he sees an almond rod, a symbol of God's judgment and imminent punishment of the people of Judah.*

In the second vision he beholds a "seething" (boiling) pot, with its opening toward the south. "Out of the north an evil shall break forth upon all the inhabitants of the land" (1:14). Some commentators have believed that these two visions predict raids from bands of Scythians (c. 625 B.C.), but it seems much more likely that they refer to the danger from the Babylonians (c. 605 B.C.).[10]

THREE ADMONITORY PARABLES (13:1-14 and 18:1-12). Jeremiah uses three illustrative stories to impress upon the people the results which are to follow God's wrath against them. In the first parable (13:1-11) the fate of the Jews is compared to that of a loincloth hidden for a while in a rock beside the Euphrates. When the cloth is recovered, it is found to be ruined. The prophet is probably preaching against Judah's allowing itself to be corrupted by alliances with Babylonia.[11]

In a short parable (13:12-14), all the people of Judah—including king, priests, and prophets—are like full wine bottles; in other words, they are drunk with their own iniquity. The Lord will "dash them one against another" and destroy them without mercy or pity.

Borrowing, perhaps, from Isaiah 29:16, Jeremiah tells the famous Parable of the Potter and the Clay (18:1-12). Just as a potter exercises sovereignty over his clay and the vessels he makes from it, so God maintains his sovereignty over human beings. If a vessel is warped or otherwise unfit for use, the potter may demolish it and rework it into a suitable shape; in like manner, God can destroy and remake Judah if it continues in its sinful ways.†

THE "FOE FROM THE NORTH" (4:5-13, 29-31; 5:14-16; 6:1-8, 22-26; 10:17-22; 21:1–22:30; 25:8-38; 27:1–28:17). In oracles apparently delivered at several different times between 609 and 587 B.C., Jeremiah predicts destruction at the hands of the Babylonians. He paints a terrifying picture:

* Compare the rod of Aaron (Num. 17:1-11) and that of Ezekiel (Ezek. 7:10). (Hyatt, exegesis, *The Interpreter's Bible*, V, 806.)

† This figure of the potter has been used not only by many other Biblical authors (see Isa. 45:9, 64:8; Wisd. Sol. 15:7; Ecclus. 33:13; Rom. 9:21) (Hyatt, exegesis, *The Interpreter's Bible*, V, 960), but also by Omar Khayyám in his *Rubáiyát* and by Robert Browning in "Rabbi Ben Ezra."

The trumpet will blast out a shrill warning, and a watchman will exhort the people to flee to the fortified cities. They will gird themselves with sackcloth, and they will "lament and howl." Neither flight nor lamentation will avail, however, for the fierce anger of the Lord will be upon them. He is sending the Babylonians like a "lion from a thicket." Changing the figure, Jeremiah says that the enemy will

> come up as clouds,
> And his chariots shall be as a whirlwind:
> His horses are swifter than eagles. (4:13)

The people of Jerusalem

> shall flee for the noise of the horsemen and bowmen;
> They shall go into thickets, and climb up upon the rocks:
> Every city shall be forsaken,
> And not a man dwell therein. (4:29)

Those who escape death will be captured and carried into Babylon as exiles.

The Grief of Jeremiah (8:18—9:11; 11:18—12:6; 14:17—15:21; 17:14-18; 18:18-23; 20:7-18; 22:20-23). One of the most memorable and characteristic features of Jeremiah's book is the deep personal grief of the prophet. He shares the sufferings of his people, and he cries out in agony each time one of his own predictions of calamity comes true. He laments the people's sinfulness, their obstinate refusal to repent and reform, and the resultant hardships which the Lord is sending upon them.

> Behold the voice of the cry of the daughter of my people
> Because of them that dwell in a far country:
> Is not the Lord in Zion?
> Is not her king in her? . . .
> The harvest is past, the summer is ended,
> And we are not saved.
> For the hurt of the daughter of my people am I hurt;
> I am black; astonishment hath taken hold on me.
> Is there no balm in Gilead?*

---

* The phrase "balm in Gilead" has become proverbial. It is the title of a famous Negro spiritual, and Edgar Allan Poe used it as a synonym for *comfort* in "The Raven." The balm referred to probably came from styrax trees in the territory of Gilead, which exported it for medical use. See Hyatt, exegesis, *The Interpreter's Bible,* V, 888.

> Is there no physician there?
> Why then is not the health of the daughter of my people
>   recovered?
> Oh that my head were waters,
> And mine eyes a fountain of tears,
> That I might weep day and night
> For the slain of the daughter of my people! (8:19—9:1)

He pleads with the Lord on behalf of Judah:

> Hast thou utterly rejected Judah?
> Hath thy soul loathed Zion?
> Why hast thou smitten us,
> And there is no healing for us?
> We looked for peace, and there is no good;
> And for the time of healing, and behold trouble! (14:19)

Sometimes Jeremiah laments his own miserable lot: he has done the best he could for his people, but they have ignored him, spurned him, hated him, and even plotted against his life. Like some of the Psalmists, he asks God to avenge the persecutions he has suffered:

> But I was like a lamb or an ox
> That is brought to the slaughter;
> And I knew not that they had devised devices against me,
> Saying, Let us destroy the tree with the fruit thereof,
> And let us cut him off from the land of the living,
> That his name may be no more remembered.
> But, O Lord of hosts, that judgest righteously,
> That triest the reins and the heart,
> Let me see thy vengeance on them:
> For unto thee have I revealed my cause. (11:19-20)

Promises of Restoration (29:1—31:40; 33:1-26). After the first deportation of the Judeans (597 B.C.), Jeremiah continued to advise the exiles by letters. His prophecies of this period hold out no false hopes of revenge on the Babylonians or of a quick return to Palestine; they do, however, promise that at some time the Jews will come back to their native land. What is more important, Jeremiah inspires in the exiles a different sort of hope, a hope based on a new relationship with God.

A LETTER TO THE EXILES (29:1-23). During the reign of Zedekiah, Jeremiah learned that two false prophets had misled the

Jews in Babylon by predicting that the period of their captivity would soon be over. In a general letter addressed to the exiles, Jeremiah warns that they will remain in Babylon "seventy years" (29:10), and he counsels them to make the best of their present lot: build houses, cultivate gardens, marry and have childen, and strive for the welfare of Babylon. As for the false prophets, God will cause Nebuchadrezzar to slay them.

Jeremiah's letter is of especial historical interest because it reflects the large degree of personal freedom which the Jews were granted while in exile.[12]

THE RETURN FROM THE DIASPORA* AND THE "NEW COVENANT" (23:5-6 and Chs. 30, 31, and 33).[13] After the long period of penance, the Lord will burst the bonds of his people, who will then return to Palestine:

For, lo, the days come, saith the Lord, that I will bring again the captivity of my people Israel and Judah, saith the Lord: and I will cause them to return to the land that I gave to their fathers, and they shall possess it. (30:3)

Like Isaiah, Jeremiah foretells the establishment of a kingdom of righteousness under the rule of a Messiah descended from David:

Behold, the days come, saith the Lord, that I will raise unto David a righteous Branch, and a King shall reign and prosper, and shall execute judgment and justice in the earth. In his days Judah shall be saved, and Israel shall dwell safely: and this is his name whereby he shall be called, The Lord Our Righteousness. (23:5-6)

In this new era the "old things will pass away." The Hebrews will no longer be put on trial as a race, nor will the sins of the fathers be visited upon their children; instead, each person will be responsible for his own acts:

In those days they shall say no more, The fathers have eaten a sour grape, and the children's teeth are set on edge. But every one shall die for his own iniquity: every man that eateth the sour grape, his teeth shall be set on edge. (31:29-30)

"The most important single teaching of Jeremiah"[14] is his proclamation of the "New Covenant." In ancient times God made

---

* *Diaspora* is a Greek word meaning "scatter." It is used to refer to the dispersion of the Jews in colonies outside Palestine after the Babylonian Exile.

the "Old Covenant" between himself and the Hebrew nation, but his Chosen People never, as a group, lived up to their part of the contract. In the future, God will establish a different kind of covenant—between himself and the people who will know and worship him as individuals:

Behold, the days come, saith the Lord, that I will make a new covenant with the house of Israel, and with the house of Judah: Not according to the covenant that I made with their fathers, in the day that I took them by the hand to bring them out of the land of Egypt; which my covenant they brake, although I was a husband unto them, saith the Lord: But this shall be the covenant that I will make with the house of Israel; After those days, saith the Lord, I will put my law in their inward parts, and write it in their hearts; and will be their God, and they shall be my people. And they shall teach no more every man his neighbor, and every man his brother, saying, Know the Lord: for they shall all know me, from the least of them unto the greatest of them, saith the Lord: for I will forgive their iniquity, and I will remember their sin no more. (31:31-34)

This passage is a significant step in the direction of the teachings of Jesus. It is quoted or referred to by several of the New Testament writers.* It lies behind the words[15] which Jesus used at the Last Supper: "This cup is the new testament [covenant]† in my blood" (I Cor. 11:25); and it "is responsible for the distinction which was eventually made between 'The Old Testament' and 'The New Testament.' "[16]

* For example, see Heb. 8:8-12 and 10:16-17; Luke 22:20; and II Cor. 3:5-14.

† It should be remembered that *covenant* and *testament* are two translations of the same Greek word.

The Exilic Prophets
Ezekiel and the Unknown Prophet (Second Isaiah)

History records little about the life of the Jewish people during the five decades of their Babylonian Captivity. A few scraps of information may be gleaned from II Kings, II Chronicles, some of the Psalms, and the books attributed to Jeremiah, Ezekiel, and the authors of Second and Third Isaiah.*

The letter of Jeremiah to the exiles in Babylon (Jer. 29) conveys the impression that the conquerors dealt rather generously and leniently with the vanquished, allowing them much personal liberty and such privileges as the maintenance of their own homes and gardens (Jer. 29:5). Even the formerly rebellious King Jehoiachin was eventually freed from prison and treated with deference (II Kings 25:27-30).

The majority of the exiles, however, never ceased to fear and loathe their captors; their fierce hatred is reflected in Psalm 137, especially verses 7-9. And the Persian overthrow of the Babylonian Empire in 539 B.C. was celebrated by the Hebrews as a great deliverance (II Chr. 36:22-23 and Isa. 45:1-8).

Two great prophets may be assigned to the period of the Exile: Ezekiel, who exhorted the Jews to remain faithful to Yahweh despite their deportation and the destruction of their Temple and who promised the restoration of their Holy City; and the author of Second Isaiah, who joyously proclaimed the end of the Exile and foretold once again the coming of the Messiah.

* The book of Daniel, although it purports to be an account of events in sixth-century Babylon, actually reflects the era of the Seleucids in the second century B.C.

EZEKIEL: PROPHET OF PERSEVERING FAITH

Contemporary with Jeremiah, Ezekiel was a priest and probably a member of the renowned family descended from Zadok,
a priest during David's time. For many centuries Biblical scholars
accepted the traditions (1) that in 597 B.C. Ezekiel was deported
to Babylon along with King Jehoiachin and about ten thousand
other Judeans; (2) that he was "called" to prophesy in 593 or
592 B.C.; and (3) that he remained in Babylon the rest of his
life. Some recent historians have argued that, although exiled in
597, he returned to Jerusalem about 593, remained there till the
city was destroyed, and then went back to Babylon. Still others
have doubted that he was ever exiled.[1] There is no record of
either the date or the place of his death.

There has been much disagreement over dates of composition
and over which parts of the book should be attributed to the
priest Ezekiel. Although the problem may never be solved, most
scholars today are inclined to believe that between 593 and
586 B.C. Ezekiel wrote most of the material in Chapters 1–32 and
that between 586 and 570 B.C. some Exilic editor in Babylon reworked Ezekiel's contributions and added most of Chapters
33–48.[2]

Several of Ezekiel's messages are so similar to those delivered
by Jeremiah that some commentators have suggested the possibility that the two prophets knew each other in Jerusalem between 593 and 586 B.C., or that one was familiar with the other's
writings. Neither prophet, however, mentions the other. Like
Jeremiah, Ezekiel (1) denounces the sins of the people of Judah,
especially their idolatry; (2) predicts that Yahweh will punish
them with exile and the destruction of Jerusalem; (3) proclaims
that Yahweh may be worshiped as well in Babylon as in Jerusalem; (4) emphasizes individual responsibility for sins; and (5)
foretells the restoration of the Hebrew nation in Palestine. *Unlike*
Jeremiah, however, Ezekiel stresses the need for communal worship, ritualism, and continual perusal of the Holy Scriptures;
he emphasizes these "priestly elements of religion"[3] in an effort
to bind together the Jewish community during their stay in a
foreign land and after their return from it. He envisages the
restored Israel as a theocratic community centering on the
Temple. Jeremiah and Ezekiel differ also in their personalities

and in their attitudes toward the people; whereas Jeremiah is warm, sympathetic, and subjective, Ezekiel is cold, stern, and objective.[4]

Most of the book of Ezekiel is in prose; a few passages are in poetic form. Many readers find it wordy and repetitious; certainly it uses stereotyped phrases over and over again: "son of man," "profane my sanctuary," "as I live, says the Lord," and "in the sight of the nations."[5] But it compensates with many colorful and extraordinary passages, some of literary excellence: vivid imagery, mystical visions, ecstatic utterances, parables, striking symbolism, allegories, and the account of dramatic activities which the prophet engages in for the purpose of driving home some point.

Compared with most of the other books of prophecy, Ezekiel is rather well organized and coherent. Four fairly distinct parts may easily be recognized: (1) Judah's iniquities and her punishment to come (Chs. 1–24); (2) oracles against foreign nations (Chs. 25–32); (3) restoration of Israel (Chs. 33–39); and (4) vision of the New Jerusalem (Chs. 40–48).[6]

The Calling of Ezekiel (Chs. 1–3). Like Isaiah, Ezekiel has a wondrous mystical vision and simultaneously receives a divine command to prophesy to the people of Judah. His vision is more elaborate and detailed than that of the earlier prophet.

In the fifth year of King Jehoiachin's exile (that is, in 593 B.C.), while he is in Babylon beside the River Chebar,* Ezekiel beholds coming out of the north a great whirlwind and a cloud flashing with fire. From the midst of the cloud emerge four cherubim, apparently arranged in a square. Each cherub has a body somewhat like that of a human being, but each has four faces—one of a man, one of a lion, one of an ox, and one of an eagle.† They have four wings apiece, which make a sound "like the noise of great waters, as the voice of the Almighty" (1:24). Beside each of these celestial beings is a shining wheel which has eyes on its rim, and another wheel inside it—"wheels within wheels."‡

* This meticulous pinning down of date and place is characteristic of the Exilic editor of Ezekiel's original oracles.

† Compare the four creatures described in Rev. 4:7. Lion, ox, and eagle symbolism was frequently associated with deities in ancient religions of the Middle East (Herbert G. May, exegesis to Ezekiel, *The Interpreter's Bible,* VI, 72).

‡ Compare the wheels of the throne described in Dan. 7:9.

Stretched above the cherubim is a "terrible crystal" firmament, and above that a sapphire throne, on which is seated Yahweh himself, encircled with a fiery brightness. He commands Ezekiel to go to the "rebellious house" of Judah and warn them that they will surely die unless they repent of their wickedness and reform. He gives the prophet a scroll (symbolizing God's judgment) and tells him to eat it; Ezekiel finds that it tastes as sweet as honey.*

The Sins and Punishments of Judah (Chs. 6—13 and 21—22). As a prophet of the defeated and deported, Ezekiel has a mission similar to that of Jeremiah. He must convince the downcast children of Israel that their misfortunes have come upon them *not* because their God is weak or has deserted them, but because *they* have deserted *him*. It is Yahweh who is punishing them— not the pagan deities of the Babylonians. Keenly aware of the dangers which threaten the survival of Judaism during the Exile, Ezekiel feels that his first objective must be to preserve Yahweh-worship. Consequently, he has less to say about personal and social ethics than some of the earlier prophets, such as Amos and Micah. To be sure, he does castigate sexual immorality, greed, extortion, bribery, and usury (22:10-12); but the sins that he attacks most vehemently are false prophesying (Ch. 13) and idolatry, both in the "high places" (Ch. 6) and in the Temple itself (Chs. 8—11). The people's apostasy from God began in Egypt, continued in the wilderness, and still persists in Judah. The people have defiled the Holy City with the blood or sacrificial offerings to idols (22:1-16). They have worshipped the Sumerian nature god Tammuz and also some solar deity (8:14-18).

The Lord will use the sword of the king of Babylon as his punitive instrument (21:18-24). Jerusalem will be besieged, its idolatrous altars will be destroyed, and its people will suffer famine and pestilence. As Yahweh pours out his indignation upon them, many will die and the others will be scattered among the alien nations (22:15).

Ezekiel's Little Dramas (Chs. 4—5 and 24:15-27). In order to impress the people with the gravity of their predicament, the Lord instructs Ezekiel to shock them with a series of six extraor-

* Compare the descriptions of God's laws and words in Pss. 19:10 and 119:103.

dinary activities; three of them pertain to the siege of Jerusalem, one to the destruction of the city, and the other two to the Exile.

THE PICTURE ON THE BRICK (4:1-3). First, Ezekiel is to portray on a brick Jerusalem under siege, encircled by fortifications and battering rams; then he is to place a pan or griddle (prototype of an "iron curtain") between himself and the picture on the brick—symbolic, perhaps, of Yahweh's estrangement from his people.

FOOD RATIONING (4:9-11). The prophet is told to mix an odd assortment of grains in a vessel, grind them, and make bread of the resultant "flour." Each day he is to limit himself to a small portion of the bread and to about a quart of water. These actions symbolize the rationing to which the inhabitants of the besieged city will be subjected.

UNCLEAN FOOD (4:12-15). Next, Ezekiel is to bake his bread over human dung. Thus he will demonstrate to the Jerusalemites that they will be reduced to eating "unclean" food.*

THE DEAD WIFE (24:15-27). Ezekiel's wife dies. In obedience to the Lord's command, the prophet neither weeps nor mourns for her. When the people ask the reason for his unconventional behavior, he explains that he is demonstrating how *they* shall act when the Temple is profaned and their sons and daughters are felled by the sword. The people will not mourn or weep but will pine away for their iniquities.

THE BOUND PRISONER (4:4-8). In another action the prophet is to lie down, tightly bound in ropes, for almost a year and a quarter—three hundred and ninety days on one side as a symbol of the years of the Northern Kingdom's exile, and forty more days on the other side, "each day for a year," to dramatize Judah's period of captivity.†

SHAVING OF FACE AND HEAD (5:1-17). Finally, Ezekiel is directed to shave off his beard and the hair of his head. After

---

* Compare Hosea's prediction about "unclean" food in Assyria (9:3); the refusal of the youths to eat alien food in Dan. 1; and modern Jewish concern over kosher foods (May, exegesis, *The Interpreter's Bible,* VI, 89).

† Biblical scholars have tried ingeniously but futilely to explain the inaccuracies of Ezekiel's predictions. Compare the prophecies of a seventy-year exile in Jer. 25:11-12 and 29:10 and in Zech. 7:5. (See May, exegesis, *The Interpreter's Bible,* VI, 87-88.)

dividing it all into three equal parts, he is to burn one part, smite a second with a sword, and scatter the remaining part to the winds; a few hairs of the last portion are to be saved and bound up in his robe. From these actions the people of Jerusalem are to learn that a third of them will die of pestilence and famine, a third will be killed by the sword, and a third will be exiled— except for a few whom God will allow to escape.

Ezekiel's Allegories (Chs. 15—17, 19, and 23:1—24:14). In addition to dramatic actions, the prophet uses several allegorical representations to add color and force to his predictions.

THE WORTHLESS VINE (Ch. 15). Like Hosea (10:1), Isaiah (5:1-7), and Jeremiah (2:21), Ezekiel compares the Israelites to a vine. Here the nation is a wild and worthless vine, unfit for any human use. Hence it will be devoured by fire.

THE FAITHLESS WIFE (Chs. 16 and 23). Borrowing, perhaps, from Hosea 2 and Jeremiah 2—3, Ezekiel employs the old allegory of the adulterous wife to chide the children of Israel for their infidelity to their God. Long ago Yahweh began to care for Jerusalem (symbol of the whole kingdom of Judah) when she was a helpless babe, a foundling. He nurtured her tenderly, brought her up to be a beautiful maiden, and made her his spouse. Now she has played the harlot with foreign lovers— Assyria, Egypt, and Babylonia. To their pagan gods she has built altars and offered sacrifices; sometimes she has even made sacrificial offerings of her own children. She has followed in the footsteps of her sister Samaria (the city, symbolizing the Northern Kingdom), who has already been punished with destruction; now it is Jerusalem's turn.*

THE EAGLES AND THE CEDAR (Ch. 17). In a rather striking allegory, Ezekiel reviews the recent history of Judah and predicts her future.

A great eagle (Nebuchadrezzar) broke the top (Jehoiachin) off a cedar tree (Judah) and carried it into a city of merchants (Babylon). Then he planted a seed of the cedar (Zedekiah) and caused it to sprout into a vine and to flourish. But a second eagle (Hophra, Pharaoh of Egypt) caused the vine to turn toward it. Shall not such a perfidious vine be uprooted and made

---

* In Ch. 23 Jerusalem is called Aholibah and Samaria, Oholah. The promises of restoration after punishment (16:53-63) are believed to be an editorial interpolation.

to wither and die? (Zedekiah not only had ungratefully plotted with Egypt against Nebuchadrezzar, his benefactor, but had also sworn *by Yahweh* to be faithful to his Babylonian overlord.) *

In a Messianic conclusion (17:22-24), Ezekiel prophesies that the Lord will eventually take another twig from the cedar and cause it to grow into a great blessing to other trees and birds (Gentile nations).[7]

THE WHELPS OF THE LIONESS (19:1-9). More Hebrew history is reviewed in the allegory of the lioness and her whelps.

A lioness (Judah) has given birth to two offspring. When the first (King Jehoahaz) has grown into a strong young lion, he begins to devour men. Alarmed, the other nations set a snare for him and, when they have captured him, surrender him to Egypt. The second whelp (King Jehoiachin) is no better than his elder brother. He too devours men and lays waste to their cities. The nations catch this one in a pit and convey him in a cage to Babylon, where he remains in captivity.

This allegory and the following one are in poetic form.

THE FRUITFUL VINE (19:10-14). A second allegory about a vine tells of the fate of King Zedekiah and of the nation after his defection. Judah is likened unto a fruitful vine, and Zedekiah is described as a strong stem of it. Now, however, the vine has been plucked up in fury, dried by the east wind (an appropriate symbol for Babylonia), and consumed by fire.

THE CALDRON AND THE FIRE (24:1-14). In an allegory reminiscent of Jeremiah's figure of the boiling caldron (Jer. 1:13-19), Ezekiel depicts once more the siege of Jerusalem. The city is compared with a rusty pot filled with pieces of flesh and bone and set upon a fire to boil. The Lord's fury has been aroused, and he has called down woe upon the bloody city. The fire will be made hot enough to consume the rust of the pot (that is, the sinfulness of the city), so that it will be thoroughly cleansed.

Responsibility of the Individual (Chs. 18 and 33). It may seem somewhat incongruous, if not inconsistent, for Ezekiel to lay special stress on both ritualism and individual moral responsibility. Closer scrutiny, however, will reveal that the double stress is in reality a support of the Law from two directions: ritualism maintains the letter of that Law, and individual re-

---

* Compare II Kings 24:20.

sponsibility is the essence of its spirit. Ezekiel perceived that the outward forms of Yahweh-worship had to be preserved if Judaism was to survive as a communal religion; hence the emphasis on ritualism in the later chapters (40—48).* But he saw, too (as Jeremiah did), that in a pagan land, where opportunities for communal worship and instruction were limited, there was an urgent need to emphasize individual morality, worship, and study of the Scriptures. Consequently his book (again like that of Jeremiah) stresses individual responsibility before God. God will deal with each person separately. Guilt is no longer a matter of group or of family accountability. A righteous son of a wicked father will be blessed, and a wicked son of a righteous father will be judged for his own sins. Neither will a man be judged by his past life; if he repents and reforms, his soul will live:

The word of the Lord came unto me again, saying, what mean ye, that ye use this proverb concerning the land of Israel, saying, The fathers have eaten sour grapes, and the children's teeth are set on edge? As I live, saith the Lord God, ye shall not have occasion any more to use this proverb in Israel. Behold, all souls are mine; as the soul of the father, so also the soul of the son in mine: the soul that sinneth, it shall die. (18:1-4)

Yahweh is a just God:

Therefore I shall judge you, O house of Israel, every one according to his ways, saith the Lord God. Repent and turn yourselves from all transgressions; so iniquity shall not be your ruin. (18:30)

Oracles against Foreign Nations (Chs. 25—32). In a long passage which holds relatively little literary or religious interest for the modern reader, Ezekiel predicts that the Lord will bring disaster on the wicked and idolatrous neighbors of the Israelites; the Babylonians, of course, will be the Lord's instruments of destruction. Ammon, Moab, Edom, Philistia, Phoenicia, and Egypt will all be judged; Nebuchadrezzar will be their scourge. The major portion of these oracles is concerned with the fall of Tyre, the famous Phoenician island-city so often mentioned in other parts of the Old Testament.† In Chapter 27 Ezekiel uses

---

* It should be remembered that a major portion of these chapters is attributed not to Ezekiel but to the priestly editor.

† See, for example, I Kings 5:1-18, 9:10-14, 26-27, and Jer. 27:3.

the now-famous "ship of state," metaphor* likening Tyre to a vessel about to founder in turbulent waters.

Restoration of the Hebrew Kingdom (Chs. 33—39). The Exilic editor (believed to be responsible for most of the last sixteen chapters of the book) strikes a comforting note. After a brief dissertation on the obligation of a prophet to deliver his message, plus a reiteration of Ezekiel's views on personal responsibility (Ch. 33), he tells the captive people that aid will soon be forthcoming, in the person of a Messiah descended from David. The widely scattered exiles will be gathered up and brought back to their own country, and God will defeat some (unidentified) fierce aggressor "from the North."

THE NEW SHEPHERD: A MESSIANIC VISION (Ch. 13). The "shepherds of the people" (their pre-Exilic rulers) have misled their flock. Instead of feeding and protecting them, each ruler has neglected them and exploited them for his own benefit. Now Yahweh himself will be the Good Shepherd.† He will lead the people back to their own land, protect the weak from their bold and ruthless fellows (the aristocracy), and eventually send them a new leader—a noble and selfless descendant of David, who will rule as the agent of God. Freedom, peace, security, and prosperity will return to the land.‡

GOD'S SELF-VINDICATION (36:22-32). An important new theological note appears in Chapter 36. God declares that he will soon punish the oppressors of the House of Israel, *not* because he pities the Israelites but because he wishes to vindicate his holy name, which has been profaned; and the Hebrews will be forgiven "for his name's sake." This is an approximation of the "doctrine of grace" to be expounded by Paul—the doctrine that man's salvation is the free gift of God rather than the reward for righteousness.[8]

---

* Alcaeus of Lesbos (*c.* 612 B.C.) was probably the first writer to employ the metaphor. It was later used by Horace in *Odes,* I, 14. Longfellow made it familiar to the modern reader in "The Building of the Ship."

† The figure of God as a kind of provident shepherd is found frequently in both the Old and the New Testaments. Perhaps the most familiar instances are in Psalm 23:1-4 and the allegory of the Good Shepherd in John 10:1-16. See also Matt. 10:6 and 25:32-33; Heb. 13:20; and I Pet. 2:25 and 5:4.

‡ The seemingly irrelevant Ch. 35, an oracle foretelling the devastation of Edom ("Mount Seir") may have been inserted by the editor as a contrast to the prediction of Judah's happy future. See W. L. Wardle, commentary on Ezekiel, *The Abingdon Bible Commentary,* p. 739.

THE VALLEY OF DRY BONES (37:1-14). In this famous passage, the Lord sets Ezekiel down in a valley full of dry, bleaching bones, apparently the bones of a slaughtered army.[9] Instructed by the Lord in an ecstatic vision, Ezekiel prophesies to the bones, and they miraculously come to life and are clothed with bodies again. The Lord then explains that the bones symbolize the two kingdoms Israel and Judah, which are about to be revived. (One should understand that this vision is a prediction of the rebirth of a nation—not a statement of belief in personal immortality.)

THE TWO STICKS (37:15-28). This oracle is similar to the preceding one in symbolizing God's promise to reunited Israel and Judah. Ezekiel is commanded to take two sticks, name them, respectively, Judah and "the children of Israel his companions [the southern tribes]" and Joseph and "the house of Israel his companions [the northern tribes]," and then place the sticks together. In like manner, God will join the two former kingdoms into one nation, to be ruled by a new David, and he will make with the people a new covenant of peace (compare 34:23-31).

GOG AND MAGOG (Chs. 38—39). Two very obscure chapters have long puzzled scholars. These passages foretell an invasion of Palestine from the north, an invasion which is to take place at some time after the restoration of the Hebrew nation. The Lord will vent his fury against the invaders by hurling rain, hail, fire, and brimstone at them. Birds and beasts will devour the flesh of their corpses, and it will take seven months for the Israelites to bury the bones. The weapons of the slain will be so numerous that they will serve as fuel for seven years. Thus Yahweh will again convince the nations of his power and of the holiness of his name (profaned by the invaders).

It seems that "Gog" is the name of the leader of the northern raiders, and "Magog" is the name of the land from which he comes. Various attempts to identify Gog and Magog have been made; it has been suggested that Gog refers to a king of Babylon, King Gyges of Lydia, Alexander the Great, or the Seleucid king Antiochus Eupator (162 B.C.), and that Magog is the land of the Scythians.[10] None of these identifications is convincing.*

Vision of the New Jerusalem (Chs. 40—48). The last nine chapters of the book of Ezekiel are concerned chiefly with the

---

* There is a close though not clearly defined relationship between this portion of Ezekiel and the book of Leviticus, especially the part known as the Holiness Code (Chs. 17—26).[11]

Temple and its ritual. Though less interesting to the modern reader than the earlier chapters, this section was of immense importance to the Jewish community in Jerusalem after the Exile.*

DIRECTIONS FOR REBUILDING THE TEMPLE (Chs. 40—43). The hand of the Lord comes upon Ezekiel and transports him from Babylon to Mount Zion, the "holy hill" whereon the Temple formerly stood. There a supernatural being, whose appearance is like brass and who holds in his hand a line of flax and a measuring reed (40:3), serves as his guide through the Temple area. The guide measures off the dimensions of the gates, the walls, the chambers of the inner and outer courts, the various rooms in the Temple proper, and the yard (Chs. 40—42).

At the eastern gate the prophet has a vision of the return of Yahweh—somewhat similar to the vision he had seen before the destruction of Jerusalem (described in Ezek. 10:1-22 and 11:22-23):

And behold, the glory of the God of Israel came from the way of the east: and his voice was like a noise of many waters: and the earth shined with his glory. And it was according to the appearance of the vision which I saw, even according to the vision that I saw when I came to destroy the city: and the visions were like the vision that I saw by the river Chebar; and I fell upon my face. (43:2-3)

The Lord gives Ezekiel instructions for making and consecrating the sacrificial altar.

THE DIVINE APPOINTMENT OF THE ZADOKITES (Ch. 44). A section of considerable significance to the history of the Jewish priesthood makes a distinction between the descendants of the priest Zadok and the Levites. God tells Ezekiel that the Levite priests have been idolatrous and henceforth will be allowed to serve only as Temple attendants. The Zadokites alone are to be elevated to the priesthood. Ezekiel receives a list of regulations governing the Zadokites' official functions and personal habits.

OTHER REGULATIONS AND ALLOTMENTS (Chs. 45—48). The book closes with a long series of miscellaneous instructions which the Lord gives to Ezekiel: (1) the allotment of land for the sacred district, for the prince, and for the various Hebrew tribes, and

* The imagery in Rev. 21:10-27 is obviously influenced by this passage. See May, exegesis, *The Interpreter's Bible*, VI, 284.

(2) regulations concerning contributions to the prince, weights, measures, feast days, sacrifices, and several other matters.

The only especially memorable passage (47:1-12) is that describing the sacred river which flows from the Temple—a wonderful river of life-giving waters:

And it shall come to pass, that every thing that liveth, which moveth, whithersoever the rivers shall come, shall live: and there shall be a very great multitude of fish, because these waters shall come thither: for they shall be healed; and every thing shall live whither the river cometh. (47:9) *

SECOND ISAIAH: PROPHET OF THE UNIVERSAL GOD
(ISA. 40—55)

Even the most casual reader is sure to be struck by the sudden changes in tone, style, historical background, and religious attitude which he encounters as he passes from the thirty-ninth to the fortieth chapter of the book of Isaiah as it appears in standard Bibles. Whereas the eighth-century prophet, Isaiah of Jerusalem, the author of Chapters 1—39, rebukes the people for their sins, warns of attacks by the Assyrians, and holds out little hope for the preservation of the kingdom of Judah, the author of Chapters 40—55 opens his message with a paean of joy and comfort; he assures the people that their sins are forgiven and that King Cyrus of Persia (600?—529 B.C.) will soon free them from their exile.

As noted previously (see p. 165), there is general agreement that the bulk of the first thirty-nine chapters is the work of the statesman-prophet of King Hezekiah; these chapters are usually referred to as "First Isaiah." Most scholars today believe that Chapters 40—55 were written about 540–538 B.C. by some exiled Jew in Babylonia; this section is usually called "Second Isaiah" or "Deutero-Isaiah." Many Biblical scholars perceive a difference between this portion and the last eleven chapters of the book, which, they claim, were written by several different authors, principally after the Jews' return to Palestine; hence Chapters 56—66 are called "Third Isaiah" or "Trito-Isaiah." These divisions will be observed in this Outline.

* Compare other Biblical descriptions of rivers in Zech. 14:18, Joel 3:18, Ps. 46:4, and especially Rev. 22. (May, exegesis, *The Interpreter's Bible*, VI, 326.)

Ezekiel had promised that eventually the Babylonians would fall and that the Israelites would be delivered from their bondage. For several decades, however, the might of Babylon seemed invincible. At last the star of a new military and political power began to rise. Little by little Cyrus, king of the small region know as Persia, extended his rule over Asia Minor. He overcame Media in 550 B.C. and Lydia in 546 B.C. The Jewish exiles watched eagerly as he moved against the sprawling Babylonian Empire, for by this time Cyrus was renowned not only as a conqueror but also as a lenient and generous ruler.

Some anonymous poet-prophet foresaw the coming triumph of Cyrus and celebrated it in Second Isaiah. It is believed that he wrote Chapters 40—48 at some time between 546 and 538 B.C. In the latter year Cyrus' famous edict freed the exiles. Shortly thereafter the same "Unknown Prophet" (as he is frequently called) wrote Chapters 49—55.

These sixteen chapters form one of the most significant documents in the development of religious thought. They present for the first time the belief in a single, universal, and everlasting Deity who created the world and has always controlled the history of every part of it. Hardly less important—especially for the Christian Church—is the conception of a vicariously suffering Servant, sent to lead all nations to salvation through the worship of the one true God.

Second Isaiah is not only a profound religious document but also one of the finest pieces of literature in the Bible. Most of it is in poetic form. Its best lyrical passages will not suffer by comparison with the finest of the Psalms or the most exalted selections from Job. Exultant over his momentous discoveries concerning the nature and purposes of God, the poet bursts into songs of solace and assurance. *Rhapsodic* is an adjective frequently used to describe his style and language. Much of his imagery is drawn "from the sphere of human emotion."[12] A fluent, legato music runs through most of his poetry; depth and sincerity of feeling, lyric warmth, verve, and majesty are its unfailing characteristics.

The End of the Exile. "Comfort ye, comfort ye my people, saith your God." With these words, the Unknown Prophet injects a new note into Hebrew prophecy. No longer is there need for threats and rebukes, warnings of calamities to come, or even

exhortations to endure bravely. The long night of suffering and
ignominy is over, and the bright day of liberation is about to
dawn.

PARDON AND RETURN (40:1-11, 41:17-20, 43:1-7, 48:20-21, 49:14
—50:3, 52:1-10, and 54:4-17). At last Israel has been sufficiently
punished for her iniquity, and God has forgiven her. Now he will
permit the exiles to return to their own land. Indeed, he himself
is going to lead them back to Jerusalem. As is the custom in
preparation for a royal journey, a herald is sent ahead to proclaim the advent of the Lord and to make sure that the road is
suitable for traveling:

> The voice of him that crieth in the wilderness,
> Prepare ye the way of the Lord,
> Make straight in the desert a highway for our God.
> Every valley shall be exalted,
> And every hill shall be made low:
> And the crooked shall be made straight,
> And the rough places plain.* (40:3-4)

Let Jerusalem rejoice, for the Lord is leading his children home:

> O Zion, that bringest good tidings,
> Get thee up into the high mountain;
> O Jerusalem, that bringest good tidings,
> Lift up thy voice with strength;
> Lift it up, be not afraid;
> Say unto the cities of Judah, Behold your God!
> Behold, the Lord God will come with strong hand,
> And his arm shall rule for him:
> Behold, his reward is with him,
> And his work before him. (40:9-10)

The prophet exhorts the people to flee from Babylon with a
song on their lips, rejoicing that they have been redeemed. Even
as the Lord in Moses' day led his children safely back from
Egypt through the wilderness, so will he now escort them
through the Syrian desert (48:20-21).†

---

* All three Synoptic Gospels quote this passage and identify John the Baptist
with the "voice crying in the wilderness" (Mark 1:2-4, Matt. 3:1-3, and Luke
3:1-6). According to Professor Bewer, the phrase *in the wilderness* really
modifies *make* instead of *voice*. (Julius A. Bewer [ed.], *The Prophets* [New
York: Harper and Brothers, 1955], p. 102.)

† In a later passage (52:11-12), apparently written after the edict of eman-
cipation, the prophet tells the people that there need be no haste in departure,

When Zion (Jerusalem) expresses fear that the Lord has forgotten and forsaken her, he reassures her tenderly:

> Can a woman forget her suckling child,
> That she should not have compassion on the son of her womb?
> Yea, they may forget, yet will I not forget thee. (49:15)

Soon the city will be rebuilt and repopulated. People of the Gentile nations will become the humble servants of the Israelites and will acknowledge God as Israel's deliverer:

> And all flesh shall know that I the Lord am thy Saviour
>   and thy Redeemer,
> The mighty one of Jacob. (49:26b)

Such a happy prospect inspires one of the prophet's finest lyrics:

> Awake, awake,
> Put on thy strength, O Zion:
> Put on thy beautiful garments, O Jerusalem, the holy city:
> For henceforth there shall no more come into thee the
>   uncircumcised and the unclean ...
> How beautiful upon the mountains
> Are the feet of him that bringeth good tidings,
> That publisheth peace;
> That bringeth good tidings of good,
> That publisheth salvation;
> That saith unto Zion, Thy God reigneth! ...
> Break forth into joy, sing together,
> Ye waste places of Jerusalem:
> For the Lord hath comforted his people,
> He hath redeemed Israel. (52:1, 7, 9)

CYRUS, GOD'S "ANOINTED" LIBERATOR (41:2-4, 44:24–45:13). The political agent by which the Lord will effect the great deliverance is Cyrus of Persia (mentioned by name in 44:28 and 45:1). The prophet is so certain that that brilliant monarch is acting under God's direction that he calls him "God's anointed" —a title given to no other non-Jew in the Bible.[13] God has raised up this righteous man from the east and made him to rule over

for they are no longer forced to flee. An interesting historical note is his instruction to them to take back to Jerusalem the sacred vessels of the Temple which Nebuchadrezzar had seized about forty-eight years before. Apparently Cyrus magnanimously restored these vessels to the Israelites. (Compare Ezra 1:7-11.)

all nations. The Lord has made him his shepherd and the instrument of his will. Obedient to the Lord, Cyrus will say to Jerusalem, "Thou shalt be built," and to the Temple, "Thy foundation shall be laid" (44:28).*

PUNISHMENT FOR BABYLONIA (47:1-15, 52:3-6). Although the Chaldeans were at one time acting under God's command in the oppression of the Hebrews, they eventually exceeded the divine intention and showed "no mercy" to Israel (47:6). Therefore they will be punished by God through Cyrus:

> Come down, and sit in the dust,
> O virgin daughter of Babylon,
> Sit on the ground:
> There is no throne,
> O daughter of the Chaldeans:
> For thou shalt no more be called tender and delicate. . . .
> Thy nakedness shall be uncovered,
> Yea, thy shame shall be seen:
> I will take vengeance,
> And I will not meet thee as a man. . . .
> Sit thou silent, and get thee into darkness,
> O daughter of the Chaldeans:
> For thou shalt no more be called, The lady of kingdoms.
>
> (47:1, 3, 5)

The Nature and the Ultimate Purposes of the Lord (40:6-8, 12-31; 41:1-7, 21-29: 43:8-13, 22-28; 44:6-20; 45:14-25; 46:1-7; 48:1-11; 49:22-23; 51:9-16; 53:1-9; 54:1-8; and 55:1-13). The restoration of Israel is only the means toward an end.[14] God loves the Hebrews and will show them everlasting mercy (54: 4-8), but his ultimate purpose, according to Second Isaiah, is far greater than the mere revival of the ancient Covenant with Israel. His purpose is no less than the salvation of all mankind. The Exile, Cyrus' victories, and the return of the Jews to their own country are all steps in one master plan directed toward that end. God has revealed the truth about himself to the Hebrews; the Exile has helped to spread that truth among the heathen nations; and now the merciful restoration of the Hebrews "will open the eyes of the nations to see the saving purpose of the Lord for themselves in His dealings with Israel."[15]

---

* Some commentators regard the passage 44:28—45:13 as evidence that Cyrus subsidized the rebuilding of Jerusalem. Compare Ezra 1:2-4. (Chamberlin and Feldman, *The Dartmouth Bible,* p. 690.)

At last all the people of the earth will be able to see and to recognize that Yahweh is not merely the Deity of the Israelites but the God of all nations (43:8-13, 45:14-25, 49:22-23, and 53:1-9), the eternal Creator of all things (40:6-8, 44:6-8, 51:12-13, and 54:1-3), perfect in power and wisdom (40:12-26), the source of all strength and hope (40:27-31 and 51:9-11). From the beginning of creation, he has been the director and controller of history (41:1-7).* He is the only true God, and soon all the worshipers of idols will see the error of their beliefs (41:21-29, 44:9-20, 46:1-7, and 48:1-11). Finally, he is the author of all free, forgiving grace (43:22-28). In an especially fine passage the prophet proclaims God's offer of that divine grace to all men:

> Ho, every one that thirsteth,
> Come ye to the waters,
> And he that hath no money;
> Come ye, buy, and eat;
> Yea, come buy wine and milk
> Without money and without price.
> Wherefore do ye spend money for that which is not bread?
> And your labor for that which satisfieth not?
> Hearken diligently unto me,
> And eat that which is good,
> And let your soul delight not in fatness.
> Incline your ear, and come unto me:
> Hear, and your soul shall live;
> And I will make an everlasting covenant with you. (55:1-3)

The divine purpose for mankind assuredly will be accomplished:

> Seek ye the Lord while he may be found,
> Call ye upon him while he is near:
> Let the wicked forsake his way,
> And the unrighteous man his thoughts:
> And let him return unto the Lord,
> And he will have mercy upon him;
> And to our God,
> For he will abundantly pardon.
> For my thoughts are not your thoughts,
> Neither are your ways my ways,
> Saith the Lord.

* This is Second Isaiah's answer to the ever vexatious "problem of evil"—the principal subject of the book of Job and of many of the Psalms. See Chamberlin and Feldman, *The Dartmouth Bible*, p. 665.

For as the heavens are higher than the earth,
So are my ways higher than your ways,
And my thoughts than your thoughts.
For as the rain cometh down, and the snow from heaven,
And returneth not thither, but watereth the earth,
And maketh it bring forth and bud,
That it may give seed to the sower, and bread to the eater:
So shall my word be that goeth forth out of my mouth:
It shall not return unto me void,
But it shall accomplish that which I please,
And it shall prosper in the thing whereto I sent it.
For ye shall go out with joy,
And be led forth with peace:
The mountains and the hills shall break forth before
    you into singing,
And all the trees of the field shall clap their hands.
Instead of the thorn shall come up the fir tree,
And instead of the brier shall come up the myrtle tree:
And it shall be to the Lord for a name,
For an everlasting sign that shall not be cut off. (55:6-13)

The Suffering Servant (42:1-9, 18-25; 43:8-13; 44:1-5, 21-22; 48:10-12; 49:1-7; and 52:13—53:12). God's message of salvation for all men finds further expression in several much-disputed passages concerning the Suffering Servant. According to Second Isaiah, God has singled out a particular Servant, whom he has tested and purified in the "furnace of affliction" (48:10) and whose sufferings have been endured meekly and vicariously so that "the nations" might be induced to take notice and to perceive, in the Lord's deliverance of his Servant, his intention of giving salvation to all men. The Servant is to be not only a savior of the "tribes of Jacob" but also "a light to the Gentiles" and a "salvation unto the end of the earth" (49:6). In an especially famous passage he is described as one

        despised and rejected of men;
    A man of sorrows, and acquainted with grief:
    And we hid as it were our faces from him;
    He was despised, and we esteemed him not.
    Surely he hath borne our griefs,
    And carried our sorrows;
    Yet we did esteem him stricken,
    Smitten of God, and afflicted.

But he was wounded for our transgressions,
He was bruised for our iniquities:
The chastisement of our peace was upon him;
And with his stripes we are healed.
All we like sheep have gone astray;
We have turned every one to his own way;
And the Lord hath laid on him the iniquity of us all.
He was oppressed, and he was afflicted,
Yet he opened not his mouth:
He is brought as a lamb to the slaughter,
And as a sheep before her shearers is dumb,
So he openeth not his mouth.
He was taken from prison and from judgment:
And who shall declare his generation?
For he was cut off from the land of the living:
For the transgression of my people was he stricken.
And he made his grave with the wicked,
And with the rich in his death;
Because he had done no violence,
Neither was any deceit in his mouth.
Yet it pleased the Lord to bruise him;
He hath put him to grief:
When thou shalt make his soul an offering for sin,
He shall see his seed,
He shall prolong his days,
And the pleasure of the Lord shall prosper in his hand.
He shall see the travail of his soul, and shall be satisfied:
By his knowledge shall my righteous servant justify many;
For he shall bear their iniquities.
Therefore will I divide him a portion with the great,
And he shall divide the spoil with the strong;
Because he hath poured out his soul unto death:
And he was numbered with the transgressors;
And he bare the sin of many,
And made intercession for the transgressors. (53:3-12)

Who *is* this Suffering Servant?

The Christian Church has traditionally identified him with
Jesus Christ and has interpreted these passages as prophecies of
Christ's ministry and Crucifixion. Most Jews and many Christian
scholars today, however, believe that the Servant represents no
one individual but the Hebrew nation, or perhaps a select group
of devout Jews in the time of the Unknown Prophet. They main-

tain that such an interpretation is more in keeping with the other passages in the book, and they cite as support the fact that in two different passages the Servant is specifically called "Israel" (41:8 and 49:3). There have been other attempts to identify the Servant as some particular historical individual: Moses, a Jewish martyr of the time of King Manasseh, Jeremiah, Jehoiakim, a fifth-century teacher, a martyr of the Maccabean era, or even Second Isaiah himself.[16]

It is significant that although many "servants" of the Lord recorded in the Old Testament (among them, Moses, Hosea, Isaiah, and Jeremiah) suffer in carrying out the divine will, the Suffering Servant of Second Isaiah was not identified with the Davidic Messiah before the Christian era.* Biblical scholars differ as to whether Jesus identified himself with the Suffering Servant, but Henry Sloane Coffin finds it "incredible" that he "did not draw inspiration" from the prophecy. Certainly many of the early Christians were deeply influenced by the Suffering Servant passages and saw in them an explanation of the otherwise baffling "passion, death and resurrection" of Christ.†

* James Muilenberg, introduction to Isaiah 40—66, *The Interpreter's Bible*, V, 412-413.

† Henry Sloane Coffin, exposition to Isaiah 40—66, *The Interpreter's Bible*, V, 630-631.

The Post-Exilic Prophetic Writings
Haggai, First Zechariah, Third Isaiah, Obadiah, Malachi, Joel, Second Zechariah, and Baruch

Soon after Cyrus freed the exiles, the great period of Hebrew prophecy came to an end; Second Isaiah was the last of the "major" prophetic works. During the four centuries that followed, no prophet of the stature of Amos or Jeremiah arose. On several occasions, however, in times of national crisis, "minor" spokesmen felt "called" to deliver to their people divine messages of warning or instruction. Some of these messages became separate books; others, as we have seen, were attached to older books of prophecy.

The topics with which these late prophets were most concerned were the new nationalism; the value of sacrifices, ritualism, and Temple worship; and most especially, the coming of God's new Kingdom. Apocalyptic and eschatological passages became increasingly frequent.

Although the Persian government encouraged and aided the exiles who returned to Palestine, they were beset by many difficulties. Their cities were in ruins, food was scarce, and the neighbors were hostile. To maintain a bare existence was hard; to reconstruct their desolate country was even harder. The new Temple was not finished until 516 B.C., and the walls of Jerusalem were not completed until about 432 B.C.* Meanwhile, adverse economic conditions and high taxes caused great suffering among the people.

During the Persian era much of the local government was left in the hands of the priests. One of the most serious problems which they had to solve was intermarriage of the Jews with non-

* See above discussion of Ezra-Nehemiah, pp. 141-147.

Hebrew peoples, a practice strenuously opposed by Ezra and Nehemiah and legislated against in the Priestly Code.*

After the Macedonian conquest of Persia (333 B.C.), the priest-rulers had to fight continually against the Hellenization of their land.†

HAGGAI: PROPHET OF THE NEW TEMPLE

Led by Sheshbazzar, the first Persian-appointed governor of Jerusalem, one band of liberated exiles returned to Palestine about 538 B.C. Hampered by the scarcity of provisions and by the hostility of the Palestinians, they made little progress in the re-building of the Temple. After the accession of Darius I (521 B.C.), a second company under the command of Zerubbabel, a grandson of King Jehoiachin, came down to Jerusalem. The prophet Haggai was probably a member of this company.[1] He prodded them on to resume the work on the Temple, and the task was at last completed.

Nothing is known of Haggai's ancestry, and except for his few months of prophetic activity in 520 B.C., nothing is known of his life.

His brief book is in prose; the fact that it is in the third person indicates that it was edited by some (anonymous) disciple.

Though monotheistic, Haggai is also fervently nationalistic. Lacking the high ethical vision of the greatest prophets, he defines blessedness chiefly in terms of material prosperity.

He is, nevertheless, a significant figure in the history of Judaism. First, in a time of deep discouragement he succeeded in persuading his compatriots to rebuild God's holy Temple and to make it once again the center of the religious life of the nation. Second, he opposed accepting the Samaritans into the restored Jewish community. In such opposition (continued into the Christian era) one may see "the beginning of that rigid exclusiveness which was to become so essential a characteristic of the postexilic community in Judah."[2]

Rebuild the Temple! (1:1—2:9, 15-19). Caustically Haggai rebukes the returnees: they have been more concerned about providing roofs for their own heads than with building a roof for God's sanctuary. Consequently, the Lord has been angry and has

---

* Preserved in the P Document and especially in the book of Leviticus.
† For a detailed discussion of the struggle, see above, pp. 153-161.

sent drought and famine upon them. Such punishment will be removed when they please the Lord by completing the Temple; then they will enjoy great prosperity.

The prophet's words so "stir up" Zerubbabel and the people that they resume the work of construction. Through Haggai the Lord promises to "shake the nations," restore the Hebrew kingdom, and renew his Covenant with it.

Exclusion of the Samaritans (2:10-14). Just as a person may contaminate consecrated food by touching it with his clothing, and as he may render himself "unclean" by touching a corpse, so everything that a Samaritan* may perform is "unclean" in the sight of the Lord. Therefore the Samaritans are not to be allowed to help the returned exiles in the rebuilding of the Temple.

Zerubbabel, the Messiah (2:20-23). Haggai hails Zerubbabel, descendant of David, as the long-awaited Messiah. God has chosen this prince as his "signet" and endowed him with divine authority and power, so that he will be able to destroy the armies of the heathen, topple their thrones, and set up his own glorious reign.

(Haggai's prophecy was never fulfilled. After the completion of the Temple, no more was heard of Zerubbabel. Perhaps the Persians suspected him of disloyalty and so removed him from office; at any rate, they never appointed any other Davidic prince governor of the region.)[3]

FIRST ZECHARIAH: PROPHET OF APOCALYPTIC VISIONS (ZECH. 1—8)

Virtually all modern scholars now assign the first eight chapters of the book of Zechariah to one author and the last six to one or more writers of a later date. The first part will be treated here as "First Zechariah," and Chapters 9—14 will be considered below as "Second Zechariah."

The historical background of First Zechariah is the same as

---

* The phrase "this people" (2:14) refers to the Samaritans, according to D. Winton Thomas (exegesis to Haggai, *The Interpreter's Bible*, VI, 1047). Julius A. Bewer (*The Prophets*, p. 570) says that the phrase refers to "the people who had remained in the land." It seems likely that the term *Samaritans* was applied not only to those people who during the Exile remained in the northern half of Palestine (around Samaria) but also to those who stayed in what had formerly been the kingdom of Judah.

that of Haggai; both books were begun in 520 B.C., and both hail
Zerubbabel for recommencing the construction of the new Temple.

The first verse of the book says that the author is the son of
Berechiah and grandson of Iddo, both priests; it is believed, however, that this passage is erroneous and that the prophet was the
son instead of the grandson of Iddo.[4] The date of his ministry
like that of Haggai, is pinpointed exactly: it began in the "eighth
month" of 520 B.C. and ended in "the ninth month" of 518 B.C.
(1:1 and 7:1).[5]

First Zechariah pays tribute to the pre-Exilic prophets and
quotes them (1:4 and 7:7-12). The author resembles a number
of them (especially Amos and Micah) in proclaiming that the
Lord is more concerned with ethics than rituals; he shares the
Unknown Prophet's belief in a single, universal God; and, like
Ezekiel, he makes extensive use of divine visions and emphasizes
the importance of the roles of both prophet and priest. He differs
from his predecessors in his feeling of the remoteness of God, his
angelology, and the frequency of his apocalyptic passages.*

The principal points of First Zechariah's message are as follows: (1) the necessity for rebuilding the Temple, (2) the necessity for moral reform among the Jews, (3) the superiority of
ethics to ritualism, and (4) the coming of the Messianic kingdom.

It would be misleading to speak of this prophet's "style," for he
has two styles. Sometimes his language is plain and prosaic but
direct and forceful. At other times, especially when he is describing his "visions," he becomes decidedly poetic; then he gives free
rein to his emotions and his pictorial imagination. Occasionally
his metaphors are fantastic and his symbology is obscure to modern readers. At its best, however, his writing aproaches the sublime.[6]

Summons to Repentance (1:1-6). Although most of First
Zechariah is comforting, it opens with a rather impatient call to
repentance. Yes (the author seems to say to the people), God has
a glorious new Golden Age ready to bestow upon you whenever
you show yourself worthy of it.

---

* It should be remembered, however, that Ezekiel, Second Isaiah, and
Haggai all contain predictions which have been considered apocalyptic.

His first address seems to show the impatience of youth with the natural pessimism of the old. They, he felt, were hindering the work [of rebuilding the Temple] by comparisons of this temple with the former. They must leave the dead past for the living present, and heed the lesson of the failure of their ancestors to listen to God's message [the teaching of the earlier prophets].[7]

Eight Apocalyptic Visions (1:7—6:8, 15). There are many problems to be solved, Zechariah believes, before God will bless his people with the Golden Age. After long meditation the prophet has a series of dream-visions (519 B.C.) in which each problem is presented and then solved.

Especially noteworthy is the difference between Zechariah and most of the earlier prophets in their methods of receiving the divine messages. Unlike Amos, for example, who hears God speak directly to him, Zechariah must rely on dream-visions and angelic messengers. The Deity is now considered too sacred for direct communication with human beings—even with his own prophets. He is no longer present to direct events on earth, but is aloof, remote, and transcendent. He uses dreams to convey information to men, and he employs angels to perform certain deeds in the world and to act as his interpreter.

Angels play a more prominent part in First Zechariah than in any other Old Testament book. We meet at least five different angelic beings (1:11, 2:1, 2:3, 3:1-2, and 3:4). The third of these passages contains the oldest reference in the Old Testament to "Satan," or "the Adversary," one of God's celestial servants, whose function is to accuse men of evil.[*] Zechariah's writing represents a significant step in the development of angelology and demonology, which were later to become important in Judaistic and Christian theology.

THE FOUR HORSES (1:7-17). The political unrest which followed the suicide of King Cambyses and the usurpation of the Persian throne by a pretender (522 B.C.) inspired hopes in the Jews that this might be the beginning of the upheaval which would lead to the establishment of the Messianic kingdom. But then Darius overcame the pretender, acceded to the throne, and brought an era of peace to his empire. The Jews' hopes had

---

[*] Compare Job 1—2, where Satan accuses Job and tests him by inflicting various disasters upon him.

proved to be vain. There was no chance that in the foreseeable future they could throw off the rule of so powerful and secure a monarch. The resultant pessimism and inertia was Zechariah's first "problem."

In order to solve this problem, God sends to the prophet a vision of four horses—two red, one speckled (or sorrel), and one white. A "man" (angel?) is sitting on one of the red horses. Another angel has to explain the meaning to Zechariah: these are God's earth-patrols, and now all the world is at peace. The angel asks the Lord how long his displeasure against Judah will continue, and the Lord answers that he is angry with the nations which have oppressed the Israelites more than he ever intended. Now he will show mercy to Judah, the Temple will be rebuilt, the cities will prosper again, and there will be comfort in Zion.

THE FOUR HORNS AND THE FOUR WORKMEN (1:18-21). Next Zechariah is shown four horns, representing the oppressor nations. Four workmen (divine retribution) come to demolish the horns.

THE CITY WITHOUT A WALL (2:1-5). An angel with a measuring line comes to measure Jerusalem, preparatory to rebuilding the walls. Another angel appears and announces that the city needs no walls, for God "will be unto her a wall of fire round about." Zechariah is here opposing the building of walls probably for two reasons: first, the people should rely on the Lord instead of on walls; and, second, the building of city walls would provide the Samaritans with good ground for accusing the Jews of disloyalty to Persia (compare Neh. 6:5-7).[8]

THE HIGH PRIEST AND THE SATAN (3:1-8, 10). In a fourth vision, Satan accuses Joshua, the High Priest, of being unfit for his office because he is clad in filthy garments (representing contamination from living in Babylon). At God's command, an angel causes the dirty clothing to be removed, for God has approved Joshua's appointment as spiritual head of the people. Furthermore, the Lord will send his servant, the Branch* (Zerubbabel) to be the political leader, the Messiah (3:8).

THE SEVEN-BRANCHED CANDLESTICK AND THE TWO OLIVE TREES (4:1-6, 10-14). In a rather obscure vision, the prophet sees a golden candlestick or lampstand, flanked on each side by an olive

---

* Compare Isa. 11:1. The "Branch" is apparently another term for the "rod of Jesse."

tree. Perhaps the candlestick represents Yahweh, who watches over the world (the seven branches of the candlestick are "the eyes of the Lord" [4:10]); and perhaps the trees represent Joshua and Zerubbabel ("the two anointed ones" [4:14]).

THE FLYING SCROLL (5:1-4). In the sixth and seventh visions, Zechariah sees Israel's sins symbolically removed. First, he sees a "roll," or scroll, flying through the air. On it is written the Lord's curse upon those guilty of theft and perjury—two sins which must be purged before the community can be ready for the Messianic Age. The scroll will consume both timber and stones of the sinners' houses.

THE WOMAN IN THE BARREL (5:5-11). Sin is next personified as a woman, who is trying to escape from a barrel ("ephah") in which she is enclosed. In a striking bit of allegory, an angel thrusts the leaden lid back on the barrel, and two women (angels?) fly away with it—Sin still inside—to the land of Shinar (Babylon). Thus Zechariah teaches that sin in general is the greatest enemy of mankind and must be overcome by God.[9]

THE FOUR CHARIOTS (6:1-8, 15). In the final vision, Zechariah beholds four chariots coming from between two brass mountains. Though the interpretation is a matter of dispute, apparently the chariots represent God's agents of force, which patrol the whole earth. One chariot is sent to "the north country" (Babylon), either to punish that nation or to round up the remaining Hebrew exiles and bring them back to their homeland.[10]

Zerubbabel as Messiah (6:9-14). Zechariah is instructed by the Lord to take some gold and silver which certain returnees have brought back from Babylon and to make therewith a crown for the head of the Branch (Zerubbabel).* After building the Temple, this Messiah will rule upon the throne, and he and the High Priest will co-operate to bring harmony and peace to the nation.

Epilogue: Fasting versus Morality (Chs. 7—8). About two years after seeing the eight visions, Zechariah is visited by a dep-

---

* Zech. 6:11 speaks of two crowns and says that they are to be set on the head of Joshua, not Zerubbabel. This confusion may be explained by the belief that the text has been tampered with. At first it mentioned only one crown, and that was for Zerubbabel. After his removal, apparently, some editor substituted Joshua's name, thereby transferring the messiahship to the high priest. The word *crowns* should read *crown*. See D. Winton Thomas, exegesis to Zechariah, *The Interpreter's Bible*, VI, 1080.

utation from Bethel, which seeks to learn from the prophet and the priests of the city whether the Lord wants them to continue the fasts observing the destruction of Jerusalem and the Temple and the assassination of Gedaliah. The inquiry gives Zechariah an excellent opportunity to express the belief (derived from the eighth-century prophets) that fasting and other rituals are unimportant in the eyes of God, who is far more interested in righteous living. He will restore joy and prosperity to the Jews when they practice justice and honesty. Then the city will be so happy that men from foreign lands will behold their joy and will join them in worshiping the great and beneficent God who has so blessed them.

THIRD ISAIAH: MISCELLANEOUS RELIGIOUS WRITINGS
(ISA. 56—66)

It is only for the sake of convenience that most commentators and exegetes refer to the last eleven chapters of the book of Isaiah as "Third Isaiah." Indeed, it would be more accurate to speak of Third, Fourth, Fifth, and Sixth Isaiahs, for these chapters were apparently written at different times not by one man but by four; they were consolidated at some time between 520 and 470 B.C.[11]

"A Praying Saint" (63:7—64:11). In a penitential prayer, obviously written during the Exile, the suppliant asks for forgiveness and aid. The Hebrews are still oppressed: Jerusalem is a "desolation," and God's "holy and beautiful house" has been "burned up with fire" (63:17, 64:10-11). The "saint" confesses the sins of the people and begs the Lord to redeem them in his love and pity as he did in the days of Moses. Emphasis is placed on God's fatherhood, his mercy, and his holiness.

"A Warner and Reprover" (56:9—57:14; 57:21—58:12; 59:1-15a; 65:1-16; 66:1-5, 17). Breathing the admonitory spirit of the pre-Exilic prophets, this stern spokesman protests vehemently against the rebuilding of the Temple for fear that the people will once again neglect true morality and devote themselves to meaningless sacrifices and other ritualistic practices. The heaven is God's throne, and the earth is his footstool; what need has he of a house built by hands (66:1-4)? The prophet also denounces as idolatrous the Jews' syncretistic practices—that is, their adaptation to pagan rites (57:3-13, 65:1-16, 66:5). He rebukes the leaders for their indolence and greed (56:9—57:2) and the people for their perverseness, vanity, injustice, deceitfulness, violence, and bloodshed (58:1-2, 59:1-8). He promises, however, that God will forgive and comfort the penitent and "revive the heart of the contrite ones" (57:14-21, 59:9-15a).

"Prophet of Hope and Consolation" (60—62, 63:1-6; 65:17-25; 66:6-16, 18-24). Very different in spirit and teaching from the stern reprover is the third of the authors presently being considered. For him the Temple is of paramount importance (60:7), and he speaks more words of comfort than of reproof. Like the author of Second Isaiah, he rejoices over God's promises of deliverance and over the glories of the New Jerusalem; but *unlike* this prophet, he is more interested in Israel's pre-eminence among the nations than in universal salvation (60:1-14, 16, 61:5). Strongly nationalistic, he exults over the Lord's vengeance which is to fall upon Israel's enemies, especially Edom (63:1-6).

"A Torah Teacher" (56:1-8, 58:13-14). Writing at some time after the completion of the new Temple and the resumption of worship there, a priestly teacher, deeply interested in the interpretation of the Law advocates that eunuchs and proselytes be allowed to worship in the Temple, "a house of prayer for all people" (56:7). True religion is determined, he says, not by race or body, but by observance of God's Sabbaths and by obedience to his Laws. "Here is the compromise between prophetic and priestly religion characteristic of most postexilic prophets."[12]

OBADIAH: PROPHET OF VENGEANCE

The short book of Obadiah is notable not as a record of lofty religious views but as a forceful expression of hatred and thirst for revenge. It is directed against Edom, the traditional enemy of Israel.* According to Genesis 25:22-23 and 27:39-40, enmity between the two nations had its origin in the strife between Jacob and Esau (legendary progenitors, respectively, of the Israelites and Edomites) even while they were together in their mother's womb. It seems likely that economic and commercial rivalry was the real cause of the enmity.[13] At any rate, David had conquered Edom in the tenth century, and it did not regain its independence until the Syro-Ephraemitic war of 735-734 B.C.[14] Especially galling to the Israelites was the fact that the Edomites

---

* Compare Ps. 137:7; Isa. 34:5-17 and 63:1-6; Lam. 4:21-22; and Ezek. 25:12-14 and 35:1—36:7.

allied themselves with the Chaldeans in 586 B.C. and occupied the southern part of Judah (the region which in Roman days was known as Idumea, after the Edomites).

Obadiah prophesies that Edom will be invaded and its people expelled as a punishment for their perfidy to Judah. Scholarly opinion is divided as to whether the first portion of the book (1-14, 15b) was written during the Exile or about 460 B.C., at which time the Nabatean Arabs were threatening the country.[15]

The second portion of the book (15a, 16-21), of uncertain date, predicts the coming of the "Day of the Lord," when the Jews themselves will drive the Edomites out of Judah and rule over them as God's deputies.[16]

MALACHI: PROPHET TO THE DISILLUSIONED

By the middle of the fifth century B.C. many of the Israelites in Jerusalem had become discouraged and disillusioned. Even after the completion of the Temple in 516 B.C., the glory and the prosperity promised by the Exilic and the early post-Exilic prophets failed to descend upon the Jews; instead there were the same old hardships: poverty, famine, and the hostility of the neighboring peoples. As in the days of Ezekiel, many began to ask, "Does God still love us? Is he entirely indifferent to our welfare? *Is* there a God, after all?" They became increasingly negligent of their religious and moral obligations. The priests, infected with the apathy and frustration of the people, neglected the performance of their official duties. Under these conditions the prophet known as Malachi delivered his message.

"Malachi" was not his real name. The term, which means "my messenger," was borrowed from 3:1 by some early editor and erroneously used in 1:1 as the appellation of the prophet. Nothing is known of his life. A reference to the defeat of Edom (by the Nabatean Arabs) indicates that the date of his ministry was *c.* 460-450 B.C.

The tone of the book is argumentative rather than revelatory. Malachi does not speak as one who expects his words to be believed because they have been dictated by God; instead he tries to persuade the people by logical disputation. Often he uses the dialectic method, quoting one of the people's questions and then answering it. As befits this method, the book is written entirely in prose.

The problem discussed by Malachi is fundamentally that of the book of Job: the "problem of evil." In effect, the people have complained that God has not dealt with them according to their deserts. Why should they suffer so greatly when they have not sinned greatly? Is God either indifferent or unjust? Malachi's book is a threefold argument in response to the people's complaint.[17]

Argument One: Some Suffering Is the Consequence of Sin (1:6—3:15). In agreement with the Deuteronomist, most of the pre-Exilic prophets, and Job's "comforters," Malachi contends that some of the Jews hardships are the just punishments for their sins. The priests have offered imperfect ("polluted") sacrifices, whereas the Law requires that each offering be "unblemished" (Deut. 15:21). Would those same priests dare to offer a lame or sick or blind animal to the Persian governor as a gift? If so, would the governor be pleased? Yet they dare to insult God with such third-rate offerings.* Furthermore, the priests have not been good instructors. They are supposed as messengers of God to teach the people to turn away from iniquity. But these priests have perverted the ancient convenant of God with the Levites (1:6—2:9).

As for the people, they have committed numerous sins. They have married Gentiles, who worship heathen gods, thereby threatening to pollute the pure Yahweh worship of the Jews (2:11-13).

Transcending the Mosaic Law (Deut. 24:1-4) and presupposing monogamy,[18] Malachi bluntly opposes the practice of divorce.† The Jewish men have been setting aside their wives unjustifiably —merely because they wanted to marry younger or more beautiful or richer women. But God hates "putting away" (2:16), for marriage is a covenant in his sight.

The people have, furthermore, been guilty of sorcery, adultery, perjury, and oppression of the poor, the widows, and the orphans (3:5). In addition, they have been negligent in tithing and in keeping their religious vows, thereby "robbing God" himself

---

* In a disputed passage (1:11), Malachi seems to intimate that those Gentiles who sacrifice earnestly and sincerely are really worshiping Yahweh—the one, universal God—whether they are aware of it or not. Compare Zeph. 2:11 and John 4:23. See Bewer, *The Prophets*, p. 594n.

† Here he anticipates Jesus' teachings. See Mark 10:2-12.

(3:6-8). If the people will bring in their offerings, God will cause them to prosper again so that all nations will see how blessed the Israelites are.

Argument Two: God Does Care for Israel, for He Has Punished Edom (1:2-5). In a brief passage, somewhat reminiscent of Obadiah, Malachi declares that God is not indifferent to Israel; He has proved his love—and his justice—by destroying the Edomites, "the people against whom the Lord hath indignation forever."

Argument Three: Full Justice Will Come in the Day of the Lord (3:16—4:6). In an apocalyptic and eschatological section, Malachi argues that although some of the people are now suffering more than they deserve, eventually God will make sure that everybody will receive his just reward or punishment. A great day of reckoning is coming, when those who have feared and served the Lord will become his "jewels"; their names are written in his "book of remembrance" (3:13-18). But as for the wicked, when the "Day" comes, they will be burned as in an oven, like stubble; of them the Lord will leave neither root nor branch (4:1).

An appendix (4:4-6), believed to be an interpolation, predicts that the prophet Elijah will return as a messenger to annouce the coming of the "dreadful day of the Lord."*

JOEL: PROPHET OF THE COMING
OF THE LORD'S SPIRIT

There is no specific evidence of historical background or date of composition for the book of Joel. Various scholars have suggested different dates, ranging from the eighth to the second century B.C. On the basis of what appear to be references to sacrifices in the Temple (1:13-14), to the Dispersion of the Jews (3:2), and to Greek slave traders (3:6), the most likely date is the period 400-350 B.C.

Outside of the book itself, nothing is known of Joel. We may infer from his exclusive interest in Judah and its capital city that he was an inhabitant of Jerusalem.

---

* Compare Mark 6:15 and 9:4, 11. It should be remembered that many Jews considered John the Baptist a reincarnation of Elijah.

The occasion for the writing of the book was an unprecedented devastation of the land by a swarm of locusts, which the prophet interprets as a forewarning of the approach of the Day of the Lord.

All but eight verses are in poetic form. The intense emotions of the author find outlet in several lyrical outbursts and in glowing and colorful figures of speech.

Joel seems more interested than most Old Testament prophets in the outward manifestation of repentance, fasting, public lamentation, mourning in sackcloth, offering of sacrifices, and assembling for religious assemblies. However, as indicated in 2:13 ("Rend your hearts and not your garments"), he views these rituals as symbols of moral reform.

The Plague of Locusts (1:1—2:27). The first portion of the book is devoted to a consideration of the devastation caused by the locusts and a plea to the people to prove their repentance by external demonstrations of grief.

The visitation of the locusts, followed by a terrible drought, has left the land desolate:

> For a nation is come up upon my land,
> Strong, and without number,
> Whose teeth are the teeth of a lion,
> And he hath the cheek teeth of a great lion.
> He hath laid my vine waste,
> And barked my fig tree:
> He hath made it clean and bare, and cast it away;
> The branches thereof are made white. (1:6-7)

(The "nation," of course, means the locusts.) The prophet pleads with the priests and the people to lament and to fast and to bring sacrificial offerings to the Lord. He prays God to deliver them from their great tribulation, and he promises the people that if they repent, God will restore their prosperity.

There have been several attempts to interpret the locust plague allegorically or apocalyptically, but these interpretations seem far-fetched and unconvincing; there is no good reason for believing that Joel's picture is anything other than a literal and realistic description of a local catastrophe in ancient Palestine.[19]

The Lord's Judgment (2:28—3:21). The latter third of the book is apocalyptic. The great Judgment Day of the Lord is approaching, an event of which the locusts have been the precursors. Other portents will signal the nearer approach of the Day:

> And I will show wonders in the heaven and in the earth,
> Blood, and fire, and pillars of smoke.
> The sun shall be turned into darkness,
> And the moon into blood,
> Before the great and the terrible day of the Lord come.* (2:30-31)

Many people will be so filled with the Spirit of the Lord that they will become prophets or seers:

> And it shall come to pass afterward,
> That I will pour out my Spirit upon all flesh;
> And your sons and your daughters shall prophesy,
> Your old men shall dream dreams,
> Your young men shall see visions ... (2:28)†

All the nations will be summoned into "the valley of decision" (3:14) and will be judged there by the Lord. There will be a great and final battle between the forces of evil (notably, the Philistines, Tyrians, Sidonians, Edomites, and Egyptians) and the forces of good (the people of Judah, aided by God.‡ Joel advises the nations:

> Beat your plowshares into swords,
> And your pruninghooks into spears. (3:10)

This is a startling adaptation of the famous words found in Isaiah 2:4 and Micah 4:3. Despite all the wicked will be able to do, God will destroy them. As for the righteous,

... it shall come to pass, that whosoever shall call on the name of the Lord shall be delivered: for in mount Zion and in Jerusalem shall be deliverance, as the Lord hath said, and in the remnant whom the Lord shall call. (2:32)§

---

* Compare the apocalyptic passages in Amos 8:9, Isa. 13:10, Ezek. 32:7-11, Mal. 4:5, Matt. 24:29, Mark 13:24-25, Luke 21:11 and 25, and Rev. 14:14-20.

† Compare the Pentecostal visitations of the Holy Spirit as recounted in Acts 2:1-4. Peter quotes this passage from Joel to the assembly on the day of Pentecost (Acts 2:17-21).

‡ Compare the description of Battle of Armageddon, Rev. 16:12-16.

§ Paul interprets this passage as an offer to all peoples (Rom. 10:13); Peter seems to limit it to the Jews (Acts 2:17-21).

At last Judah and Jerusalem will enter the glorious Golden
Age:

> And it shall come to pass in that day,
> That the mountains shall drop down new wine,
> And the hills shall flow with milk,
> And all the rivers of Judah shall flow with waters, . . .
> But Judah shall dwell for ever,
> And Jerusalem from generation to generation. (3:18, 20)

SECOND ZECHARIAH: PROPHECY OF THE
HUMBLE MESSIAH (ZECH. 9—14)

Virtually all modern scholars believe that the last six chapters
of the book of Zechariah (often called "Second Zechariah") were
not written by the author of the first eight chapters. There are
linguistic, ideological, and historical differences between the two
parts. There is much disagreement, however, over the date of
composition, historical background, and authorship of Second
Zechariah. The matter is far too complicated to be explored in
detail here.[20] Suffice it to say that a number of comentators have
reached the following concusions: (1) Second Zechariah was
written during some period of oppression between the Macedonian defeat of Persia (333 B.C.) and the beginning of the Maccabean era (*c.* 165 B.C.), and (2) the work falls into three distinct
parts (Chs. 9—11, 12—13, and 14), each by a different author.
Sometimes Chapters 12—14 are considered a unit designated as
Third Zechariah.

As a whole, the book adds little to the development of Hebrew theology. Like several other prophetic books, it foretells the
coming of the Messiah, the victorious war against God's enemies,
and the establishment of the Messianic kingdom with Jerusalem
as center. Its teachings, however, are on a relatively low theological level: the Messiah is depicted as pre-eminently a political
leader; there is a revival of the conception of Yahweh as the God
of war; and the New Jerusalem is not primarily the center of
universal brotherhood and love but rather a shrine to which all
nations will be required to make an annual pilgrimage in observance of the Jewish "Feast of the Tabernacles."[21]

Although Second Zechariah does not help to ennoble the Hebrew conception of God and his ways, it does contain four sig-

nificant passages—significant because the authors of the New
Testament interpreted them as prophecies about Jesus.

The Humble Messiah (9:9-10). The prophet calls upon the
people to rejoice, for their Messiah is coming. But his arrival will
not be accompanied by pomp and fanfare. Instead he will come

> Lowly, and riding upon an ass,
> And upon a colt the foal of an ass. (9:9)

Both Matthew (21:5) and John (12:12-15) quote this passage
and consider it a specific prediction of Jesus' Triumphal Entry
into Jerusalem.

**The Rejected Shepherd and the Thirty Pieces of Silver (11:4-
14).** An enigmatic and variously interpreted passage tells about
a good shepherd who tried vainly to lead the people, was
rejected by them, and was sold for thirty pieces of silver.[22]
Matthew's Gospel (27:3-10) considers Jesus' rejection by the Jews
and his betrayal by Judas a fulfillment of this prophecy.

The Pierced Body (12:10—14). The prophet predicts a "great
mourning" for some man who is going to be murdered:

And I will pour upon the house of David, and upon the inhabitants of
Jerusalem, the spirit of grace and of supplications: and they shall look
upon me whom they have pierced, and they shall mourn for him, as one
mourneth for his only son, and shall be in bitterness for him, as one that
is in bitterness for his firstborn. (12:10)

The Gospel of John (19:37) and the book of Revelation (1:7)
see in this passage an allusion to the wounding of Christ on the
Cross.

**The Death of the Shepherd and the Scattering of the Sheep
(13:7).**[23]

> Awake, O sword, against my shepherd,
> And against the man that is my fellow,
> Saith the Lord of hosts:
> ᾽Smite the shepherd,
> And the sheep shall be scattered:
> And I will turn my hand upon the little ones.

According to the Gospels of Matthew (26:31) and Mark (14:27),
Jesus himself quoted this passage as a prediction of his death
and the scattering of his disciples.

BARUCH, WITH THE EPISTLE OF JEREMIAH:
LAST OF THE BOOKS OF PROPHECY

The only book of the Apocrypha which may be classified as prophetic literature is ascribed to Baruch, the amanuensis of the prophet Jeremiah (see Jer. 36:4-10). It purports to have been written about 582 B.C. (1:1-3). Actually the book is a composite, made up of four parts and written by at least three different hands; none of the parts was composed before the fourth century B.C., and one may have been as late as the first century A.D. Whether the original language of the first three parts was Hebrew or Greek is still a matter of dispute; the fourth section was probably written first in Hebrew or Aramaic.[24]

Repentance and Redemption (1:1—3:8). This part is in prose. The opening passage (1:1-13) states that the book was written by Baruch in the fifth year after the fall of Jerusalem and that it has been read to some of the exiles, who have been so moved that they are sending a collection of money to the sufferers in the stricken capital of Judah. The remainder of this part (which contains several echoes of the book of Daniel) consists of two confessions of the Hebrews' sins, with a brief review of their history (1:15–2:10, 2:20-26); two prayers for God's mercy (2:11-19, 3:1-8); and a prediction that the people will repent and be allowed to return to their own land (2:27-35).

God's Wisdom (3:9—4:4). The second section is poetry and is evidently *not* by the author of the first. It praises God for his everlasting wisdom and for revealing part of that wisdom to the Hebrews in the Law. Israel has been punished because she has disobeyed that Law and forsaken her God.

Words of Comfort (4:5—5:9). Strongly reminiscent of Second Isaiah, the third division (in poetic form) consists chiefly of songs of hope and comfort. Its picture of Jerusalem lamenting for its children (4:9-29) recalls the book of Lamentations. Although God reproaches the Jews for their sins, he promises them that Jerusalem will be restored, that they will return to Palestine, and that their enemies will be humbled. Some portions of this section achieve real lyrical excellence.

The Letter of Jeremiah (Ch. 6). The final section* purports to be a letter from Jeremiah to the Babylonian exiles. A vehement sermon against idolatry, it is based on one verse from the canonical book of Jeremiah: "Thus shall ye say unto them, 'The gods that have not made the heavens and the earth, even they shall perish from the earth, and from under these heavens'" (10:11). The letter points out the utter folly of worshiping idols, for every one of them is as useless "as a scarecrow in a garden of cucumbers."[25] The only pagan deity singled out for condemnation (v. 4) is Bel (or Marduk, or Tammuz), the Babylonian god of vegetation. Early Christian apologists found this Hebrew polemic useful in their attacks on paganism.[26]

---

* In some Greek, Syriac, and Arabic manuscripts this letter is placed after Lamentations. In some other Greek and Syriac versions, in the Latin, and in most English Bibles that include the Apocrypha it is appended to the book of Baruch; in the King James Version it is Ch. 6 of Baruch. The Revised Standard Version makes it a separate book. See Bruce M. Metzger, *An Introduction to the Apocrypha* (New York: Oxford University Press, 1957), p. 95.

Part Four
Lyric Poetry

The Bible abounds in lyric poetry. Numerous songs adorn the even essentially prose books—hymns of praise, victory songs, dirges, and other types. Lamech's Song of the Sword (Gen. 4: 23-24), Deborah's Song (Judges 5:2-31), David's Lament for Saul and Jonathan (II Sam. 1:19-27), the Song of Vanity (Eccles. 1:2-11), Mary's Magnificat (Luke 1:46-55) and the angel's prophetic song (Luke 1:32-35), the Destruction of Babylon (Rev. 18:21-24)—these examples give some idea of the prevalence and the variety of Biblical lyrics. In addition to the hundreds of songs interspersed throughout the Scriptures, much of the prophetic and "wisdom" literature of the Bible is lyrical in nature.

Although scholars recognized long ago that many Biblical passages were poetic, it was not until relatively recent years that in some editions of the Bible these passages were printed in verse form. This fact becomes more understandable when we examine the techniques and devices conventionally employed by the Hebrew poets.

Unlike modern English poetry, Hebrew verse depends neither on rhyme nor on a regular arrangement of accented and unaccented syllables; it relies, instead, on (1) parallelism, (2) rhythm, (3) strophic division, and (4) sometimes acrostic structure or other stylistic devices.[1]

(1) *Parallelism* means the similarity in grammatical structure of two or more thought-units which are similar, complementary, or antithetical in meaning. It was Bishop Robert Lowth who (in 1753) first called attention to parallelism as the most prominent feature of Hebrew poetry. He recognized the first three characteristics listed below; later scholars have added the others.

237

(*a*) *Synonymous*: using different words but similar structure to express two or more similar ideas:

> The heavens declare the glory of God;
> And the firmament sheweth his handywork. (Ps. 19:1)

(*b*) *Antithetical*: expressing in similar structure two ideas which are antithetic to (or in contrast with) each other:

> For the Lord knoweth the way of the righteous:
> But the way of the ungodly shall perish. (Ps. 1:6)

(*c*) *Synthetical*: supplementing one thought-unit by another of similar structure:

> I cried unto the Lord with my voice,
> And he heard me out of his holy hill. (Ps. 3:4)

(*d*) *Introverted*: in a four-line strophe, having corresponding structure of the first line with the fourth and of the second with the third:

> My son, if thine heart be wise,
> My heart shall rejoice, even mine.
> Yea, my reins shall rejoice,
> When thy lips speak right things. (Prov. 23:15-16)

(*e*) *Stairlike*: repeating words or their equivalents with some additions to express a progression in thought:

> Give unto the Lord, O ye mighty,
> Give unto the Lord glory and strength.
> Give unto the Lord the glory due unto his name. (Ps. 29:1-2)

(*f*) *Emblematic*: using similar structure for both the literal description of an idea and a metaphor or simile based on it:

> As a dog returneth to his vomit,
> So a fool returneth to his folly. (Prov. 26:11)

(2) *Rhythm.* To speak of the meter of Biblical poetry would be somewhat misleading, for the ancient Hebrews were unacquainted with "meter" in the modern sense of the term. Their verse, however, does have rhythm. As in Old English poetry, this rhythm is achieved by using in each line a fixed number of accented syllables and an indeterminate number of unaccented ones. Each rhythmical unit—called a *stich*—contains two, three, or four strongly accented words (or phrases); the unaccented

words vary not only in number but also in arrangement. The most common verse form is the *distich*, or couplet, made up of two stichs; there are also the *tristich* (three stichs) and the *tetrastich* (four stichs). In each of these groups the stichs are usually bound to each other by parallelism. The rhythm which occurs most frequently in the distich is 3+3; that is, three accents appear in each stich. Other common rhythms are 3+2, 2+3, 2+2, 4+4, and 2+2+2.* Here are some examples:

> A soft-answer turneth-away wrath:
> But grievous-words stir-up anger. (3+3, Prov. 15:1)

> As coals are to burning-coals, and wood to fire;
> So is a contentious man to kindle strife. (4+4, Prov. 26:21)[2]

(3) *Strophic division.* In addition to the groupings determined by rhythm and parallelism, larger units (not always of equal length), which may be called "strophes" or "stanzas," are sometimes indicated by the nature of the contents or by the use of a refrain. For example, Psalm 19 consists of five strophes, the breaks coming after verses 4a, 6, 10, and 13; and Psalm 23 is probably divided into three strophes: verses 1-3, 4, and 5-6.

(4) *Acrostic structure.* Some Hebrew poems (Pss. 9, 10, 25, 34, 37, 111, 112, 119, and 145; Prov. 31:10-13; and Lam. 1–4)[3] employ the acrostic principle; that is, each stich, line, or group of lines begins with a selected Hebrew letter; usually the arrangement follows alphabetical sequence.

In addition to these four most important poetic devices—parallelism, rhythm, strophic division, and acrostic structure—Hebrew poetry occasionally makes use of assonance, alliteration, and rhyme. These features, along with the acrostics, are seldom preserved in English translations.

Although numerous Biblical books contain lyrical passages, only four books fall definitely into the category of lyric poetry. These are Psalms, Lamentations, The Song of the Three Holy Children, and The Prayer of Manasses.

---

* Although most English translators have made no attempt to reproduce the patterns of accents found in the Hebrew text, rhythmical structure similar to that of the original is generally observable in the translations—especially so in the King James Version.

The Psalms: A Hymnbook for Jews and Christians

One of the most widely read and most beloved books in the Bible is Psalms. The ancient Hebrews, the early Christians, and all succeeding generations, both Jewish and Gentile, have turned to it for poetic expression of their religious sentiments. It and the Gospels were the Biblical books most frequently translated into Middle English; a crudely metrical version intended for singing to English tunes was the first book published in America*; and even today Psalms is sometimes singled out as the only Old Testament book to be bound in one volume with the New. Martin Luther called it a "Bible in miniature" and "the immortal song book of the human heart," and John Calvin praised it as "the mirror of man."

The title *Psalms* is derived from Latin *psalmi,* which in turn comes from the Greek *psalmoi,* "sacred songs chanted with accompaniment";[4] this word is a derivative of the classical Greek *psalmos,* signifying the "twanging of strings."[5] The Septuagint uses *psalmoi* to translate the Hebrew title *Tehillim,* meaning "Praises."[6] One manuscript of the Septuagint (Codex Alexandrinus) entitles the book *Psalterion* (whence our word *Psalter*); originally *psalterion* denoted a stringed instrument, but eventually it came to mean the songs sung or chanted to such an instrument.[7]

The Psalms were the products of numerous poets. By tradition seventy-three are ascribed to David, twelve to one Asaph, eleven to the "sons of Korah," two to Solomon, and one each to Moses, Heman the Ezrahite, and Ethan the Ezrahite; the other forty-nine Psalms are called the "orphans," for they have not been

* *The Bay Psalm Book,* 1640.

traditionally assigned to any author.[8] However, most modern scholars doubt the accuracy of the ancient attributions of authorship. It seems exceedingly unlikely that Moses or Solomon wrote the Psalms ascribed to them. As for David, it is possible that he wrote some; certainly he had the reputation of being a musician and poet (see, for example, I Sam. 16:16-18, II Sam. 1:19-27, and Amos 6:5). But few critics today believe that he wrote very many of the seventy-three Psalms attributed to him, and not a single Psalm "can be pointed out which everyone would recognize as David's."[9]

Ascertaining the dates of composition of the individual Psalms is usually impossible. A few can be ascribed to certain eras with confidence. For example, the yearning for Jerusalem and the violent hatred for the Babylonians expressed in Psalm 137 are convincing evidence that this poem was written during the Exile —between 586 and 538 B.C.; but most of the Psalms are less specific in reference. Some literary historians believe that a small number were originated as far back as the days of David and Solomon and that many are pre-Exilic. Other commentators doubt such antiquity and maintain that all the poems in the Psalter were composed either during or after the Exile—some, perhaps during the Maccabean period.[10] It seems likely that "generally the psalms came from postexilic times and represent the life of the Jews during this troubled period of history."[11]

There are many indications that the Psalms were collected from a variety of sources over a long period of time: repetitions, duplications, superscriptions assigning specific Psalms to authors of different periods, the use of *Yahweh* in one group and of *Elohim* in another. Professors C. A. Dinsmore and J. R. Macarthur think that the formation of the Psalter extended over a period of eight centuries.[12] Almost everybody agrees that the Psalms —at least some of them—were the "hymnbook of the Second Temple."[13] The collection was complete and the canon closed by 100 B.C.—and perhaps several decades earlier.[14]

The literary excellence of these poems lies principally in (1) the concreteness of their imagery, (2) the simplicity and naturalness of their diction, (3) the sincerity of their convictions, and (4) the universality of the emotions which many express.

More successfully than most other poets, the Psalmists were able to "visualize their emotions,"[15] to transform their thoughts and feelings into concrete images and compelling metaphors. For example, instead of saying, "I was greatly relieved," the Psalmist exclaims:

> Thou hast turned my mourning into dancing;
> Thou hast put off my sackcloth and girded me with gladness.
>
> (30:11)

God is not only the Creator, but also a shepherd, a refuge, a fortress, a sun, a shield, a rock, a tower, and a dwelling place for all generations; these are objects which we can see and touch —not abstractions.[16] Incidentally, this pictorial method of describing the emotions simplifies a translator's task of carrying over into another language the beauty and the force of the original Hebrew.[17]

Two of the greatest sources of the power of the Psalms are their simplicity and their sincerity. "Born in extreme crises, they came from the heart and are not the efflorescence of the imagination."[18] They are not the creations of "an idle singer of an empty day," nor are they the products of poets who sought deliberately to win literary distinction by "making something fine." Instead, the Psalms "are the embodiment of intensely real emotions."[19] Like most great lyrics, they are the "spontaneous overflow of powerful feeling."

The fervent and profound emotions which flowed from the Psalmists are usually the emotions common to all mankind.

The Psalms find people because they express in such worthy form the emotions which are both universal and elemental—thirst for God, the sense of unworthiness, the struggle with doubt, the confidence and peace which come from hiding in the shelter of the Most High. They place man directly before the Eternal and then utter the moods arising from this relationship.[20]

It is the "variety of mental and spiritual attitude that gives the Psalter its universal quality. It becomes the mirror of the soul."[21] In it we find a reflection of nearly every type of religious experience: trust in God, gratitude to God, remorse for sin, yearning for forgiveness and cleansing, love for God's law, the mystical communion with God, praise of God, adoration of God, impatience with God, hatred for God's enemies—the list could go on and on.[22]

Although the Psalms are the records of many different moods,

attitudes, and points of view, there are several basic concepts and
beliefs which the majority of the Psalmists share:[23] (1) God is
the one and only God, the creator and ruler of heaven, earth,
and man. He is the controller of history and natural phenomena. His attributes are power, justice, mercy, and love. He
has concern for each individual, but is especially interested in
the Israelites, whom he has chosen to reveal him to the rest of
the world. Despite the prevailing monotheism, there are a few passages (for example, Pss. 82:1, 86:8, 89:6, 95:3, and 138:1) which
"imply a polytheistic theology"[24]—probably a carry-over from
early times; but even these passages make Yahweh supreme—"a
great God, and a great King above all gods" (95:3). (2) Man
is God's most wonderful creation. He has been endowed with
reason, a conscience, and freedom of the will. He suffers when
he breaks God's laws, but is restored to God's favor when he
repents. Often it is difficult to determine whether a Psalmist is
speaking of man or of himself as an individual or is speaking
symbolically of the Hebrew nation. (3) Rewards and punishments are meted out in this life. (The Psalms present no clear
notion of immortality, but a few passages may hint at a life
after death.) (4) Righteousness will triumph eventually. Several
Psalms (for example, Psalm 2) seem to be Messianic, and some
have been interpreted from time to time as prophecies of Jesus.
(5) External nature, though under God's control, has been given
to man for his sustenance, protection, and enjoyment. It should
be noted that there is little or no "pure" nature poetry in the
Psalms; that is, the Psalmists rarely refer to such phenomena as
mountains, flowers, rocks, and thunderstorms except as manifestations or illustrations of God's power or goodness.

The ancient Hebrew canon divided the Psalter into five sections (probably to correspond vaguely with the five books of
the Law): Psalms 1–41, 42–72, 73–89, 90–106, and 107–150;
each section ends with a doxology. Such a division was arbitrary.
Psalms of many sorts are "scattered promiscuously"[25] throughout all five sections, and little attempt is made to preserve the
integrity of the several collections which were combined to form
the Psalter. Various scholars have tried to classify the Psalms
according to their contents, but the diversity of the subject
matter makes classification difficult.[26] This Outline will not endeavor to classify every Psalm, but will discuss representative
Psalms under the following headings: (1) community songs of

praise, thanksgiving, and trust; (2) monodies of praise, thanks-giving, and trust; (3) laments of the community; (4) laments of the individual; (5) royal Psalms; (6) blessings and curses; (7) pilgrim Psalms; (8) legends; and (9) Psalms of "wisdom" and philosophic meditation. It should be kept in mind that these classes are not mutually exclusive; many Psalms might logically be assigned to two or more groups. Psalm 137, for example, could be labeled either a lament or a curse, and Psalm 134 is both a hymn of praise and a pilgrim song.

GROUP I. COMMUNITY SONGS OF PRAISE, THANKSGIVING, AND TRUST

One of the largest categories consists of congregational or community hymns exhorting worshipers to praise, offering thanks to God for his manifold blessings, and expressing confident trust in him.

Psalm 8: The Majesty of God.[27] This is one of the most sublime Psalms. God's name is glorified all over the world, the Psalmist sings, because of the magnificence of his creation of the earth and the heavens. And what is man's place in this cosmic order? He is the greatest of God's handiwork—only "a little lower than the angels," "crowned . . . with glory and honor," and dignified by having authority over all other living creatures. The Psalm ends with the doxology which opens it—as if to warn man against allowing the contemplation of his own greatness to cause him to forget to praise and glorify God.[28]

Psalm 24: The King of Glory. Obviously a processional an-them, this Psalm was probably once part of an important liturgi-cal rite. Originally it may have been sung at the annual Jewish festival of the New Year, in which God was symbolically en-throned as king of the universe—a rite practiced also by the Egyptians and the Babylonians.[29] Some commentators suggest that the last four verses may even date from the days of King Solomon and celebrate the bringing of the Ark into the new Temple at Jerusalem (I Kings 8).[30]

The Psalm consists of three strophes. The first (vv. 1-2), like Psalm 8, praises God as Creator of the universe. The second (vv. 3-6), in question-and-answer form, describes those people who are suitable to worship in God's Temple—those who are free of sin and who have pure hearts. The third strophe (vv. 7-10) is antiphonal (that is, sung by a choir divided into two

parts which sing in response to each other).* As the procession
nears the gates of the Temple, it requests those gates to open
themselves, so that the King of Glory can come in. The gates
(personified, and represented by the other half of the choir,
which is perhaps already inside the Temple) ask repeatedly
who the King of Glory is. The approaching procession answers
with the triumphant paean:

> The Lord strong and mighty,
> The Lord mighty in battle. . . .
> The Lord of Hosts, he is the King of Glory.

Psalm 46: "Luther's Psalm." This is the anthem which Martin
Luther transmuted into the powerful Reformation hymn "A
Mighty Fortress" (*Ein' Feste Burg*). Originally it may have com-
memorated some particular crisis in Jewish history—Sennacherib's
invasion of the eighth century B.C., the Alexandrian wars of the
fourth century, or the post-Alexandrian revolutions of the early
third century. Some commentators have called attention to the
eschatological elements in the poem (that is, those elements concerned with the "end of things," the end of the world, or God's
final judgment). One critic considers it another "enthronement
hymn," like Psalm 24.[31]

Whatever its origin, certainly the Psalm is a majestic lyric
proclaiming trust in God in time of peril and tribulation, and
expressing confidence that at some time God will cause wars to
cease and will be recognized by all the nations as Ruler of the
universe.

Some especially familiar lines are the following:

> God is our refuge and strength,
> A very present help in time of trouble. . . .
> Be still, and I know that I am God. (Vv. 1, 10)

Psalm 100: "Old Hundred." Known also as the *Jubilate* (from
the first word of the Latin version, meaning "Rejoice"), this

---

* The word *Selah*, which occurs at the end of vv. 6 and 10 (and at sixty-eight
other places in the Psalter and at three in Habakkuk) is obscure in meaning.
It is probably either a direction to the singers to lift their voices or a "rest,"
indicating an instrumental interlude. See Chamberlin and Feldman, *The
Dartmouth Bible*, p. 468, and W. Stewart McCullough, introduction to Psalms,
The Interpreter's Bible, IV, 6.

Psalm was originally a processional hymn to be sung at the presentation of the thank offering and is still often used at Thanksgiving services. The Psalmist exhorts the worshipers to enter the Temple with praise and thanks, remembering that God is our Creator; that we are his people, "the sheep of his pasture"; that he is good; and that his mercy and faithfulness endure forever.

Psalms 113—118: The "Little" or "Egyptian" Hallel.* As the name indicates, these Psalms may be classified as hymns of praise. Psalm 114, the most artistic of the group, recalls how God delivered the Israelites from Egyptian bondage and then made Israel his dominion and his sanctuary. At his approach,

> The sea saw it, and fled:
> Jordan was driven back.
> The mountains skipped like rams,
> And the little hills like lambs. (Vv. 3-4)

Psalm 117, the shortest chapter in the Bible (only two verses, thirty-three words), calls on all nations—not the Israelites alone—to praise God for his kindness and trustworthiness.

Psalm 136: "The Great Hallel." The most memorable feature of this liturgical Psalm is that the second part of each two-line verse consists of the refrain: "For his mercy endureth forever." Perhaps the first was sung by the leader and the refrain by the remainder of the choir, or perhaps the Levites sang the first and the congregation sang the refrain.[32] The Psalm lists one by one many of God's gifts: the earth itself, the "great lights" in the heavens, "food to all flesh," delivery from the Egyptian bondage, the conquest of Canaan. The poem rises to a climax with "O give thanks unto the God of heaven."

Psalm 150: The Final Doxology. The short hymn which closes the Psalter is exuberant. It opens with a "Hallelujah" ("Praise ye the Lord"). It calls on men to praise God in his sanctuary and in the "firmament of his power," to praise him for his might and for his "excellent greatness," to praise him with

---

* Hebrew *hallel* means "praise." Hence the word *hallelujah,* meaning "praise ye Yahweh" (*jah* or *yah* is a shortened form of *Yahweh*); this exhortation, translated in the King James Version as "Praise ye the Lord," once appeared in all six of these Hallel Psalms. (Chamberlin and Feldman, *The Dartmouth Bible,* p. 510.)

trumpet, psaltery, harp, timbrel, stringed instruments, cymbals, and dancing. It ends with one last, all-inclusive exhortation:

> Let everything that hath breath praise the Lord.
> Praise ye the Lord!

GROUP II. MONODIES OF PRAISE, THANKSGIVING, AND TRUST

Generally quieter and more serene than the communal Psalms of Praise—but no less magnificent—are the Psalms of individual worship. In this group are some of the finest expressions of man's adoration of God and personal communion with him.

Psalm 19: The Glories of God's Universe and the Excellence of His Law. In this majestic hymn the Psalmist combines the sentiments found in Psalms 8 and 119: he praises God first as Creator of the universe (vv. 1-6) and then as Author of the Law (vv. 7-10). He concludes with a prayer to "keep back thy servant also from presumptuous sins."

Joseph Addison's well-known hymn is a free paraphrase of the first part of the Psalm:

> The spacious firmament on high,
> With all the blue ethereal sky,
> The spangled heav'ns, a shining frame,
> Their great Original proclaim.

Compare this with the first verse of the Psalm:

> The heavens declare the glory of God;
> And the firmament sheweth his handywork.

Addison's hymn, says Professor C. A. Dinsmore, is "second-class" compared with the Biblical lyric, and he continues:

Twenty-one words are used where the Bible requires but thirteen; the rhyme detracts from the majesty of the affirmation; the adjectives add feet to the meter, but nothing to the picture, and 'great Original' is a poor substitute for 'God.'[33]

The Psalmist's admiration of God's physical universe is paralleled by his admiration of God's Law, which is perfect so that it converts the soul, trustworthy so that it makes the simple wise, and right so that it rejoices the heart; it is more precious than gold, and sweeter than honey.

The Psalm ends with the familiar prayer:

> Let the words of my mouth,
> And the meditation of my heart,
> Be acceptable in thy sight,
> O Lord, my strength and my redeemer.

Psalm 23: God as Good Shepherd and Gracious Host. The Twenty-third Psalm has probably been memorized by more people than has any other passage of Scripture except the Lord's Prayer. Its simplicity, its calm assurance, and its joyous trust in God have made it the best loved of all the Psalms.

The poem falls into two parts, each being the elaboration of a metaphor. In the first (vv. 1-4), the helpless sheep (representing the Psalmist) is happy, because his kind shepherd (God) provides him with all the necessities of life—food, water, rest, and wise guidance; the sheep is free from fear, because even though he sometimes wanders through dark and dangerous regions, he knows that he can rely for protection on the rod and staff of the shepherd.

In the second part (vv. 5-6), the figure changes. Now God is a gracious host, who offers to his guest (the Psalmist) not only sanctuary from enemies but also a table full of food, an overflowing wine cup, and oil to anoint the head. Since the guest receives such treatment at all times, he confidently looks forward to dwelling in the host's house forever.

Psalm 91: Refuge in the Shadow of the Almighty. This poem expresses assurance that whoever abides "under the shadow of the Almighty" and who trusts in God as his "refuge and fortress" will be protected against all sorts of ills—disease ("pestilence"), man-made dangers ("the arrow that flieth by day"), and perilous beasts ("lion and adder"). Although a thousand men may fall at his side and ten thousand at his right hand, God will cover him with his wings and send angels to guard him.

Psalm 104: Hymn to Creation. This superb hymn of praise is similar to—and perhaps dependent on—an Egyptian hymn to the sun god attributed to the Pharaoh Ikhnaton (c. 1375-1358 B.C.).[34] The Psalm opens with one of the most beautiful of all Biblical passages glorifying God:

> Bless the Lord, O my soul.
> O Lord my God, thou art very great;

Thou art clothed with honor and majesty:
Who coverest thyself with light as with a garment:
Who stretchest out the heavens like a curtain:
Who layeth the beams of his chambers in the waters:
Who maketh the clouds his chariot:
Who walketh upon the wings of the wind:
Who maketh his angels spirits; his ministers a flaming fire. (Vv. 1-4)

The five succeeding strophes tell once again the story of Creation: the foundation of the earth, with its mountains and valleys;
the sending of springs of water; the growth of vegetation; the
establishment of the moon and the sun; and the creation of the
ocean and its inhabitants.* The next strophe (vv. 27-30) shows
how all living creatures are dependent on God:

Thou hidest thy face, they are troubled:
Thou takest away their breath, they die, and return to their dust.
Thou sendest forth thy spirit, they are created.
And thou renewest the face of the earth. (Vv. 29-30)

The poem ends with a joyous doxology (vv. 31-35).[35]

Psalm 119: Love for God's Law. This great Psalm is unique in
many respects. In the first place, it is the longest chapter in the
Bible (176 verses). Secondly, it consists of twenty-two strophes,
each headed by a different letter of the Hebrew alphabet; each
strophe is made up of eight verses, and each of these verses
begins with the Hebrew letter which heads the strophe; thus the
Psalm is an alphabetic acrostic. Thirdly, *every verse* refers in
some way to the Law; it is remarkable that ten different words
are used to mean "Law." (They are distinguished in the King
James Version by the following near synonyms: "Law, Word,
Saying, Commandment, Statutes, Ordinances, Precepts, Testimony, Way, and Path."[36])

"Saturated with the teachings of Deuteronomy,"[37] the author
devotes most of the verses to his adoration for God's Word. "O
how I love thy law!" he says; "it is my meditation all the day"
(v. 97). It brings him strength and comfort in times of trouble;
it is his guide through life—a lamp unto his feet and a light unto
his path (v. 105). When he breaks God's statutes, rivers of waters
run down his eyes, and he feels like a lost sheep (vv. 136 and

* Compare this account of Creation with those found in Gen. 1–2.

176). He prays that the Lord will give him understanding and obedience.

Psalm 139: God's Care for the Individual. Hailed as "the crown of the Psalter," this poem is one of the best expressions in the Old Testament of God's interest in each individual human being.

In the first section (vv. 1-6)[38] the Psalmist marvels at God's knowledge of him. God has "searched" him and knows all his actions and all his thoughts. "Such knowledge," says the Psalmist, "is too wonderful for me; it is high, I cannot attain unto it."

The theme of the second section (vv. 7-12) is God's omni presence. As in Francis Thompson's "The Hound of Heaven," the poet cannot escape from God:

> Whither shall I go from thy spirit?
> Or whither shall I flee from thy presence?
> If I ascend up into heaven, thou art there;
> If I make my bed in hell, behold, thou art there. (Vv. 7-8)

God is not only always present but also always a source of help:

> If I take the wings of the morning,
> And dwell in the uttermost parts of the sea;
> Even there shall thy hand lead me,
> And thy right hand shall hold me. (Vv. 9-10)

The third section (vv. 13-18) tells of God's making and intimate knowledge of the Psalmist's body, before as well as after its birth.

The fourth section (vv. 19-24)—thought by some commentators to be an interpolation by a later poet[39]—calls down a curse on the heads of those who speak wickedly against so wise and good a God, and the Psalmist fiercely proclaims his "perfect hatred" for such sinners. He ends the poem with a prayer that God may know his heart and thoughts, test him, and lead him "in the way everlasting"—that is, the paths of eternal righteousness.

GROUP III. LAMENTS OF THE COMMUNITY

The Hebrew poets often bemoaned the disasters suffered by their nation or their community. A famine, an epidemic, or an inroad by an enemy was frequently regarded as the Lord's punishment of the people for some sin; then the Psalmists would cry out to God for forgiveness and relief. Sometimes, however (as in Psalm 44:17-18), the poet protests that the people are

innocent of wrongdoing and seems puzzled over the reason for
their calamities. Often he reminds God that the sufferers are his
Chosen People and that he should help them for his own sake.[40]

Psalm 44: National Defeat and Disgrace. Scholarly opinions
have differed as to the period in Jewish history which is reflected
by this Psalm. Some critics have argued that it laments a military
disaster during the Maccabean struggle; others have maintained
that the circumstances which it describes fit better the latter part
of the Persian period (*c.* 350 B.C.).[41]

The poem, apparently spoken by a military leader in the
presence of his prostrate army, recalls to God that he has been
Israel's help in ages past and has made the nation victorious
over its enemies. Israel still worships him and depends on him
alone—not on its own prowess. But now God has cast the nation
off, caused its retreat, given it into the hand of the enemy, and
made it the object of derision among the nations. The Psalmist
cannot discern any reason for God's defection, for the people are
still loyal; they have not forgotten God nor broken the Covenant.
He pleads with God:

> Awake, why sleepest thou, O Lord?
> Arise, cast us not off for ever. . . .
> Arise for our help,
> And redeem us for thy mercies' sake. (Vv. 23 and 26)

Psalm 74: Desecration of the Temple. Like Psalm 44, this
lament tells of some national catastrophe: God's enemies have
destroyed the Temple and blasphemed God's holy name. The
Psalmist asks how long such insults will be allowed to continue.
He praises God's power: it is God who has divided the sea,
broken the heads of dragons and the leviathan,* created springs,
dried up rivers, established night and day, set the borders of the
earth, and made winter and summer. He appeals to God to
avenge himself on the evil ones who have blasphemed his name.

The descriptions of the Temple indicate that the occasion for
the writing of this Psalm was the Babylonian raid of 586 B.C.
rather than the polluting by Antiochus Epiphanes in 167 B.C.[42]

---

* A primeval water monster. Perhaps the word refers to a pagan sea god.
(W. Stewart McCullough, exegesis to Psalms, *The Interpreter's Bible,* IV,
397.)

GROUP IV. LAMENTS OF THE INDIVIDUAL

Similar to the communal lament, the lament of the individual sufferer usually confesses a sin and asks for God's forgiveness, or it pleads the sufferer's innocence and begs God to reveal the cause of the affliction. The penitential Psalms may have been sung or recited as part of the ritual accompanying the sin offering.[43]

Psalm 3: Prayer for Deliverance from Foes. The Hebrew superscription asserts that this Psalm was written by David while he was fleeing from Absalom (see II Sam. 15–17), but modern scholars find little evidence to support such a traditional belief.

The author bewails the fact that a multitude of enemies are threatening him; they think that he is powerless to withstand them. He relies on God as his shield, and he cries aloud to God for help. God answers "out of his holy hill." Then the afflicted one is comforted and reassured, so that he is able to lie down and sleep; no longer is he afraid of the ten thousand enemies who surround him. Confidently now he petitions God to save him and thereby prove to godless foes that "Salvation belongeth to the Lord" (v. 8).

Psalm 32: A Prayer of the Sick. Though usually classified as a penitential prayer, this is also a Psalm of blessing (Group VI) and a "wisdom" piece (Group IX). It is especially interesting as an expression of the prevalent Hebrew attitude toward misfortune: that suffering is sent as a punishment for sin.

It opens with the general observation that that man is happy ("blessed") who has repented of his sin and has been forgiven (vv. 1-2). The author then illustrates his point by relating a personal experience. Once he was very ill. As long as he refused to confess that he was guilty of sin, his "bones waxed old" from his "roaring all the day long," and God's hand was heavy upon him (vv. 3-4). But when he acknowledged his transgressions, the Lord forgave him and cured him. Therefore he urges his listeners not to act "as the horse, or as the mule, which have no understanding," but to learn the obvious lesson:

> Many sorrows shall be to the wicked:
> But he that trusteth in the Lord, mercy shall
> compass him about. (V. 10)

Psalm 51: A Broken and a Contrite Heart. In this poignant poem the Psalmist laments not so much any physical or material misfortune as he does the fact that his sins have caused a breach between himself and God. He confesses his iniquities—even from the day that his mother conceived him. He begs the Lord to take away his sin, to forgive him, and to restore him:

> Purge me with hyssop, and I shall be clean:
> Wash me, and I shall be whiter than snow. . . .
> Create in me a clean heart, O God;
> And renew a right spirit within me. (Vv. 7 and 10)

He asserts that God does not want ceremonial sacrifices and burnt offerings, but values humility and penitence:

> The sacrifices of* God are a broken spirit:
> A broken and a contrite heart, O God, thou wilt not despise. (V. 17)

The last two verses of the Psalm are believed to be an interpolation, for they differ in tone from the rest of the poem and flatly contradict verse 17 (quoted above).[44] Apparently some Priestly editor, fearing the effect of the attack on sacrificial rites, sought to modify it by praying for the rebuilding of the walls of Jerusalem:

> Then shalt thou be pleased with the sacrifices of righteousness,
> With burnt offering and whole burnt offering:
> Then shall they offer bullocks upon thine altar. (V. 19)

Psalm 73: Faith in Spite of Suffering. A striking contrast to Psalm 32 is this lyric, whose author, like Job, finally decides to trust in God even though the innocent suffer and the wicked prosper. He almost lost faith when he observed that the iniquitous were happy and arrogant, whereas he himself had lived a pure and innocent life and yet was "plagued" all day long and "chastened every morning." He began to doubt whether God knows or cares about human beings and their action. Then, while worshiping in the Temple one day, he suddenly understood: the success of the wicked is ephemeral and passes away like a dream; those who put their trust in God have a certain and enduring recompense. He now deplores his former stupidity and ignor-

---

* Acceptable to.

ance—he was acting like a beast. His faith in God is restored. Henceforth, he promises,

> God is the strength of my heart,
> And my portion for ever. (V. 26)

GROUP V. ROYAL PSALMS

A few of the Psalms are concerned with a king, "and it may be assumed that the reference is to a king of Judah."[45] Some in this group (Pss. 2, 18, 20, 21, 72, 101, 110, 132, and 144:1-11) invoke the aid of the Lord during some emergency, especially a military undertaking; two poems (Pss. 18 and 144) offer thanks to God for a victory. One "Royal Psalm" (Ps. 45) is a wedding song.[46]

Psalm 2: The King as God's Son. This controversial Psalm warns the "heathen" nations and the "kings of the earth" against opposing God's anointed king. The Lord laughs at such enemies, and the king will say to them:

> The Lord hath said unto me,
> 'Thou art my Son;
> This day have I begotten thee.
> Ask of me, and I shall give thee the heathen for thine inheritance,
> And the uttermost parts of the earth for thy possession.
> Thou shalt break them with a rod of iron;
> Thou shalt dash them in pieces like a potter's vessel. (Vv. 7-9)

Many Christians have interpreted the poem as a prophecy of the coming of Christ as the Messiah; Jewish commentators consider it a good description of the Hebrews' conception of their monarchs' role as the leaders of God's Chosen People.

Psalm 45: A Prothalamion. This is perhaps the only secular poem in the Psalter; even so, three of its verses (in the King James Version) refer to God and his blessings.

It celebrates the marriage of some Israelitish king to a "daughter of Tyre." Hence many scholars have thought that it was composed for the wedding of Ahab and the Tyrian (or Sidonian) princess Jezebel (see I Kings 16:31); other commentators have suggested that it celebrated the wedding of some other Hebrew monarch.[47]

After a brief introduction (v. 1) in which the poet tells of his own overflowing joy occasioned by the wedding, the king is praised for his beauty, grace, glory, majesty, power, and righteousness. Next the bride is warned that she must forget about her native country; she is lauded for her own loveliness and for that of her clothing. The poem closes with a prediction that the people will praise the royal pair forever and ever and that their offspring will be "princes in all the earth."

A Targum (see p. 27) of the Psalm interprets the king to be the Messiah and the bride to be Israel.[48]

GROUP VI. BLESSINGS[49] AND CURSES

This relatively small class of Psalms contains descriptions of the happy state of certain persons and invocations of God's wrath upon the wicked. Most of the "blessing" Psalms are distinctly didactic and might be classified as "wisdom" poetry.

Psalm 1: The Righteous and the Wicked. This brief poem serves as an excellent introduction to the entire Psalter—a warning that there are only "two ways of life" [50]—the good and the evil; the reader must choose one or the other.

The first three verses discuss the nature and the rewards of the righteous man: *he* refuses to follow the advice of the ungodly, to meet with sinners, and to associate with the arrogant or "scornful." Instead he loves God's Law and meditates upon it day and night. God will prosper such a man so that he shall flourish "like a tree planted by the rivers of water."

In contrast is the wicked man, who will be unable to stand up before God's judgment or to remain in the congregation of good men. *He* will be driven out of God's presence, like chaff before a mighty wind.

God will recognize and reward the "way of the righteous," but "the way of the ungodly shall perish."

Psalm 109: "Words of Hatred." This is an imprecation so full of hatred and bitterness that many readers have wondered how it found its way into the Hebrew canon. Before condemning such a poem, however, one should remember that the ancient Israelites lived by more primitive standards of conduct than those existing today (which are themselves, of course, frequently violated).

The Psalm opens with a petition that God refrain no longer from action. The author lists his grievances: his enemies have lied about him, encircled him with words of hatred, fought him without provocation, and rewarded him evil for good. Then the real curse begins: May the Lord cause the enemy* to be brought to court and condemned:

> Let his days be few; and let another take his office.
> Let his children be fatherless, and his wife a widow. (Vv. 8-9)

Let all his possessions be seized by creditors and strangers, so that his children will be beggars. "Let his posterity be cut off," so that even his name will be blotted out and forgotten. Let the sins of his parents be visited upon him. Even let his prayers be considered a sin. Because he has loved cruelty, show him no mercy.

> As he clothed himself with cursing like as with his garment,
> So let it come into his bowels like water, and like oil into his bones.
> (V. 18)

Again the Psalmist calls attention to his own miserable state and asks the Lord's aid. He is so sure that that aid will be granted that in the last two verses he offers praise and thanks to God.

Psalm 137: A Curse for a Nation. This Psalm is sometimes classified as an elegy or a lament, for the first portion bewails the captivity of the Jews in Babylon. Their captors ask them to sing a song of Zion; but the exiles, having no heart for songs or mirth, have hung up their useless harps on willow trees and have sat down and wept. They will never forget Jerusalem, but will prefer her above their highest joy.

Abruptly the Psalmist drops the plaintive strain and utters what is perhaps the most violent curse in the Bible. He urges God to remember the Edomites' pleasure over the destruction of Jerusalem and its Temple; and as for Babylon herself—

> Happy shall he be, that rewardeth thee as thou hast served us.
> Happy shall he be, that taketh and dasheth thy little ones
> against the stones. (Vv. 8-9)

---

* Here the Psalmist shifts his number, perhaps referring to all his enemies collectively as a single person or perhaps merely retaining the words of a "traditional curse formula." (McCullough, exegesis, *The Interpreter's Bible*, IV, 582.)

GROUP VII. PILGRIM PSALMS*

There is a group of fifteen consecutive Psalms (120–134) which is generally believed to be a collection of songs sung by pilgrims going up to Jerusalem to attend religious festivals. Some scholars think that these Psalms were used by the exiles returning from Babylon in the days of Nehemiah and Ezra; others believe they are of later date.⁵¹ Some critics hold that a few of the poems in the group (for example, Ps. 120) were not originally pilgrim songs at all inasmuch as they are not necessarily related to a journey.⁵²

Psalm 121: God as Protector. This favorite Psalm may have been sung by pilgrims approaching the mountainous regions around Jerusalem:

> I will lift up mine eyes unto the hills,
> From whence cometh my help. (V. 1)

It is a song of trust (and so might be placed in Group I):

> My help cometh from the Lord,
> Which made heaven and earth. (V. 2)

The Lord will not fall asleep while watching over his people, but will protect them from all evil and all calamities, such as stroke by the sun or moon.† He will preserve them in their "going out" and their "coming in" "from this time forth, and even for evermore."

Psalm 122: A Prayer for Peace. Indubitably the song of pilgrims, this is a hymn of praise and thanksgiving and a prayer for Jerusalem's peace and welfare.

> I was glad when they said unto me,
> Let us go into the house of the Lord.
> Our feet shall stand within thy gates, O Jerusalem. . . .
> Peace be within thy walls, and prosperity within thy palaces.
>   (Vv. 1-2, 7)

---

* The Hebrew superscription attached to each of these Psalms is translated in the King James Version as "A Song of Degrees"; the English Revised Version and the Revised Standard Version translate it "A Song of Ascents."

† It was a popular belief that sunstroke and "moonstroke" (certain diseases, such as epilepsy and fever) were caused by demons in the sun and moon. (William R. Taylor, exegesis to Psalms, *The Interpreter's Bible,* IV, 646-647.)

Psalm 130: De Profundis. This is a short but forceful Psalm, sung by a penitent pilgrim. "Out of the depths" of remorse for sins, the Psalmist calls upon the Lord for help. Fortunately, he says, God forgives man's iniquities instead of condemning him for each one. The Psalmist's soul waits for God's pardon more impatiently than a sentinel watches for the first ray of dawn. This Psalm closes with a plea to Israel to "hope in the Lord."

GROUP VIII. LEGENDS

Three of the Psalms (78, 105, and 106) are predominantly narrative rather than lyrical. They tell about some events in Jewish history, especially during the centuries covered by the Hexateuch; and they emphasize God's role in the events.

Psalm 78: Escape from Egypt and Conquest of Canaan. In this long and rather prolix ballad, the Psalmist retells the familiar old story of the Egyptian oppression of the Hebrews, the plagues sent upon the oppressors, the Hebrews' flight through the Red Sea, their hardships and backslidings in the wilderness, and their successful battles against the Canaanites. The main didactic theme is similar to that of the book of Judges: the people sin, God chastises them, and then he relents and shows them mercy.[53] The tribe of Judah is pointed out as God's favorite, because it built the Temple in Jerusalem (vv. 68-72); and the tribe of Ephraim is censured for disobeying God's Law and for cowardice in battle (vv. 9-11).

Psalm 105: God's Covenant through the Centuries. After an introductory doxology (vv. 1-6) this Psalm reviews God's dealings with the Hebrews from the time of Abraham through the conquest of Canaan. The establishment of the Covenant with Abraham and its confirmation with Isaac and Jacob, the migration to Egypt, the story of Joseph, the Exodus and wanderings in the wilderness, and the inheritance of Palestine—all these are briefly related. The author's purpose is to show that God has

> ... brought forth his people with joy,
> And his chosen with gladness ...
> That they might observe his statutes,
> And keep his laws. (Vv. 43 and 45)

GROUP IX. PSALMS OF "WISDOM" AND
PHILOSOPHIC MEDITATION

Another group of Psalms consists of didactic and reflective poems. Some of these (for example, Pss. 37, 127, and 128) consist largely of short, epigrammatic sayings which we usually label "proverbs"; others (such as Pss. 49 and 90) are more extensive discussions of some profound ethical, religious, or metaphysical problems.

Psalm 37: "Fret Not Thyself Because of Evildoers." This is an acrostic Psalm; each of its twenty-two brief strophes begins with a different Hebrew letter and the strophes are arranged in alphabetical order. Its theme, announced in the first line, is the ever-recurrent "problem of evil"—why the evil thrive and the good suffer. This author's solution is that although the wicked may prosper temporarily, they will eventually be punished, and the righteous will be vindicated.[54]

The Psalm resembles many passages in the book of Proverbs. It is filled with brief, pithy bits of wisdom such as an old man might jot down as guides for his children or grandchildren:

> Fret not thyself because of evildoers,
> Neither be thou envious against the workers of iniquity.
> For they shall soon be cut down like the grass,
> And wither as the green herb.
> Trust in the Lord, and do good;
> So shalt thou dwell in the land,
> And verily thou shalt be fed. . . .
> A little that a righteous man hath
> Is better than the riches of many wicked. . . .
> The wicked borroweth, and payeth not again:
> But the righteous showeth mercy, and giveth. . . .
> I have been young, and now am old;
> Yet have I not seen the righteous forsaken,
> Nor his seed begging bread. (Vv. 1-3, 16, 21, and 25)

Psalm 90: A Funeral Hymn. The fact that this Psalm was ascribed to Moses is sufficient evidence of the esteem in which it was held by the ancient Jews. It has been called "the greatest funeral hymn in all the world,"[55] and it is the basis for Isaac Watts' noble hymn "O God, Our Help in Ages Past."

The Psalm may be divided into two parts, vv. 1-12 and 13-17.

Some scholars believe that the two sections are by different authors, but of this there is no conclusive evidence.[56]

The first part is a contrast of God's eternal nature with man's transitory one. Before the mountains were created, God existed, for

> Even from everlasting to everlasting, thou art God. (V. 2)

In God's sight a thousand years are like one day or a short watch in the night. Man, on the contrary, is like grass, which flourishes in the morning and is cut down in the evening. Man's allotted life is threescore years and ten—or at the most fourscore—and this brief span is passed under the shadow of God's anger, for man is sinful. The Psalmist's prayer is that God will keep us aware of the brevity of our life so that "we may apply our hearts unto wisdom" (v. 12).

The second section of the poem is a prayer for God's love and mercy. It appears to be the reflection of an era of great tribulation:

> Return, O Lord, how long?
> And let it repent thee concerning thy servants.
> O satisfy us early with thy mercy;
> That we may rejoice and be glad all our days....
> Let thy work appear unto thy servants,
> And thy glory unto their children.
> And let the beauty of the Lord our God be upon us. . .
>
> (Vv. 13-14, 16-17)

12

Minor Lyrical Books

Lamentations, The Prayer of Manasses,
and The Song of the Three Holy Children

Psalms is incomparably the most significant book of lyrics in the Bible. There are, however, three other lyrical books, which will be discussed in this chapter.

LAMENTATIONS: A DIRGE FOR JERUSALEM

Every year on August 9, Jewish people all over the world still gather to observe the anniversary of the fall of Jerusalem and the burning of its Temple. Tradition holds that the city was destroyed on that day in 586 B.C. by the Babylonians and again on the same day in A.D. 70 by the Romans. To commemorate the double catastrophe, Jews in Jerusalem proceed to the famous Wailing Wall, and elsewhere they congregate in synagogues; wherever they gather on the sad anniversary, an important part of the ceremony is the recital of the series of elegiac poems known as the book of Lamentations.[1]

In the Hebrew version these poems make up the third of the five *Megilloth*, or "Rolls." There its title is derived from its first word *Echah*, meaning "Ah, how." There is no naming of an author.[2]

In the Septuagint the book is called *Threnoi* ("Lamentations," or "Dirges"), and it follows the prophecy of Jeremiah.* Prefaced to the first chapter in this version are the following words: "And it came to pass after Israel was taken captive and Jerusalem made desolate, Jeremiah sat weeping and lamented with this lamentation and said." Why the author of this preface ascribed

* The order adopted by the Latin, Syriac, and most English versions.

the book to the old prophet is unknown, unless it was because Jeremiah had a reputation for weeping and lamenting (see, for example, II Chr. 35:25). At any rate, the ascription has stuck, and most non-Jewish Bibles call the lyrics "The Lamentations of Jeremiah."

Most modern scholars, however, doubt that Jeremiah wrote any part of the book. The style of the book of prophecy which bears his name is natural and spontaneous, whereas that of Lamentations is decidedly artificial.

The five chapters of Lamentations are actually five separate and distinct poems. Considerations of diction, style, and mood make it appear most likely that Chapters 2 and 4 were written by one poet and that each of the other chapters had a different author.

The dates of composition and compilation are uncertain. Most authorities agree that Chapters 2 and 4 were the earliest and that they were written soon after the fall of Jerusalem in 586 B.C. —not later than 573 B.C. The order and the dates of the other chapters seem to be as follows: Chapter 1, between 570 and 540 B.C.; Chapter 3, uncertain (speculations vary from *c.* 540 B.C. to *c.* 325 B.C.); and Chapter 5, *c.* 540 B.C.[3] Perhaps Chapters 1, 2, and 4 were consolidated *c.* 425, *and* Chapters 3 and 5 were added *c.* 300 B.C.[4]

Each of the first four chapters is an acrostic of twenty-two strophes; each strophe begins with a different Hebrew letter and the order of strophes is generally alphabetical (in Chs. 2—4 the letters *'ayin* and *pe* are transposed). In Chapters 1 and 2 every strophe makes up one verse, and all but two verses contain three lines (1:7 and 2:19 have four lines each). In Chapter 3 every strophe has three lines, but all the lines in each strophe begin with the same letter; in English Bibles each line is a separate verse, making sixty-six verses. In Chapter 4 each strophe consists of only two lines, and each strophe is a separate verse. Chapter 5 has twenty-two verses but no acrostic structure; perhaps this is a "first draft" which the author intended later to change into an acrostic.[5]

Most of the lines in Chapters 1—4 are in the rhythm (or "meter") known as the "*qînāh*" (*kinah, qina*), or "limping verse"; this is the 3+2 distich, frequently used for Hebrew elegiac poetry. The lines in Chapter 5 have the 3+3 rhythm.

One would expect poems subject to the exigencies of so strict a rhythmical and acrostic pattern to be too artificial for adequate expressions of deep and passionate grief. Certainly "they are not the unstudied effusions of natural emotion,"[6] nor were they intended to be. Instead, they are the elaborate products of conscious and painstaking artistry. One should remember that Milton's "Lycidas," Shelley's "Adonais," and Tennyson's *In Memoriam* conform to rigid conventions, too, but are, nevertheless, elegiac masterpieces. In like manner, the authors of Lamentations —especially of Chapters 2 and 4—were successful in molding their ideas to fit the chosen verse forms. Perhaps the restrictions imposed by the forms helped to achieve a desirable artistic restraint, so often lacking in inferior elegiac verse. At any rate, in Lamentations the intensity of the poets' sorrow is still present. That, plus the use of many descriptive details and much vivid coloring, makes the book "one of the most heartrending accounts ever written of the anguish of a people."[7]

God's Punishment of the Jerusalemites (Chs. 2 and 4). As has been stated, these two poems were written very near the time of the Babylonian destruction of the Holy City. They bear every indication of being the accounts of an eyewitness of the atrocities and the suffering. Perhaps they are the only "contemporaneous picture of the thoughts and emotions aroused by the Fall of Jerusalem."[8]

With regard to the catastrophe the poet takes the traditional Hebraic point of view, held by many of the historians, prophets, and Psalmists—that adversity comes from God as a punishment for man's sins. Because God is angry with Israel for her wickedness, he has become her enemy instead of her protector (2:1-5). He has carried out his threat against her, delivered by numerous prophets. He has repudiated his own anointed king and his priests, the Law "is no more," and the prophets (2:9) are given no vision; false prophets and sinful priests have led the people astray.

Retribution, executed by the Babylonians, has been terrible; and the suffering has been made worse by contrast with the joy of former days: those who in the past fed on delicate dishes are now starving in the streets; those who dressed in fine garments are found on dunghills; the handsome young men, whose faces were whiter than snow and whose bodies were more ruddy than coral, now—

> Their visage is blacker than coal;
> They are not known in the streets:
> Their skin cleaveth to their bones;
> It is withered, it is like a stick. (4:8)

Those who have been slain by the sword are lucky, for they do not have to endure slow death by starvation. Some loving mothers have become so maddened by hunger that they have boiled their own children and eaten their flesh.

In vain the remnants of the population have watched for help from some other nation. The Babylonians have hunted them down in the streets and pursued them into the mountains and the wilderness (4:18-19). Now the city is desolate. All who see it

> . . . hiss and wag their head
> At the daughter of Jerusalem,*
> Saying, "Is this the city that men call
> The perfection of beauty,
> The joy of the whole earth?" (2:15)

The elders of the city sit in silence on the ground, cover themselves with sackcloth, and cast dust upon their heads; the young maidens hang their heads down to the ground; and as for the poet himself—

> Mine eyes do fail with tears,
> My bowels are troubled,
> My liver is poured upon the earth,
> For the destruction of the daughter of my people. (2:11)

He ends his two poems with a bit of grim consolation: the thought that Edom, the most bitterly hated neighbor of the Jews, will soon suffer the fate of Jerusalem:

> He will visit thine iniquity, O daughter of Edom;
> He will discover thy sins. (4:22)†

* "The daughter of Jerusalem" is a conventionalized phrase denoting the city. Similar phrases with the same meaning are "daughter of my people," "daughter of Judah," and "daughter of Zion." (Henry T. Fowler, A History of the Literature of Ancient Israel [New York: Macmillan Co., 1922], p. 248.)

† Compare Ps. 137:7, Isa. 34, Jer. 25:15-29, and Hab. 2:15-16.

The Empty City and Her Scattered Citizens (Ch. 1). The themes of Chapters 2 and 4 are found also in Chapter 1—God's anger and the people's suffering. But now the tone is somewhat subdued; searing anguish has given way to aching sorrow.

In vv. 1-11 and 17 the poet tells of the grief-stricken city, personified as a woman:

> How doth the city sit solitary,
> That was full of people!
> How is she become a widow!
> She that was great among the nations,
> And princess among the provinces,
> How is she become a tributary! (V. 1)

She weeps for her people, but they are all dispersed, "like harts that find no pasture." She deserves her misery, however, for there has been "filthiness in her skirts."

In verses 12-16 and 18-22 the city voices her own complaints, admits her transgressions, and begs the Lord for relief.

Resignation and Hope (Ch. 3). Although in the form of "a personal lament and prayer," [9] Chapter 3 may be intended to represent the sentiments not of an individual sufferer but of the Hebrew community.[10] The mourner bewails his pains and his outcast state, but he knows that the Lord is merciful as well as just and will eventually deliver him. He prays for that deliverance.

This poem is the most artificial and the least original of the five in the book.

A Community Prayer (Ch. 5). The last of the poems appears to be the petition not of the exiles in Babylon but of those Jews left in Jerusalem. Once more it lays before the Lord their pitiable condition: their disgrace, their poverty, their dependence on Egypt and Assyria for food, their helplessness before bands of marauders. The women of the city have been raped or abducted, the princes hanged, and the young men enslaved. Foxes roam over Mount Zion!

The sufferers beg the Lord to relent:

> Wherefore dost thou forget us for ever,
> And forsake us so long time?
> Turn thou us unto thee, O Lord,
> And we shall be turned;
> Renew our days as of old. (Vv. 20-21)

THE PRAYER OF MANASSES*:
CONFESSIONS OF A PENITENT SINNER

Manasseh, son of the good King Hezekiah, was one of the worst monarchs ever to rule over Judah. According to II Kings 21:1-18 and II Chronicles 33:1-20, he practiced magic and "dealt with familiar spirits and wizards," he worshiped all the "host of heaven" (Assyrian astral deities), he rebuilt the altars to Baal and the "high places" which Hezekiah had destroyed, he set up a graven image and altars to pagan gods in Yahweh's own Temple, and he even made his son "pass through fire" (that is, he sacrificed him as a burnt offering). In these ways he led the peopel of his kingdom to sin. As recompense, God decided to cause Babylon to destroy the Temple and to exile the people of Judah (II Kings 24:1-4). Manasseh himself was given a foretaste of the national disaster by being carried into captivity by the Assyrians (see II Chr. 33:10-13 and 18-19).

"The Book of the Kings of Israel" and "The Sayings of the Seers" have been lost, and so we have no copy of Manasseh's prayer of repentance mentioned by the Chronicler (II Chr. 18). An attempt to supply such a prayer was made by an anonymous poet at some undetermined time during the last two centuries B.C. It is unknown whether this poem was originally composed in Hebrew, Aramaic, or Greek.[11]

Perhaps the author chose Manasseh as the speaker of the Prayer in order to stress his belief that God is merciful to even the worst of sinners if they truly repent. Especially noteworthy is his emphasis on the superiority of repentance and contrition to sacrificial offerings.

The Prayer may be divided into four parts. In the first (vv. 1-8) Manasseh praises God for his creation of the universe and for his mercy toward repentant sinners. Next he confesses his manifold sins (vv. 9-10). The Prayer closes with a petition for forgiveness and a short doxology:

> Now therefore I bow the knee of mine heart,
> Beseeching thee of grace.
> I have sinned, O Lord, I have sinned,

---

* *Manasses* is the Apocryphal spelling of *Manasseh,* the name as it appears in the canonical books. The latter spelling will be used in this summary.

And I acknowledge mine iniquities:
Wherefore I humbly beseech thee,
Forgive me, O Lord, forgive me,
And destroy me not with mine iniquities.
Be not angry with me for ever,
By reserving evil for me;
Neither condemn me into the lower parts of the earth.
For thou art the God,
Even the God of them that repent;
And in me thou wilt shew all thy goodness:
For thou wilt save me, that am unworthy,
According to thy great mercy.
Therefore I will praise thee forever
All the days of my life:
For all the powers of heaven do praise thee,
And thine is the glory for ever and ever. Amen. (Vv. 11-15)

Professor B. M. Metzger calls this poem "one of the finest pieces in the Apocrypha ... [a] little classic of penitential devotion."[12]

THE SONG OF THE THREE HOLY CHILDREN: A HYMN FROM THE FIERY FURNACE

The third chapter of the canonical book of Daniel tells how Nebuchadrezzar, king of Babylon, threw the Jews Shadrach, Meshach, and Abednego into a fiery furnace because they refused to worship a golden image of him; the Lord sent an angel to protect them so that the fire did them no harm.[*] In the Vulgate there appears after Dan. 3:23 a long passage consisting of a prayer uttered by Azariah (the Hebrew name of Abednego)[†] and a hymn sung by all three Jews when the angel joined them in the furnace. In Protestant Bibles this long interpolation became a separate Apocryphal book, entitled The Song of the Three Holy Children.[‡]

The author of the book is unknown. The afflictions of the Hebrews described in v. 9 are similar to those suffered at the hands of Antiochus Epiphanes. It is therefore believed that the date of the book is *c.* 165 B.C.[13]

[*] See p. 313, below, for a discussion of this story.

[†] *Azarias,* the Grecized form of *Azariah,* is the name used in the Apocrypha.

[‡] The Revised Standard Version calls it The Prayer of Azariah and the Song of the Three Young Men.

Azariah begins his prayer as soon as he and his companions are cast into the furnace. The prayer is not, as one might expect, a petition to be freed from the flames; in fact, Azariah does not even mention the fire. Instead, he praises God for his many mercies, confesses the sins of the Israelites, and begs the Lord to deliver them from bondage (vv. 2-22). The theology of one pasage recalls that of The Prayer of Manasses and of Psalm 51:

> Neither is there at this time prince, or prophet, or leader,
> Or burnt offering, or sacrifice, or oblation, or incense,
> Or place to sacrifice before thee, and to find mercy.
> Nevertheless in a contrite heart and an humble spirit let us
> be accepted. (Vv. 15-16)

Nebuchadrezzar's men pour more fuel into the furnace,

So that the flame streamed forth above the furnace forty and nine cubits. And it passed through, and burned those Chaldeans it found about the furnace. But the angel of the Lord came down into the oven together with Azarias and his fellows, and smote the flame of the fire out of the oven; and made the midst of the furnace as it had been a moist whistling wind, so that the fire touched them not at all, neither hurt nor troubled them. (Vv. 24-27)

Then the three young men sing their hymn. In the first six verses (29-34) they proclaim the Lord's "blessedness"; each of these verses ends with the refrain "and to be praised and exalted above all for ever." The singers exhort all the universe to join in blessing the Lord—the heavens, the angels, the waters above the heavens, the planets, the winds, the mountains, all sea animals, all fowls, all land animals, and all men. Each of these verses (35-65) closes with the refrain "Praise and exalt him above all for ever." These exhortations owe much to Psalm 148, which urges various natural objects to praise God, and to Psalm 136, in which the refrain "For his mercy endureth for ever"* appears twenty-two times.[14] The last three verses (66-68) offer praise and thanksgiving to God for preserving the three young men.

This hymn is obviously of the same genre as those Psalms classified as Community Hymns of Praise, Thanksgiving, and Trust (see p. 245); and it is worthy to stand beside the best of

---

* This refrain appears verbatim at the end of the last two verses of the "children's" hymn.

them. The quotation of a few lines will suffice to illustrate its "majestic rhythm":[15]

> O all ye works of the Lord, bless ye the Lord:
> Praise and exalt him above all for ever.
> O ye heavens, bless ye the Lord:
> Praise and exalt him above all for ever.
> O ye angels of the Lord, bless ye the Lord:
> Praise and exalt him above all for ever.
> O all ye waters that be above the heaven, bless ye the Lord:
> Praise and exalt him above all for ever. (Vv. 35-38)

Part Five
Dramatic Literature

Since the ancient Hebrews had no theater, their literature contains no actual stage play. It would be a mistake, however, to suppose that they were lacking in dramatic instinct. Professor Laura H. Wild maintains:

The Israelites were a dramatic folk, much more so than are western peoples to-day. They thought in pictures even in their ordinary transactions and they accompanied their words with gesticulations and significant tones of the voice; they even acted out the news of the day or prophecies of future events.[1]

When suffering from great tribulation, they "acted out" their distress by clothing themselves in sackcloth and pouring ashes and dust upon their heads. The prophet Zedekiah demonstrated with "props" (horns of iron) how Ahab would defeat the Syrians (I Kings 22:11). For three years Isaiah dressed in the garb of a captive and went from house to house in an effort to warn the people that *they* would soon be captives and exiles unless their rulers reformed their ways (Isa. 20:2-6). And Ezekiel is told to shave off the hair from his head and his face and to burn some of it and scatter the rest to the winds—as a symbolic warning of how the Israelites will be destroyed (Ezek. 5:1-4).[2] Furthermore, the Bible includes many examples of dramatic lyrics, dramatic visions, and dramatic prophecies.[3]

Although these strong histrionic tendencies resulted in no play for the stage, two Biblical books may justifiably be classified as dramatic literature. These are the book of Job and The Song of Solomon.

Job: A Drama of the Inner Life

So many superlatives have been used in praise of the book of
Job that it is difficult to find a fresh one. Many critics believe
that the book is the supreme literary masterpiece of the Bible,
and some consider it the greatest single work in world literature.
Luther called it "magnificent and sublime as no other book of
Scripture"; Tennyson thought it "the greatest poem of ancient
and modern times"; and Carlyle said of it: "A noble Book; all
men's Book! ... There is nothing written, I think, in the Bible or
out of it, of equal literary merit." [4]

The book is anonymous. Because the action apparently takes
place in Edom,* several commentators have argued that the author was an Edomite, but the nature of most of the contents is
thoroughly Hebraic. [5]

Biblical scholars have gathered an impressive amount of material which may have been influential on the author of Job. It
is possible that he knew Greek tragedy, but the evidence is inconclusive.† He may have borrowed from Edomitic wisdom,
Egyptian pessimism, Babylonian skepticism, and international
folklore. The two closest parallels to the Biblical book are the
Babylonian works known as "The Poem of the Righteous Suf-

---

* Eliphaz, one of Job's friends, comes from Teman, a region in Edom
(Job 2:11).

† There are some interesting parallels between the Hebrew book and
Aeschylus' *Prometheus Bound:* both Prometheus and Job are good heroes who
suffer at the hands of a superhuman power, and both are visited during the
period of torture by groups of friends; Job is restored to happiness and prosperity, and in the lost sequel to *Prometheus Bound,* the hero is believed to have
been freed from his suffering by the aid of Hercules. Further similarities
between Job and Greek tragedies are the use of a prologue and messengers;
and the coming of the Voice out of the Whirlwind (Job 38–41) resembles the
Greek *deus ex machina* device.

ferer" (or "The Babylonian Job") and an "Acrostic Dialogue on Theodicy."[6]

Few facts are known about the history of the composition of Job, but many conjectures have been made. The majority of modern commentators seem to think that at some time between 580 and 400 B.C. a Hebrew poet took an old folk tale (in prose) about an innocent sufferer, used parts of this as an introduction and a conclusion (Chs. 1—2 and 42:7-17), and inserted his own philosophic considerations (in poetic form) as the main body of his composition (Chs. 3—27, 29—31, and 38—42:6). The praise of wisdom (Ch. 28) and the discourse of Elihu (Chs. 32—37) are believed to be additions interpolated at some unknown dates between 400 and 200 B.C.[7]

There is even less scholarly agreement about the classification of Job than about its date and authorship. Some critics have labeled it a Platonic-type dialogue, but it has more narrative content than most of that genre. Others have classified it as "wisdom" literature, made up of a series of lyric, didactic, and reflective poems; but it has more organic unity than would be expected of a series. Long ago Professor J. F. Genung described the book as an "epic of the inner life," but an actual epic it is not if an epic depends on a long, dignified narrative full of *events*, with a hero who embodies national or racial virtues and performs great feats of daring. Finally, it has been called a drama. More than a hundred years ago Bishop Robert Lowth compared it with Sophocles' *Oedipus at Colonus;*[8] and in the early part of this century H. M. Kallen maintained that it was a tragedy modeled on the plays of Euripides; he shifted certain lines to form choral interludes and rearranged other parts to meet the requirements of the stage.[9] At least two different groups have performed the work as a drama.[10] Professor George Sprau refuses to call it a drama because, he says, it lacks plot;[11] but Professor S. R. Driver claims that it has entanglement, development, and solution.[12] Professor R. G. Moulton calls it a "wisdom drama,"[13] and E. S. Bates, "a philosophical drama."[14] Although the book does not fit precisely into any literary category, it comes closest to being a drama. This Outline will endeavor to show that it contains most of the elements of the drama as listed by Aristotle in the *Poetics*.*

---

* Aristotle said that the six "parts" of a drama are plot, character, thought, diction, song, and scenery or "spectacle." He discusses these only in relation to tragedy, but all except song are indispensable elements of any sort of drama.

First, let us consider the matter of *plot*. Job does have a plot, if by that term we mean a story built around an unstable situation which by its very nature must be resolved, and which, until the resolution, holds the audience or reader in suspense. The "unstable situation" is Job's prolonged indecision, following his afflictions, whether to continue as a faithful worshiper of God. The inciting force is Satan's wager with God that adversity will make Job "renounce God to his face." The crises are Job's various misfortunes, including the exasperating speeches of the "Comforters." The climax is Job's decision to remain true to God, based on his recognition that God himself will be his "vindicator" (19:25-29). Significant events in the dénouement are the humbling of Job by the Voice out of the Whirlwind and the restoration of Job's prosperity. Now, it is readily admitted that there is little physical action in the drama, but there is about as much as in Aeschylus' *The Persians* and *Prometheus Bound* or in Browning's *A Soul's Tragedy*, yet no one hesitates to call these compositions "dramas." The most important happenings in the book of Job take place inside the hero's mind; hence we have ventured to alter Genung's phrase and designate the book "a *drama* of the inner life."

Next, there are the *dramatis personae*. Several of the characters are skillfully drawn and are given clearly individualized personalities: (1) *God*. In the Prologue and the Epilogue (presumably taken from the folk tale) he is depicted as an Oriental potentate, proud of the loyalty of his vassal Job; benevolent, but not too merciful to allow his faithful vassal to be tried by the most terrible afflictions. In the passages consisting of the Voice out of the Whirlwind, he more nearly resembles the Yahweh of the historians and the prophets—eternal, omnipotent, capable of fierce wrath but concerned for each individual that he has created. (2) *Satan*. This character is not to be identified with Lucifer, the archenemy of God. On the contrary, he is apparently one of God's servants; he goes to and fro in heaven as well as on earth, and he associates on equal terms with the "sons of God" (1:6). He is a "sort of *agent provocateur*,"[15] whose function is to observe man, report on his behavior, and test the genuineness of his righteousness. Hence it is better to refer to him as *the* Satan (or the "Adversary," the true meaning of the Hebrew name)—the opponent of mankind. (3) *Job*. It is necessary to keep in mind that at the beginning of the book the hero is a *completely* upright and God-fearing man, who suffers calamities through no fault of his own. In his speeches he shows himself to be highly intelligent, intellectually honest, and capable of deep philosophical reflection. He is *not,* however, the personification of patience, as implied by the proverbial expression "as patient as Job." Like most people, he becomes furiously *im*patient when his friends "needle" him, and he comes close to blasphemy when he dares to question the justice of God's treatment of human beings. (4) *The Four "Comforters."* These so-called "friends" are, of course, not really comforters at all, but "hecklers." Instead of bringing Job solace, they add to his misery by refusing to believe his claims of innocence and by accusing him of deceit, pride, and stubbornness. All of them are incorrigible supporters of the traditional view that suffering is proof of guilt. (*a*) *Eliphaz* is the least obnoxious of the four and the only one who seems to feel any genuine sympathy for Job. He is an old man and a mystic: he has visions, sees spirits gliding past his face, and hears a mysterious voice conveying the truth to him (4:12-21). (*b*) *Bildad* relies not on mystical visions but on the stored-up traditions of the past. He is middle-aged, dogmatic, and scholarly. (*c*) *Zophar* is younger and even more dogmatic than Bildad and, in addition, is narrow-minded, irascible, and vituperative. (*d*) *Elihu,* the youngest of the four, is conceited and self-confident. He thinks that he can succeed in persuading Job although his three elder friends have failed. His speeches are prolix and flatulent.

Such is the cast of characters. Now for the *thought* or theme of the drama.

The book is a profound treatment of the age-old problem of evil: Why do the innocent suffer and the wicked prosper? Now, everybody recognizes (as certainly the ancient Hebrews did) that many sufferings are the result of misdeeds, and most people will agree that few human beings are entirely innocent of wrongdoing; but rewards and punishments in this world do not appear to be commensurate with deserts. How can this fact be reconciled with the belief in a benevolent, just, and omnipotent Deity? This is perhaps the most fundamental question in the philosophy of religion, for it is, in effect, an attempt to ascertain both the nature of God and his purpose for the universe: If God is all-powerful and all-good, why did he not create a universe in which there would be no suffering and no sin? Almost all thinking adults have considered this perplexing problem, and philosophers and theologians have offered numerous solutions; but most of these solutions are variations of those suggested by the book of Job: suffering is (1) a test of man's goodness and faith, (2) a punishment for sin, (3) an admonition and restorative from God, (4) a part of the "unfathomed mystery" of the universe, in which evil as well as good is an ingredient, and (5) a challenge to man to remain faithful to God and at the same time to preserve his intellectual honesty.[16]

Aristotle lists *diction* as the fourth element of drama. The language of the King James version of Job is unsurpassed—and unsurpassable—in its dignity and power. Especially noteworthy are the passages known as Job's Curse (Ch. 3), Job's Oath of Clearing (Ch. 31), and the Voice out of the Whirlwind (38:1–42:6). The discourse of Elihu (Chs. 32–37) is of lower literary quality than other portions of the book.

Aristotle's last two requirements for a drama are *song* and *scenery* (or *spectacle*). Having no chorus, Job lacks the former; and inasmuch as the drama was not written for the stage, there is no concern for "scenery" or props. The author clearly indicates, however, that there are three places where the action occurs: heaven, Job's domicile in Uz, and the ash heap outside the city; the last is an appropriate site for the debate which rages between the wretched Job and his "friends."

The book is not divided into the traditional five "acts" of Senecan and later drama, nor yet into the prologue, the episodes, and the exodus of Greek tragedy. The following division seems logical and appropriate: (1) The Prologue (Chs. 1–2); (2) Job's Curse (Ch. 3); (3) The Debate (Chs. 4–27); (4) Hymn on Wisdom (Ch. 28); (5) Job's Peroration (Chs. 29–31); (6) Elihu's Interposition (Chs. 32–37); (7) The Divine Intervention (38:1–42:6); and (8) The Epilogue (42:7-17).[17]

THE PROSE (OR FOLK-TALE) PROLOGUE
(CHS. 1—2)

The drama opens with a prologue in prose. After an introductory character sketch of the hero, there are four "scenes"—the first and third in heaven and the second and fourth on earth.

Introduction of Job (1:1-5). The protagonist of the drama is introduced as a prominent sheikh—"the greatest of all the men of the east." He is blessed with seven sons and three daughters,* and he is very rich, possessing seven thousand sheep, three thousand camels, five hundred yoke of oxen, five hundred she-asses, and "a very great household." Furthermore, he is an exceptionally good man, "perfect and upright, and one that feared God, and eschewed evil." Not only is he righteous, devout, and humble himself, but also he is so deeply concerned for his children's acceptability to God that he presents burnt offerings to the Deity for any possible secret thoughts of his children which may have been offensive. Such is the hero of the story—a man of high estate who, up to this point, has shown no "tragic flaw."

The First Challenge by the Satan (1:6-12). The first scene of the Prologue reveals God in conference with the Satan and the "sons of God" (apparently angelic creatures). The Deity asks the Satan whether he has observed that Job is "a perfect and an upright man." The Satan acknowledges Job's goodness, but suggests cynically that Job has every reason to be good: he is rich, secure, and happy. If he were to lose his prosperity, he would lose also his faith in God. God accepts the challenge and gives the Satan permission to do as he wishes with Job's possessions; the Satan must not, however, harm Job's person.

Job's First Round of Afflictions (1:13-22). The second scene takes place at Job's home. Without any forewarning, four messengers present themselves to Job in quick succession, each bearing news of a disaster: (1) the theft of all Job's oxen and asses by a band of Arabs ("Sabeans"), who slew all the attending servants; (2) the destruction of all his sheep and shepherds by lightning ("fire of God"); (3) the seizure of all his camels by three bands of Arameans ("Chaldeans"), who killed the camel drivers; and (4) the death of all his children as the result of a great hurricane. Each messenger declares himself the only survivor of the disaster which he reports—presumably spared by the Satan for the sole purpose of delivering the bad tidings.[18]

Although bereft of all his sons and daughters and reduced to poverty, Job neither sins nor accuses God of wrongdoing. He tears his robe and shaves his head (Oriental expressions of deep

* Large numbers of children were considered blessings in ancient days. Compare the classic myth of Niobe, who boasts that she is superior to Leto because she (Niobe) has fourteen children whereas Leto has only two (Apollo and Artemis).

mourning); then he falls upon the ground and worships God, and in a famous passage expresses his resignation to God's will:

> Naked came I out of my mother's womb,
> And naked shall I return thither:
> The Lord gave,
> And the Lord hath taken away;
> Blessed be the name of the Lord. (1:21-22)

The Second Challenge by the Satan (2:1-6). In the third scene the Adversary confesses defeat, but is still unconvinced of Job's integrity. He offers a second challenge: If God will permit Job's body to be tortured, then Job will cease being faithful and will curse God to his face. Again God agrees to the test, but he forbids the Satan to take Job's life.

Job's Second Round of Afflictions (2:7-13). In the final scene of the Prologue Job is smitten from head to foot with boils.* The formerly happy and prosperous sheikh, now reduced to a sick and miserable beggar, scrapes his loathsome body with a potsherd and deserts his own house to take up his abode on a pile of dung ashes† outside the city walls. His wife advises him to relinquish his "integrity" and to "curse God and die." Rebuking her for foolish words, Job retains his trust in God. We receive good from God's hands, he says; shall we not also expect to receive evil?

Hearing of his sad plight, three of Job's friends—Eliphaz, Bildad, and Zophar—come to commiserate with him. Job's suffering and their grief for him are so overwhelming that for seven days and seven nights the four men maintain an eloquent silence.

JOB'S CURSE (CH. 3)

Having lost by this time his former submissive resignation, Job bursts into a terrible imprecation—"a curse, not against God, but against his own existence":[19]

> Let the day perish wherein I was born,
> And the night in which it was said, "There is a man
>   child conceived."‡ (3:3)

* Many scholars have tried to diagnose Job's malady. Leprosy and various skin diseases have been suggested. See Samuel Terrien, exegesis to Job, *The Interpreter's Bible*, III, 920.

† Such an ash heap, known as a *mazbala,* still exists today outside some Arabian towns. (Terrien, exegesis, *The Interpreter's Bible*, III, 920.)

‡ A memorable borrowing of this awesome curse appears in Thomas Hardy's *Jude the Obscure*, when Jude uses Job's words to curse his own miserable existence.

He wishes he had died at birth, and he yearns to die now:

> Wherefore is light given to him that is in misery,
> And life unto the bitter in soul;
> Which long for death, but it cometh not;
> And dig for it more than for hid treasures;
> Which rejoice exceedingly,
> And are glad, when they can find the grave? (3:20-22)

THE DEBATE (CHS. 4—27)

Following the lament of Job, there is a series of arguments between Job and his group of friends—a discussion somewhat similar to the *agon* of an Aristophanic comedy. This debate has three rounds or cycles; in each cycle each of the three friends speaks and (except in one instance) in answered by Job (according to the arrangement proposed by Professor Moulton).[20] As the discussion progresses, Job grows more and more impatient and angry with his friends, and they become ever more denunciatory and abusive.

The First Cycle (Chs. 4—14). Tactfully but patronizingly, Eliphaz opens the debate with a long and dignified statement of the traditional Hebrew view of suffering (Chs. 4—5); God is righteous and just; therefore we may be sure that every affliction suffered by a man is a punishment for some deed of iniquity. God uses suffering to humble the wicked. If a sinner will accept God's chastening and repent of his sins, God will again become his benefactor and give him a long and happy life. Eliphaz ends his speech with the dogmatic pronouncements that he is among those who have studied these matters and that therefore he *knows* that what he has said is true; he advises Job to profit by his teachings (5:27).

Job's reply (Chs. 6—7) is addressed "partly to Eliphaz, partly to God."[21] He bemoans his miseries and attributes them to God's cruelty. He accuses his friends—whom he still calls "brethren"—of heartlessness, willful misunderstanding, and even treachery. In his anguish he engages in a very human inconsistency: one moment he is pleading with God to destroy him (6:9), and the next he is deploring the brevity of man's life:

> My days are swifter than a weaver's shuttle,
> And are spent without hope. (7:6)

Perhaps parodying Psalm 8,[22] he sarcastically asks why God should so exalt man as to "try" him every minute (7:17-18). Without admitting that he has sinned, he wonders why God, in his mercy, has not pardoned whatever transgression he may have committed. He warns God to hurry, for Job will soon descend into Sheol, and then it will be too late for forgiveness. "Thus the poet twists man's desperate clinging to the belief in God's love into a grim joke upon the Deity's frustration."[23]

Bildad now (Ch. 8) enters the debate. Angrily he accuses Job of rashness and folly:

> How long wilt thou speak these things?
> And how long shall the words of thy mouth be like a strong wind?
> Doth God pervert judgment?
> Or doth the Almighty pervert justice? (8:2-3)

The wisdom of the ages has declared that, since God is just, the wicked will not prosper or the righteous go unrewarded.

Job's rejoinder (Chs. 9–10) is a reply not so much to Bildad as to Eliphaz, whose words he is apparently still pondering. God, he says, is fearfully powerful, but also capricious and devoid of interest in moral behavior. Formerly he has seemed to be Job's friend, but now he is his tormentor. And why? Since Job has not sinned, there is no reason for the change in God's treatment of him. Job begs God to let him alone and give him a short period of comfort before eternal death (10: 18-22).*

At this point (Ch. 11), Zophar joins the fray. Fiercely he attacks Job's speeches, which he considers blasphemous babble. Without adding anything new to the discussion, he reasserts belief in God's goodness and wisdom, and he urges Job to repent of his sins.

In a rather lengthy rebuttal (Chs. 12–14) Job declares his Comforters' arguments to be worthless. The very fact that he is suffering *proves* God's lack of justice. Again he contrasts God's power with man's weakness, and he laments the misery and the transiency of man's life:

> Man that is born of a woman is of few days, and full of trouble.
> (14:1)

---

* It should be noted that in this portion of the book there is no trace of a belief in life after death.

Feeling that the end of his life is near, he hurls one more challenge at the Deity: even if it should mean his death, he would like to meet God face to face and there defend his innocence.* The cycle ends with a groan of despair.

The Second Cycle (Chs. 15—21). Discarding his former gentleness and courteousness, Eliphaz opens his second discourse with a blunt indictment of Job, who, he says, is only deluding himself. He paints a gruesome picture of the fate of the wicked (Ch. 15).

Hotly Job upbraids his friends for their heartlessness and God for his cruel injustice. Then a new idea occurs to Job (16:18-22). In Jewish law a *goël*[24] or "avenger of blood" took up the cause of a man who had been murdered or had lost his property or been sold into slavery. So Job envisages some equivalent redeemer to vindicate him to God after his death. (The occurrence of this idea is a major crisis in the drama and leads directly to the climax, as will be seen.) At the moment, however, death is all that Job has to look forward to.

Bildad's second speech (Ch. 18) merely emphasizes that a sinner's lot is unhappy while he is on earth and that he will be utterly forgotten after his death.†

The turning point of the play comes in Job's second reply to Bildad (Ch. 19). Indignant with his friends, to whom he has vainly looked for comfort, Job feels his complete alienation from unsympathetic man. While brooding over his ideas concerning a *goël*, he makes a sudden shift in his thinking. He concludes that somehow God himself will ultimately be his *goël*, his vindicator, champion, and defender.‡[25] In this "leap of faith," Job claims that after the worms have eaten his body, he himself will plead his case before God. (Perhaps the author of the drama intends

* The King James translation of 13:15a ("Though he slay me, yet will I trust him"), though sublime, is indefensible on either linguistic or psychological grounds. The correct meaning is that God is surely going to slay Job, who has abandoned all hope. See W. F. Lofthouse, commentary on Job, *The Abingdon Bible Commentary,* p. 494, and Terrien, exegesis, *The Interpreter's Bible,* III, 1003-1005.

† Compare Psalm 109.

‡ The King James translation of 19:25 ("I know that my redeemer liveth") has been believed by many Christians to be a prophecy of Christ's redemption of mankind.

this speech as a foreshadowing of Job's encounter with the Deity when the latter addresses him from the Whirlwind.)

Zophar's second speech (Ch. 20) virtually ignores everything that Job has been saying. Instead it harps on the same old theme that the wicked, though temporarily prosperous, will inevitably be given their just deserts.

In his retort (Ch. 21) Job asks his friends to be honest for a while—to withhold their pious condemnations and to listen open-mindedly to his words. He adduces as evidence for his view about suffering the facts that the wicked are unpunished, enjoy life, and thrive; that the prayers of the good often go unanswered, and their lives are made bitter; and that evil men are honored after their death. He ends the cycle by branding all the friends' opinions as falsehoods.

The Third Cycle (Chs. 22—27). The last round of speeches is largely repetitious of the first two rounds and so requires only brief comment. As usual, Eliphaz speaks first, accusing Job of wickedness and urging him to repent (Ch. 22). In a familiar passage (23:1—24:17) Job laments that he is unable to discover God:

> O that I knew where I might find him!
> That I might come even to his seat! (23:3)

God is elusive and goes away whenever Job tries to seek him out.

Bildad (Ch. 25 and 26:5—14*) does not reply to Job, but extols God's great power and knowledge.

Job answers that such considerations are of little help to him, and again he reaffirms his own integrity (26:1-4 and 27:1-12).

Zophar merely reiterates his own preceding speech (24:18—24 and 27:13—23).[26]

A HYMN ON WISDOM (CH. 28)

Following the three cycles of debate, there is a fine chapter dealing with man's inability to acquire wisdom, which is attainable by God alone. The hymn is clearly not a part of the debate between Job and his friends; Bildad might conceivably have

* Attributed by modern scholars to Bildad, though following Job's retort without an indication of change of speaker.

spoken it, but it is really irrelevant to the topic being debated. Most Biblical scholars consider it an interpolation.

JOB'S PERORATION (CHS. 29—31)

In a long monologue—apparently *not* addressed to the three friends, but spoken as if in soliloquy—Job offers a final summary of his plight. He recalls his former days of prosperity, when God was with him; then his children were about him, he had material wealth, he was a benefactor to the needy, and men respected his counsels (Ch. 29). Now, he says, people mock at him and abhor him; he is a derelict; pain racks his body; God has cruelly cast him into the mire; he is like dust and ashes; when he has waited for the light, he has received only darkness (Ch. 30). His famous "oath of clearing" (Ch. 31) is one last, exalted protestation of his innocence. He lists sixteen different sinful acts and swears that he is not guilty of any one of them. He wishes that God would confront him with a bill of indictment; he would display it in public, answer it like a prince, and so clear himself of all charges.

ELIHU'S INTERPOSITION (CHS. 32—37)

At the end of the oath of clearing, the dramatic tension is very great. The three self-righteous Comforters have spoken their pieces, and Job has wound up the whole debate like a lawyer summarizing his case before a jury. In fearful suspense the reader awaits the dread decision of the judge. Instead, however, there bursts upon the scene a young man named Elihu, who has not even been mentioned earlier in the drama. He delivers a windy and tedious monologue, six chapters long, which repeats much of what the other three Comforters have already said; his one contribution to the discussion is the suggestion that God uses suffering to warn and restore men.[27] By sending tribulations, God opens the ears of men, shows them what is right, perhaps through a "messenger" or "interpreter," and so saves them from Sheol (33:16—24).

Most modern Biblical scholars consider Elihu's discourse a late interpolation. This belief is borne out by the facts (1) that none of the other persons of the drama replies to Elihu or in any other way acknowledges his presence and (2) that God's reply out of the Whirlwind seems to be in response to Job's words which precede Elihu's interruption.

THE DIVINE INTERVENTION (38:1—42:6)

The most powerful and exalted passage in the drama—often regarded as the finest piece of poetry in the whole Bible—is God's reply spoken to Job from a Whirlwind. Time after time Job has begged that he might be allowed to meet God face to face, plead his cause, and accuse the Deity of injustice. Now his prayer is answered, in effect, except that after God finishes speaking, Job does not feel like hurling further charges.

Most of God's discourse consists of a series of rhetorical questions. He begins by asking wrathfully and contemptuously:

> Who is this that darkeneth counsel by words without knowledge?
> Gird up thy loins like a man;
> For I will demand of thee, and answer thou me. (38:2-3)

The torrent of questions that follows (38:4—41:34)* holds up vain and puny man in contrast with the Creator of the universe:

> Where wast thou when I laid the foundations of the earth?
> Declare, if thou hast understanding.
> Who hath laid the measures thereof, if thou knowest?
> Or who hath stretched the line upon it?
> Whereupon are the foundations thereof fastened?
> Or who laid the corner stone thereof;
> When the morning stars sang together,
> And all the sons of God shouted for joy? (38:4-7)

It is God who has created the earth and the sea and the sky, day and night, snow and hail and lightning, rain and ice and mist, the constellations, and the wild and domestic animals.† Does Job understand these things—was he around when they were created?

Job is utterly, abjectly humbled. He confesses that he has spoken ignorantly. He abhors himself and repents "in dust and ashes." Whereas he has formerly received his conception of God

---

* God's discourse is broken into two parts by Job's meek acknowledgment of his own worthlessness (40:3-5).

† The passages on Behemoth (the hippopotamus?) (40:15-24) are believed to be interpolations by some late (second century B.C.?) editor.

at second hand ("by the hearing of the ear"), now (42:5) he himself has encountered God directly ("now mine eye seeth thee"). At last he perceives that he *has* been sinful. For so insignificant a creature to dare to question the purposes of the Almighty is pride of the most presumptuous sort.

This is the drama's final answer to the question of why the innocent suffer; and it is, of course, no solution. The dramatist seems to be saying that man can never discover a logical solution to the problem. God is the Creator of all things and beings with their potential for good and evil; yet he is also the Redeemer, who cares for man; and an encounter with him brings faith in his purpose and submission to his will.

THE PROSE (OR FOLK-TALE) EPILOGUE (42:7-17)

A prose epilogue completes the plot—and virtually refutes the philosophical point made in the preceding passage. By allowing God to restore Job's prosperity, the dramatist is, in effect, proving the Comforters' contention that the innocent do not actually continue to suffer, but are rewarded with material things for their goodness. Job begets ten more children, and his former wealth is doubled. This conclusion doubtless was part of the old folk tale used as the material for the drama, and perhaps the dramatist felt that it was needed to round out the action and bring the story to a happy ending. At any rate, he warns us that the Comforters' views are wrong; God himself condemns them and praises Job for his honest quest of the truth (42:7).

The Song of Solomon: A Wedding Idyl[1]

During the "revolt of the intellectuals" in the 1920's, many young skeptics boasted that the only part of the Bible which they read was The Song of Solomon, or The Song of Songs. The reason for this partiality was that the book is entirely secular. It is a group of highly erotic lyrics, filled with romantic descriptions of the human body. How this book (which never even mentions God) found its way into the Hebrew* and the Christian canons is a fascinating story.

To begin with, the book opens with an announcement that its author is King Solomon. Such authorship, though it would not establish the *sacredness* of the work, certainly would lend it enormous prestige. Attribution to Solomon is owing to the facts (1) that the book itself mentions that ancient monarch as one of its two leading characters (3:7, 9, 11; 8:12), and (2) that Solomon, like his father David, was traditionally regarded as a great poet (I Kings 4:32 says that he wrote a thousand and five songs). But most modern scholars believe that Solomon had nothing to do with the composition of the book.

As we shall see, there is good evidence that the poems belong to the realm of folk song and that they are of north Palestinian or Syrian provenance. That they were transmitted orally for several centuries seems likely. Linguistic considerations (especially the presence of Aramaisms) indicate that they were written down in their present form between 350 and 250 B.C.[2]

The question of canonicity leads us to a consideration of the important matter of interpretation, for it was one of the early interpretations which induced Jewish scholars to accept the book

* The book is the third part of the Hebrew canon known as the Writings. It is read today, either publicly or privately, as part of the Passover service.

as a piece of sacred literature near the end of the first century
A.D. Since that time there have been numerous other attempts
to explain and classify it. Most of these suggestions are included
under the following five headings:

"*Allegorical explanation*"[3]: Some ancient Hebrew commentators interpreted The Song of Songs as an allegory of the love
of God for the Israelites; God was represented by King Solomon
and the Hebrews by the Shulamite, and the love described in
the poems was to be understood as spiritual rather than physical.
This symbolic interpretation was adapted by the early Christians
to fit their own beliefs: the book celebrated the mystical union
of Christ and the Church. This interpretation was in keeping
with various New Testament references to the Church as the
bride of Christ (see, for example, II Cor. 11:2 and Rev. 19:7–8,
21:9, and 22:17). It was almost universally accepted by Christians down through the eighteenth century; the King James
translators followed it when writing the outlines prefixed to
each chapter. Few modern scholars accept the allegorical interpretation.

"*Natural explanation*": Some students have believed that the
book is simply a collection of separate secular love lyrics. The
principal objections to this view are that there is more continuity
in the poems than one generally finds in a "collection" or anthology and that there is a chorus—rarely, if ever, found in individual love lyrics.

"*Anthropological explanation*": A third suggestion is that The
Song of Songs is an adaptation to Yahweh-worship of a part of
a ritual belonging to the cult of some pagan fertility god. Such
a ritual usually included singing and dancing (sometimes by a
chorus of women). The annual spring festival celebrating the
wedding of the Babylonian sun god Tammuz (Adonis) and
the goddess Ishtar (Astarte), for instance, might have been the
source of the Hebrew poems. Comparable celebrations were held
in honor of the Greek Dionysus and the Egyptian Osiris.

"*Literary explanation*": An attractive interpretation is that The
Song of Songs is a full-fledged drama. The explicators who hold
this view are divided into two groups: (1) those who recognize
three principal characters—King Solomon, the shepherd lover,
and the Shulamite shepherdess; the two men vie with each other
for the hand of the maiden, and the shepherd finally wins "ac-

cording to the best democratic tradition";[4] and (2) those who think that the shepherd is really King Solomon in disguise; he masquerades as a swain in order to win the shepherdess and then reveals his identity and makes her a member of his harem.

"*Sociological explanation*": The interpretation which probably best explains the form and the contents of the book is that it is a quasi-dramatic series of songs once used as a part of Oriental wedding celebrations. In 1873 J. G. Wetzstein called attention to the survival in some rural parts of Syria of customs which are believed to be very ancient (and which, incidentally, are extant today). The nuptial festivities continue for a whole week, during which period the bride and the groom are treated as "queen" and "king," with the local peasantry serving as their "attendants." Each of the principals praises the other's physical beauty, and sometimes the "queen" performs a sword dance. In 1894 Karl Budde argued convincingly that The Song of Songs was a sort of "script" for one of these ancient rural pageants. This view would explain the shepherd's role as King Solomon, the presence of the choruses of maidens and young men, and the pastoral setting.

This "sociological explanation" seems to be the one most widely held today by reputable scholars, and this Outline will assume that it is the right one.

As a piece of literature The Song of Songs ranks very high. It is not extravagant to say that no other composition in world literature can surpass it as an expression of the exuberance of pure, connubial love. Compared with it, even so excellent a love song as Spenser's "Epithalamion" seems artificial and a bit tame. The Song of Songs is inspired with the frank, unself-conscious passion of the Oriental lover and his bride. It is unrestrained but not crude, fleshly but not bawdy, intimate but not vulgar. Not only is the book filled with descriptions of the persons of the bride and groom, but also it breathes the atmosphere of the Palestinian (or the Syrian) countryside—the roes upon the mountains, the flocks of sheep and goats beside the tents of the shepherds, the lilies in the fields, the orchards with their clusters of grapes and their pomegranates, the joyous song of the turtledove, the bright spring weather succeeding the winter-long rains.

The descriptions are made especially vivid by the use of innumerable fresh and daring similes and metaphors: the groom is like a bundle of myrrh that lies between the breasts of the bride, he is like a bouquet of henna flowers in the vineyard, his cheeks are like a bed of spices, his body is like ivory overlaid with sapphires, his legs are like pillars of marble, and even his name is like ointment poured forth. The bride is a garden that has been carefully protected from would-be spectators, she is an enclosed spring of water, her lips are like a thread of scarlet, her temples are like a piece of pomegranate, honey and milk are under her tongue, and the fragrance of her breath is like apples. Occasionally the poet uses figures of speech which would seem ludicrous in a modern work; for example, the bride's breasts are like two fawns, her teeth are like a flock of ewes, and—worst of all—her nose is like the tower of Lebanon! Assuredly, however, these similes did not seem grotesque either to the poet or to the Hebrew wedding guests, but were intended—and recognized— as phrases expressive of the highest degree of perfection.

The predominant "meter" in The Song of Songs is that of the *qînôh*.* Most of the lines form distichs of 3+2 accents; some are 2+3 or 2+2. Tristichs are fairly frequent (3+2+3, 3+2+2, or 3+3+3).[5] There is less parallelism in the book than in most other Hebrew poetry—perhaps evidence that it is of non-Palestinian origin.

The cast of characters in the little "idyl" is small: King Solomon, the groom; the Shulamite, the bride; a chorus of the "Brothers," friends of the groom; and a chorus of "Daughters of Jerusalem," friends of the bride.[6] There are six "scenes": (1) 1:2—2:7, (2) 2:8—3:5, (3) 3:6—5:1, (4) 5:2—6:3, (5) 6:4—8:4, and (6) 8:5-14.[7] It seems likely that each of the scenes is presented on a separate day and that the closing lines of every scene mark the end of the day's public celebration and serve as a prelude to the approach to the marriage bed.

SCENE ONE: INVITATION TO LOVE (1:2—2:7)

The participants in the first tableau are the Shulamite, the Daughters of Jerusalem, and King Solomon. The Shulamite opens the scene with an invitation, addressed partly to the Daughters and partly to her beloved:

> Let him kiss me with the kisses of his mouth:
> For thy love is better than wine.

* See p. 263 for a discussion of this meter.

After the Daughters rejoice with her, she and King Solomon take turns eulogizing each other. She addresses a beautiful amatory passage to the Daughters:

> He brought me to the banqueting house,
> And his banner over me was love.
> Stay me with flagons,
> Comfort me with apples:
> For I am sick of love.*
> His left hand is under my head,
> And his right hand doth embrace me. (2.4-6)

She ends the scene with an injunction (perhaps relating to a rite) not to "stir up" or "awake my love till he pleases."†

SCENE TWO: "REMINISCENCES OF THE COURTSHIP"⁸
(2:8—3:5)

One of the loveliest passages in the book is the bride's recollection of a visit from her lover during the days of their courtship:

> The voice of my beloved!
> Behold, he cometh leaping upon the mountains,
> Skipping upon the hills. . . .
> My beloved spake, and said unto me,
> Rise up, my love, my fair one, and come away.
> For, lo, the winter is past,
> The rain is over and gone;
> The flowers appear on the earth;
> The time of the singing of birds is come,
> And the voice of the turtle‡ is heard in our land.
> The fig tree putteth forth her green figs,
> And the vines with the tender grape give a good smell.
> Arise, my love, my fair one, and come away. (2:8, 10-13)

The reverie is broken by the harsh voice of the Brothers, crying that the foxes have broken into the vineyard and are spoiling the grapes (2:15).

The Shulamite tells about a dream she has had: she dreamed that she was seeking her lover and could not find him. She asked the night watchmen, but got no help. At last she found him whom

* "Sick of love" means, of course, "sick *with* love."
† The Revised Standard Version translates, "Stir not up nor awaken love till it pleases."
‡ Turtle dove.

she sought, held him close, and would not release him till she had brought him into her mother's house.

The story of the dream finished, she repeats the 2:7 refrain.

SCENE THREE: THE WEDDING DAY (3:6—5:1)

The Daughters of Jerusalem open the third scene by proclaiming the approach of the groom, who comes in from the wilderness "like pillars of smoke, perfumed with myrrh and frankincense," borne on a litter by "threescore valiant men."

The groom responds with an exquisite lyric praising his bride: "Behold, Thou Art Fair, My Love" (4:1-15). The Shulamite compares herself to a garden and welcomes her lover into it:

> Let my lover come into his garden,
> And eat his pleasant fruits. (4:16)

Eagerly King Solomon accepts the invitation:

> I am come into my garden, my sister, my spouse:
> I have gathered my myrrh with my spice;
> I have eaten my honeycomb with my honey;
> I have drunk my wine with my milk ... (5:1)

He urges all the guests to join in the day's festivities by eating and drinking.

SCENE FOUR: A NIGHTMARE OF THE BRIDE'S (5:2—6:3)

In the fourth tableau the bride tells of another dream she has had. She dreamed that one night her lover knocked at the door. Her fingers dripping with myrrh, she opened the door, but her beloved had departed. She sought him in the streets. Again she met the night watchmen, but on this occasion they beat and wounded her and took away her veil. She found herself face to face with the Daughters and requested their aid, for she was sick with love. They asked her in what ways her sweetheart was superior to any other young man; she quickly seized this opportunity for another eulogy of his charms. The nightmare had a happy ending. With the illogicality that is characteristic of dreams, the Daughters next asked *her* where her lover was, and then she knew the answer: he had gone into the garden to feed his flocks and to gather lilies. Once again she was happy.

SCENE FIVE: LOVE IN THE ROYAL COURT CONTRASTED WITH LOVE IN THE VILLAGE (6:4—8:4)

In the fifth scene the newlyweds begin to drop the "play-acting" as king and queen. The groom commences with a superb poem praising the loveliness of his bride:

> Thou art beautiful, O my love, as Tirzah,*
> Comely as Jerusalem, terrible as an army with banners.

Perhaps it is the reference to the two great cities that suggests to the groom the contrast of the pomp and turmoil of the court with the idyllic serenity of his own village, and of the *real* King Solomon's love life with his own. Whereas the great monarch has sixty queens, eighty concubines, and "virgins without number,"

> My dove, my undefiled is but one. (6:9)

(It would be difficult to find elsewhere so eloquent, so restrained, and so poetic a glorification of single-hearted devotion.) The youth continues with a catalogue of the maiden's beauties—her feet, her navel, her belly, her breasts, her neck, her nose, her head, her hair, and even the roof of her mouth.

The Shulamite replies with a rededication of herself to her lover, and she exhorts him to wander away with her to the fields and vineyards, where the grapes and the pomegranates are in bloom and the mandrakes offer their fragrance. She will take him to her mother's house and give him spiced wine and pomegranate juice. His left hand will be under her head, and his right will embrace her. Again the refrain of 2:7 is repeated.

SCENE SIX: RENEWAL OF LOVE AT HOME (8:5-14)

The last tableau is a sort of finale, in which the bride and the groom are welcomed to their own house by both choruses. With exultation the Shulamite describes the eternity of true love:

> Set me a seal upon thine heart,
> As a seal upon thine arm:
> For love is strong as death;
> Jealousy is cruel as the grave:
> The coals thereof are coals of fire,
> Which hath a most vehement flame.

* Tirzah was at one time the capital of the Northern Kingdom.

> Many waters cannot quench love,
> Neither can the floods drown it:
> If a man would give all the substance of his house for love,
> It would be utterly contemned.* (8:6-7)

Once more the bride offers her body (her "vineyard") to her beloved, who begs to be allowed to hear her voice call again. She complies:

> Make haste, my beloved,
> And be thou like to a roe
> Or to a young hart
> Upon the mountains of spices. (8:14)

* *Contemned* here means "rejected."

Part Six
Short Stories and Tales

In our survey of history and biography we have encountered many short narratives which could be—and which indeed often have been—removed from context and appreciated purely for the sake of the stories.* In the next two chapters we shall consider some unique post-Exilic tales which, whatever their basis in historical fact and whatever their immediate theological purpose, were calculated in Jewish religious communities to "hold children from play and old men from the chimney corners." Because of their distinctive settings, their psychologically well-developed characters, and their suspenseful plots, several (Ruth, Jonah, Tobit, Susanna, and Esther) are full-fledged short stories by almost any modern definition. The more stylized tales of Daniel 1–6 and of Bel and the Dragon, however they may be classified, rank among the great legends of antiquity.†

---

* The following types (with representative examples given in parentheses) have been commented upon in previous chapters: *myth* (The Story of Creation, Gen. 1–2), *folk legend* (The Story of Samson, Judg. 13–16), *historical tale* (The Story of Joseph, Gen. 37–50), and *fable* (Jotham's Fable, Judg. 9:7-15).

† The Song of the Three Holy Children (which has to do with Daniel's companions) has been treated as lyric poetry (see p. 268). The fragmentary Apocryphal book called The Rest of Esther will be considered together with the canonical story of Esther (see p. 328).

Fourth-Century Stories
Advocating Tolerance
Ruth and Jonah

The books of Ruth and Jonah represent a reaction against the understandably bitter racial prejudices and religious exclusiveness which were prevalent in Jerusalem after the return from the Babylonian Captivity.* Although many political leaders and priests of the fourth century B.C. encouraged a discriminatory attitude against foreigners, some thinkers, deeply rooted in the spirit of the Prophets (see especially Isa. 42:1-7), believed that the Chosen People had been elected as a missionary light to all nations and looked forward to an age when a united world would live in peace, with Jerusalem as its religious center. They felt it a mistake to regard an all-merciful Creator as being interested only in the salvation of the Jews and in the welfare of Palestine. At least two such thinkers chose the short story as an effective means of promoting the humane and tolerant aspects of Jewish theology.

RUTH: AN IDYL WITH A GENTLE PROTEST
AGAINST NATIONAL PREJUDICE

Ruth, one of the most beautiful and beloved books of the Old Testament, was admitted late to the Hebrew canon and was classed among the "Writings." Because its story is set in the time

* It should be recalled that Ezra and Nehemiah believed that Yahweh-worship and the purity of ancient Hebrew blood were endangered by any intermingling with neighboring populations. Hence they took stringent measures (for example, laws requiring the divorce of alien spouses) to exclude foreigners from the Jewish community and from participation in the Hebrew religious services.

of the Judges (c. 1100 B.C.) and because its heroine is said to
have been an ancestress of King David, the Greek, Latin, and
English Bibles have traditionally placed it after the book of
Judges. Its language, style, and allusions indicate that it was
probably written at some time between 450 and 250 B.C.; and its
message concerning the intermarriage of Jews and aliens probably narrows the date to the half-century of 400-350 B.C. The
anonymous author may have used an ancient tale as his source;
but if he did, he adapted the tale very skillfully to his immediate
purpose. That purpose is accomplished so tactfully and so unobtrusively that a casual modern reader is likely to overlook it entirely and to conclude with Goethe that here is the "daintiest of
love idyls." Yet the author did time and again remind his original
readers that the heroine was a foreigner—a Moabitess*—who em-
braced Judaism and contributed to the blood of the Hebrew
royal line.

The Story of Ruth. The reader of the story must bear in mind
an ancient marital custom (the "levirate law" of Deut. 25:5-6)
and an ancient Jewish property law (Lev. 25:25). The former,
as it seems to have been understood by the author of Ruth, may
be stated thus: If a man died childless, his nearest kinsman was
obligated to marry the widow and to consider the first-born son
as the dead man's heir.[1] The second decreed that if a poor man
was forced to sell his land, a near kinsman was obligated to buy
it back ("redeem" it).

THE ADVERSITIES OF AN UPRIGHT FAMILY (Ch. 1). Elimelech,
with his wife Naomi and two sons, is compelled by famine to em-
igrate from Bethlehem in Judah to the land of Moab. There he
dies, and some ten years later his sons (both of whom have married Moabitish girls) die. Naomi starts home to Bethlehem. When
she advises the younger widows to return to their parents and
seek new husbands, one tearfully obeys; but the other, Ruth, insists upon accompanying her and adopting her people and her
God.† Arriving among the welcoming townsmen, the elderly

* The people of Moab were hated by many Jews; see, for example, Deut.
23:3. The author's reminders of Ruth's Moabite blood occur in Ruth 1:22, 2:2,
2:6, 2:10, 2:21, 4:5, and 4:10.

† The verses beginning "Entreat me not to leave thee" (1:16-17) are justly
celebrated as a supremely beautiful expression of human affection.

widow requests to be called no longer *Naomi* ("Pleasant") but *Mara* ("Bitter").

THE FORTUNES OF RUTH AND NAOMI (Ch. 2). Ruth follows the hired reapers in the barley field to glean their leavings,* and she happens to select land belonging to Boaz, a wealthy kinsman of Elimelech. Boaz learns her identity and assumes some special responsibility for her welfare, commanding that she be permitted to share the midday meal of the regular workers and that his men let a considerable amount of grain fall so that she may pick it up. When Ruth returns home with a large amount of grain and tells Naomi that it is from the field of Boaz, Naomi at once recognizes the relationship and blesses the Lord, "who hath not left off his kindness to the living and the dead."

NAOMI'S PLAN (Ch. 3). By the end of the reaping session, Naomi has decided upon a wise course: Ruth shall go by night to the threshing floor, lie down at the feet of Boaz, and await his instructions. Boaz praises Ruth for seeking his protection and professes his readiness to marry her and redeem certain land that had belonged to Elimelech—provided that a still nearer kinsman will relinquish priority.

RUTH'S MARRIAGE AND ITS LESSON FOR THE HEBREWS (Ch. 4). In the morning Boaz and the unnamed kinsman appear before the city elders. The nearer relative would be willing to redeem the land for Naomi, but not to complicate the legal status of his first-born. So Boaz redeems the property and marries Ruth. Their first son is named Obed—"and Obed begat Jesse, and Jesse begat David."

Literary Qualities. Having noted its moral lesson, let us look at the story as a specimen of fictional art. Its main excellence lies in the tenderness, serenity, and nobility which pervade the entire narrative; in the exquisiteness and delicacy with which details are handled; and in the suspense which is continuously maintained. There has been a tendency among Western admirers to regard it as a sort of religious fairy tale in which a Cinderella meets and weds her Prince Charming, but perhaps the fourth-century Hebrew writer had a different conception of romance. His lovers have seen trouble and known loneliness, and at last

* The right of the poor to glean was established by law—Deut. 24:19-22.

they find security and peace; and the justice of the Lord toward Naomi and toward the upright dead are a part of the happy ending.

SETTING. The setting is "in the days when the judges ruled"— the bygone age when manners and speeches and the observance of Jewish customs were supposedly at the best. "Now this was the manner in former time," says the author (implying that the name of God was not taken in vain even in legal testimony), "a man plucked off his shoe and gave it to his neighbor; and this was a testimony in Israel" (4:7). It was a model age of family loyalty, when the young showed proper respect for the old and when property rights were strictly regarded. The author includes pleasant background vignettes of village life as it used to be and of work in the grainfield and on the threshing floor.

CHARACTERS. Nothing is said about Ruth's being either physically beautiful or in the first bloom of youth; her virtues are her love for her mother-in-law, her fortitude in times of trouble, and her ready acceptance of the Hebrew God. Boaz seems from his speeches to be middle-aged, and there is something wistful in his astonishment that Ruth should turn to him rather than give her attention to young men "whether poor or rich" (3:10). He is the soul of piety, honor, and dependable responsibility; that he is kind and well loved is shown in his first greeting to the reapers (2:4). Naomi is the really complicated character of the story. She is the pioneer mother who has followed her husband to a strange land and who determines to return to Bethlehem only after making certain that bread is plentiful there (1:6). She is the resourceful mother-in-law and matchmaker (who, in 3:3, even thinks to warn Ruth against approaching Boaz until he has dined and is in a fine humor). She can be melodramatic about her misfortunes (1:20), but fundamentally she is the humble woman who accepts all troubles as the will of God. There is no villain in this idyl, but there is some artful pointing up of the virtues of the leading characters through contrast with those not so outstandingly noble (through contrast of Ruth with the less devoted daughter-in-law and contrast of Boaz with the more cautious kinsman).

PLOT. The author is a master at introducing human interest naturally and unobtrusively: the welcoming of Naomi by her former neighbors, Ruth's saving a part of her lunch for Naomi, the concern of the city elders for the welfare of a widow, the excitement of the women when a child is born. The author also knows how to introduce new elements of suspense at times: Will the Moabitess make a living in Judah? will she fall a victim to the young men? will Boaz assume his obligations? will the nearer kinsman spoil Naomi's plan? And there is the surprise ending which tells us so briefly, in the style of Chronicles, of Ruth's real importance in Hebrew history.

JONAH: AN ADVENTURE STORY EXPOSING
THE FOLLY OF BIGOTRY

When the Hebrew Prophetic canon was compiled (c. 200 B.C.), the book of Jonah was included among the "Latter Prophets." During the last hundred years, however, both theologians and literary critics have leaned increasingly toward the view that the work was originally intended as pure fiction (whether allegory, parable, or satire) with a strong religious message for the fourth-century rebuilders of Jerusalem.

A historical "Jonah, the son of Amittai" is briefly mentioned in II Kings 14:25 as a prophet who delivered divine messages in the reign of Jeroboam II (c. 785 B.C.), when Assyria, with its capital Nineveh, was rising to international prestige. We do not know whether this historical Jonah was actually sent upon some mission to Nineveh, nor do we know whether his name may have later figured in folk legends about a disobedient prophet. We next meet him as the hero of the book, which is almost certainly post-Exilic in composition.[2] Most scholars date the writing about 350 B.C.

Had the book of Jonah been presented as a historical and scientific monograph, even fourth-century B.C. readers might well have questioned whether the idolatrous Ninevites had ever been converted to Judaism, whether a man could live for three days within a fish, or whether a gourd or any other plant could spring up overnight and give shade. No such questions could arise if the book were understood to be a work of fiction written by a religious teacher who held (with Hosea and Isaiah) that a merciful God loves all creation and has chosen Jerusalem to be a missionary center for the conversion of the entire world. In such a view, it is the author of the story of Jonah (rather than the titular hero) who is the real *prophet,* the true human spokesman of God's will.

The Story of Jonah. The author was not interested in teaching history—his story does not mention Jeroboam or name the so-called King of Nineveh. His purpose rather was to inculcate the religion of a merciful, loving, and just God—his story attributes this doctrine directly to God. He was interested in exposing and criticizing any tendency in Jerusalem toward racial and religious exclusivism; his hero, however admirable in many respects, is an old-fashioned preacher with a hatred for foreigners that in the author's view was theologically anachronistic.

JONAH'S REBELLIOUSNESS (Ch. 1). Rather than obey God's command to go as a missionary to the sinful Ninevites, Jonah takes ship in the opposite direction. The ship is caught in a terrible storm. The polytheistic sailors cast lots to discover who among them has offended a deity. When the lot falls on Jonah, he confesses that he has offended the God of Heaven who created both sea and land; and he demands to be thrown overboard. The sailors try hard to bring the ship to land, but the sea becomes more tempestuous. Then, after praying to Jonah's God, they reluctantly throw the prophet into the sea. As soon as this is done, a calm comes and the sailors offer sacrifices. Meantime, Jonah is swallowed by a fish which the Lord has prepared for this purpose; he remains within the fish three days and three nights.

JONAH'S PRAYER (Ch. 2). The prayer which Jonah utters "out of the fish's belly" is a conventional psalm of thanksgiving for deliverance from trouble. (Although Jewish storytellers frequently introduced versified interludes into their prose, Chapter 2 is thought to be an editor's insertion, because it scarcely fits an otherwise well-unified plot.)

THE CONVERSION OF NINEVEH (Ch. 3). Vomited up by the fish and finding himself upon dry land, Jonah again hears God's word to preach to Nineveh. This time he obeys, and when he arrives in that great city, he shouts his warning of imminent doom. Contrary to his hopes, the king instantly repents and commands the inhabitants, "man and beast," to fast, wear sackcloth, and pray to the Lord for mercy. Seeing their repentance, the Lord determines to be merciful.

THE LORD'S ANSWER TO JONAH (Ch. 4). Jonah admits having known all the time that God is gracious and merciful, and he is disgusted that God's love should extend to the Ninevites. Demanding to be killed rather than see his oracle of doom unfulfilled, he sits outside the city and awaits developments. The Lord answers Jonah first with a divine action and then with patient reasoning. First, he ordains that a vine* spring up overnight and briefly shelter the prophet from the heat, but that the vine be just as suddenly killed by a worm. To Jonah's indignant outburst, the Lord replies in effect: It is I and not you who created the Ninevites, and it is I and not you who created the vine; though you would have destroyed the people and spared the plant, should I not prefer to spare "more than sixscore thousand persons . . . and also much cattle?"

Literary Qualities. As a tale of imaginative adventure, Jonah has ever-popular folk elements,† a realistic storm scene, and continual suspense. But no book was included in the Bible simply for the sake of entertainment.

CHARACTERS. The character of Jonah is worth looking into for what it must have meant to citizens of fourth-century B.C. Jerusalem. Here is a fundamentally honest Jew who would give his life to save Gentile shipmates or even to restore a plant, but who so blindly hates a whole foreign nation that he would rather die than see its people spared. Here is a missionary who does not want his listeners to be converted and saved. Here is a theologian who believes God to be Creator and ruler of land and sea, but who tries to escape God simply by leaving Palestine. In short, here is an upright man whose prejudices are in direct opposition to his beliefs. Could it be, the author seems to ask, that many of the rulers, priests, and average citizens of Jerusalem were just as incongruous?

As in Ruth, we have a story that lacks a villain. Jonah is a valiant and (in his way) a tender man. The heathen sailors are good fellows who will row with hopeless energy rather than desert a dangerous passenger, but they have never been taught about the

---

* The King James Version translates "gourd."

† For later restatements of the ancient motifs of human beings swallowed and delivered alive or of great plants springing up overnight, one need read no further than "Little Red Ridinghood" and "Jack and the Beanstalk."

God of Heaven. The King of Nineveh is a conscientious monarch in a land where people have never had a chance to "discern
between their right hand and their left hand" (4:11). God is
the unseen protagonist whose will directs human affairs.

CLASSIFICATION. Jonah has been called the most misunderstood
book in the Bible. Difficulties have arisen from the fact that it
became classified as a work of prophecy although its methods of
teaching (not its doctrines) were distinct from those of Hebrew
prophetic literature.* Hence some early Christians regarded the
three days in the "great fish" as symbolic of Christ's burial and
Resurrection.† Further misunderstandings have arisen from the
assumption that the work was historical simply because the name
of Jonah was historical and because the author saw no need
for spoiling his story with prefatory explanations.

Hebrews of the fourth century B.C. who knew their national literature were acquainted with many examples of what we now
call *allegory, parable,* and *satire*—all literary devices for winning
audiences to the truth by making them decide for themselves instead of by asking them to listen to logical arguments or to base
judgments upon documentable facts. The terms are not mutually
exclusive, and all three literary methods may be included within
a story.

Some critics think that the character Jonah allegorized the Hebrew people, that the "great fish" allegorized Babylon, that the
swallowing of the hero allegorized the period of the Babylonian
Captivity, and that Jonah's obligation to preach to the Ninevites
allegorized the Hebrews' obligation to spread the knowledge of
God to pagan peoples. Such an interpretation may well have occurred to the original readers of Jonah.

Some think of Jonah as a parable, as a story which teaches
moral or spiritual truths in terms of human experience. They see
Jonah as a figure of self-righteousness, like the elder brother of
the Prodigal Son (Luke 15:11-32) or the sanctimonious priest
and Levite of The Good Samaritan story (Luke 10:25-37). Admirers of Cervantes' *Don Quixote* and Swift's *Tale of a Tub* may

---

* For a discussion of the methods of prophetic literature, see p. 163.

† The authors of Matt. 12:39-41 and 16:4 and of Luke 11:29-30 may have
so regarded this one episode in the story. On the other hand, they may have
looked upon Jonah merely as a classical tale suitable for illustrative allusion;
see James D. Smart, introduction to Jonah, *The Interpreter's Bible,* VI, 872.

view Jonah as a stubborn fighter for a lost cause, a likeable human anachronism. The story resembles these works in being told as a corrective satire; it holds the mirror of truth before a narrow-minded nation which has not yet realized the contradiction between its belief in a universal God and its worship of a purely Jewish Deity.

16

Second- and First-Century Stories Encouraging Integrity

Tobit, Daniel Cycle, Judith, and Tales of Esther

Whereas Ruth and Jonah reflect a period of revived independence and patriotism, the later fictional works of the Old Testament and Apocrypha reflect the long period of Grecian (Macedonian and Seleucid) occupation of Palestine. Tobit seems to date from the relatively calm era before the Seleucid ruler Antiochus Epiphanes attempted to impose Hellenic culture and religion upon the Jews. Most of the others appear to have been written in the time of bitterness and hatred for oppressors which came to a head in the Maccabean Revolt (see p. 150). All encourage Jews to remain true to their traditional faith and religious customs and to resist assimilation. The storytellers' "long ago" is no longer the idyllic age of Judges or Kings, but the time of the Exile, when the uncompromising righteousness of certain national heroes and heroines had, according to legend, frustrated pagan overlords.

TOBIT: AN ORIENTAL ROMANCE WITH HEBREW IDEOLOGY

Although less well known today when many English Bibles omit the Apocrypha, Tobit was dearly beloved in ancient times, in the Middle Ages, and in the Reformation. Its ancient popularity is attested by the facts that three texts have been preserved in Greek, two in Latin, two in Syriac, four in Hebrew, and one in Ethiopic, and that Hebraic and Aramaic fragments have recently been discovered among the Dead Sea Scrolls. In the Middle Ages it was regarded as instructive reading for young married couples (and sometimes is still so regarded today).[1] Toward the beginning of the Reformation, Martin Luther called it "a truly beautiful, wholesome, and profitable fiction, the work of a gifted poet, . . . a book useful and good for us Christians to read."

This book was written, most commentators agree, in the early years of the second century B.C.—possibly in the decade of 185-175. Its anonymous author was evidently a pious Jew with a knowledge of the Law, the Prophets (including a version of Jonah), and at least some of the Writings (Psalms, Proverbs, and Job); he seems to have been acquainted with Egyptian folklore (the Tractate of Khons and the Story of the Grateful Dead), with Babylonian folklore (the Story and Wisdom of Ahikar), and with Persian ideas about demonology.

The Story of Tobit. Apart from the purpose of encouraging Jews to withstand oppression, the main didactic purposes are to emphasize that the prayers of the faithful will be heard in time of affliction and that good works are eventually rewarded. The tale is set in the early years of the Exile—mainly in the reign of Sennacherib's successor; but the author is more concerned with moral lessons and with pictures of righteous conduct than with historical accuracy. His action shifts between the legendary city of Nineveh in Assyria and the legendary city of Ecbatana in Media.

GOD'S CONCERN WITH THE PRAYERS OF TOBIT AND SARAH (Chs. 1–3). Unlike many other Jewish exiles in Assyria, Tobit has remained letter-true to the traditional religion. As a boy, during the reign of the idolatrous Jeroboam II, he made pilgrimages to Jerusalem on holy days; in exile he has kept strict kosher diet and at great personal risk has buried the bodies of Jewish victims of atrocity.[*] Under one Assyrian king ("Shalmanezar" or Sargon), he held a governmental office and was in a position to perform many charities for his people; under a succeeding king (Sennacherib), his property was confiscated and he was driven into hiding for burying the dead; and now, under a third (Esarhaddon), he is at liberty but very poor. One day while sitting down

---

[*] Many ancient peoples believed that the dead could not rest until properly interred (cf. Sophocles' *Antigone* or the last book of Homer's *Iliad*). Hebrew custom, whether or not connected with this belief, emphasized various requirements for proper burial and regarded a man who had touched a corpse as ceremonially unclean for a specified time.

to a Pentecostal dinner, he learns that a Jew has been slain, and
he rushes away to bury the body. Returning ceremonially defiled
from contact with a corpse, he lies down to sleep outside his
house. The droppings of sparrows fall in his eyes and cause a
blinding film (cataract?). When even his wife mocks him, the
righteous Tobit blesses the Lord, asks forgiveness, and prays for
death.

Meanwhile Tobit's unknown kinswoman Sarah (daughter of
Raguel, who is exiled in Ecbatana) has been persecuted by a
demon who seven times has prevented her from consummating
marriage by killing her bridegrooms on the wedding nights.
Taunted by her handmaids, Sarah blesses the Lord and, like
Tobit, asks to be released from life.

God hears the prayers simultaneously and sends his angel Raphael to see that Tobit's health and prosperity be restored, that
Sarah become the wife of Tobias, and that the demon (Asmodeus) be bound.*

TOBIAS' JOURNEY TO MEDIA (Chs. 4–6). As if by divine inspiration, Tobit recalls having deposited ten talents of silver for safe-
keeping with a relative in Media and determines to send his son
Tobias after this sizable fortune. His parting advice to the youth
is in the spirit of Hebrew "wisdom" literature: Take care of your
mother when I am dead, remember the Lord, give alms to all
who deserve them, marry a Jewish girl, pay every employee adequately and promptly, what you hate do not do to anyone (a
negative version of the Golden Rule), never drink too heavily,
and ignore no wise counsel. Giving Tobias a receipt for the
money, he tells his son to find a competent guide. The guide
whom Tobias selects is none other than the angel Raphael in disguise.

Tobias and Raphael, followed by the young man's dog, set
forth and camp one night on the banks of the Tigris. When a fish
leaps up, Tobias (at his guide's instigation) catches it and saves
its heart and liver, which the angel explains are effective in chasing away demons, and its gall, which is effective in removing
films from eyes. Raphael tells Tobias that they shall stop at the
house of Raguel and recommends that the young man marry
Sarah because, as the only surviving eligible relative, he is en-

* Though immortal, demons could be chained and rendered powerless.

titled to her, because she is beautiful and sensible, and because she has a large inheritance.

THE COURTSHIP; THE EXORCISING OF THE DEMON; THE MARRIAGE (Chs. 7—10). Introductions are made, Raphael arranges with Sarah's parents for an immediate wedding, and a ram is killed for the betrothal feast. Calming Sarah's apprehension that he suffer the fate of the previous husbands, Tobias that night burns the heart and liver of the fish in the ashes of incense. The smell (whether good or bad) drives Asmodeus into Egypt—where he is bound by the angel. Tobias offers a marriage prayer. In the morning, Raguel (who has spent the night digging a grave) learns that Tobias is still alive and offers a prayer of thanksgiving. Raphael goes to collect Tobit's money and gets the bag with seals intact upon presenting the proper receipt. Meanwhile back in Nineveh, Tobit and his wife have become anxious at their son's long absence. Tobias, sensing his parents' concern, sets out for home with bride and a fortune (Raguel gives him half of his property).

THE REUNION OF TOBIT'S FAMILY (Chs. 11—12). In Nineveh Tobias' eager mother and blindly stumbling father rush forth to greet their son. Tobit's sight is restored by the fish gall, and he blesses God and the angels for their mercy. Raphael declines the generous offer of half the young man's fortune, reveals himself to be an angel, and states the moral of the story: Do good, and evil will not overcome you; prayer is effective when accompanied by fasting, almsgiving, and righteous conduct; God is ever aware of human good deeds.

EPILOGUE (Chs. 13—14). The closing chapters contain a verse psalm by Tobit and also the dying words of that good man, who has lived a long and satisfying life. He advises his son and six grandsons to depart from Nineveh before that city is destroyed. He predicts that the Jews will be scattered but that Jerusalem and her Temple will be rebuilt and the whole world will be converted to her God. The other characters, too, grow old with honor and receive magnificent funerals. Tobias, who has returned with his wife and children to Ecbatana, hears of Nebuchadrezzar's capture of Nineveh.

Literary Qualities. Historians and anthropologists are particularly indebted to the book of Tobit for hints about the theories of angels and demons which (probably under the influence of the dualistic religious doctrines of the Persians [2]) had developed in Hebrew thinking by the second century B.C. Demons appear infrequently in the Old Testament, but are taken for granted in the New.*

All readers are indebted to the book for its portrayal of loyalties and affections among a persecuted, scattered people. With their frank desire for economic success, the Jews of the second century B.C. retained a scrupulous sense of ethics and belief in honest dealings; with their love for good living, they wanted always to share their fortunes with the poor; with all their ceremonial piety, they clung to the hope that some day the benefits of Judaism might be extended to the Gentile world.

Students of literary technique are indebted for a well-told tale which gives fresh expression to various types of Hebrew art: psalmody, wisdom literature, prophecy, and theological teaching.

CHARACTER. The conflict relates to social oppression and demonic activities as they affect the fortunes of an exiled people. Although the protagonists are idyllically good, each is an individual and reacts to adversity in his own way. At the opening, Tobit speaks in monologue, revealing himself to be a friendly and garrulous old man, not too strait-laced to tell a joke on himself (for example, the humiliating result when he rashly accused his wife of theft [Ch. 2]). Tobit's wife is equally human—dutiful to the point of working for hire when her husband is incapacitated, but sharp-tongued. The other characters, too, have colorful touches: Tobias' devotion to his dog,† Sarah's correction of impudent servants or slaves, Raguel's need for working off nervousness by digging a grave at night.

PLOT. Despite a duo-setting (Assyria and Media) and despite three plot threads (God's rewards to Tobit, the love story of Tobias and Sarah, and the binding of Asmodeus), Tobit is a closely knit.‡ All threads come together in Chapter 3, when God hears the simultaneous prayers of Tobit and Sarah, and the rest of the

* Readers of the Gospels will recall that possession by demons was associated with madness, and sometimes with the compulsion to do violence to others or to oneself (Matt. 12:24, Mark 5:2-5, 9:18). Can there be a latent suggestion that the usually gentle Sarah was subject to violent seizures before the demon was exorcised? Certainly, the servants accused her of having strangled her husbands, and she herself contemplated suicide.

† Nowhere else in the Bible is the dog mentioned as a pet.

‡ The first twelve chapters come far nearer to being a modern short story than do many of the medieval English romances which add episode to episode

story leaves few loose ends. Even the depositing of Tobit's money is mentioned early so that it does not happen as a miraculous coincidence, the fish is introduced because it will be significant to the plot,* and Tobit's garrulous self-introduction is made significant in Raphael's summing up of events.

STYLE. The model prayers (which begin by blessing and thanking God instead of by requesting favors) would not be included in a modern short story; but to the Hebrew reader they were perhaps the best parts of Tobit; so, too, must have been the wisdom speeches of the elderly men to the young and of the angel to human beings. The model conduct (proper burials, proper weddings, proper financial dealings) is always subordinate and always contributory to the plot. There are occasional flashes of humor: a reader who has been let in on the truth can appreciate the irony of Tobit's cross-questioning an angel and of Raguel's exclamation of meeting Tobias: "How like my cousin Tobit you look!"

THE DANIEL CYCLE†

A series of short stories and semi-narrative visions revolves around Daniel, a legendary Jewish hero who reputedly lived throughout most of the Babylonian Captivity and held high governmental office under various Babylonian and Median potentates. Very likely there had been a famously wise and just worthy named Daniel;‡ but there is ample reason to believe that the mar-

---

until the author decides to finish. The concluding chapters provide a sequel for readers who want to know what happened later.

* Even the fish is motivated—in most versions by a desire to swallow Tobias, but in one by a desire to snatch Tobias' bread.

† This cycle includes the Hebrew book of Daniel plus several works from the Septuagint which are regarded as independent books in the Protestant Apocrypha but as special chapters of Daniel in the Roman Catholic Douay Bible. The latter are the lyric Song of the Three Holy Children (Dan. 3:24-90 in the Douay), the stories of Bel and the Dragon (Dan. 14 in the Douay), and the story of Susanna (Dan. 13 in the Douay).

‡ The name occurs twice in Ezekiel: in Ezek. 14:14 Daniel is mentioned together with Noah and Job as one of the three most righteous worthies of Israel; and in Ezek. 28:3 there is a reference to his proverbial wisdom. A legendary "Danel" appears in Ugaritic tablets unearthed at Ras Shama in Syria as recently as 1929 and bears some resemblance to the Old Testament Daniel. On the other hand, Daniel is never mentioned by writers of Biblical history; and there are no nonscriptural records of such an outstanding Hebrew in the time of the Captivity.

velous tales and visions of the Hebrew book which bears his
name were written between 167 and 165 B.C., during the Maccabean Revolt and that they were intended to convey messages of
encouragement to Jews who were robbed of their liberties and
persecuted for their faith under Antiochus Epiphanes. The tale
of Bel and the Dragon may well have been written by a different
author at a different time, for none of its episodes seems political in purpose. The highly developed short story of Susanna con-
cerns Daniel only incidentally; it introduces him as a famous
judge whose wisdom saves the heroine from injustice, and there
is doubt as to whether this story had any special message for
Maccabean sympathizers.

Daniel: Legends of an Upright Sage (Chs. 1—6). To keep
alive faith in the Jewish God and respect for the Jewish Law, the
author of Daniel told legends of olden times, but almost undoubtedly slanted the legends in such a way that his purpose
would be plain to second-century Jews. None of his tyrannical
kings so closely resembled Antiochus Epiphanes as to render the
stories subversive or treasonable. Yet each somehow represented
one of more of the bad sides of Antiochus (for example, Nebuchadrezzar was a figure of intolerance and pride; Belshazzar, of
dissoluteness and sacrilege; and Darius, of credulity and dependence on political informers). Let us review the six legends in
the light of the messages which they must have conveyed to Jews
living in an age of rebellion against persecution.

THE REFUSAL OF DANIEL AND HIS FRIENDS TO BREAK MOSAIC
LAW (Ch. 1). The first tale drove home the moral that God expected faithful Jews to maintain their religious laws even in captivity. One of the Jews' grievances against Antiochus was that he
tried to make them eat "unclean" food; indeed, compliance in food
matters seems to have been used as a test of loyalty to the king.

In the days of Nebuchadrezzar some high-born and gifted Jewish captives are selected to study Chaldean wisdom in order that
they may become counselors to the ruler. All except Daniel and
his three friends (best known by their Babylonian names of Shadrach, Meshach, and Abednego) break Jewish law by eating the
"king's meat"; but these particular youths insist upon kosher fare,
however meager. At the end of a ten-day test period, it is these
who show mental and physical superiority. Especially is this true
of Daniel, who in wisdom and understanding continues to prove

"ten times better" than all the magicians and astrologers in Babylonia.

NEBUCHADREZZAR'S DREAM OF A MESSIANIC AGE (Ch. 2). The second tale was intended to demonstrate the incomparable superiority of divinely inspired wisdom to human wisdom and of divine will to human will (such as that asserted by Antiochus). Furthermore, it advanced a theory of the past, present, and future history which was calculated to raise the Hebrews' hope for a Messianic deliverer.

Troubled by a dream which he can no longer remember, Nebuchadrezzar orders his court sages to recall it and interpret it for him. When the sages are nonplussed, Daniel, together with his three friends, promises to tell the king the meaning of the dream. That night, after prayer, Daniel receives a vision of the dream and is able to interpret it. First, Nebuchadrezzar has seen a huge image with head of gold (representing the then current Babylonian Empire), with breast and arms of silver (prefiguring a future Median Empire), with belly and thighs of brass (prefiguring a still more remote Persian Empire), and with legs of iron and feet of clay mixed with iron (prefiguring a Greco-Macedonian or Seleucid era). Second, Nebuchadrezzar has seen a marvelous stone strike the fragile feet so that the whole image falls and crumbles; and then he has seen the stone turn into a mountain which covers the whole earth (prefiguring a universal and final Messianic age).* The king then acknowledges the supremacy of Yahweh as "a God of gods, and a Lord of kings, and a revealer of secrets," and rewards the young men with high positions, making Daniel ruler of Babylon and chief of the sages.

THE FIERY FURNACE (Ch. 3). The third legend had a particular message for the Jews who had been commanded by Antiochus to worship images of Grecian gods. It is a miracle story.

Because they refuse to worship an image which Nebuchadrezzar has set up, Shadrach, Meshach, and Abednego are cast into a

---

* The author of Daniel knew that there had been Babylonian and Persian empires. He lived in the Seleucid era and was confident that it would soon be destroyed and replaced by a divinely ordered era. This was his theory of history from the time of the Dispersion: four successive empires, each worse than its predecessor, had ruled the world, and the fourth was about to be destroyed by a Messianic deliverer.

seven-times heated furnace.* Guarded by a celestial being, who appears in the fire, they emerge unharmed. Nebuchadrezzar is so impressed that he decrees death for anyone who speaks against the God of the Israelites.

NEBUCHADREZZAR'S INSANITY (Ch. 4). In its fictional way, the fourth legend reassured the Jews that earthly existence is controlled by an all-powerful, all-knowing, and ever-just God. Ostensibly the story dealt with Nebuchadrezzar, but it must have thrilled those who were hoping for the sudden downfall (perhaps through mental collapse) of the erratic and violent Antiochus.

The author cast his tale partly in the form of an epistle, written by Nebuchadrezzar to the peoples of the world, in which the king confesses how he in all his pride had suddenly gone mad and had remained so for "seven times" (seven years?) because he had placed himself too nearly on a level with God and because he had shown no mercy to the oppressed. It includes two prayers by Nebuchadrezzar and a sermon by Daniel on the value of repentance.†

The epistle tells how Nebuchadrezzar had a dream which none of his wise men can interpret: he had seen a tree so tall as to be visible from all parts of the earth; he had heard a voice command that the proud tree be hewn down and made into a groveling beast. Daniel explained that the tree symbolized the king, who was about to lose his reason and eat grass in the wastelands until he "know that the most High ruleth in the kingdom of men." All this has come to pass and the humbled king writes his epistle in praise of God.

BELSHAZZAR'S FEAST (Ch. 5).‡ In the fifth legend, the author must have had in mind Antiochus' profanation of the Temple (see p. 154). Let Antiochus, too, look out for "handwriting on the wall."

---

* In the Septuagint, the Vulgate, and the Douay Bible (vv. 25-90), The Song of the Three Holy Children is included at this point. (See p. 268.)

† The art of Biblical storytellers is ever worth attention. Let us note that the casting of an improbable tale in the form of documents is a permanently effective literary method for achieving verisimilitude, and it is so used in *Dr. Jekyll and Mr. Hyde* and many other modern tales of the supernatural.

‡ This ever-popular tale has furnished subjects for many works of literature, music, and painting—for example, Handel's oratorio *Belshazzar,* Sibelius' tone poem *Belshazzar's Feast,* a novel by W. S. Davis, and two well-known poems by Byron.

Belshazzar (unhistorically represented as son and successor of Nebuchadrezzar) indulges in a drunken orgy and sacrilegiously pledges pagan gods with cups from the Jerusalem Temple. At the height of the revelry a ghostly hand appears and writes upon the wall the ominous words: "*Mene, Mene, Tekel, Upharsin.*" None of the court sages can read the characters or explain the meaning to the terrified monarch.* Then the queen (the monarch's mother?) remembers Daniel and suggests that this wise Hebrew be summoned. After boldly upbraiding Belshazzar for pride, sacrilege, and idolatry, Daniel reads the oracle and explains its significance: the days of the Babylonian kingdom have been numbered and are at an end; Belshazzar has been weighed and found wanting (worth only a shekel as compared with Nebuchadrezzar?); and the kingdom will be divided between the Medes and the Persians.† Before the night is over, Babylon is invaded by Darius and Belshazzar is killed.

THE LIONS' DEN (Ch. 6). The final legend re-emphasized the lesson that pious Jews should permit no human ordinance to restrain them from proper worship—whether their portion might be life or death. It was set in the period of "Darius the Mede."‡

Daniel has been appointed one of three satraps of the land. Fearing that he may soon become their superior, but at a loss to find fault with his character or ability, the rival satraps seek to catch him up on the basis of religion. They persuade the gullible Darius to proclaim himself sole deity for one month and to decree that any who pray to other deities be cast to the lions. When Daniel continues his regular devotions, they arrest him, and the king must abide by the edict.§ Protected by an angel, Daniel re-

* The words themselves appear to be Aramaic terms for certain Babylonian monetary weights: *mene* = "mina" (one-sixtieth of a talent); *tekel* = "shekel" (one-sixtieth of a mina); and *parsin* = "two half-minas." Even had they succeeded in translating the words, the sages would still have been faced with the problem of interpreting the oracle.

† The *peres* (singular of *parsin*) of v. 28 is Aramaic for "division."

‡ A similarity of purpose and event is often noted between this chapter and Ch. 2. Here Daniel appears without his friends, and there the friends appear without Daniel; here the instrument of martyrdom is the animal den, and there the fiery furnace; here the king is Darius, and there Nebuchadrezzar. Perhaps the author consciously drove home the same message through repetition, seeking variety only by a change of detail.

§ The "laws of the Medes and the Persians" were considered inviolable.

mains in the lions' den overnight and emerges unscathed. Darius then commands that the accusers and their families be thrown to the lions, and all these are devoured instantly. Darius issues a decree commanding everyone under his rule to "tremble and fear before the God of Daniel: for he is the living God and stedfast for ever" (6:26).

LITERARY QUALITIES. The legends of Daniel 1–6 are highly schematized: always there are (1) a prologue setting forth the luxury and paganism of an Oriental court, (2) a marvelous fable in which God's will is asserted in human affairs, and (3) an epilogue picturing the humiliation of the oppressor and the rewards of the righteous.

The characters are not psychologically complicated. Daniel and his three friends know no human fear and rise to any occasion in which righteousness is called for. The kings are tyrannical figureheads whose ethics and wisdom never go beyond observance of official decorum and a display of crude justice. The pagan villains are schemers and informers who deserve the fates they prepare for others. The swift-moving plots depend upon no great subtlety of expression and could easily be borne in mind and retold among a persecuted people.

Daniel: Apocalyptic Visions (Chs. 7–12). The second half of Daniel consists of four visions in which the sage (writing supposedly in various periods of the Capitivity) looks into the future and predicts the growth and downfall of Babylonian, Median, Persian, and Greek empires. During the last of these, a Messiah will take over and usher in the permanent kingdom of God. The author of Daniel has told his pointed legends, and now he is engaging in a more dangerous discussion*; hence he adopts a new and more cryptic literary form. Only the introductory verse pretends that the visions are to be regarded as fiction: "Daniel had a dream and visions ... : then he wrote the dream, and told the sum of the matters" (7:1). The visions are written in the first person, and they provide one of the earliest examples of the Biblical type known as *apocalypse* or *apocalyptic* (see p. 357).

In the apocalypse we ... see a union of the symbolism and myths of Babylonia with the religious faith of the Jews. . . it was the literary

---

* We do not know whether the visions were originally circulated all at one time. They could (like Thomas Paine's *Crisis*) have been issued periodically to keep up the spirit of the people to whom they were addressed.

means of setting forth by the use of symbols the certainty of Divine judgment and the equal certainty of Divine deliverance. The symbols are usually animals of various sorts, and frequently involve composite creatures whose various parts represented certain qualities of the animals from which they were derived.

Apocalyptic is akin to prophecy. Its purpose was fundamentally to encourage faith in Jehovah on the part of those who were in distress, by "revealing" the future. . . .

The parent of apocalyptic is the book of Daniel, which, by the almost unanimous consensus of scholars, appeared in the Maccabean period.[3]

Since the apocalyptic visions are an integral part of the book of Daniel, we shall briefly summarize them here; but we should realize that their literary method has more in common with the books of Second Esdras and Revelation than with "short stories."

THE FOUR BEASTS (Ch. 7). Reverting to his theory (Ch. 2) about four world empires, the author sought to encourage the Jews by predicting that their tribulations were almost at an end.

Daniel dreams of four beasts: a lion with eagle's wings which are suddenly plucked (Babylonia), a bear with ribs in its mouth (Media), a winged leopard with four heads (Persia), and a monster with iron teeth and ten horns (the Greco-Macedonian Empire). Presumably the horns represent the ten kings who followed Alexander. A new "little" horn (Antiochus Epiphanes represented here as a usurper and an upstart?) sprouts and uproots three of its predecessors. In v. 9 the vision shifts, and an enthroned "Ancient of Days" (the all-ruling God?) slays the fourth beast. "One like the Son of man" is appointed to rule the world.*

THE RAM AND THE HE-GOAT (Ch. 8). The second vision (as do the third and the fourth) supplements and reinforces the message of the first.

Daniel sees a ram with two horns (the Median and Persian empires?). A goat (the Macedonian Empire?) with a horn between its eyes (Alexander the Great?) defeats the ram. Then the horn is broken and replaced by four more horns (sections into which Alexander's empire was divided after his death?). From

---

* The vision is a prediction set against a review of history. If "a time and times and the dividing of time" (v. 25) means a three-and-a-half-year respite before judgment, the prediction was fairly accurate, for the Maccabean Revolt had begun in 168, the Temple was repaired and rededicated to Yahweh in 165 B.C., and Antiochus was to be killed in 164 B.C.[4]

one of these (the Seleucid Empire?), a "little" horn (Antiochus?) sprouts and grows so strong that it arrogantly attacks even the stars of heaven and also the Jewish Temple. Daniel hears a holy voice predict that within a certain time* the atrocities will end and the sanctuary be purified. The angel Gabriel interprets the vision to Daniel.

THE SEVENTY WEEKS (Ch. 9). The third vision ventured a forecast about when the new era was to be expected and how it would begin.†

Perplexed by a seemingly unfulfilled promise of Jeremiah that the Jews would be liberated after seventy years of captivity, Daniel devotes himself to a prayer of penitence and supplication on behalf of his people.‡ He is rewarded by the appearance of the heavenly messenger Gabriel, who enlightens him by explaining that Jeremiah's "seventy years" meant "seventy weeks of years" (RSV).§ In the last "week" there will be war and destruction; but God's judgment will fall upon the enemies of Jerusalem.

THE ANGEL BY THE RIVER (Chs. 10–12). The fourth and last vision added climactic appeal to what the author had previously said. Not merely does it give additional interpretations of history and some specific predictions about the death of Antiochus, but it assures the Jews that there is heavenly warfare on their behalf, that the righteous will be resurrected and eternally rewarded on the Day of Judgment, and that the wicked will be doomed to eternal punishment.‖ In 10:13, 21, and in 12:1 we are told that the angel Michael is heavenly patron of the Jews and that he fights victoriously against demonic powers who would harm them. In 12:2 we are told that "many of them that sleep in the dust of the earth shall awake, some to everlasting life, and some to shame and everlasting contempt."

---

* If the 2300 "days" of v. 14 refer to the twice-a-day sacrificial services, the time would be about three years and two months.

† For a consideration of variant modern interpretations, see Arthur Jeffery, exegesis to Daniel, *The Interpreter's Bible*, VI, 484-499.

‡ See Jer. 25:11-12 and 29:10. The author of Jeremiah probably had no calculable period in mind, but simply meant a very long time (J. P. Hyatt, exegesis to Jeremiah, *The Interpreter's Bible*, V, 1000). The author of Daniel uses Jeremiah's prophetic sayings as authority for his own predictions.

§ That is, 7×70, or 490 years, which (if calculated from the fall of Jerusalem in 586 B.C.) would bring the final week close to Maccabean times.

‖ These concepts of angelology and resurrection after death are not found in earlier Hebrew Scripture.

Whereas the first and second visions had been set in the time of Belshazzar and the third in the reign of "Darius the Mede," this one was set in the third year of Cyrus—that is, at the time of Ezra and Nehemiah, when the Jews were being allowed to return to Palestine. Its perspective is closer to the Maccabean era, and it can give greater attention to recent history (even to Antiochus' war with Egypt which had begun in 171 B.C.).*

In the vision, while walking by a river, Daniel meets an unnamed angel who tells him of events about to happen in the Persian, Macedonian, Seleucid, and Ptolemaic (Egyptian) empires. He learns that Michael and other celestial beings are protecting the Jews. He is told that a king (Antiochus) will defeat the Egyptians and then return to the north (Palestine) and shortly die.† There will be further tribulations for the Jews, but the permanent age of righteousness and justice is at hand.

LITERARY QUALITIES. The visions of Daniel are as schematized as the legends. All are told in the first person; all have a prologue which gives the time; all recount the vision and then interpret it; and all except Chapter 9 conclude with Daniel's own comment upon his mystical experience.

Because they expressed revolutionary views in a time when freedom of speech was not countenanced, they probably had to be cast in a pseudo-historical, mystical, and symbolic form. The writing was no doubt plain enough to cheer the special group for whom the work was written, though it leaves many unsolved problems for those who seek to understand them today.

The author's view of history as a series of empires leading toward the permanent empire of God, which is not out of keeping with the views of the prophets, is noteworthy as an attempt to find direction and meaning in human affairs. His special method of writing history—always as if it were something predetermined and to happen in the future—is no doubt grounded in his belief in God's omniscience. The near accuracy of some of

* For a succinct identification of many of the historical events alluded to, see Jeffery, exegesis, *The Interpreter's Bible,* VI, 347-348. As usual, the author of Daniel reviews the past as if it had not yet taken place; and then he proceeds to forecast the future.

† Dan. 11:21-45 is generally thought to summarize the career of Antiochus. Hopeful predictions have always circulated among the downtrodden in times of unbearable persecution. This one, though inaccurate in detail (Antiochus' campaign in Egypt was to be unsuccessful, and he was to die in Persia instead of Palestine), was accurate enough in its general forecast.

his predictions about Antiochus shows that he was an acute analyst of political trends.

As previously mentioned, Chapters 7–12 of Daniel have extra literary importance in that they helped to establish the apocalypse—a semi-narrative, semi-prophetic form of writing which was to remain popular in New Testament times.* Why did the apocalypse remain popular? Sometimes because it served as a medium for disseminating the ideas that could not be expressed openly; but also, perhaps, because the Hebrew people (like the Greeks of classical times, like the Anglo-Saxons, like the Elizabethans, and like many of us today) loved riddles, allegories, and other works with hidden meanings.†

Bel and the Dragon: Legends Contrasting Paganism with True Religion. The Apocryphal book Bel and the Dragon (or in the Douay version, the concluding chapter of Daniel) is generally thought to be of later origin than the canonic Hebrew stories. From the scant evidence available, it could have been written as late as the first century B.C. and could have been written in Hebrew or Aramaic or Greek.[5] Its anonymous author may have woven together some ancient legends about Daniel (including a variant of "The Lion's Den") or may simply have adopted the popular folk hero for an entertaining tale with a religious rather than a political theme.

Bel and the Dragon exposes the falsity of pagan deities, the chicanery and greed of pagan priests, and the gullibility of those who trust in either. By way of contrast, it asserts the author's faith in a living God who can send protective angels when the righteous are endangered. Incidentally, it may also give a folk explanation for the ruins of an ancient Babylonian temple.‡

* See pp. 357-358 for a discussion of apocalyptic literature.

† We may assume that Samson's riddle (Judg. 13:28-18), the riddle of the Sphynx in the Oedipus legend, and the riddles of Old English and Middle English literature reflect an abiding human interest in riddles. The visions of Daniel and the allegories of Spenser's *Faerie Queene* and of *Gulliver's Travels* reflect a perennial delight in riddles which convey opinions upon political and moral affairs.

‡ The Temple of Marduk (sometimes listed among the "Seven Wonders of the Ancient World") had been built by Nebuchadrezzar and, according to Green history, looted and torn down by Xerxes I. At all events, it was in ruins by the time of Alexander the Great. The story of Bel and the Dragon says that it was torn down by Daniel.

PLOT. Cyrus the Persian is King of Babylon, and his favorite companion is Daniel. The two have a running argument about religion: sometimes it consists of friendly raillery and the laying of wagers, and sometimes it bursts into violent anger.

Daniel's Destruction of the Idol and Temple of Bel (Vv. 1–22). Daniel worships only the living God. When Cyrus argues that the Babylonian statue of Bel is "living" because it regularly consumes quantities of flour, meat, and wine, Daniel jeers and undertakes at forfeit of his life to prove it inanimate. The seventy priests of the Babylonian temple agree to the following test: Cyrus himself shall place the nightly rations before the idol, shall seal the door, and shall find in the morning whether or not the offering has been devoured. On the next morning the seals are found to be untampered with, and the food and the wine to have disappeared. Cyrus triumphantly bursts into praise of Bel, "in whom there is no deceit." Then Daniel, who has secretly scattered ashes on the floor, points to the footprints of men, women, and children and proves that the sacrifice has been stolen by the priests and their families and that the temple is "rigged" with concealed doors. The outraged king orders death for the priests and their families and authorizes Daniel to destroy both idol and temple.

Daniel's Slaying of the Sacred Dragon (Vv. 23–27). When Cyrus argues that a dragon worshiped by the Babylonians is a "living" god, Daniel offers to prove its mortality by killing it without sword or club. By feeding it a cake made of pitch, fat, and hair (ingredients which, like the fish entrails in Tobit, may or may not have been popularly credited with supernatural power), he causes it to burst open and die; and to the king he says, "See what you have been worshiping."

The Rescue of Daniel from a Lions' Den (Vv. 28–40).† Because Cyrus has allowed Daniel to destroy their idol and their dragon, the Babylonians accuse the king of having become a Jew

---

* Bel (or Marduk in later mythology) had been worshiped by the Babylonians. There is no record that these people had ever worshiped dragons or serpents, but there are Biblical suggestions that Hebrews may have done so. However, dragon stories were well known by the first century B.C., and the author of Bel and the Dragon is contemptuous of any sort of sacred animal.

† Opinions differ as to whether this tale and the tale of Dan. 6 have a common origin.

and compel him to throw Daniel into a den of lions. After surviving unharmed for six days, Daniel is fed by the prophet
Habakkuk—who has been miraculously conveyed from Judea by
an angel. On the seventh day he is released, and the Babylonian
ringleaders are thrown to the lions and instantly devoured.

LITERARY QUALITIES. Bel and the Dragon is a connected tale
with three episodes which may once have been independent
legends. The first has to do with an inanimate idol which works
fake miracles because operated by deceitful priests; the second
has to do with a strange animal that is no more divine than any
other mortal creature; the third illustrates the author's faith in
the power of an unseen and ever-living God to perform real
miracles.

We can, if we choose, call two of the episodes "ancient detec-
tive stories"—they represent a type of legend in which a sage
(through accurate observation, common sense, or some homely
ruse) upsets or refutes the judgments of his less discerning contemporaries. The third is a miracle legend showing the increasing
popularity of the belief that God governs the world through
angels. From a purely literary point of view, then, Bel and the
Dragon is interesting as a surviving example of a type of oral or
written stories which may have circulated very widely among
Hebrews of the first century B.C. (Perhaps there was even a cycle
of no-longer-existent legends about the prophet Habakkuk.)

Stylistically, the narrative is a bare sketch; but it is something
that could be dressed up and made suspenseful and significant
by gifted raconteurs.

Susanna: An Idyl in Which Justice Is Achieved by Prayer.
There have been many tales of chaste wives who are slandered
by rejected suitors, and there have been many of wise judges
who deliver the innocent from trumped-up charges. The superbly
written "History of Susanna" combines these universal motifs
with a background of Jewish community life and Jewish religious beliefs. At the same time, it is a story of Daniel.

As with Bel and the Dragon, we do not know who wrote the
story, precisely when in the first century it was written, or in
what language it was originally set down.[6] Probably because it
introduces the sage as an unknown youth, the Septuagint places
it at the beginning of the book of Daniel; inasmuch as it had no
canonic Hebrew standing, Jerome placed it near the end; and
Protestants have traditionally considered it to be an independent

work of literature. Certainly it seems to bear more resemblance to the affectionately idyllic genre of Ruth and Tobit than to the rather starkly purposeful legends which constitute the Hebrew book of Daniel.

THE STORY OF SUSANNA. For once, we have a tale set in the Babylonian period in which the villains are not foreign oppressors or pagan priests, but local Jewish officials in a Jewish community.

While bathing in her garden, Susanna, the beautiful wife of a prominent Jew, is waylaid by two lecherous elders—both recently appointed judges. If she will not submit to their lust, they will testify in court that they have found her committing adultery. Though the punishment of an adultress is execution by stoning, she chooses to risk death and public shame rather than to sin in the sight of God. Brought to trial and condemned, she prays. The Lord hears her cry and, while she is being led to execution, sends a youth named Daniel to defend her.

Daniel cross-questions each of the accusers separately. The first swears that Susanna's alleged misconduct took place under a mastic tree, and the second that it took place under a holm (evergreen oak). Upon hearing such conflicting testimony, the court, which is made up of righteous elders, acquits Susanna and has the accusers put to death.

LITERARY QUALITIES. The story emphasizes the rewards of virtue and God's attention to the prayers of the righteous, although its plot turns upon the celebrated wisdom and justice of Daniel.* Certainly it teaches two of the Ten Commandments: "Thou shalt not commit adultery" and "Thou shalt not bear false witness." Opinions differ as to whether it goes further and criticizes the Talmudic regulation allowing judges to send an accused person to death on the testimony of two witnesses. (Some critics have thought that v. 48 advocates the desirability of thorough cross-examination where tangible evidence is lacking.) Some have suggested that the author was really condemning miscarriage of justice in Greek law courts, but carefully disguising his criticisms by mentioning only Jewish administration. These theories are possible, but the author's literary approach (unlike that in the Hebrew book of Daniel) does not suggest hidden meanings. Admirers of humanistic fiction agree that "plot, surprise, struggle,

* Shylock's "A Daniel come to judgment!" (*Merchant of Venice*, IV, i, 223) refers to the story of Susanna rather than to the Old Testament book of Daniel.

unfolding of character, are present here in just the right proportion."[7]

SETTING. The setting is that of a peaceful Jewish community in which the people carry on their local affairs without interference from Babylonian overlords. And a general pleasantness of life is suggested.

CHARACTERS. Susanna has been brought up by her parents according to the Law of Moses (v. 3); she is a mother (v. 30); no scandal has ever involved her (v. 27); and she suspects no evil in others. She is so unprepared for calumny that her only resource is prayer to God; but in time of trouble that resource is sufficient.

The two hypocritical elders are scarcely representative of the Jewish community. One is a relic of wicked days, and the other an offspring of Canaan (vv. 52, 56). Both have been appointed recently to judgeship, and power has gone to their heads (v. 5); one has used his office to seduce Israelitish women through threats of blackmail (v. 57). The author shows touches of psychology and perhaps of humor in noting how each distrusts the other, how each hides his own wickedness from the other, and how the two come face to face in a compromising situation.

Daniel (as a figure well known to readers) is given little characterization, but his deeds and words are in keeping with the established conception. His nobility is recognized at once by the righteous elders of the community, and the young man is immediately invited to sit among them.

PLOT. The plot is concisely and neatly constructed. It shows how the evil pair happened to be in the house of Susanna, how they watched her day after day, and how they contrived matters so that she would have no chance of escape. The references to the gossip of servants and the solicitude of kinsmen and townspeople advance the narration and give variety to the style. The use of Daniel as a human agent for divine intervention keeps the climax within the realm of the possible, as opposed to the miraculous.

JUDITH: A WAR STORY INCULCATING VALOR AND TRUST IN GOD

Judith is a patriotic tale holding out the belief that God will protect the entire Jewish nation in its darkest hours if the people will remain faithful. It is usually thought to have been written about 150 B.C.—that is, about a decade after the great victories of Judas Maccabeus but while the Jews were still struggling for independence and religious freedom against the successors of Antiochus Epiphanes. And it is usually thought to have been written in Hebrew by a Palestinian Jew.

That it is fiction rather than history is accepted by virtually all Jewish and Protestant scholars. Its exaggerations, anachronisms, and geographical inaccuracies seemed so conspicuous to Martin Luther that he suspected them of having been introduced purposely to warn readers against literal acceptance.*

The Story of Judith. The tale has two parts: (1) a (pseudo-historical) account of Nebuchadrezzar's victory over Media and of a punitive expedition against countries which had denied him military aid, and (2) the legend of Judith's heroism just as Israel was about to surrender. These are followed by an epilogue which reinforces the author's lessons with a psalm and which provides a brief dénouement.

THE SIEGE OF ISRAEL (Chs. 1–7). After conquering Media, the "Assyrian" king sends Holofernes† to humble the nations which had refused their support. In quick succession such nations are overrun, their shrines destroyed, and their people forced to worship Nebuchadrezzar as "God."

Laying siege to the strategic border city of Bethulia,‡ Holofernes questions a captive Ammonite named Achior and is told that the Hebrews have remained and will always remain undefeated except when they sin against their God. Contemptuously, he binds Achior and casts him where the Israelites can take him in; then he shuts off the water supply of the city. After a long

---

* For instance, the action takes place in the time of Nebuchadrezzar (c. 580 B.C.); yet the Hebrews are depicted as having already returned from the Exile and as having already rebuilt the Temple (finished c. 516 B.C.). Nebuchadrezzar is called king of Assyria, and his capital is said to be Nineveh, though original readers must have known that he had been king of Babylonia and that Nineveh had been destroyed before he came to the throne. The Jews are portrayed as governed from Jerusalem by a high priest and Sanhedrin—a type of civil government that did not come into existence until several centuries after Nebuchadrezzar.

† Such a commander is not known to historians. For attempts to identify him, see James Hastings (ed.), *Dictionary of the Bible,* revised by F. C. Grant and H. H. Rowley (New York: Charles Scribner's Sons, 1963), p. 388.

‡ A fortified hill city elsewhere unnamed in the Bible. Attempts have been made to identify it with Shechem; see C. C. Torrey, *The Apocryphal Literature* (New Haven: Yale University Press, 1945), pp. 91-92.

period of fasting and prayer,* Bethulia is ready to surrender; but the ruler Uzziah (Ozias) stipulates that the Lord be given another five days to save the people.

JEWISH VICTORY THROUGH THE FAITH AND HEROISM OF JUDITH (Chs. 8–15). At this critical point, Uzziah and the elders are approached by Judith. She upbraids them for putting the Lord to the test in place of trusting him to save his people in his own good time; nevertheless, she promises, with God's aid, to rescue the city within the stipulated five days.

Her first act (Ch. 9) is to offer a prayer praising the all-knowing and all-powerful God, stating the cause of the Israelites and asking that she—a helpless widow—may achieve a victory that will teach everybody that God protects the people of Israel.

Then she dresses in finery and sets out for the Assyrian camp with one slave girl and a bag of kosher food. Her beauty captivates the enemy soldiers, who escort her to their general. She flatters Holofernes, telling him that she has fled to his camp because she knows him to be the greatest of military conquerors. Confirming Achior's insistence that the Jews cannot be vanquished unless they sin, she professes to know that they are about to sin through eating consecrated grain; and she offers to aid the Assyrians by praying to God each night and reporting the sin as soon as it is committed. Various of her promises are spoken with double meaning though literally true.†

Accepting the lecherous commander's invitation to a private banquet in his tent, she encourages him to drink heavily. When he is stupefied, she cuts off his head with his own sword, puts the head into her bag (which is carried by the maid), and returns triumphantly to her city.

After identification by Achior, the head is placed on the city wall; the leaderless Assyrians are routed and their camp looted by the Jews. Judith presents her share of the treasure to the Temple in Jerusalem.

EPILOGUE (Ch. 16). Judith sings a psalm in praise of the Creator, who demands obedience even more than sacrifices (v.

---

* As in Jonah, even the animals are made to wear sackcloth.

† For example, she promises that God will "accomplish something" if Holofernes follows her advice (11:6) and will carry out "what he has determined to do" (12:4). This type of cunning is popular in Jewish legends; compare Judg. 14, where Samson wagers thirty changes of raiment with the Philistines and pays his wager by killing and stripping thirty of them.

16) and who dooms nations that attack Israel. She lives to a great age, refuses many offers of marriage, frees her faithful slave, and at her death is nationally honored. The nation enjoys an era of peace.

Literary Qualities. With its realistic description of war, Judith adds a new element to Hebrew fiction which, in the stories so far considered, has dealt with peaceful countrysides, commercial centers, or Oriental courts. Judith was based upon the same doctrine which inspired the authors of Ruth and Tobit to write idyls of human kindness, the author of Daniel to write miracle legends, and the author of Susanna to write a tale of divine concern for purity and innocence—the doctrine that God will protect those Jews who remain true to their faith however much their fortitude be tested. Judith, however, was written in an era when violence and murder could be glorified in the name of righteousness.

SETTING. Although it is not to be inferred that the author revels in bloodthirsty detail,* it can be deduced from the long "historical" introduction that he has some interests in common with the great epic poets. He takes an imaginative interest in re-creating the movements of troops, the sacking of cities, the burning of fields, the wrangling of diplomats, the boasting of champions, and the triumphal processions of victors. Against this background, he contrasts the terror of ordinary human beings fainting from thirst in a besieged town.

CHARACTERS. As in modern wartime writings, the characterization seems influenced by general conceptions of national traits. The Assyrians (represented by the background figure of Nebuchadrezzar, the fully delineated Holofernes, and the undistinguishable common soldiers) are all barbarians—savage, arrogant, self-indulgent, and susceptible to flattery. Israel's nearer neighbors (particularly the Moabites) are perhaps less brutish than the Assyrians, but they are treacherous and envious of the Jews. Among foreigners, only Achior the Ammonite has some saving virtues; better informed and wiser than the rest, he reminds us of the soothsayer Balaam (Num. 23–24), who cannot tell a lie when speaking of Israel; and he is glad to become a naturalized Jew when given a chance. By way of contrast, the Israelites are a civilized and noble people; their leaders (Uzziah and the city

---

* Such reveling remained for the medieval and Renaissance painters and Anglo-Saxon poets who turned to the story of Judith for subject matter.

fathers) are compassionate, honorable men even though they may lack resourcefulness and need to have their faith prodded in in time of crisis.

Reading Judith, one is almost inevitably reminded of Joan of Arc—the lonely woman whose wisdom, piety, and courage succeeded where politicians and men of valor failed. Judith's name means simply "Jewess" (it is the feminine counterpart of "Judas" and was perhaps intended to call to mind the name of Judas Maccabeus, the national hero). She would prefer to spend her life in retirement, wearing widow's clothes and quietly serving God; but when duty demands, she knows precisely what to do. The author impresses her magnificence upon the reader not merely by description, not merely by her speeches, not merely by her deeds—but also by the effect which she has upon other characters in the story. Uzziah regards her with utmost respect (8:28–29), the elders of the city cannot turn their eyes from her when she passes (10:10), and the Assyrian soldiers confess that Hebrew women, if all were like her, could beguile the whole world (10:19).

PLOT. Judith is not a simple tale set down for oral retelling, but an intricate narrative composition with shifting points of suspense. In the opening chapters interest is centered upon the Jews as a nation: when all neighboring peoples have capitulated, can their border fortress hold out against seemingly overwhelming odds? Their chances of survival are summed up in Achior's statement that they will be undefeatable so long as they do not sin; but they have weakened to the point of allowing God five days in which to perform a miracle, and they are brought to the verge of surrender. Not until then does the heroine appear; and the rest of the story rises to still greater tension with the account of her personal risks.

ESTHER: A PATRIOTIC LEGEND WITH A SECULAR AND A RELIGIOUS VERSION
(ESTHER; "THE REST OF ESTHER" OR ESTHER 10:4—16:24)

The stirring legend of Esther, whether read in the Hebrew or the Greek version, might well be subtitled "The Origin of Purim" —the gay festival celebrated on the fourteenth and the fifteenth of Adar (February—March of the Western calendar). Unlike other Jewish holidays, Purim was not established in the Law of

Moses, but came into existence during the Dispersion.* If derived
from the Assyrian *puru,* the word *Purim* means "Lots"; and the
legend does tell how anti-Semites cast lots to determine an auspi-
cious date for massacring all Jews and how (by a turning of
tables) they themselves were massacred on that date. The national festival of Purim has some resemblance to the American
Independence Day and Thanksgiving Day and to the British
Guy Fawkes Day: it commemorates a "day of deliverance" and
is an occasion for feasting, noise-making, masquerading, gift-
giving, and charity to the poor.

Some regard the story as true history, and some as fiction
which makes use of historical background and historical characters. All admit it to be a story of adventure with sociological
significance. Whether its events be true or fanciful, its background of racial hatred is tragically real; and its picture of how
the suspicions, jealousies, and perhaps inherited enmities of a
few individuals can spread among peacefully coexistent peoples
is real. It raises the problem of whether an ethnic minority who
hold to their own culture may still be loyal citizens of a state,
and it seems to imply that such a minority can be more loyal to
the state than are the ambitious politicians who attack them.

The legend is particularly intriguing to literary scholars because it survives in two distinct versions. The Hebrew version
(which constitutes the book of Esther in Protestant Old Testaments and Esther 1:1—10:3 in Roman Catholic ones) appears to
be a studiously secular patriotic narrative: it never specifically
mentions God or prayer, and it shows no influence of the prophetic doctrines about sin and punishment or about the divine
mission of the Chosen People. Did its immediate author write at
a time when advocation of Jewish religion might have given
enemies an excuse for attacking Jewish holy places, or was that
author writing fiction for which he claimed no religious authority? The Greek version (preserved in the Septuagint) is equally
patriotic; but it is framed by a prologue and epilogue which
interpret the whole action as a working out of divine providence
in human affairs, it contains prayers, and again and again it

* Attempts have been made to show that Purim was a Jewish adaptation of
a Persian festival depicting the victory of the Babylonian deities Marduk
(Mordecai?) and Ishtar (Esther?) over the Elamite deities Humman
(Haman?) and Masti (Vashti?). The theory is not widely accepted today.

refers to God as omniscient and omnipotent. Did its immediate author restore passages that had been omitted from the Hebrew, or did he (as perhaps the majority of modern scholars assume) seek to remedy deficiencies in the legend by altering passages and adding material that would give it religious significance?

Both versions are set in a Persia of long ago: the Hebrew, in the reign of "Ahasuerus" (probably Xerxes I, who ruled 486—465 B.C.) and the Greek, in the reign of "Artaxerxes" (probably Artaxerxes II, 404—358 B.C., but possibly Artaxerxes I, 464—424 B.C.). For linguistic and other reasons, both are thought to have been composed in the second century B.C.[8]

Western Bibles print the Hebrew story in full. They include only the variant readings of the Greek, and they number these Esther 10:4—16:24. Protestant translations place the variants in a separate book of the Apocrypha and call them "The Rest of Esther" or "Additions to the Book of Esther"; the Douay version places them at the end of the Hebrew story. Since the fragments are disarranged and make little sense in themselves, many modern Protestant and Roman Catholic editions tell the reader how to fit them into the Hebrew or how to substitute them for the Hebrew.*

The Story of Esther in Its Two Versions. The present summary emphasizes the Hebrew short story, but calls attention in footnotes to the most significant Greek differences. Students will find a fascinating example of how a single legend may take two forms if they read the Hebrew version first and regard it as a self-sufficient secular short story, and if they then reconstruct the Septuagint version and regard it as an equally self-sufficient religious short story. To reconstruct the latter, they must take a copy of the "Rest of Esther" and correlate its chapters and verses with those of Esther in the following order:

Chs. 11:2—12:6
Chs. 1:1—3:13

---

* The disarrangement came about in the following way. When preparing the Vulgate text, St. Jerome translated the Hebrew narrative into Latin. He then appended variant passages from Latin editions of the Septuagint and indicated how these were to be correlated with the Hebrew story. His notes were often omitted by ancient scribes; and during the Middle Ages (when chapter-and-verse numbers were given to the Bible) the variants came to be treated as if they were a continuation of the story. During the Reformation, Protestant scholars relegated the fragmentary variants to the Apocrypha but did not change the traditional numbering or try to straighten out the order.

Ch. 13:1-7
Chs. 3:14—4:14
Chs. 13:8—15:16
Chs. 5:3—8:12 (Ch. 5:1—3 is not found in the Greek)
Ch. 16
Chs. 8:13—10:3
Ch. 10:4-13
Ch. 11:1.

ESTHER'S ENTHRONEMENT AND MORDECAI'S SERVICE TO THE KING (Chs. 1—2). Ahasuerus of Persia deposes Queen Vashti and orders that all eligible virgins in his capital (Shushan, Susa) be put into his harem until he selects a new queen from among them. Esther, cousin and adopted daughter of the Jewish official Mordecai, is finally selected. Mordecai overhears a conspiracy to assassinate Ahasuerus and sends warning to the king; the conspirators are executed, and Mordecai's service is set down in the court records but otherwise forgotten.*

HAMAN'S PLOT TO MASSACRE THE JEWS AND ESTHER'S DECISION TO INTERCEDE (Chs. 3—4). Haman the Agagite is made grand vizier of Persia, and all are commanded to bow in his presence. Because Mordecai refuses to bow, Haman informs Ahasuerus that a "certain people" within the empire hold to their own laws and disregard those of the land; and he secures written authority to kill these people on the thirteenth of Adar (a date chosen by lot) and to confiscate their property. Mordecai persuades Esther to intercede. Although she knows that to intrude upon the king without invitation may bring death, she reluctantly agrees, saying, "If I perish, I perish." (The king, it should be noted, is unaware that the condemned people are the Jews, that Esther is a Jewess, or that his own life has been saved by a Jew.)†

---

* *Chs. 11:2—12:5.* The Septuagint story opens with a vision: Mordecai dreams that two dragons are about to fight, that evil nations are about to attack a righteous nation, and that a tiny spring turns into a great river. He overhears the conspiracy to assassinate the king (here Artaxerxes), reports it, and is rewarded.

† *Chs. 12:6—15:16.* In the Greek, Haman has been in league with the conspirators and now seeks to avenge them. (Thus it is he—not the Jewish people—who is disloyal to the state.) The text of the royal edict for the pogrom is given in full (13:1-7). Mordecai prays for the protection of the Jews, explaining that he has not bowed because he would not set the glory of man before the glory of God. Esther prays that true religion may not be extinguished in the land, explaining that she has adhered strictly to the kosher food laws and that

THE TURNING OF THE TABLES UPON HAMAN (Chs. 5–8). Welcomed by the king and offered her choice of gifts, Esther asks only the privilege of entertaining him and Haman at a banquet. The banquet is held, and a second banquet is arranged for the next day. Between banquets Haman goes home to boast of his greatness at court; his only grief is that he has again encountered Mordecai and that the Jew has again refused to bow. On the advice of his wife and friends he erects a high gallows tree upon which to hang Mordecai.

Chapter 6 tells how Ahasuerus is unable to sleep on the night before the second banquet and how he asks that the court records be read to him. For the first time he learns that Mordecai has saved his life; and he is dismayed that such service has gone unrewarded. Just at this moment Haman enters, expecting to ask permission to hang Mordecai. Instead, he is consulted about how best to reward a man whom the king wishes to honor. Assuming the man to be himself, Haman suggests royal robes and a horse with crown-like headgear. When ordered to confer these honors upon Mordecai, he runs home and is taunted by his wife and friends. An escort arrives at his house to take him to the second banquet.

Chapters 7–8 complete the downfall of Haman. Esther reveals the grand vizier's evilness; Haman is hanged upon the gallows prepared for Mordecai, and his property and court position are bestowed upon the Jew. Esther also reveals that she herself is a Jewess and cousin of Mordecai and that both are members of the "certain people" condemned to mass execution. By Persian law Ahasuerus cannot revoke his own edict, but he can and does issue a counteredict permitting the Jews to arm and defend themselves.*

THE TURNING OF THE TABLES UPON ALL ANTI-SEMITES; THE INSTITUTION OF THE TWO-DAY FESTIVAL OF PURIM (Ch. 9). The Jews proceed to slay all who would have slain them, although they refrain from taking loot. On the thirteenth and fourteenth

---

she is distressed at being married to a Gentile. She goes to the throne room, and her intrusion arouses the king's fury until God transforms the wrath into gentleness. She swoons.

* *Ch. 16.* The Greek version is documented with the full text of the new edict: King Artaxerxes has discovered how the Jews have been misrepresented to him, how instead of being disloyal to the civil law they are loyal to the righteous law of God.

of Adar those living in the city kill hundreds; and on the thirteenth those living in the provinces kill thousands. Each of these victories is followed by a day of national celebration: this is the origin of Purim.

EPILOGUE (Ch. 10). Mordecai, grand vizier and second only to Ahasuerus in rank, spends the rest of his life promoting the welfare and peace of the Jewish people.*

Literary Qualities. Such are the two versions of Esther—a book of the Bible which, however popular among Jewish laymen on their only secular holiday, has been generally unpopular among theologians. Of the two versions, the Greek is the more violent in that it insists upon God's approval of the vengeance and in that it claims to provide documentary evidence for the truth of the events. The Hebrew version, claiming neither divine inspiration nor documentable historicity, can be taken as a pure folk story; and folk stories have a universal way of not stopping until the biter is thoroughly bitten, the hangman thoroughly hanged, and would-be murderers thoroughly murdered.

SETTING. Both versions contain some accurate description of the Persian Empire with its badly governed territories, its court intrigues, its official decorum, its architecture, its horses with crownlike headgear, and so on. But perhaps even more than the other books which we call "short stories," Esther makes free with historical fact and chronology.†

CHARACTERS. Since the psychological motivations of the protagonists differ greatly in the Hebrew and Greek versions, while the story remains pretty much the same, we must consider the characters to be types rather than fully drawn personalities. Their deeds rather than their thoughts and emotions constitute the short story.

Evaluated by her deeds, Esther is a legendary heroine who

* Ch. 10:4-13 and Ch. 11:1. The Greek version finishes its frame story: Mordecai's vision of the two dragons symbolized Haman and himself; the nations, the anti-Semites and the Jews; the spring which turned into a river, Esther. Ch. 11:1 is a colophon certifying that the legend is genuine history.

† There is no record that Xerxes or Artaxerxes (I or II) had a Jewish queen, authorized a Jewish minority to massacre Gentile subjects, or was so much concerned with affairs of the harem as to forget affairs of state. There is some evidence that a Mordecai was an official at the court of Xerxes; but if (as the story says) he had been brought to Persia as a captive of Nebuchadrezzar, he would have been at least a hundred years old, and the seductive Esther would not have been much younger, in the time of Xerxes.

uses her beauty and shrewdness to save her people. In the Hebrew (4:13) she has to be prodded into action by a reminder that she herself is under death sentence if Jews are to be exterminated. In the Greek (Ch. 14) she leads a double life—rubbing dung into her hair in private lamentations and then appearing clean and perfumed before the husband she secretly loathes.

Evaluated by *his* deeds, Mordecai is a staunch patriot, loyal to the Persian king, loyal to the Jews, and too noble to bow to an upstart. In the Greek, he is also a sort of Daniel who sees visions and risks martyrdom for his faith.

Haman in either version is a villain who schemes, gloats, brags, grovels, and deserves to be hanged. The Hebrew version stigmatizes him as an Agagite (an ignominious last survivor of an accursed race of anti-Semites); the Greek version makes him a Macedonian, one of the Grecian overlords who were persecuting Jews in Seleucid times.

The king is substantially the same Oriental potentate that we have seen in the Daniel legends: here he is Ahasuerus or Artaxerxes, and there he is Nebuchadrezzar, Belshazzar, or Darius. He is intoxicated by wine, women, and pride in a godlike way of expressing pleasure or displeasure with a gesture. He can be deceived by false counselors, but if convinced that villainy is taking place under his nose, he will declare an edict that sets matters to right.

PLOT, SITUATION, AND DIALOGUE. Until Chapter 9, where interest in the authenticity of Purim takes over, elements of suspense are kept ever going. Will Esther be chosen queen, and will she fare any better than her capriciously dethroned predecessor? Will Mordecai survive the enmity of Haman? Will the Jewish nation be obliterated? The story is told with artful teasing, switching scenes whenever excitement is at high pitch.

The author has a great sense for ironic situation, in which events turn out to be just the reverse of what the villain schemes, Haman erects a gallows only to be hanged on it. Haman casts lots to choose a date for exterminating the Jews, only to have his own people exterminated on that date. Haman parades his honors before his wife and friends, only to be reviled by them within twenty-four hours. Haman seizes Esther's feet and grovels for mercy, only to be suspected of trying to assault her sexually.

The speeches, if translated into dialogue, are spirited—whether we consider them dramatic or melodramatic:

Esther: We are sold, I and my people, to be destroyed, to be slain and to perish.
King: Who is he and where is he, that durst presume?
Esther: The adversary and enemy is this wicked Haman.
King: Hang him.

And the prayers and royal decrees of the Greek version are certainly intended as model compositions.

Both versions are tales of intrigue and revenge. The Hebrew is almost straight adventure story: the hard-pressed heroine and hero trust to their own prowess and are helped by a series of lucky coincidences (for example, by the fact that the king happens to read the court records at just the right time). The Greek is classifiable as a miracle story motivated by divine foreordination of history and by a series of divine interventions in human affairs.

Part Seven
Wisdom Literature

"For the law shall not perish from the priest, nor counsel from the wise, nor the word from the prophet" (Jer. 18:18). Thus does the seer Jeremiah call attention to the three types of moral and spiritual leaders of ancient Israel: first, the priest, whose primary functions were to teach and to enforce the Law; second, the "wise man," who dispensed practical advice on how to live successfully in the world which God has created; and third, the prophet, whose duty was to recall men to ethical behavior and right worship by revealing to them the profound truths which God himself had delivered to the prophet.

The "wise man" was the Oriental philosopher. Unlike his Greek counterpart, he had little enthusiasm for metaphysics or theoretical speculation. He did, however, take all human *experience* as his province, and he tried to deduce from his observations the rules which, if followed, would assure a man of a long, prosperous, and happy life. His attitude was utilitarian and pragmatic, and his quest for "the good life" has led many commentators to call him a humanist. He has often been censured for emphasizing man rather than God and for harping too exclusively on the theme that it pays to be good. It should be remembered, however, that he began with the assumption that God made the universe and established the rules for man's conduct. If honesty turns out to be the best policy, it is because God has ordained that it be so; God rewards those who obey his laws and punishes those who transgress them.* Therefore it is wise to observe God's rules and foolish to disobey them:

> The fear of the Lord is the beginning of knowledge:
> But fools despise wisdom and instruction. (Prov. 1:7)

* It should be noticed that this belief is similar to those of the Deuteronomist and of Job's "Comforters."

The practical philosophy of the sages appears in a number of literary forms—the proverb, the essay, the fable, the parable, and even the riddle. Often it is attached to or made a part of a work of some other genre.

It should not be supposed that the ancient Hebrews had a monopoly on wisdom literature. It has been produced by thoughtful writers in almost every country, beginning at the very dawn of civilization and continuing down to the present day. The "world's oldest book," *The Precepts* of the Egyptian Ptahhotep (fl. *c.* 2650 B.C.), is a collection of shrewd and homely reflections on life, its conduct, and its meaning. Some other notable examples in world literature are the *Analects* of Confucius, the *Fables* of Aesop, the *Dialogues* and *Moral Epistles* of Seneca, the *Meditations* of Marcus Aurelius, the *Maxims* of La Rochefoucauld, and *Poor Richard's Almanac* of Benjamin Franklin.

Like most other nations, Israel showed profound respect for the dispensers of wisdom, who are mentioned frequently throughout the Bible. Wise women tried to reassure the mother of Sisera (Judg. 5:28-30), and David's Generàl Joab sought the advice of a female sage (II Sam. 14:14). The Hebrew most renowned for sagacity was Solomon, whose "wisdom excelled the wisdom of all the children of the east country, and all the wisdom of Egypt" (I Kings 4:30). Daniel, Shadrach, Meshach, and Abednego surpassed all the magicians and astrologers of Babylon "in all matters of wisdom and understanding" (Dan. 1:20).

Four Biblical books may be classified as wisdom literature: Proverbs, Ecclesiastes, Ecclesiasticus, and The Wisdom of Solomon. Two others, Job and the Epistle of James, are sometimes placed in this category. In addition, there are many parts of other books which qualify as "sapiential" writing: Jotham's Fable (Judg. 9:8-15); Psalms 1, 15, 16, 24, 37, 49, 50, 73, and 112; Baruch 3:9–4:4; and some precepts of Jesus' Sermon on the Mount, especially those about money (Matt. 5–7 *passim*).

It is noteworthy that Hebrew wisdom literature is addressed to the individual and not to the nation as a group. It contains no reference to the Covenant, to the Israelites as the Chosen People, or to the expected Messiah. Hence it is less national and of more general application than much Old Testament literature.

Ethical Precepts and Cynical Pessimism
Proverbs, Ecclesiastes, Ecclesiasticus,
and the Wisdom of Solomon

Three of the Biblical wisdom books consist largely of short aphoristic sayings based on the traditional Hebrew belief that God rewards the righteous with prosperity and punishes the wicked with adversity; the fourth wisdom book, Ecclesiastes, is a philosophical essay, written by a world-weary agnostic.

PROVERBS: A TREASURY OF WISE PRECEPTS

The book of Proverbs is a compilation of several collections of ancient wise sayings:

(1) The oldest collection (10:1—22:16), consisting of 375 proverbs, may have come down from the tenth century B.C. It is the nucleus of the book. Probably because Solomon was traditionally considered the greatest Hebrew sage and because I Kings 4:32 says that he "spake three thousand proverbs," this section (and sometimes the whole book) has been ascribed to him. Although no single precept can definitely be assigned to Solomon, some modern scholars think that he may have written a considerable percentage of this section of the book, for it reflects the social, political, and economic conditions of his era.[1] Nearly all of these proverbs are two lines long, and many of them employ antithetic parallelism,* holding up the fool in contrast with the wise man, the rich with the poor, the lazy with the industrious, and so on.

(2) The second section (Chs. 25—29) claims to consist of "the proverbs of Solomon, which the men of Hezekiah king of Judea

---

* See discussion of parallelism as a poetic device above (pp. 237-238).

copied out" (25:1). It was probably collected in the eighth century B.C.

(3) The third group (22:17–23:34) is made up of four parts: an introduction (22:17-21); a series of short warnings (22:22–23:14), similar to those in an Egyptian collection of 800–600 B.C. entitled "The Teaching of Amen-em-ope"; a third division (23:15–24:22); and the last (24:23-34).

(4) The fourth section (30:1-33) is called "The words of Agur the son of Jakeh" (30:1), which title may apply only to vv. 1-14, a series of "personal reflections"[2] of the author. Verses 15-33 consist of a series of lists of things remarkable for one reason or another. "Agur" was probably an Edomite or an Arabian. The date of the collection is uncertain.

(5) The fifth collection (31:1-9), also of uncertain date, consists of "The words of king Lemuel" (31:1) which his mother taught him—a warning against the dangers of alcohol and bad women. Lemuel, too, was probably an Edomite or an Arabian.

(6) Probably later than the "words of Lemuel" is the description of a virtuous woman (31:10-31), a Hebrew acrostic.

(7) A large collection (1:7–9:18) is entitled "The proverbs of Solomon the son of David, king of Israel" (1:1). Though parts of this section, notably Chapters 8 and 9, may have originated in the tenth century B.C., matters of style suggest Greek influence and indicate a post-Exilic date for the final version. Much of the section discusses the nature and merits of wisdom, and it warns against the snares of immoral women.

From this brief summary one concludes that the process of composition covered a period of several hundred years, perhaps from the tenth to the third century B.C. Many of the proverbs were probably transmitted orally for a long time before being written down. Linguistic peculiarities (such as the use of certain Aramaisms) and ideological considerations indicate that the date of final compilation was post-Exilic and probably between 300 and 200 B.C.[3]

Theme and Literary Qualities. The theme of the book is the value, the worth of wisdom—primarily because it assures a man of happiness and prosperity in life.

Proverbs defines wisdom as "the fear of God," and it glorifies wisdom as the rational principle of the universe. Wisdom, therefore, = goodness, and folly = sin.

The book tells little about the nature and purposes of God except insofar as those are inherent in the doctrine that he will reward with material blessings those who are wise (that is, good) and will withhold those blessings from the foolish (or wicked). The book has little or nothing to say about personal immortality. It does, however, teach many *ethical* if not theological lessons. It attacks, for example, the vices of pride, dishonesty, drunkenness, and sexual promiscuity; and it advocates such virtues as industriousness, thrift, generosity, and kindness.

Its tone is that of an old man to a young, a father to a son, a man who has experienced life and who wants those who come after him to walk in the paths of wisdom.

Some of the literary merits of the book of Proverbs are epigrammatic conciseness, balance, and the use of many homely but arresting figures of speech drawn from the everyday life. All of it is in poetic form, and it often employs parallelism, the principal literary device of Hebrew poetry.

Contents. The compiler of the book of Proverbs apparently made no attempt to arrange the sayings topically. Maxims on the same or similar subjects are scattered throughout different chapters, and some chapters contain proverbs on a wide variety of topics. The following summary is an attempt to bring together related ideas found in various parts of the book.[4]

THE NATURE OF WISDOM (1:1-7, 20-33; 4:7-9; 8:1-31). True wisdom is knowledge of, and obedience to, the commandments of the Lord. Wisdom and righteousness are one and the same. Wisdom (personified) was created by God himself; she is older than the universe:

> The Lord possessed me in the beginning of his way, before
> his works of old.
> I was set up from everlasting, from the beginning, or ever
> the earth was. (8:22-23)

She cries out from high places, at the city gates, and in the streets, warning men and directing them in the way of righteousness. She helps kings and princes to rule justly.

THE WISE MAN CONTRASTED WITH THE FOOL (1:5-7, 22; 9:8-9; 10:2; 11:1; 12:15; 13:15, 20, 25; 15:21, 29; 16:6; 17:3, 10, 12, 21, 24; 24:19-20; 26:3-7; 28:1, 13). The wise man seeks instruction, counsel, knowledge, understanding, and discretion; he welcomes reproofs and rebukes. A fool, on the contrary, scorns learning and delights in his own simplicity; his way is right in his own eyes; he hates reproof. It is good to associate with the wise man,

> But a companion of fools shall be destroyed. . . .
> Let a bear robbed of her whelps meet a man, rather than
>   a fool in his folly. (13:20, 17:12)

THE REWARDS OF WISDOM (1:33; 2:10-11; 3:1-8, 13-18; 4:7-9; 8:32-36; 9:1-6; 13:7; 14:30; 15:16-17, 27; 16:8, 19; 17:1; 22:1; 23:4-5; 28:6). "Happy is the man that findeth wisdom" (3:13), for wisdom brings long life, riches, honor, and peace. It provides for one's head "an ornament of grace" and "a crown of glory" (4:9). The various forms of folly (unrighteousness)—hatred, envy, greed, bribery, pride, strife—all bring unhappiness. But wisdom (righteousness) is more precious than silver and rubies, for it brings life itself, "the favor of the Lord" (8:35), and tranquility of spirit.

THE TRAINING OF A CHILD (1:8-9; 3:11-12; 4:10, 12-13; 13:24; 19:18; 20:29; 22:6, 15; 23:13-14, 22; 29:15). A young child is foolish; but instruction in the laws of the Lord makes him wise. Train him right while he is young, and when he is old he will continue his righteous ways. Reproof and punishment will bring him wisdom and will deliver his soul from hell. Let the father not withhold correction from his child—

> If thou beatest him with the rod, he shall not die. (23:13)

Administering such punishment is simply emulating God,

> For whom the Lord loveth he correcteth. (3:12)

TREATMENT OF THE POOR (14:21, 31; 17:15; 19:17; 21:13; 22:2, 22-23, 28; 28:27; 30:13-14; 31:8-9). There is a generation who pretend piety but who in reality stop their ears to keep out the cries of the poor and who close their eyes so as not to see the suffering of the needy; their

> teeth are as swords,
> And their jawteeth as knives,
> To devour the poor from off the earth. (30:14)

Woe be unto him who either robs the poor or refuses them aid, for the Lord will not hear *his* cries but will despoil him. But blessed be the man who pleads the cause of the poor; the Lord will hear *his* cause in time of trouble.

> He that hath pity upon the poor lendeth unto the Lord;*
> And that which he hath given will he pay him again. (19:17)

TREATMENT OF FRIENDS AND NEIGHBORS (3:27-28; 10:12; 17:9, 17; 18:24; 25:17; 27:5, 10, 19). The best way to win friends is to show yourself friendly. Deal justly with everybody; do not withhold from a man anything that is due him. When you have money, do not hesitate to lend it to a neighbor. Do not forsake your friend when he needs you; stick by him in adversity. Do not stir up strife; overlook your friends' faults. Refrain from repeating gossip or derogatory remarks.

TREATMENT OF ENEMIES† (24:17-18, 29; 25:21-22). Do not rejoice over misfortune to your enemy lest the Lord become angry with *you* and cease his anger at your enemy. But be kind to your enemy: feed him when he is hungry, and give him water when he is thirsty; in this way you will make him ashamed ("heap coals of fire upon his head"‡), and God will reward you.

> Say not, I will do so to him as he hath done to me:
> I will render to the man according to his work. (24:29)⁵

THE FOLLY OF ANGER (14:17, 29; 15:1; 16:32; 17:14; 18:19; 19:11; 20:3; 22:24-25; 25:28; 26:21, 27; 27:4). A man acts foolishly when he is angry; he who is slow to anger is wise and "better than the mighty" (16:13). It is discreet to ignore an injury or an insult. Avoid association with contentious men, for you may learn their ways; if, however, you must come into contact with them, try to calm their wrath by speaking softly and gently. Meddlers and irritable men are fools, but

> It is an honor for a man to cease from strife. (20:3)

THE FOLLY OF TALK WITHOUT THOUGHT (12:23; 13:3; 14:23; 15:2, 4; 16:21-23; 17:28; 18:7, 13, 21; 21:23; 25:11; 29:11, 20). The wise man learns much but says little and speaks judiciously.

---

* Compare the saying of Jesus: "Inasmuch as ye have done it unto the least of these my brethren, ye have done it unto me." (Matt. 25:40.)

† These precepts are perhaps the source of Jesus' commandments about loving one's enemies, Matt. 5:21-26, 38-47. But in Jesus' teachings there is no consideration of prudence or self-interest.

‡ Quoted by Paul in Romans 12:20.

Heedless loquacity leads to trouble—penury, shame, even destruction. Even a fool is considered wise when he keeps his mouth shut.

THE FOLLY OF LYING AND SLANDER (11:9, 13; 12:22; 18:8; 19:9; 20:17; 23:6-7; 25:9-10, 18-19; 26:20; 29:5). "Lying lips are an abomination to the Lord" (12:22). Do not spread malicious tales which may wound another; conceal the matter if you can. A perjurer is like a sword or a sharp arrow; he shall not go unpunished, but shall perish. Settle your case with your neighbor and do not air it in public. Deceit may seem sweet temporarily, but eventually it shall be as gravel in the mouth.

THE SLOTHFUL AND POOR CONTRASTED WITH THE DILIGENT AND RICH (6:6-11; 10:4-5, 26; 12:9, 24; 13:4, 11; 14:4, 20; 18:1-23; 19:4, 6-7, 15, 24; 20:13; 22:7, 13, 29; 24:10, 30-34; 26:16; 27:8, 23-27; 30:24-28).

> Go to the ant, thou sluggard;
> Consider her ways, and be wise. (6:6)

Industry and diligence are among the surest marks of the wise man. The fool spends his time in idleness and procrastination. He allows thorns and nettles to cover his field and vineyards, and he lets his stone walls tumble down. In times of adversity his strength shall be small, and he shall come to poverty. The poor man is despised even by his neighbors; he has to "use entreaties" and be a servant to the rich. In contrast, the industrious man will enjoy plenty—hay and tender grass, lambs and goats, herds and flocks. He will always have many friends, and he will be a ruler among men.

THE USE AND ABUSE OF ALCOHOL (20:1; 21:17; 23:20-21, 29-35; 27:20; 31:4-7). "Wine is a mocker" (20:1), and whoever is deceived by it is not wise. It bites like a serpent and stings like an adder. Drunkenness causes red eyes, babbling, contention, brawling, wounds without cause, sorrow, woe, and poverty. Rulers especially should never drink wine, for it makes them forget the law and pervert justice.

Nevertheless, wine encourages him whose heart is heavy, makes the poor man forget his poverty, causes the miserable man to forget his misery, and comforts him who is about to die.

THE WISDOM OF RULERS AND NATIONS (11:14; 14:34; 19:12; 20:5, 28; 23:1-3; 24:21-22; 25:2-7; 29:2, 18). A steadfast and merciful king will be safe upon his throne, and wise people will dwell in safety and honor. Because a king is strong, a private man is foolish to covet his delicacies, meddle with his rule, or put himself forward in the royal presence. A nation's strength lies in righteousness and wise counsel, and "where there is no vision,* the people perish" (29:18).

THE EVIL WOMAN CONTRASTED WITH THE VIRTUOUS WOMAN (5:15, 18-19; 6:20-35; 7:1-5, 24-27; 9:16-17; 11:16; 12:4; 18:22; 19:14; 21:9, 19; 27:15; 30:21-23; 31:2-3, 10-31). A young man should remember the commandments of his father and mother— "bind them continually" in his heart and "tie them about [his] neck" (6:21) so as to preserve himself "from the evil woman" (6:24). She can beguile him by flattery; her beauty will make him lust after her; and her eyelids can "take" him (6:25)!

> Can a man take fire in his bosom,
> And his clothes not be burned?
> Can one go upon hot coals,
> And his feet not be burned? (6:27-28)

Adultery wounds and dishonors a man and destroys his soul. A wicked woman leads a man astray:

> Her house is the way to hell,
> Going down to the chambers of death. (7:27)

A prudent and virtuous woman, on the contrary, is a gift from the Lord, and "her price is far above rubies" (31:10). She arises from the bed while it is still dark, and she labors hard all day. She prepares food for her household. She plants vineyards. She spins wool and flax; she makes clothing for her own family and sells some to outsiders. She appraises and buys real estate. She is never idle, even after dark—

> Her candle goeth not out by night. (31:18)

She is generous to the poor and needy. When she speaks, kindness and wisdom flow from her lips. "Strength and honor are her clothing" (31:25). Her husband praises her, and

> Her children arise up, and call her blessed. (31:27)

* The Revised Standard Version translates "prophecy."

ECCLESIASTES: THE PESSIMISM OF A WISTFUL CYNIC

"Vanity of vanities; all is vanity." This motto, which appears at the beginning of the book and again near the end (1:2 and 12:8), establishes its tone and epitomizes its philosphy. Ecclesiastes is a prose essay (interrupted here and there with bits of poetry), expressing the skeptical pessimism of a man who for many decades has sought the meaning of life, only to conclude that life has no meaning and no purpose.

Title, Authorship, and Date. The word *Ecclesiastes* is a Greek translation of the Hebrew *Koheleth,* or *Qohéleth,* which means "one who participates in, or speaks to, an assembly." The King James translation of the word is "Preacher" (1:1).

Like the book of Proverbs and The Song of Songs, this essay is attributed to Solomon, "the son of David, king in Jerusalem" (1:1); but both subject matter and linguistic considerations have led most modern scholars to conclude that Solomon had nothing to do with its composition and that its principal author was a learned Jew, either Palestinian or Alexandrian, writing in the latter part of the third century B.C.

The "Original" Essay. The presence of (1) a rather large number of "pious" passages which appear to be in conflict with the generally pessimistic and agnostic philosophy of the book and (2) some more or less irrelevant aphoristic verses has caused most modern scholars[6] to believe that the nucleus of the book was a fairly homogeneous essay on the vanity of human life and that later editors interpolated passages in order to make the book more acceptable to Jewish believers. Without the interpolations it would probably never have been received into the Hebrew (or Christian) canon. Morris Jastrow characterized three types of interpolation: (1) "Additions by 'Pious' Commentators"; (2) "Additions by the 'Maxim' Commentators"; and (3) "Miscellaneous Comments and Glosses."[7]

Literary Qualities. The body of Ecclesiastes is a personal essay in prose, more unified than the book of Proverbs, but not a "systematic development of thought" nor a "consciously ordered arrangement of material."[8] Rather, it consists of the melancholy broodings of a perceptive and open-minded man who has been puzzled by the presence of both joy and sorrow "under the sun" and who has resolved to find out life's meaning if he can. Poetic passages of varying length are scattered throughout the twelve chapters; some of them, especially the longer ones coming near the end, are of great beauty.

The author moves somewhat desultorily from one area of life to another, often returning to a topic for further comment. The lament, "This, too, is vanity," frequently appears as a refrain. The book ends appropriately (if one disregards the extraneous interpolations) with some wistful comments about old age and death.

Koheleth's Thought.* Numerous commentators have called attention to the similarity of Koheleth's conclusions to those reached by Omar Khayyám in the *Rubáiyát*. Both authors temper their pessimism with a mild epicureanism. The poems of A. E. Housman also invite comparison, but Housman's melancholy appears to be that of a disillusioned young man, whereas both Koheleth and Omar seem to speak with the wisdom of old age.

All creation, says Koheleth, is an endless round of futility.

> One generation passeth away,
> And another generation cometh:
> But the earth abideth forever.
> The sun also ariseth,
> And the sun goeth down,
> And hasteth to his place where he arose. . . .
> The thing that hath been,
> It is that which shall be;
> And that which is done
> Is that which shall be done:
> And there is no new thing under the sun. (1:4-5, 9)

Koheleth has sought everywhere to find "the good life" and to discover whether life has any meaning or purpose. He has tried every realm wherein man is supposed to find contentment, but in vain.

He has tried hard work (Thomas Carlyle's panacea), but

> What profit hath a man of all his labour
> Which he taketh under the sun? . . .
> I have seen all the works that are done under the sun;
> And, behold, all is vanity and vexation of the spirit. (1:3, 14)

He has amassed great wealth: silver, gold, houses, vineyards, forests, and servants. Although this brought temporary satisfac-

---

* This summary will disregard the "pious" and incongruous interpolations which contradict Koheleth's main thesis.

tion, his joy evaporated when he began to think that he would have to die and leave all his possessions—eventually to a stranger.

He tried such sensuous pleasures as food, wine, and music. These brought as much contentment as anything he found; but, again, the satisfaction will not last.

Finally, he sought comfort in wisdom, only to discover that, although wisdom is superior to folly, both the wise man and the fool come to the same ending—the grave. Therefore even wisdom is vanity.

There is nothing beyond the grave, no immortality. To be dead, however, is better than to live, because dead men are unaware of the suffering and injustice in this world, "the evil work that is done under the sun" (4:3).* There is a God, but he gives no comfort to the oppressed. He treats the just and the unjust alike; he hands out his blessings and punishments capriciously. He is all-powerful, in control of all things; and he pre-determines the recurrence of what is past in an endless cycle.

What, then, should a man do? Recognizing that all things are in God's hands, he should submit and cease "striving after wind." He should confess that he is unable to solve the riddle of the universe or reconcile its incongruities. He should practice moderation, find what physical and emotional pleasures he can in life, and accept what is,

> Or ever the silver cord be loosed,
> Or the golden bowl be broken,
> Or the pitcher be broken at the fountain,
> Or the wheel broken at the cistern.
> Then shall the dust return to the earth as it was:
> And the spirit return unto God who gave it.
> Vanity of vanities, saith the preacher;
> All is vanity. (12:6-8)

ECCLESIASTICUS: A HANDBOOK OF PRACTICAL ETHICS

The Apocryphal book of Ecclesiasticus is often considered a "second collection" of wise sayings, comparable to the canonical book of Proverbs.

Title, Authorship, and Date. There are variant titles for this book in the extant texts. In the Douay Version it is called "The Wisdom of Jesus (or Jeshua), the Son of Sirach (or Sira)." The

* Compare A. E. Housman's "Be Still, My Soul."

word *Ecclesiasticus* means "church book"[9] and seems to bear testimony to the value assigned to the book by the early Christian Church; that is, although not a part of the canon, it was apparently considered so excellent a volume of instruction that it became a sort of handbook to be used by leaders and members of the Church.

It is the only Apocryphal book whose author and date we know. The grandson of that author added a prologue, which tells us that his grandfather, Jesus Ben Sira (that is, "son of Sira") of Jerusalem wrote the book in Hebrew about 180 B.C. The grandson himself translated it into Greek in 132 B.C. in the land of Egypt. He pleads for the leniency of the reader in criticizing the translation, for, he says, it is very difficult to carry over exact shades of meaning from one language to another.

Literary Qualities. Like the book of Proverbs, Ecclesiasticus is written chiefly in couplets of parallel lines, but unlike the canonical book, it is *not* made up principally of short, pithy apothegms, although a great many of these are present; instead, it consists chiefly of essays or discourses of varying lengths. Some of the passages are poetry of a very high order—for example, the praise of the universe as the handiwork of God (43:13-20), a passage comparable in beauty to Psalm 19.

The defects of Ecclesiasticus are its loose organization, its occasional repetitiousness, and its lack of any new or deep philosophy. It is, nevertheless, unfailingly interesting, giving "pungent expression" to even "the most hackneyed themes."[10]

The author was manifestly a man of wide experience and learning, mature intelligence, and penetrating powers of observation. He is sure of himself; he speaks with great confidence, naive candor, and a genial wit. Written before the beginning of the persecutions of Antiochus Epiphanes, the book "breathes a serenity which would hardly be possible later on."[11]

Significance. For three reasons Ecclesiasticus should be recognized as perhaps the most significant book in the Apocrypha: (1) It is filled with sound practical advice on hundreds of matters, advice which is pertinent today; (2) it gives an intimate and detailed account of Palestinian life in the era when it was written; and (3) it serves as an important link between early Judaism and the beliefs and attitudes which developed into Sadduceeism and "Talmudic rabbinism."[12]

Contents. Ecclesiasticus may be divided into five parts of varying length:[13]

PART I. THE PROLOGUE. Here the grandson of the author tells (in prose) about the writing and translating of the book.

PART II. PROVERBS (1:1–42:14).* By far the longest section, this contains many short maxims and precepts similar to those in the book of Proverbs. There are also many longer discussions of various religious and ethical matters. There is little attempt on the part of the author to organize his meditations on any logical or topical principle.

PART III. HYMN OF CREATION (42:15–43:33). This is a rhapsodic poem praising God for creating the "world of physical nature."[14]

PART IV. HISTORY OF THE HEBREWS (Chs. 44–49). Here the poet glorifies God for his wondrous providence in directing the course of Hebrew history. Of special interest is the "Praise of Famous Men," a eulogy of twenty-nine of the great heroes of the Old Testament, from Adam down through Nehemiah; included are Abraham, Joseph, Moses, David, and Elijah. Notably missing from this list is Ezra, evidently omitted because he propagated beliefs that grew into Pharisaism, which Ben Sira opposed.

PART V. EPILOGUE: TEMPLE SERVICES AND PRAISE OF THE HIGH PRIEST (50:1–51:30). The book closes with a eulogy of the High Priest Simon, the most complete description of Temple services that has come down to us from ancient times, and some short concluding authogiographical remarks.

Ben Sira's Thought. So numerous and so miscellaneous are the topics discussed in this book—the longest in the Apocrypha—that an attempt to summarize or even to categorize them in this Outline would be impractical. It gives advice on almost every area of life, advice which "is usually full of good sense and as applicable today as it was two thousand years ago."[15] Self-control, almsgiving, table etiquette, family relations, avarice, hypocrisy, standing surety for another's debt, mourning for the dead—these are a few of its topics. Some of the most significant ones have been selected for discussion here.

* Some scholars divide this into two sections, Chapters 1–23 and 24:1–42:14, which may have been published separately. See *The Interpreter's Dictionary of the Bible,* II, 17.

THE NATURE OF WISDOM. Following the example of Proverbs, Ecclesiasticus attempts to define *wisdom* and also personifies it. At times Ben Sira identifies wisdom with the Law which God gave to Moses on Mount Sinai (19:20; 24:23). (A century or so later, the Sadducees were to accept only the written "Law of Moses" [the Pentateuch], as their guide.) Elsewhere Ben Sira shows a much broader conception of wisdom, as including the right way to conduct all the activities of man. This is a more worldly wisdom than one finds either in Proverbs or in the later Apocryphal book The Wisdom of Solomon. Ben Sira says, in effect, "Put your trust in the Lord . . ., but trust also the wisdom that comes from experience."[16] An example of his advice might be: When you are sick, "pray to the Lord . . . and then put yourself in the hands of a physician, for God created him."[17] According to Ecclesiasticus, "worldly wisdom is the same in kind as divine wisdom, and differs from it only in degree."[18]

THE EDUCATION OF CHILDREN (30:1-13). Ben Sira urges the father to maintain strict discipline: Whip your son often so that he will turn out well; be severe with him while he is young so that he will not become stubborn and cause you grief later on.

WOMEN AND MARRIAGE. The author generally takes a dim view of women. He had rather keep house with a lion or a serpent than with a wicked woman; her malice makes all other malice seem small. And her husband groans bitterly among his neighbors whenever he thinks about her (25:13-26, 26:7-12). But there are *some* virtuous women, and a happy marriage is one of life's greatest blessings (25:1; 26:1-4, 13-18). Marital infidelity will be punished (23:18-26).

DINNER ETIQUETTE (31:12—32:13). Ben Sira writes an extended essay on how to behave at a dinner party: Don't be greedy and don't gulp your food down. Don't reach too far for dishes. Don't drink too much wine. If you are asked to be master of ceremonies—an after-dinner speaker—be concise; speak few words; and don't be the last to go home!

DOCTORS (38:1-15). A fine passage in praise of medical doctors claims that God has entrusted to the physicians the work of diagnosing and healing illnesses and of preserving life. They will pray to God for assistance in these endeavors. (In some churches this passage, known as "The Praise of the Physician," is read on the Feast of St. Luke, Paul's "beloved physician."[19])

MAN'S FREE WILL AND GOD'S JUSTICE (15:11-20; 16:1-14; 17:7-32; 35:1-20). Ben Sira says that God's Law is a powerful deterrent to evil and that prayer helps man to avoid sin. But God has given man freedom of the will, and if man chooses evil, he will be judged according to his deeds. God holds man responsible for his sins, but he is also merciful and forgiving. When man repents, he receives him again unto himself.

SADDUCEEISM. Ben Sira is clearly of the Sadducean persuasion. He rejects belief in angels and spirits, the resurrection of the dead, and the mass of rabbinical interpretations of the Hebrew Law. His emphasis is on "good works" rather than rituals or doctrine. Men's rewards and punishments are meted out to him in this world, for "the son of man is not immortal" (17:30). Therefore, one should not fear death, the common lot of all men; God has so planned it, and it is the end of everything for every man:

> There is no inquisition in the grave,
> Whether thou have lived ten, or an hundred,
>   or a thousand years. (41:4)

THE WISDOM OF SOLOMON: A TREATISE ON GOD, ETHICS, AND IMMORTALITY

Generally considered the most important *theological* book in the Apocrypha, The Wisdom of Solomon is a fusion of Greek philosophy with orthodox Judaistic beliefs, and it casts considerable light upon the New Testament doctrines of the Logos (especially as propounded in the Gospel of John) and personal immortality.

Date, Authorship, and Language. There is no evidence to pinpoint the date of composition. Scholarly guesses have ranged from 150 B.C. to A.D. 40. Late in the first century B.C. seems a reasonable conjecture.[20]

Although the title attributes the authorship to Solomon and although the author speaks in the character of that monarch (for example, in 7:1-8; 8:9-11; and 9:7-8, 12), it is obvious that the writer had no intention to deceive, but was simply following a literary tradition which ascribed to Solomon numerous pieces of wisdom literature, including the canonical books of Proverbs and Ecclesiastes. The real author is unknown, but internal evidence indicates that he was an Alexandrian Jew, orthodox in his

religious beliefs, but familiar with the philosophy of Plato and the Stoics.

A few scholars have argued that the first nine chapters differ so greatly from the last ten in style and originality that the two parts must be by different authors. The first part, according to this view, was written in Hebrew by one person and later edited and translated into Greek by another, who added (in Greek) the relatively undistinguished second part.[21] The consensus, however, seems to be that one author wrote all (or nearly all) originally in Greek.

Literary Qualities. Most of the book is poetic in form,[22] consisting largely of parallel couplets such as are common in Proverbs and the Psalms. The first section (through Ch. 9) is lively, imaginative, and original; the remainder is generally dull, lacking in spontaneity, and sometimes bombastic.

Contents. Thematically the book may be divided into three parts.

PART I. REWARDS OF WISDOM (1:1–6:11). The theme of this part is that wickedness results in spiritual death, whereas wisdom and righteousness lead to immortality. Speaking to the Jews, "King Solomon" urges them to worship God and show reverence for his laws. He rebukes those apostates who have turned their backs on goodness and sought worldly pleasures. (Here the author seems to be deliberately trying to refute the hedonism of Ecclesiastes.) The wicked will suffer great anguish and remorse at the Day of Judgment. As for the righteous, their suffering is a cleansing which prepares them for immortality with God.

PART II. HYMN TO WISDOM (6:12–9:18). This section is made up of a hymn in praise of Wisdom (6:12–7:30), here personified, as in Proverbs 8, and a prayer for Wisdom (Chs. 8–9).

PART III. HISTORY OF THE HEBREWS (Chs. 10–22). This consists of a long review of Jewish history, which aims to demonstrate the superiority of Judaism to paganism. It makes a careful distinction between the two kinds of idolatry: worship of elements of nature, such as the sun and the moon which were created by God and reflect his glory, and worship of idols fashioned by the hand of man. Both kinds of idolatry lead to moral corruption, but the latter is far worse.

Doctrine and Influence. Before the Macedonian conquest in the fourth century B.C. brought Greek culture to Palestine, the

afterlife had received little emphasis in Hebrew theology. Sheol
was vaguely depicted as a shadowy place in which both good
and bad persons were "gathered to their fathers" after death,
lingering in a semi-conscious state. The author of The Wisdom
of Solomon introduces a Platonic "idea which is entirely new in
the Old Testament tradition: that man is by nature immortal."[23]

> For God created man to be immortal,
> And made him to be an image of his own eternity. (2:23)

For the first time in Hebrew thought we find a fully developed conception of a final judgment following death, of heaven
as a realm of bliss for the righteous, and of hell as a realm of
eternal torment for the wicked (3:1-5, 14, 18; 4:18-20; 5:15-16;
17:21). It seems likely that some of these ideas are derived from
the Greek conceptions of the afterlife in Elysium (the abode of
the good) and Tartarus (the infernal regions where sinners were
punished).

Two more views derived from Platonic thought (found chiefly
in the *Apology* and the *Phaedo*) appear in The Wisdom of
Solomon: (1) The soul is entrammeled by the body and is free
to attain truth only after death:

> For the corruptible body presseth down the soul,
> And the earthly tabernacle weigheth down the mind
> That museth upon many things.
> And hardly do we guess aright at things that are upon earth,
> And with labour do we find the things that are before us:
> But the things that are in heaven
> Who hath searched out? (9:15-16) °

(2) The soul has had a pre-existence in a world-soul:

> For the spirit of the Lord filleth the world:
> And that which containeth all things
> Hath knowledge of the voice. . . .
> A good soul fell to my lot;
> Or rather, being good, I entered an undefiled body. (1:7; 8:19-20)

Finally, there is the conception of wisdom (again personified
as in Proverbs and in Ecclesiasticus) as the divine principle of

---

° This idea, when further developed, led to the Gnostic "heresies" in the
first century A.D.—heresies attacked by Paul in the Epistle to the Colossians
and by the author of the First Epistle of John.

order and rationality which permeates and governs the whole universe:

> For she is the breath of the power of God,
> And a pure influence flowing from the glory of the Almighty. (7:25)

She is the

> all powerful word that leaped from heaven,
> From the royal throne into the midst of the land. (18:15)

This conception is closely akin to the idea of the Logos as held by the Stoics and the Alexandrian philosopher Philo Judaeus— an idea later to be altered by the author of the Gospel of John in an attempt to explain the Incarnation of Jesus Christ ("And the Word was made flesh, and dwelt among us . . ." [John 1:14]).

Part Eight
An Apocalyptic Literature

Apocalyptic writing has sometimes been considered a type of prophecy but it is actually a different literary genre. Derived from the Greek *apocalypsis,* which means "a revealing," an apocalypse is a revelation of "things to come," the preview of the end of an age and the establishment of a new one. Usually appearing in an era of great oppression and persecution, it has as its "single theme . . . the ultimate certainty of God's triumph over the forces of evil."[1] It is nearly always filled with graphic and terrifying accounts of disasters which will put an end to the persecution. R. C. Dentan recognizes three other characteristics of the genre[2]: (1) Most apocalypses are pseudonymous, being attributed to someone who lived in an era preceding that of the actual author, usually a famous and worthy man—Daniel, Enoch, Ezra, St. John, and so on. (2) All are written in cryptic or symbolic language. Because predictions of judgment in times of persecution are always dangerous for the author, a secret sort of writing is employed—symbols and words which will be understood by the persecuted but not by the oppressors. Hence we find strange beasts, angels, mystical numbers, vials, the falling of stars and large hailstones, the turning of the moon into blood, and such phrases as "the son of man," "the ancient of days," "locusts of torment," and so on. The use of this language and symbology explains why apocalyptic writing is so puzzling to many readers: it was *intended* to puzzle the uninitiated. (3) Many apocalpyses are composite: that is, made up of a number of writings fused together.

The Bible contains many examples of apocalyptic writing. In the Old Testament we find Isaiah 24–27, written during the Assyrian harassment in the seventh century B.C.; Ezekiel 37, written during the tribulations inflicted by the Babylonians in the sixth century B.C.; and Daniel 7–12, written during the persecutions of Antiochus Epiphanes in the middle of the second century B.C. Zechariah 9–14 and Joel 3 also contain apocalyptic elements. In the New Testament the book of Revelation is, of course, the most noteworthy apocalypse; other apocalyptic passages are Mark 13, Matthew 24, Luke 21, I Corinthians 15, Jude, II Peter, II Thessalonians 1–2, and scattered passages in some of the other epistles. The Second Book of Esdras is the only full-fledged apocalypse in the Apocrypha, but Baruch has a few apocalyptic passages.

II Esdras: Visions Attributed to Ezra

As noted previously (see p. 147). Esdras is the Greek form of Ezra. II Esdras is an apocalyptic work which tells of visions attributed to this post-Exilic priest (see p. 141).

COMPOSITION AND TRANSMISSION

The history of the composition of II Esdras is an exceedingly complicated story, covering a period of perhaps two centuries.[3] The core of the book consists of Chapters 3–14. The first verse of this section says that it was composed in Babylon "in the thirtieth year of the ruin of the city (Jerusalem)" (that is, about 556 B.C.) by one Salathiel.* Biblical scholars believe that this section was actually written in either Hebrew or Aramaic near the end of the first century A.D., possibly during the reign of Domitian.† Somewhat later it was translated into Greek. In the middle of the second century some unknown Christian author added (in Greek) Chapters 1–2. About a hundred years later, another unknown writer, also a Christian, composed Chapters 15–16, again in Greek. None of the Aramaic (or Hebrew) text is extant, and only a few verses of the Greek text have survived. Except for a sizable portion of Chapter 7, the book was preserved for the Western world in Old Latin versions, which St. Jerome used in preparing the Vulgate. In 1874 Robert L. Bensly discovered a ninth-century Latin text which included about

---

* The Hebrew form of the name is *Shealtiel*. A later editor (3:1b) added the clause "who am also Ezra."

† The New Testament book of Revelation also was composed during this period. However, II Esdras 3–14 is the product of Judaism and reflects the centuries-old longing for a Messiah, whereas Revelation is a distinctly *Christian* apocalypse and prophesies the Second Coming of Jesus Christ.

seventy lost verses, apparently belonging between verses 35 and 36 of Chapter 7 of the King James Version. In 1895 these were included for the first time in an English Bible (English Revised Version).

LITERARY QUALITIES

Like most other apocalyptic writings, II Esdras contains much elaborate and confusing symbolism, part of which may be lost to the modern reader. Nevertheless, the author is able to transmit effectively his own deep sorrow for his suffering people, his hatred for Rome, and his dogged faith in the God of Israel. Despite some trivial, wordy, and repetitious passages, "a real vein of poetry runs throughout the book."[4] In an attempt to answer the old, old question asked long before by Job, "Why do God's righteous people suffer?" the author's reply "is a lofty justification of the ways of God to man."[5]

CONTENTS

Most of II Esdras consists of a series of seven visions which came to Salathiel (Chs. 3–14), plus the two Christian additions noted above (Chs. 1–2 and 15–16).

Prologue: Warning to Israel (Chs. 1—2). The prologue establishes Ezra's (Esdras') credentials as a priest by opening with his genealogy, which traces his descent from Aaron, the brother of Moses. Ezra is depicted as a captive in the land of the Medes during the reign of Artaxerxes (the Second?), king of Persia. In a passage reminiscent of Old Testament prophecy, the Lord commands Ezra to denounce the Israelites for their sins and to warn them that God will scatter them among "the nations" and replace them in His favor with Gentile peoples. Ezra is shown a vision of risen "saints" (Christian martyrs?) being crowned on Mount Zion by a young man "of lofty stature"—"the Son of God" —whom they have acknowledged as their Lord on the earth. Ezra is instructed to tell the people about the wonders he has seen.

The First Vision: Original Sin and the Problem of Evil (3:1—5:20). Bewailing the miseries suffered by Jerusalem and the Israelites, Ezra asks God to explain why Adam's sin has been transmitted to his descendants and why, therefore, all men have an inborn tendency toward evil. ("This is the first known ap-

pearance of the doctrine of original sin in Jewish literature."[6])
In a passage similar to God's reply to Job from the Whirlwind (Job 38—41), the angel Uriel points out that Ezra cannot understand even the simple things in his own life—the
weight of fire, the measuring of the wind, where past days go.
How, then, can he expect to understand the ways of God? In
the great age to come, Uriel says, Ezra will be given the answers,
and he elaborates upon a series of portents that will precede
the end of this present age.

The Second Vision: The Future of the Living and the Dead
(5:21—6:34). After another complaint about the lot of the
Hebrews, Ezra asks what will happen to those who die before
the New Age comes. Uriel assures him that both the living and
the dead will be treated alike. He lists more omens of the new
era.

The Third Vision: The Messiah and the Final Judgment
(6:35—9:25). Once again Ezra asks God to explain about the
saved and the damned. Uriel reappears and foretells that the Messiah will come and reign four hundred years (compare the
millennium foretold in Revelation 20:1-6); then he (the Messiah) and all human beings will die. Next will come the resurrection of all men and the final judgment. Uriel gives a lengthy
account of the joys of the few who will be saved and of the
torments of the many who will be damned. When Ezra objects
to God's cruelty in causing so many to suffer, Uriel (rather
unsatisfactorily) replies bluntly that that is the way God wills it.
The vision closes with Uriel's disclosure of more signs of the
approach of the Judgment Day.

The Fourth Vision: The Mourning Woman (9:26—10:59).
Ezra is shown a vision of a woman mourning for the death of
her only son. While Ezra is pointing out to her that she should
be weeping for all Zion instead of merely her son, she vanishes,
and a beautiful city appears. Uriel explains that the woman *was*
Zion and the son was Jerusalem, now in ruins. The splendid new
city was the New Jerusalem which will replace the old.

The Fifth Vision: The Eagle from the Sea (Chs. 11—12).
An elaborate and entirely different sort of vision is shown to
Ezra: an eagle with three heads, twelve large wings, and eight
small wings rises from the sea. A lion appears from the forest
and accuses the eagle of cruelty and oppression. One by one,

eighteen of the wings disappear; one of the heads eats the last two wings and the other two heads. At last the body of the eagle is burned. Upon awakening, Ezra is told by "a voice" that the eagle represents the fourth kingdom foreseen by Daniel (Dan. 7:7—8:23); the heads and wings were the various Roman emperors, and the lion was God's promised Messiah. The voice tells Ezra to write in a book what he has seen.

The Sixth Vision: The Militant Messiah (Ch. 13). Ezra sees a vision of a Man rising from the sea; everything the Man looks upon trembles, and all who hear his voice melt as wax before a fire. A great multitude gathers to war upon the Man, but without the use of any weapon he destroys his enemies by breathing fire upon them. Thereupon a joyful and peaceable multitude assemble about him. The Voice of the Most High explains that the Man represents the Messiah; the enemy multitude, the Gentiles; and the joyful multitude, the Ten Lost Tribes of Israel.

The Seventh Vision: The Voice from the Bush (Ch. 14). God speaks to Ezra from a bush (compare Ex. 3:2) and tells him that the end of the old age is near. He instructs Ezra to rewrite the books of the Old Testament, which have been destroyed by the Babylonians. Ezra enlists the services of five scribes, to whom he dictates continuously for forty days. The result is not only the twenty-four books of the Hebrew canon but also seventy additional works—presumably apocalyptic and instructional books such as II Esdras. (At this point some Oriental versions of II Esdras tell of Ezra's being carried up into heaven.)

Epilogue: Punishment of the Wicked (Chs. 15—16). In a rather long and tedious passage, Ezra is once more assured that the wicked nation (Rome) will soon be destroyed and Babylon, Asia, Egypt, and Syria subjected to devastation. Iniquity will disappear from the earth. The righteous have nothing to fear, but the wicked will be as a grainfield covered by thorns, abandoned to a consuming fire.

Notes

NOTES TO CHAPTER 1: PALESTINE AND ITS PEOPLE

[1] See W. F. Albright in *The Old Testament and Modern Study,* ed. H. H. Rowley (London: Oxford University Press, 1951), pp. 6 ff.

[2] George Sprau, *Literature in the Bible* (New York: Macmillan Co., 1932), p. 41, doubts that all the tribes left Palestine and suggests that the whole account of the Egyptian residence may have been merely a symbolic representation of Egyptian supremacy over Palestine. Edgar J. Goodspeed, *How to Read the Bible* (Philadelphia: John C. Winston Co., 1946), p. 212, seems to accept the Biblical account literally when he says: "The Hebrews, enslaved and overworked in Egypt by Rameses II, in the thirteenth century before Christ, escaped from the country toward 1200 B.C." A number of scholars interpret pre-Mosaic accounts as symbology or as tribal rather than personal history. See Theodore H. Robinson, "The History of Israel," *The Interpreter's Bible* (Nashville, Tenn.: Abingdon Press, 1952), I, 273.

[3] For the date and identity of Moses' Pharaoh, see W. F. Albright, *op. cit.*, pp. 9-11; see also Chapter 3, note 13.

[4] William F. Albright, "The Old Testament World," *The Interpreter's Bible*, I, 235-236.

[5] For a detailed discussion of Hebrew faith and conception of God, see James Muilenburg, "The History of the Religion of Israel," *The Interpreter's Bible*, I, 292-389.

NOTES TO CHAPTER 2:
THE NATURE, ORIGINS, AND CONTENTS OF THE BIBLE

[1] I am indebted for this point to J. H. Gardiner, *The Bible as English Literature* (New York: Charles Scribner's Sons, 1927), p. 1. Pages 1-12 of this book argue eloquently for the unity of the Bible.

[2] Stanley Rypins, *The Book of Thirty Centuries* (New York: Macmillan Co., 1951), p. 22.

[3] Rypins, *op. cit.*, p. 310.

[4] Allen P. Wikgren, "The English Bible," *The Interpreter's Bible* (Nashville, Tenn.: Abingdon Press, 1952), I, 91. See also F. F. Bruce, *The English Bible* (New York: Oxford University Press, 1961), pp. 86-92.

[5] Wikgren, *The Interpreter's Bible*, I, 91.

[6] Wikgren, *The Interpreter's Bible*, I, 93.

[7] For the best discussion of what the King James Version owes to each of its English predecessors, see Charles C. Butterworth, *The Literary Lineage of the King James Bible, 1340-1611* (Philadelphia: University of Pennsylvania Press, 1941), p. 111.

[8] Wikgren, *The Interpreter's Bible*, I, 94-95.

[9] *The Holy Bible*, ed. John P. O'Connell (Chicago: The Catholic Press, 1950), p. x. For a list of revisions of Catholic Bibles, see Wikgren, *The Interpreter's Bible*, I, 100.

[10] Ira Maurice Price, *The Ancestry of Our English Bible*, ed. William A. Irwin and Allen P. Wikgren (3rd rev. ed.; New York: Harper & Brothers, 1956), p. 297.

[11] Price, *op cit.*, p. 297.

[12] See Wikgren, *The Interpreter's Bible*, I, 99, for a brief summary. For a far longer account, see Max L. Margolis, *The Story of Bible Translations* (Philadelphia: Jewish Publication Society, 1917).

[13] See *The Holy Scriptures* (Philadelphia: Jewish Publication Society, 1917), preface, pp. vi-vii.

[14] Quoted by Price, *op. cit.*, p. 310.

NOTES TO CHAPTER 3:
THE FOUNDING OF THE HEBREW NATION

[1] See Cuthbert A. Simpson, "The Growth of the Hexateuch," *The Interpreter's Bible* (Nashville, Tenn.: Abingdon Press, 1952), I, 185, for a discussion of the traditional authorship of the Pentateuch.

[2] For an exciting account of the growth of the Hexateuch, see Simpson, *The Interpreter's Bible*, I, 185-200. This Outline is indebted to Simpson's account for much material on this topic.

[3] For the date of the J Document and its two editions (J[1] and J[2]), see Simpson, *The Interpreter's Bible*, I, 192-196; and Harold H. Watts, *The Modern Reader's Guide to the Bible* (rev. ed.; New York: Harper & Brothers, 1959), p. 55.

[4] See Simpson, *The Interpreter's Bible*, I, 194, 200.

[5] William Owen Sypherd, *The Literature of the English Bible* (New York: Oxford University Press, 1938), p. 54. For a more nearly complete list of J passages, see Julius A. Bewer, *The Literature of the Old Testament* (rev. by Emil G. Kraeling; New York: Columbia University Press, 1962), footnotes to pp. 69-71.

[6] For the date of the E Document, see Simpson, *The Interpreter's Bible*, I, 197, 200; and Watts, *op. cit.*, p. 55. Bewer, *op. cit.*, p. 85, and Alice Parmelee, *A Guidebook to the Bible* (New York: Harper & Brothers, 1948), p. 33, suggest 750 B.C. as a more likely date.

⁷ Sypherd, *op. cit.*, p. 54. For a more nearly complete list, see Bewer, *op. cit.*, pp. 79-88, *passim* and especially footnotes to pp. 82, 83, and 84.

⁸ For a discussion of the virtual identity of Josiah's book of law and our Deuteronomy, see Simpson, *The Interpreter's Bible*, I, 197-198.

⁹ For a list of passages from the P Document, see Bewer, *op. cit.*, footnotes to pp. 260-264.

¹⁰ Edgar J. Goodspeed and J. M. Powis Smith (eds.), *The Short Bible* (Chicago: University of Chicago Press, 1933), p. 148.

¹¹ Theodore, H. Robinson, "The History of Israel," *The Interpreter's Bible*, I, 273. For a slightly different chronology of early Biblical events, see Watts, *op. cit.*, p. 70; and George A. Barrois, "Chronology, Metrology, etc.," *The Interpreter's Bible*, I, 142-152.

¹² Circumcision was also widely practiced by other Semites and by the Egyptians. See Cuthbert A. Simpson, Exegesis to Genesis, *The Interpreter's Bible*, I, 613-614.

¹³ For the identity of the oppressor and for that of the Pharaoh of the Exodus, see Robinson, *The Interpreter's Bible*, I, 274; see also the discussion and bibliography given by J. Coert Rylaarsdam, Introduction to Exodus, *The Interpreter's Bible*, I, 836. Rameses II (*c.* 1290-1224 B.C.) is usually recognized as the oppressor; Seti I (1319-1301) and Tutmose III (*c.* 1450) have also been suggested.

¹⁴ An interesting analogue is the birth story of Sargon of Agade. See J. Coert Rylaarsdam, Exegesis to Exodus, *The Interpreter's Bible*, I, 859. For a list of other "mysterious birth" stories, see Sypherd, *op. cit.*, p. 58. One should also note the parallel of the saving of the baby Jesus after the decree of Herod (Matt. 2).

¹⁵ The Egyptian form of the name seems to have been *Mes.* The Hebrew was *Môsheh*, from *māsāh*, meaning "to draw out." Perhaps this refers to Moses' drawing his people out of Egypt, or maybe to Pharaoh's daughter drawing Moses out of the water. See Rylaarsdam, Exegesis, *The Interpreter's Bible*, I, 861.

¹⁶ Mary Ellen Chase, *The Bible and the Common Reader* (rev. ed.; New York: Macmillan Co., 1952), p. 98.

¹⁷ For other explanations of the rite of Unleavened Bread, see Rylaarsdam, Exegesis, *The Interpreter's Bible*, I, 922.

¹⁸ Scholars believe that perhaps only the portions of the lyric in 15:1 should be attributed to Moses. (This is a quotation from the Song of Miriam, Ex. 15:20-22.) The following seventeen verses were probably added many centuries later.

¹⁹ Apparently *Sinai* and *Horeb* are two names for the same mountain. Documents J and P use *Sinai*; E and D use *Horeb*. Some scholars think that there are two mountains referred to. For discussions of this

question and of the identity of the mountain, see Rylaarsdam, Introduction, *The Interpreter's Bible*, I, 836-837.

[20] Ernest Wright, Exegesis to Deuteronomy, *The Interpreter's Bible* (Nashville, Tenn.: Abingdon Press, 1953), II, 454.

[21] Rylaarsdam, Exegesis, *The Interpreter's Bible*, I, 1042.

[22] Rylaarsdam, Introduction, *The Interpreter's Bible*, I, 842-843.

[23] *New Analytical Indexed Bible* (Chicago: John A. Dickson Co., 1931), p. 120.

[24] The Ark was probably originally a mere box. Later on in Hebrew history the Ark was of immense significance as the abode of God himself. It was sometimes carried into battle and even captured by the enemy (see I Sam. 4:11). Such a palladium was often carried about by nomadic tribes. See Rylaarsdam, *The Interpreter's Bible*, I, Introduction and Exegesis, 844-845 and 1022.

[25] The Tabernacle as described in Exodus would be far from a portable structure, but the description is anachronistic, being an idealized conception of the Tabernacle based on later writers' knowledge of the Temple in Jerusalem. See Rylaarsdam, Introduction, *The Interpreter's Bible*, I, 845.

[26] Roy B. Chamberlin and Herman Feldman (eds.), *The Dartmouth Bible* (2nd ed.; Boston: Houghton Mifflin Co., 1961), p. 146. See Numbers 1:50-54 for the functions of the Levites.

[27] George Sprau, *Literature in the Bible* (New York: Macmillan Co., 1932), p. 85.

[28] Nathaniel Micklem, Introduction to Leviticus, *The Interpreter's Bible*, II, 3.

[29] Chamberlin and Feldman, *op. cit.*, p. 118.

[30] John Marsh, Exegesis to Numbers, *The Interpreter's Bible*, II, 170.

[31] Charles Allen Dinsmore, *The English Bible as Literature* (Boston: Houghton Mifflin Co., 1931), p. 156.

[32] Divisions suggested by Ray Freeman Jenney, *Bible Primer* (New York: Harper & Brothers, 1955), pp. 35-36.

[33] Ernest S. Bates (ed.), *The Bible Designed to Be Read as Living Literature* (New York: Simon and Schuster, 1936), p. 120.

[34] Dinsmore, *op. cit.*, p. 157.

[35] Jenney, *op. cit.*, p. 39.

[36] Drawn chiefly from Chamberlin and Feldman, *op. cit.*, pp. 115, 118-119, and 150. See also *Webster's New International Dictionary*, (2nd ed.; Springfield, Mass.: G. & C. Merriam Co., 1934), "Law," p. 1401.

[37] Jenney, *op. cit.*, p. 39.

[38] Sprau, *op. cit.*, p. 90.

[39] John Bright, Introduction to Joshua, *The Interpreter's Bible*, II, 548.

[40] Chase, *op. cit.*, pp. 100-101.

NOTES TO CHAPTER 4: RISE AND FALL OF THE MONARCHY

[1] See Jacob M. Myers, Introduction to Judges, *The Interpreter's Bible* (Nashville, Tenn.: Abingdon Press, 1953), II, 677-682.

[2] See, for example, 2:11, 14 and 3:15.

[3] Mary Ellen Chase, *The Bible and the Common Reader* (rev. ed.; New York: Macmillan Co., 1952), pp. 103-105.

[4] *Ibid.*

[5] Jacob M. Myers, Exegesis to Judges, *The Interpreter's Bible*, II, 730.

[6] This element and the two following ones are all suggested by Wilbur Owen Sypherd, *The Literature of the English Bible* (New York: Oxford University Press, 1938), p. 61.

[7] S. R. Driver, *An Introduction to The Literature of the Old Testament* (rev. ed.; New York: Charles Scribner's Sons, 1920), p. 168.

[8] Richard G. Moulton (ed.), *The Modern Reader's Bible* (New York: Macmillan Co., 1952), p. 1347.

[9] For a detailed discussion, see George B. Caird, Introduction and Exegesis to I and II Samuel, *The Interpreter's Bible*, II, 855-865. Most of the information in this Outline concerning the date and authorship of I and II Samuel is derived from Caird.

[10] Alice Parmelee, *A Guidebook to the Bible* (New York: Harper & Brothers, 1948), p. 26.

[11] For a list of the principal later additions, see Caird, Introduction, *The Interpreter's Bible*, II, 862-865.

[12] George Sprau, *Literature in the Bible* (New York: Macmillan Co., 1932), pp. 124-125.

[13] Title suggested by Ray Freeman Jenney, *Bible Primer* (New York: Harper & Brothers, 1955), p. 47.

[14] Title borrowed from Chase, *op. cit.*, p. 121.

[15] Chase, *op. cit.*, p. 122.

[16] See Caird, Introduction, *The Interpreter's Bible*, II, 863-864.

[17] Chase, *op. cit.*, pp. 133-134.

[18] See Caird, Exegesis, *The Interpreter's Bible*, II, 1059.

[19] Caird, Exegesis, *The Interpreter's Bible*, II, 1124-1125.

[20] There is some doubt whether there had ever been a promise. David seems to be confused and is convinced by Bathsheba and Nathan that he should favor Solomon's claims. See Norman H. Snaith, Introduction and Exegesis to I and II Kings, *The Interpreter's Bible* (Nashville, Tenn.: Abingdon Press, 1954), III, 23-24.

[21] See Snaith, Exegesis, *The Interpreter's Bible*, III, 34.

[22] Most of the material for this section and that on the purpose and the method of the authors is based upon Snaith, Introduction, *The Interpreter's Bible*, III, 3-18.

[23] Sprau, *op. cit.*, p. 128.

[24] Snaith, Introduction, *The Interpreter's Bible*, III, 9-10. This procedure had to be abandoned, of course, after 722 B.C., when there were no longer any kings of Israel.

[25] Ernest Sutherland Bates (ed.), *The Bible Designed to Be Read as Living Literature* (New York: Simon and Schuster, 1936), p. 296.

[26] A contrary view of Solomon's wisdom is held by modern historians. Theodore H. Robinson says: "A wise man might have preserved and strengthened the new Israelite state, but Solomon was quite unfit for the task. Vain, ostentatious, shortsighted, selfish, and cowardly, he was unscrupulous in the attainment of his ends." ("The History of Israel," *The Interpreter's Bible* (Nashville, Tenn.: Abingdon Press, 1952), I, 282.

[27] The dates given in the parentheses refer to the years of the reign of each sovereign. These dates do not correspond exactly to those given by the Biblical historian but follow the chronology given by Harold H. Watts, in *The Modern Reader's Guide to the Bible* (rev. ed.; New York: Harper & Brothers, 1959), pp. 128-130. Robinson ("The History of Israel," *The Interpreter's Bible*, I, 282) gives the date of the death of Solomon and the accession of Rehoboam as 936 B.C.

[28] Frederick Carl Eiselen, Edwin Lewis, and David G. Downey (eds.), *The Abingdon Bible Commentary* (Nashville, Tenn.: Abingdon Press, 1929), p. 424.

[29] For a different conception of Jeroboam—as a good king who did what he thought was best for his people—see Eiselen, Lewis, and Downey, *op. cit.*, p. 424.

[30] The purpose in beautifying herself was probably to prepare her body for the next life. See Snaith, Exegesis, *The Interpreter's Bible*, III, 236.

[31] Snaith, Exegesis, *The Interpreter's Bible*, III, 194.

[32] Chase, *op. cit.*, p. 136.

[33] See *ibid.*

[34] Chase, *op. cit.*, p. 139.

[35] Snaith, Exegesis, *The Interpreter's Bible*, III, 212.

[36] For a thorough discussion of the origin of Deuteronomic reform, see G. Ernest Wright, Introduction to Deuteronomy, *The Interpreter's Bible*, II, 323-326.

NOTES TO CHAPTER 5:
ESTABLISHMENT OF A CHURCH STATE AFTER THE EXILE

[1] Theodore H. Robinson, "The History of Israel," *The Interpreter's Bible* (Nashville, Tenn.: Abingdon Press, 1952), I, 287. The summary of the history of Palestine and the Hebrews included here is drawn chiefly from Robinson.

[2] George Sprau, *Literature in the Bible* (New York: Macmillan Co., 1932), pp. 124-125.

[3] For a detailed discussion of this vexing problem, see W. A. L. Elmslie, Introduction to I and II Chronicles, *The Interpreter's Bible* (Nashville, Tenn.: Abingdon Press, 1954), III, 345-347. Elmslie argues for an early date, *c.* 400-350. See also John Robinson Macarthur, *Biblical Literature and Its Backgrounds* (New York: Appleton-Century-Crofts, 1936), p. 175.

[4] It is believed that the Chronicler did not write these genealogies but began his narrative at 10:1. See Elmslie, Exegesis, *The Interpreter's Bible*, III, 349.

[5] Elmslie, Exegesis, *The Interpreter's Bible*, III, 349.

[6] For a full discussion of the sources, see Raymond A. Bowman, Introduction to Ezra and Nehemiah, *The Interpreter's Bible*, III, 554-560.

[7] Bowman, Introduction, *The Interpreter's Bible*, III, 555. Bowman places Neh. 7:1-73a in the Nehemiah narrative.

[8] For these and many more cogent arguments against the priority of Ezra, see Bowman, Introduction, *The Interpreter's Bible*, III, 562-563; and Roy B. Chamberlin and Herman Feldman (eds.), *The Dartmouth Bible* (rev. ed.; Boston: Houghton Mifflin Co., 1961), p. 346. If Ezra preceded Nehemiah, then the order of the material, according to Professor Macarthur (*op. cit.*, pp. 185-186), should be as follows: Ezra 1:1-11; I Esdras 4:47b-56; I Esdras 4:62—5:6b; Ezra 2:1—8:36; Neh. 7:73b—8:18; Ezra 9:1—10:44; Neh. 9:1—10:39; Neh. 7:5—73a; Neh. 1:1—7:4; and Neh. 11:1—13:30.

[9] Approximately this arrangement is suggested by Bowman (Introduction, *The Interpreter's Bible*, III, 560).

[10] The Chronicler makes Sheshbazzar (Ezra 1:8) and Zerubbabel (Ezra 2:2) the same person. For a discussion of the matter, see Bowman, Exegesis, *The Interpreter's Bible*, III, 574-576.

[11] Chamberlin and Feldman, *op. cit.*, p. 837.

[12] *Ibid.*

NOTES TO CHAPTER 6: THE MACCABEAN REVOLT

[1] The facts in this table are drawn from Robert H. Pfeiffer, "The Literature and Religion of the Apocrypha," *The Interpreter's Bible*

(Nashville, Tenn.: Abingdon Press, 1952), I, 415-419. The dates given in Pfeiffer's article differ slightly from those given by Theodore H. Robinson, "The History of Israel," *The Interpreter's Bible*, I, 288-291.

² Roy B. Chamberlin and Herman Feldman (eds.), *The Dartmouth Bible* (rev. ed.; Boston: Houghton Mifflin Co., 1961), p. 735.

³ *Ibid.*

⁴ Chamberlin and Feldman, *op. cit.*, p. 734.

⁵ Chamberlin and Feldman, *op. cit.*, pp. 765-766; and Harold H. Watts, *The Modern Reader's Guide to the Bible* (rev. ed.; New York: Harper & Brothers, 1959), p. 316.

⁶ See Chamberlin and Feldman, *op. cit.*, pp. 734-735, 739, and 766; Wilbur Owen Sypherd, *The Literature of the English Bible* (New York: Oxford University Press, 1938), pp. 149-150; and Bruce M. Metzger, *An Introduction to the Apocrypha* (New York: Oxford University Press, 1957), p. 131.

⁷ Sypherd, *op. cit.*, p. 150; Chamberlin and Feldman, *op. cit.*, p. 739; and John Robertson Macarthur, *Biblical Literature and Its Backgrounds* (New York: Appleton-Century-Crofts, 1936), p. 358.

⁸ Chamberlin and Feldman, *op. cit.*, p. 739.

⁹ *Ibid.*

¹⁰ Chamberlin and Feldman, *op. cit.*, p. 767.

¹¹ Macarthur (*op. cit.*, p. 359) suggests 125-75 B.C.; Sypherd (*op. cit.*, p. 150) places it "near the close of the first century B.C."; and Chamberlin and Feldman (*op. cit.*, p. 769) say that some authorities date the book *c.* 40 B.C.

¹² John C. Thirlwall and Arthur Waldhorn (eds.), *A Bible for the Humanities* (New York: Harper & Brothers, 1954), p. 310.

NOTES TO PART THREE INTRODUCTION
AND TO CHAPTER 7: EIGHTH-CENTURY PROPHETS

¹ Roy B. Chamberlin and Herman Feldman (eds.), *The Dartmouth Bible* (2nd ed., Boston: Houghton Mifflin Co., 1961), p. 531. My introduction to the prophets is greatly indebted to this work and to Hughell E. W. Fosbroke, "The Prophetic Literature," *The Interpreter's Bible* (Nashville, Tenn.: Abingdon Press, 1952), I, 201-211.

² Chamberlin and Feldman, *op. cit.*, p. 531.

³ See Fosbroke, "The Prophetic Literature," *The Interpreter's Bible*, I, 204-206.

⁴ Fosbroke, *op. cit.*, p. 206.

⁵ Chamberlin and Feldman, *op. cit.*, p. 532.

⁶ Suggested by John Robertson Macarthur, *Biblical Literature and Its Backgrounds* (New York: Appleton-Century-Crofts, 1936), p. 288.

See also Wilbur Owen Sypherd, *The Literature of the English Bible* (New York: Oxford University Press, 1938), pp. 72-73.

[7] See Hughell E. W. Fosbroke, Exegesis to Amos, *The Interpreter's Bible* (Nashville, Tenn.: Abingdon Press, 1956), VI, 829.

[8] H. Wheeler Robinson, Commentary on Amos, *The Abingdon Bible Commentary* (Nashville, Tenn.: Abingdon Press, 1929), p. 782.

[9] R. B. Y. Scott, Introduction to Isaiah, *The Interpreter's Bible* (Nashville, Tenn.: Abingdon Press, 1956), V, 161.

[10] Macarthur, *op. cit.*, p. 240.

[11] Chamberlin and Feldman, *op. cit.*, p. 534.

[12] Macarthur, *op. cit.*, p. 241.

[13] For some of these points and for other comments on Isaiah's style, see Sypherd, *op. cit.*, pp. 75-76; Macarthur, *op. cit.*, p. 241; and S. R. Driver, *An Introduction to the Literature of the Old Testament* (rev. ed.; New York: Charles Scribner's Sons, 1920), pp. 227-229.

[14] These words also appear in Micah 4:1-5; scholars disagree as to which book of prophecy borrows from the other. See Chamberlin and Feldman, *op. cit.*, p. 578.

[15] For these and many others, see Macarthur, *op. cit.*, pp. 242-244.

[16] R. B. Y. Scott, Exegesis to Isaiah, *The Interpreter's Bible*, V, 251.

[17] Sypherd, *op. cit.*, p. 74, and Scott, Introduction, *The Interpreter's Bible*, V, 155-156.

[18] Seraphim probably symbolized lightning. See Scott, Exegesis, *The Interpreter's Bible*, V, 208.

[19] This interpretation of the familiar passage (1:18) is derived from Scott, Exegesis, *The Interpreter's Bible*, V, 174-175.

[20] Scott, Exegesis, *The Interpreter's Bible*, V, 240.

[21] Others have suggested that the passages (especially 9:1-7) were written about the coronation of another king—Ahaz, Jehoash, or possibly some post-Exilic monarch in whom the author hoped that the Davidic line would be restored. See Scott, Exegesis, *The Interpreter's Bible*, V, 231-232.

[22] Title from Chamberlin and Feldman, *op. cit.*, p. 581.

[23] For a more thorough discussion of Micah's dates and public activities, see Rolland E. Wolfe, Introduction to Micah, *The Interpreter's Bible* (Nashville, Tenn.: Abingdon Press, 1956), VI, 897-898.

[24] Wolfe, Introduction, *The Interpreter's Bible*, VI, 899-900. The most important post-Exilic passages (2:12-13, 4—5, and 7:5-20) are believed to be the work of several anonymous authors; one portion (Chs. 4—5) appears to be "almost a review of Isa. 40—44" (Rolland E. Wolfe, Exegesis to Micah, *The Interpreter's Bible*, VI, 921). These interpolations purport to foretell the return from the Babylonian Captivity and the rebuilding of Jerusalem and the Temple; God him-

self will be the people's king and judge, and he will inaugurate an era of peace, justice, and righteousness. See Isa. 2:4 and note 16 above.

25 Chamberlin and Feldman, *op. cit.*, p. 581.

26 Wolfe, Exegesis, *The Interpreter's Bible*, VI, 936.

NOTES TO CHAPTER 8: JUDAH'S PRE-EXILIC PROPHETS OF THE SEVENTH AND SIXTH CENTURIES

1 Although there has been some dispute about Zephaniah's lineage, most commentators seem to agree that the Hezekiah mentioned in Zeph. 1:1 is the king of Judah who ruled during Isaiah's time. See Charles L. Taylor, Jr., Introduction to Zephaniah, *The Interpreter's Bible* (Nashville, Tenn.: Abingdon Press, 1956), VI, 1009; and Roy B. Chamberlin and Herman Feldman (eds.), *The Dartmouth Bible* (2nd. ed.: Boston: Houghton Mifflin Co., 1961), p. 633.

2 See Taylor, Introduction, *The Interpreter's Bible*, VI, 1008-1009.

3 John Robertson Macarthur, *Biblical Literature and Its Backgrounds* (New York: Appleton-Century-Crofts, 1936), p. 308.

4 Charles L. Taylor, Jr., Exegesis to Zephaniah, *The Interpreter's Bible*, VI, 1018.

5 For a long discussion of the complicated problem of authorship, date, and growth of the book, see Charles L. Taylor, Jr., Introduction to Habakkuk, *The Interpreter's Bible*, VI, 973-977, from which pages this Outline has drawn most of its information.

6 James Philip Hyatt, Introduction to Jeremiah, *The Interpreter's Bible* (Nashville, Tenn.: Abingdon Press, 1956), V, 778.

7 The traditional dating is based upon the statement in 1:2 that the "word of the Lord came to" Jeremiah in the thirteenth year of the reign of Josiah (that is, 627-626 B.C.), plus the assumption that the prophet must have been about twenty-three or twenty-four years old when he began his ministry. The scholars who argue for the later date believe that the verse quoted above refers to Jeremiah's birth itself—a belief strengthened by the fact that 1:5 asserts that God chose him to be a prophet even before he was born. See Hyatt, Introduction and Exegesis to Jeremiah, *The Interpreter's Bible*, V, 779 and 796-798. Most of the information in this Outline concerning Jeremiah's life has been derived from Hyatt (*The Interpreter's Bible*, V, 778-782).

8 Chamberlin and Feldman, *op. cit.*, p. 589.

9 Hyatt, Introduction, *The Interpreter's Bible*, V, 787. Most of the material concerning the composition of the book is derived from Hyatt (*The Interpreter's Bible*, V, 787-791; see these pages for verse-and-chapter references to the authors of various portions of Jeremiah).

¹⁰ For both points of view, see Hyatt, Introduction, *The Interpreter's Bible*, V, 779.

¹¹ Hyatt, Exegesis, *The Interpreter's Bible*, V, 921-922. This exegete lists other possible interpretations.

¹² Hyatt, Exegesis, *The Interpreter's Bible*, V, 1018.

¹³ What portion of these three chapters was written by Jeremiah is a matter of dispute. Many scholars believe that a large percentage was added by later editors. See Hyatt, Exegesis, *The Interpreter's Bible*, V, 1022-1042 and 1049-1053, *passim*.

¹⁴ Hyatt, Exegesis, *The Interpreter's Bible*, V, 1037.

¹⁵ *Ibid.*

¹⁶ *Ibid.*

NOTES TO CHAPTER 9: THE EXILIC PROPHETS

¹ For a detailed summary of these various biographical arguments, see Herbert G. May, Introduction to Ezekiel, *The Interpreter's Bible* (Nashville, Tenn.: Abingdon Press, 1956), VI, 51-53.

² Wilbur Owen Sypherd, *The Literature of the English Bible* (New York: Oxford University Press, 1938), p. 81. For a more detailed discussion of the theories of authorship, see May, Introduction, *The Interpreter's Bible*, VI, 41-51 and 53-62.

³ John Robertson Macarthur, *Biblical Literature and Its Backgrounds* (New York: Appleton-Century-Crofts, 1936), p. 268.

⁴ Macarthur, *op. cit.*, p. 269.

⁵ May, Introduction, *The Interpreter's Bible*, VI, 50-51; and Sypherd, *op. cit.*, p. 81.

⁶ Sypherd, *op. cit.*, pp. 80-81; and May, Introduction, *The Interpreter's Bible*, VI, 64-66.

⁷ W. ʼL. Wardle, Commentary on Ezekiel, *The Abingdon Bible Commentary* (Nashville, Tenn.: Abingdon Press, 1929), p. 725.

⁸ See Herbert G. May, Exegesis to Ezekiel, *The Interpreter's Bible*, VI, 259 and 263; and Wardle, *op. cit.*, p. 740.

⁹ Wardle, *op. cit.*, p. 740.

¹⁰ May, Exegesis, *The Interpreter's Bible*, VI, 273.

¹¹ For a full discussion of this relationship, see May, Introduction, *The Interpreter's Bible*, VI, 53-56.

¹² Sypherd, *op. cit.*, p. 83.

¹³ Julius A. Bewer (ed.), *The Prophets* (New York: Harper & Brothers, 1955), p. 117.

¹⁴ Bewer, *op. cit.*, p. 100. For much of the material in this paragraph I am indebted to Professor Bewer's introduction and his notes to Second Isaiah, *op. cit.*, pp. 99-139.

¹⁵ Bewer, *op. cit.*, p. 100.

[16] See Bewer, *op. cit.*, p. 101; and Roy B. Chamberlin and Herman Feldman (eds.), *The Dartmouth Bible* (2nd ed.; Boston: Houghton Mifflin Co., 1961), p. 690.

NOTES TO CHAPTER 10: THE POST-EXILIC PROPHETS

[1] Julius A. Bewer (ed.), *The Prophets* (New York: Harper & Brothers, 1955), p. 567. I am indebted to Bewer, pp. 567-568, for several points in my introduction to Haggai.

[2] D. Winton Thomas, Introduction to Haggai, *The Interpreter's Bible* (Nashville, Tenn.: Abingdon Press, 1956), VI, 1039.

[3] Bewer, *op. cit.*, p. 571, and Thomas, Introduction, *The Interpreter's Bible*, VI, 1039.

[4] See Nehemiah 12:16, and D. Winton Thomas, Introduction to Zechariah 1–8, *The Interpreter's Bible*, VI, 1053.

[5] Bewer, *op. cit.*, p. 573.

[6] John Robertson Macarthur, *Biblical Literature and Its Backgrounds* (New York: Appleton-Century-Crofts, 1936), pp. 314-315.

[7] Irving Francis Wood and Elihu Grant, *The Bible as Literature* (Nashville, Tenn.: Abingdon Press, 1914), p. 88.

[8] D. Winton Thomas, Exegesis to Zechariah 1–8, *The Interpreter's Bible*, VI, 1064.

[9] J. E. McFadyen, Commentary on Zechariah, *The Abingdon Bible Commentary* (Nashville, Tenn.: Abingdon Press, 1929), p. 823.

[10] See McFadyen, *The Abingdon Bible Commentary*, p. 823; and Thomas, Exegesis, *The Interpreter's Bible*, VI, 1078.

[11] Bewer, *op. cit.*, p. 141. The assigning of the specific chapters and verses to each author and the labels, in quotation marks, for the four writers (used in this Outline as headings for the subdivisions of Third Isaiah) are derived from Bewer, pp. 141-142. I am indebted to Professor Bewer for much of my discussion of Third Isaiah.

[12] Bewer, *op. cit.*, p. 145.

[13] Bewer, *op. cit.*, p. 585.

[14] Bewer, *op. cit.*, p. 585. See also II Kings 16:6.

[15] Bewer, *op. cit.*, p. 585.

[16] Bewer, *op. cit.*, p. 586.

[17] I am indebted for my organization of this discussion to Robert C. Dentan, Introduction to Malachi, *The Interpreter's Bible*, VI, 1118-1120.

[18] Bewer, *op. cit.*, p. 599.

[19] For several suggested interpretations of the plague of locusts, see John A. Thompson, Introduction to Joel, *The Interpreter's Bible*, VI, 733-734.

[20] For a detailed discussion, see Robert C. Dentan, Introduction to Zechariah 9–14, *The Interpreter's Bible*, VI, 1089-1091; and J. E.

McFadyen, Commentary on Zechariah, *The Abingdon Bible Commentary*, pp. 825-826.

21 Bewer, *op. cit.*, pp. 619-620.

22 For explanations of the passage and for attempts to identify the shepherd, see Dentan, Exegesis to Zechariah 9—14, *The Interpreter's Bible*, 1103-1105.

23 The New Testament references to the four passages from Zechariah are cited by Bewer, *op. cit.*, p. 620.

24 For discussions of the dates and languages of the book, see Bruce M. Metzger, *An Introduction to the Apocrypha* (New York: Oxford University Press, 1957), pp. 90, 96; Charles C. Torrey, *The Apocryphal Literature* (New Haven: Yale University Press, 1945), pp. 62, 65-66; and Edgar J. Goodspeed (ed.), *The Apocrypha* (New York: Random House, 1959), p. 329.

25 Torrey, *op. cit.*, p. 65.

26 Metzger, *op. cit.*, p. 98.

NOTES TO PART FOUR INTRODUCTION
AND TO CHAPTER 11: THE PSALMS

1 Wilbur Owen Sypherd, *The Literature of the English Bible* (New York: Oxford University Press, 1938), pp. 91-92; W. Stewart McCullough, Introduction to Psalms, *The Interpreter's Bible* (Nashville, Tenn.: Abingdon Press, 1955), IV, 11-12; and Theodore H. Robinson, *The Poetry of the Old Testament* (London: Gerald Duckworth and Co., 1947), pp. 20-46. Most of the information in this Outline on parallelism and rhythm is derived from Sypherd and Robinson.

2 Both examples suggested and marked by Sypherd, *op. cit.*, pp. 95-96.

3 Sypherd, *op. cit.*, p. 92.

4 Roy B. Chamberlin and Herman Feldman (eds.), *The Dartmouth Bible* (2nd ed.; Boston: Houghton Mifflin Co., 1961), p. 467.

5 George Sprau, *Literature in the Bible* (New York: Macmillan Co., 1932), p. 195.

6 Elmer A. Leslie, Commentary on the Psalms, *The Abingdon Bible Commentary* (Nashville, Tenn.: Abingdon Press, 1929), p. 509.

7 Leslie, *The Abingdon Bible Commentary*, p. 509.

8 The ascriptions to these authors are very ancient, dating at least as far back as the Septuagint (McCullough, Introduction, *The Interpreter's Bible*, IV, 8. Although Ps. 43 has no superscription, it and Ps. 42 are obviously one song, and therefore Ps. 43 is considered one of the songs of the Sons of Korah. Asaph, Ethan, and Heman have not been satisfactorily identified; the Sons of Korah were probably a guild of temple singers (McCullough, pp. 8-9).

The "orphans" are Pss. 1, 2, 10, 33, 66, 67, 71, 91—100, 102, 104—107, 111—121, 123, 125, 126, 128—130, 132, 134—137, and 146—150.

The Psalms ascribed to David are 3—9, 11—32, 34—41, 51—65, 68—70, 86, 101, 103, 108—110, 122, 124, 131, 133, and 138—145.

The Psalms of the Sons of Korah are 42—49, 84, 85, and 87.

Those by Asaph are 50 and 73—83.

Those ascribed to Solomon are 72 and 127.

The others are as follows: Heman, Ps. 88; Ethan, Ps. 89, and Moses, Ps. 90.

[9] Julius A. Bewer, *The Literature of the Old Testament* (3rd ed., revised by Emil G. Kraeling; New York: Columbia University Press, 1962), p. 362.

[10] Sprau, *op. cit.*, pp. 198-199. See also Sypherd, *op. cit.*, p. 111, and McCullough, Introduction, *The Interpreter's Bible*, IV, 10-11.

[11] Sprau, *op. cit.*, p. 199.

[12] Charles Allen Dinsmore, *The English Bible as Literature* (Boston: Houghton Mifflin Co., 1931), p. 180; John Robertson Macarthur, *Biblical Literature and Its Backgrounds* (New York: Appleton-Century-Crofts, 1930), p. 205.

[13] Dinsmore, *op. cit.*, p. 180. See also Sypherd, *op. cit.*, p. 108, and Macarthur, *op. cit.*, p. 205.

[14] Alice Parmelee, *A Guidebook to the Bible* (New York: Harper & Brothers, 1948), p. 122. See also Sypherd, *op. cit.*, p. 111; Sprau, *op. cit.*, p. 198; Harold H. Watts, *The Modern Reader's Guide to the Bible* (New York: Harper & Brothers, 1949), p. 210. McCullough (Introduction, *The Interpreter's Bible*, IV, 11) says that the Psalms may have canonized by the early part of the second century B.C.

[15] Dinsmore, *op. cit.*, p. 183.

[16] Parmelee, *op. cit.*, pp. 128-129, and Dinsmore, *op. cit.*, p. 183.

[17] Parmelee, *op. cit.*, p. 128.

[18] Dinsmore, *op. cit.*, p. 184.

[19] J. H. Gardiner, *The Bible as English Literature* (New York: Charles Scribner's Sons, 1927), p. 129.

[20] Dinsmore, *op. cit.*, p. 182.

[21] Leslie, *The Abingdon Bible Commentary*, p. 514.

[22] Leslie, *The Abingdon Bible Commentary*, p. 514; Robinson, *op. cit.*, pp. 154-162; and Macarthur, *op. cit.*, pp. 210-211.

[23] These "basic concepts and beliefs" have been gleaned from several sources: Dinsmore, *op. cit.*, pp. 186-188; Leslie, *The Abingdon Bible Commentary*, p. 514; Robinson, *op. cit.*, pp. 152-162; and Sprau, *op. cit.*, pp. 201-206.

[24] Sprau, *op. cit.*, p. 205.

[25] McCullough, Introduction, *The Interpreter's Bible*, IV, 5.

[26] For two of the most widely recognized attempts at classification —those by Hermann Gunkel and Sigmund Mowinckel—see McCullough, Introduction, *The Interpreter's Bible*, IV, 6-7. For other commentators' classifications, see Richard G. Moulton (ed.), *The Modern Reader's Bible* (New York: Macmillan Co., 1952), pp. 1433-1440, 1726-1728; Leslie, *The Abingdon Bible Commentary*, pp. 513-514; Dinsmore, *op. cit.*, p. 181; Macarthur, *op. cit.*, p. 210; Bewer, *op. cit.*, pp. 341-362; Sypherd, *op. cit.*, p. 111; and Robinson, *op. cit.*, pp. 125-145.

[27] Title suggested by William R. Taylor, Exegesis to Psalms, *The Interpreter's Bible*, IV, 48.

[28] Taylor, Exegesis, *The Interpreter's Bible*, IV, 53.

[29] Taylor, Exegesis, *The Interpreter's Bible*, IV, 131-132.

[30] Chamberlin and Feldman, *op. cit.*, p. 507.

[31] For these suggested interpretations, see Leslie, *The Abingdon Bible Commentary*, p. 539, and McCullough, Exegesis, *The Interpreter's Bible*, IV, 240-241.

[32] W. A. Shelton, Commentary on Psalms 73-150, *The Abingdon Bible Commentary*, p. 593.

[33] Dinsmore, *op. cit.*, p. 98.

[34] Chamberlin and Feldman, *op. cit.*, p. 510.

[35] These divisions of the Psalm are suggested by McCullough, Exegesis, *The Interpreter's Bible*, IV, 552-557.

[36] Shelton, *The Abingdon Bible Commentary*, p. 584.

[37] *Ibid.*

[38] This division of the Psalm is suggested by Shelton, *The Abingdon Bible Commentary*, p. 595.

[39] Shelton, *The Abingdon Bible Commentary*, p. 595. For other comments on the unity of the Psalm, see McCullough, Exegesis, *The Interpreter's Bible*, IV, 712-713.

[40] Robinson, *op. cit.*, p. 129.

[41] Leslie, *The Abingdon Bible Commentary*, p. 538, and Taylor, Exegesis, *The Interpreter's Bible*, IV, 227-228.

[42] McCullough, Exegesis, *The Interpreter's Bible*, IV, 394.

[43] See Robinson, *op. cit.*, p. 131.

[44] Taylor, Exegesis, *The Interpreter's Bible*, IV, 272.

[45] Robinson, *op. cit.*, p. 129.

[46] Gunkel's classification, followed by Robinson, *op. cit.*, pp. 129-131.

[47] Taylor, Exegesis, *The Interpreter's Bible*, IV, 234-235.

[48] Taylor, Exegesis, *The Interpreter's Bible*, 235.

[49] Here the word *blessing* refers not to a prayer for God's favor but to a description of the people who deserve such favor. When the poet

says: "Blessed is the man . . .," the first word "is almost an interjection" (Robinson, *op. cit.*, p. 139).

[50] Taylor, Exegesis, *The Interpreter's Bible*, IV, 17.

[51] Taylor, Exegesis, *The Interpreter's Bible*, IV, 638.

[52] See Robinson, *op. cit.*, p. 140.

[53] McCullough, Exegesis, *The Interpreter's Bible*, IV, 423.

[54] See Taylor, Exegesis, *The Interpreter's Bible*, IV, 192.

[55] Chamberlin and Feldman, *op. cit.*, p. 509.

[56] McCullough, Exegesis, *The Interpreter's Bible*, IV, 487.

NOTES TO CHAPTER 12: MINOR LYRICAL BOOKS

[1] Roy B. Chamberlin and Herman Feldman (eds.), *The Dartmouth Bible* (2nd ed.; Boston: Houghton Mifflin Co., 1961), p. 522.

[2] S. R. Driver, *An Introduction to the Literature of the Old Testament* (rev. ed.; New York: Charles Scribner's Sons, 1920), p. 456.

[3] Theodore H. Robinson, *The Poetry of the Old Testament* (London: Gerald Duckworth and Co., 1947) pp. 215-216, suggests the following dates: Chs. 2 and 4, *c.* 586 B.C.; Ch. 1, *c.* 570-560 B.C.; Ch. 5, *c.* 540 B.C.; Ch. 3, *c.* 540-520 B.C. W. G. Jordan, Commentary on Lamentations, *The Abington Bible Commentary* (Nashville, Tenn.: Abingdon Press, 1929), p. 709, suggests Chs. 2 and 4, *c.* 573 B.C.; Chs. 1 and 5, *c.* 540 B.C.; Ch. 3, *c.* 325 B.C. For some unusual suggestions made by Wilhelm Rudolph, see Theophile J. Meek, Introduction to Lamentations, *The Interpreter's Bible* (Nashville, Tenn.: Abingdon Press, 1956), VI, 4-5.

[4] Jordan, *The Abingdon Bible Commentary*, p. 709.

[5] Meek, Introduction, *The Interpreter's Bible*, VI, 3.

[6] Driver, *op. cit.*, p. 459.

[7] Chamberlin and Feldman, *op. cit.*, p. 523.

[8] Jordan, *The Abingdon Bible Commentary*, p. 709.

[9] Theophile J. Meek, Exegesis to Lamentations, *The Interpreter's Bible*, VI, 23. This commentator suggests that the speaker may have in mind the experiences of Jeremiah and may be playing that prophet's role in the poem.

[10] Jordan, *The Abingdon Bible Commentary*, p. 711.

[11] The information in this paragraph is derived from Bruce M. Metzger, *An Introduction to the Apocrypha* (New York: Oxford University Press, 1957), pp. 124-125.

[12] Metzger, *op. cit.*, p. 123.

[13] Metzger, *op. cit.*, pp. 103-104.

[14] Pointed out by Metzger, *op. cit.*, pp. 102-103.

[15] Metzger, *op. cit.*, p. 102.

NOTES TO PART FIVE INTRODUCTION
AND TO CHAPTER 13: JOB

[1] Laura H. Wild, *A Literary Guide to the Bible* (New York: Harper & Brothers, 1922), p. 192.

[2] These examples from Isaiah and Ezekiel are cited by Wild, *op. cit.*, pp. 192-193.

[3] See Richard G. Moulton, *The Literary Study of the Bible* (rev. ed.; Boston: D. C. Heath & Co., 1899), pp. 515 and 524.

[4] All these eulogies are quoted by Samuel Terrien, Introduction to Job, *The Interpreter's Bible* (Nashville, Tenn.: Abingdon Press, 1954), III, 877.

[5] See Terrien, Introduction, *The Interpreter's Bible*, III, 878-880.

[6] Terrien, Introduction, *The Interpreter's Bible*, III, 880-884. "The Poem of the Righteous Sufferer" is of uncertain date but was well known in the seventh century B.C., and the acrostic dates from the ninth century B.C.

[7] For specific suggestions concerning the dating of the various parts, see Terrien, Introduction, *The Interpreter's Bible*, III, 890; Theodore H. Robinson, *The Poetry of the Old Testament* (London: Gerald Duckworth and Co., 1947), p. 81; Wilbur Owen Sypherd, *The Literature of the English Bible* (New York: Oxford University Press, 1938), p. 128; Roy B. Chamberlin and Herman Feldman (eds.), *The Dartmouth Bible* (2nd ed.; Boston: Houghton Mifflin Co., 1961), p. 431; John Robertson Macarthur, *Biblical Literature and Its Backgrounds* (New York: Appleton-Century-Crofts, 1936), p. 197; and Alice Parmelee, *A Guidebook to the Bible* (New York: Harper & Brothers, 1948), p. 112.

[8] Terrien, Introduction, *The Interpreter's Bible*, III, 878.

[9] *The Book of Job as a Greek Tragedy* (New York: Moffat, Yard & Co., 1918).

[10] Macarthur, *op. cit.*, p. 198, and Henry Thatcher Fowler, *A History of the Literature of Ancient Israel* (New York: Macmillan Co., 1922), p. 333. *J.B.*, by Archibald MacLeish, is a drama that retells the story in a modern setting.

[11] George Sprau, *Literature in the Bible* (New York: Macmillan Co., 1932), p. 220.

[12] S. R. Driver, *An Introduction to the Literature of the Old Testament* (rev. ed.; New York: Charles Scribner's Sons, 1920), p. 411.

[13] Richard G. Moulton (ed.), *The Modern Reader's Bible* (New York: Macmillan Co., 1935), p. 1041.

[14] Ernest Sutherland Bates (ed.), *The Bible Designed to Be Read as Living Literature* (New York: Simon and Schuster, 1936), p. 698.

[15] Chamberlin and Feldman, *op. cit.*, p. 462.

¹⁶ Paraphrased from Moulton, *The Literary Study of the Bible*, pp. 6, 7, 20, 22, and 24. It should be observed that "solutions" 4 and 5 are not "solutions," but are theological interpretations first suggested in the Bible by the book of Job.

¹⁷ A combination of the suggestions by Moulton, *The Modern Reader's Bible*, p. 1037, and Terrien, Introduction, *The Interpreter's Bible*, III, 902-905.

¹⁸ Samuel Terrien, Exegesis to Job, *The Interpreter's Bible*, III, 915.

¹⁹ Terrien, Exegesis, *The Interpreter's Bible*, III, 925.

²⁰ Moulton, *The Modern Reader's Bible*, pp. 1042-1069 and 1656-1657.

²¹ W. F. Lofthouse, Commentary on Job, *The Abingdon Bible Commentary* (Nashville, Tenn.: Abingdon Press, 1929), p. 491.

²² Terrien, Exegesis, *The Interpreter's Bible*, III, 965-966.

²³ Terrien, Exegesis, *The Interpreter's Bible*, III, 969.

²⁴ For an enlightening discussion of the function of the *goël*, see Robinson, *op. cit.*, pp. 97-98.

²⁵ Some exegetes deny that God is the *goël* envisioned by Job, and in support of their view they point out (1) that Job's speeches in the remainder of the debate reflect no confidence on his part that his problems have been solved and (2) that God (as in the Voice out of the Whirlwind) is still Job's accuser, not his vindicator. See Terrien, Exegesis, *The Interpreter's Bible*, III, 1052. For the opposite view, see Robinson, *op. cit.*, pp. 97-99.

²⁶ According to the text of the King James Version, Zophar does not speak in the third cycle. Most scholars, however, believe that the text is corrupt and that some of the speeches apparently attributed to Job are inconsistent with his other discourses. Terrien (Exegesis, *The Interpreter's Bible*, III, 1098-1099) suggests that 24:18-24 and 27:13-23 should be assigned to Zophar. See also Lofthouse, *The Abingdon Bible Commentary*, pp. 498-499. There is no reply of Job to Zophar in the third cycle.

²⁷ Moulton, *The Literary Study of the Bible*, p. 20.

NOTES TO CHAPTER 14: THE SONG OF SOLOMON

¹ Ernest Sutherland Bates, ed. (*The Bible Designed to Be Read as Living Literature* [New York: Simon and Schuster, 1936], p. 772) calls it "a fragmentary wedding idyll"; and Professor Richard G. Moulton (*The Literary Study of the Bible* [rev. ed.; Boston: D. C. Heath & Co., 1899], p. 207) calls it a "lyric idyl."

² For discussions of origin, date, and authorship, see Bates, *op. cit.*, p. 771; Robert H. Pfeiffer, Commentary on The Song of Songs, *The Abingdon Bible Commentary* (Nashville, Tenn.: Abingdon Press, 1929), pp. 622-623; and Theophile J. Meek, Introduction to The Song

of Songs, *The Interpreter's Bible* (Nashville, Tenn.: Abingdon Press, 1956), V, 96-97.

[3] These headings are quoted from Roy B. Chamberlin and Herman Feldman (eds.), *The Dartmouth Bible* (2nd ed., Boston: Houghton Mifflin Co., 1950), pp. 512-513. Discussions of the various interpretations are derived not only from this work but also from Meek, Introduction, *The Interpreter's Bible*, V, 92-96; and Pfeiffer, *The Abingdon Bible Commentary*, pp. 622-623.

[4] Bates, *op. cit.*, p. 771.

[5] See Meek, Introduction, *The Interpreter's Bible*, V, 97-98.

[6] Suggested by Bates, *op. cit.*, p. 772.

[7] Division suggested by Bates (*op. cit.*, pp. 772-785), who also breaks the lines up into separate speeches and assigns a speaker to each. This Outline will follow Bates' arrangement. For a division of the book as a drama (rather than a wedding pageant), see Chamberlin and Feldman, *op. cit.*, pp. 513-521.

[8] Title suggested by Moulton, *op. cit.*, p. 215. My interpretations of the various scenes owe much to Professor Moulton's analyses (pp. 212-220).

NOTES TO CHAPTER 15:
FOURTH-CENTURY STORIES ADVOCATING TOLERANCE

[1] *Levirate marriage* has been defined more technically as: "a custom or law . . . according to which the brother of a man who died leaving a widow but no children (or no male child) was obliged to marry the widow. Her children (or, under the later law, the first-born male child) from such marriage were considered as heirs to the dead brother's estate and perpetuators of his name. Release from this obligation could, under the later law, be obtained by a special ceremony, and it was finally abolished." *Webster's New International Dictionary* (2nd ed.; Springfield, Mass.: G. & C. Merriam Co., 1934), p. 1422.

[2] Necessarily, the book was written between the time of Jeroboam and the compilation of the Hebrew canon. The following cumulative evidence supports mid-fourth century authorship: (1) Except for the psalm of Chapter 2, the entire story is told in the third person and is told as a story about an old-time prophet. (2) The psalm seems to be based upon Jer. 51:34 or upon similar passages which occur in the Psalter. See James D. Smart, Introduction to Jonah, *The Interpreter's Bible* (Nashville, Tenn.: Abingdon Press, 1956), VI, 874. (3) The author seems to be unconcerned with geographical or historical accuracy; rather he is dealing with a "long ago" when Nineveh was a city of fabulous circumference and fabulous population, when it was ruled by its own king, and when king and populace were converted in one day to Judaism. None of these details is substantiated by

Biblical history, by ancient documents, or by modern archaeology.
(4) Linguistic evidence (late Hebrew and Aramaic words and expressions not found elsewhere in the Old Testament) points to about
350 B.C. though it does not rule out the possibility that the author
was retelling an older story. (5) The most nearly conclusive evidence
lies in the religious doctrines which the author attributes directly to
God, which were in keeping with the teachings of post-Exilic prophets rather than with those of Jeroboam's time and which had particular appropriateness for the embittered rebuilders of Jerusalem in the
fourth century B.C.

NOTES TO CHAPTER 16: SECOND- AND
FIRST-CENTURY STORIES ENCOURAGING INTEGRITY

[1] See Bruce M. Metzger, *An Introduction to the Apocrypha* (New
York: Oxford University Press, 1957), pp. 40-41.

[2] Roy B. Chamberlin and Herman Feldman (eds.), *The Dartmouth
Bible* (2nd ed.; Boston: Houghton Mifflin Co., 1961), p. 785.

[3] Shailer Mathews and Bruce M. Metzger, "Pseudepigrapha," in
James Hastings (ed.), *Dictionary of the Bible* (rev. ed. by Frederick
Grant and H. H. Rowley; New York: Charles Scribner's Sons, 1963),
p. 821.

[4] Arthur Jeffrey, Introduction and Exegesis to Daniel, *The Interpreter's Bible* (Nashville, Tenn.: Abingdon Press, 1956), VI, 347-348
and 466-467.

[5] For the language and the date of composition, see Metzger, *op.
cit.*, p. 100, and Chamberlin and Feldman, *op. cit.*, p. 802.

[6] See Metzger, *op. cit.*, pp. 100, 107-108; Edgar J. Goodspeed
(ed.), *The Apocrypha* (New York: Random House, 1959), p. 347;
and Chamberlin and Feldman, *op. cit.*, p. 802.

[7] Metzger, *op. cit.*, p. 110.

[8] For the dates of composition, see Robert H. Pfeiffer, Commentary
on Esther, *The Abingdon Bible Commentary* (Nashville, Tenn.:
Abingdon Press, 1929), p. 477; Metzger, *op. cit.*, p. 55; and Charles
G. Torrey, *The Apocryphal Literature* (New York: Random House,
1959), p. 58.

NOTES TO CHAPTER 17:
ETHICAL PRECEPTS AND CYNICAL PESSIMISM

[1] Charles T. Fritsch, Introduction to Proverbs, *The Interpreter's
Bible* (Nashville, Tenn.: Abingdon Press, 1955), IV, 774-775.

[2] Charles T. Fritsch, Exegesis to Proverbs, *The Interpreter's Bible*,
IV, 947.

[3] For detailed discussions of the dating and authorship of Proverbs,
see Fritsch, Introduction, *The Interpreter's Bible*, IV, 774-775; Theodore H. Robinson, *Poetry of the Old Testament* (London: Gerald

Duckworth and Co., 1947), pp. 190-191; and Roy B. Chamberlin and Herman Feldman (eds.), *The Dartmouth Bible* (2nd ed.; Boston: Houghton Mifflin Co., 1961), p. 394.

[4] Based to some extent upon the rearrangement made by Chamberlin and Feldman, *op. cit.*, pp. 395-420.

[5] "A negative form of the Golden Rule (Mt. 7:12 . . .)," Chamberlin and Feldman, *op. cit.*, p. 406.

[6] See especially A. H. McNeile, *Introduction to Ecclesiastes* (Cambridge, England: G. P. Putnam's Sons, 1904); and Morris Jastrow, *A Gentle Cynic* (Philadelphia and London: J. B. Lippincott Co., 1919).

[7] Jastrow, *op. cit.*, pp. 245-254. According to Jastrow, the "pious" interpolations are as follows: 1:13, 16, 17; 2:3, 9, 12, 26; 3:11, 14, 15, 17; 5:6; 7:1-3, 18, 26, 29; 8:2, 3, 5, 8, 11-13; 9:1, 18; 10:5; 11:9, 10; 12:1, 7, 12-14. The maxim additions: 1:15, 18; 2:14; 3:3-8; 4:5, 9-12, 14; 6:7; 7:5-9, 11, 12, 19; 8:1; 9:17, 18; 10:1-3, 8-15, 18; 11:3, 4; 12:11. The miscellaneous additions: 1:1, 2, 5; 2:6; 3:12, 17, 18, 21; 4:15, 16; 5:3, 8, 12; 6:3; 7:12, 25, 27; 8:6, 7, 12; 9:1, 9, 12; 10:10, 13-15, 19; 11:12; 12:2, 8-10.

[8] George Sprau, *Literature in the Bible* (New York: Macmillan Co., 1932), p. 250.

[9] Robert C. Dentan, *The Apocrypha, Bridge of the Testaments* (Greenwich, Conn.: Seabury Press, 1954), p. 78.

[10] Charles C. Torrey, *The Apocryphal Literature* (New Haven: Yale University Press, 1945), p. 96.

[11] Dentan, *op. cit.*, p. 78. Much of the criticism in these paragraphs is derived from Dentan, pp. 77-78; Bruce M. Metzger, *An Introduction to the Apocrypha* (New York: Oxford University Press, 1957), pp. 81-82; Chamberlin and Feldman, *op. cit.*, p. 108; and Charles C. Torrey, *The Apocryphal Literature* (New Haven: Yale University Press, 1945), p. 96.

[12] Metzger, *op. cit.*, p. 88.

[13] Division suggested by Dentan, *op. cit.*, p. 79.

[14] *Ibid.*

[15] Metzger, *op. cit.*, p. 81.

[16] Torrey, *op. cit.*, p. 94.

[17] *Ibid.*

[18] Metzger, *op. cit.*, p. 77.

[19] Metzger, *op. cit.*, p. 83.

[20] See Metzger, *op. cit.*, p. 67; Torrey, *op. cit.*, pp. 102-103; Chamberlin, *op. cit.*, p. 827; and George A. Buttrick (ed.), *The Interpreter's Dictionary of the Bible* (Nashville, Tenn.: Abingdon Press, 1962), IV, 862.

²¹ Torrey, *op. cit.*, pp. 98-102, and Edgar J. Goodspeed (ed.), *The Apocrypha* (New York: Random House, 1959), p. 177.

²² Goodspeed's translation makes all of it poetry. *The Dartmouth Bible* (2nd ed.; Boston: Houghton Mifflin Co., 1961) considers some passages prose.

²³ Dentan, *op. cit.*, p. 85.

NOTES TO PART EIGHT INTRODUCTION AND TO CHAPTER 18: II ESDRAS

¹ Robert C. Dentan, *The Apocrypha, Bridge of the Testaments* (Greenwich, Conn.: Seabury Press, 1954), p. 94.

² *Ibid.*

³ For a more detailed account of the composition and transmission of II Esdras, see Dentan, *op. cit.*, pp. 94-97, and Bruce M. Metzger, *An Introduction to the Apocrypha* (New York: Oxford University Press, 1957), pp. 22-24.

⁴ Metzger, *op. cit.*, p. 30.

⁵ Edgar J. Goodspeed (ed.), *The Apocrypha* (New York: Random House, 1959), p. 39.

⁶ Dentan, *op. cit.*, p. 98.

Bibliography

REFERENCE WORKS

The Abingdon Bible Commentary. Nashville, Tenn.: Abingdon Press, 1929. Articles and commentaries on Biblical topics by a number of authorities.

Chamberlin, Roy B., and Herman Feldman (eds.). *The Dartmouth Bible.* 2nd ed. Boston: Houghton Mifflin Co., 1961. An abridgment of the King James Version, with introductions, prefaces, notes, and annotated maps.

Douglas, James Dixon (ed.). *The New Bible Dictionary.* Grand Rapids, Mich.: William B. Eerdmans Publishing Co., 1962.

Ellison, John W. *Nelson's Complete Concordance of the Revised Standard Version.* New York: Thomas Nelson & Sons, 1957.

Hastings, James (ed.). *Dictionary of the Bible.* Rev. ed. by Frederick C. Grant and H. H. Rowley. New York: Charles Scribner's Sons, 1963.

The Interpreter's Bible. 12 vols. Nashville, Tenn.: Abingdon Press, 1951-1957. The King James Version and the Revised Standard Version side by side, with an introduction, interpretation, and notes for each book of the Bible, general articles, and outline maps. 148 editors, consulting editors, and contributors, representing a cross section of Protestant scholarship.

The Interpreter's Dictionary of the Bible. Edited by George A. Buttrick. 4 vols. Nashville, Tenn.: Abingdon Press, 1962. Entries for Biblical persons, places, objects, terms, and doctrines. Maps and illustrations.

The Jerusalem Bible. General editor, Alexander Jones. Garden City, New York: Doubleday & Co., 1966. A new translation, based on (1) a French text prepared by the Dominican Biblical School in Jerusalem and (2) Hebrew, Aramaic, and Greek texts.

The Layman's Bible Commentary. General editor, Balmer H. Kelly. 25 vols. Richmond, Va.: John Knox Press, 1959-1964. Prepared by numerous scholars and editors. Learned yet simple discussions of all the canonical books.

May, Herbert G., and Bruce M. Metzger (eds.). *The Oxford Annotated Bible.* New York: Oxford University Press, 1962. The Revised

Standard Version, with introductions, notes, general articles, and maps.

Miller, Madelaine S. and J. Lane. *Encyclopedia of Bible Life*. Rev. ed. New York: Harper & Brothers, 1955.

———. *Harper's Bible Dictionary*. 6th ed. New York: Harper & Brothers, 1959.

Moulton, Richard G. (ed.). *The Modern Reader's Bible*. New York: Macmillan Co., 1952. The text of the English Revised Version, with introduction and notes.

Neil, William. *Harper's Bible Commentary*. New York: Harper & Row, 1962.

New Analytical Index Bible. Chicago: John A. Dickson Co., 1931.

Westminster Dictionary of the Bible. Rev. ed. Philadelphia: Westminster Press, 1944.

THE BIBLE: GENERAL BOOKS

Bates, Ernest S. (ed.). *The Bible Designed to Be Read as Living Literature*. New York: Simon and Schuster, 1936.

Chase, Mary Ellen. *The Bible and the Common Reader*. Rev. ed. New York: Macmillan Co., 1952. Reprinted in paperback.

Dinsmore, Charles Allen. *The English Bible as Literature*. Boston: Houghton Mifflin Co., 1931.

Gardiner, J. H. *The Bible as English Literature*. New York: Charles Scribner's Sons, 1927.

Goodspeed, Edgar J. *How to Read the Bible*. Philadelphia: John C. Winston Co., 1946.

———, and J. M. Powis Smith (eds.). *The Short Bible*. Chicago: University of Chicago Press, 1933. Reprinted by Modern Library (Random House).

Grant, Frederick C. *How To Read the Bible*. New York: Morehouse-Gorham Co., 1956. Reprinted in paperback by Macmillan Co.

Jenney, Ray Freeman. *Bible Primer*. New York: Harper & Brothers, 1955.

Keller, Werner. *The Bible as History*. Translated by William Neil. New York: William Morrow & Co., 1956.

Landis, Benson Y. *An Outline of the Bible, Book by Book*. New York: Barnes & Noble, Inc., 1963.

Macarthur, John R. *Biblical Literature and Its Backgrounds*. New York: Appleton-Century-Crofts, 1936.

Moulton, Richard G. *The Literary Study of the Bible*. Boston: D. C. Heath & Co., 1894.

Neil, William. *The Rediscovery of the Bible*. New York: Harper & Brothers, 1955.

Parmelee, Alice. *A Guidebook to the Bible*. New York: Harper & Brothers, 1948. Reprinted in paperback.

The Reader's Bible. New York: Oxford University Press, 1951.

Sprau, George. *Literature in the Bible*. New York: Macmillan Co., 1932.

Sypherd, Wilbur Owen. *The Literature of the English Bible*. New York: Oxford University Press, 1938.

Thirwall, John G., and Arthur Waldhorn (eds.). *A Bible for the Humanities*. New York: Harper & Brothers, 1954.

Watts, Harold H. *The Modern Reader's Guide to the Bible*. Rev. ed. New York: Harper & Brothers, 1959.

Wild, Laura H. *A Literary Guide to the Bible*. New York: Harper & Brothers, 1922.

THE OLD TESTAMENT: GENERAL BOOKS

Bewer, Julius A. *The Literature of the Old Testament*. 3rd ed. rev. by Emil G. Kraeling. New York: Columbia University Press, 1962.

Chase, Mary Ellen. *Life and Language in the Old Testament*. New York: W. W. Norton & Co., 1955. Reprinted in paperback.

Driver, S. R. *An Introduction to the Literature of the Old Testament*. Rev. ed. New York: Charles Scribner's Sons, 1920. Reprinted in paperback by Meridian Books (World Publishing Co.).

Fowler, Henry T. *A History of the Literature of Ancient Israel*. New York: Macmillan Co., 1922.

Gaer, Joseph. *The Lore of the Old Testament*. Boston: Little, Brown and Co., 1952.

Goodspeed, Edgar J. *The Story of the Old Testament*. Chicago: University of Chicago Press, 1934.

Heaton, E. W. *Everyday Life in Old Testament Times*. New York: Charles Scribner's Sons, 1956.

James, Fleming. *Personalities of the Old Testament*. New York: Charles Scribner's Sons, 1939.

Gottwald, Norman. *Light to the Nations: An Introduction to the Old Testament*. New York: Harper & Brothers, 1959.

Muilenburg, James. "The History of the Religion of Israel," *The Interpreter's Bible*. Nashville, Tenn.: Abingdon Press, 1952. I, 292-389.

Oesterley, W. O. E., *An Introduction to the Books of the Old Testament*. Naperville, Ill.: Alec R. Allenson, 1934.

Pfeiffer, Robert H. *Introduction to the Old Testament*. Rev. ed. New York: Harper & Brothers, 1948. Abr. ed. in paperback.

Robinson, Henry Wheeler. *Inspiration and Revelation in the Old Testament*. London: Oxford University Press, 1946. Reprinted in paperback.

Robinson, Theodore H. "The History of Israel," *The Interpreter's Bible*, I, 272-291.

Rowley, Harold H. *The Growth of the Old Testament*. London and New York: Hutchinson's University Library, 1950.

——— (ed.). *The Old Testament and Modern Study: A Generation of Discovery and Research*. Oxford: Clarendon Press, 1951. Reprinted in paperback.

Sandmel, Samuel. *The Hebrew Scriptures: An Introduction to Their Literature and Religious Ideas*. New York: Alfred A. Knopf, 1963.

Schultz, Samuel J. *The Old Testament Speaks*. New York: Harper & Brothers, 1960.

THE APOCRYPHA: GENERAL BOOKS

The Apocrypha: An American Translation. Edited by Edgar J. Goodspeed, with an Introduction by Moses Hadas. New York: Random House, 1959. Reprinted in paperback.

Dentan, Robert C. *The Apocrypha, Bridge of the Testaments*. Greenwich, Conn.: Seabury Press, 1954. Reprinted in paperback.

Goodspeed, Edgar J. *The Story of the Apocrypha*. Chicago: University of Chicago Press, 1939.

Metzger, Bruce M. *An Introduction to the Apocrypha*. New York: Oxford University Press, 1957.

The Oxford Annotated Apocrypha. Edited by Bruce M. Metzger. New York: Oxford University Press, 1965.

Pfeiffer, Robert H. "The Literature and Religion of the Apocrypha," *The Interpreter's Bible*. Nashville, Tenn.: Abingdon Press, 1952. I, 391-419.

CHAPTER 1: PALESTINE AND ITS PEOPLE

Aharoni, Y., and M. Avi-Yonah. *The Macmillan Bible Atlas*. New York: Macmillan Co., 1968.

Albright, William F. "The Old Testament World," *The Interpreter's Bible*. Nashville, Tenn.: Abingdon Press, 1952. I, 233-271.

———. *From the Stone Age to Christianity*. 2nd ed. Baltimore, Md.: Johns Hopkins Press, 1957. Reprinted in paperback by Anchor Books (Doubleday).

Baly, Denis. *The Geography of the Bible*. New York: Harper & Brothers, 1957.

Browne, Lewis. *The Graphic Bible*. New York: Macmillan Co., 1928.

Burrows, Millar. *What Mean These Stones?* New Haven, Conn.: American Schools of Oriental Research, 1941. Reprinted in paperback by Meridian Books (World Publishing Co.).

De Vaux, Roland. *Ancient Israel: Its Life and Institutions.* Translated by John McHugh. New York: McGraw-Hill Book Co., 1961. Reprinted in paperback.

Finegan, Jack. *Light from the Ancient Past.* 2nd ed. Princeton, N. J.: Princeton University Press, 1959.

Finkelstein, Louis (ed.). *The Jews: Their History, Culture, and Religion.* 2 vols. 3rd ed. New York: Harper & Brothers, 1949.

Gordon, Cyrus H. *World of the Old Testament.* Rev. ed. New York: Doubleday & Co., 1958.

Grant, Elihu. *The Orient in Bible Times.* Philadelphia: J. B. Lippincott Co., 1920.

Grollenberg, L. H. (ed.). *Atlas of the Bible.* New York: Thomas Nelson and Sons, 1957.

Guignebert, Charles. *The Jewish World in the Time of Christ.* Translated by S. H. Hooke. New York: E. P. Dutton & Co., 1939.

Kenyon, Kathleen. *Archaeology in the Holy Land.* 2nd ed. New York: Frederick A. Praeger, 1960. Reprinted in paperback.

———. *Digging up Jericho.* New York: Frederick A. Praeger, 1957.

Kraeling, Emil G. H. *The Rand McNally Bible Atlas.* 2nd ed. New York: Rand McNally and Co., 1962.

May, Herbert (ed.). *Oxford Bible Atlas.* New York: Oxford University Press, 1962. Reprinted in paperback.

Smith, George Adam. *The Historical Geography of the Holy Land.* 4th ed. New York: George H. Doran Co., 1896. Reprinted in paperback by Torchbooks (Harper & Row).

Wright, G. Ernest, and Floyd Vivian Filson (eds.). *The Westminster Historical Atlas to the Bible.* Rev. ed. Philadelphia: Westminster Press, 1956.

———, and David Noel Freedman (eds.). *The Bible Archaeologist Reader.* New York: Doubleday & Company, 1961. Paperback reprint of articles from *The Biblical Archaeologist.*

CHAPTER 2: THE NATURE, ORIGINS, AND CONTENTS OF THE BIBLE

Bowie, Walter R. *The Story of the Bible.* Nashville, Tenn.: Abingdon Press, 1934.

Bruce, F. F. *The English Bible: A History of Translations from the Earliest English Versions to the New English Bible.* New York: Oxford University Press, 1961.

Butterworth, Charles C. *The Literary Lineage of the King James Bible 1340-1611.* Philadelphia: University of Pennsylvania Press, 1941.

The Cambridge History of the Bible. 3 vols. Cambridge, England: Cambridge University Press, 1963–. (In progress.)

Coggan, Frederick D. *The English Bible.* London: Longmans, Green, 1963.

Colwell, Ernest C. *The Study of the Bible.* Chicago: University of Chicago Press, 1937. Reprinted in paperback.

Herklots, H. G. G. *How Our Bible Came to Us.* New York: Oxford University Press, 1954. Reprinted in paperback.

Jeffery, Arthur. "The Canon of the Old Testament," *The Interpreter's Bible.* Nashville, Tenn.: Abingdon Press, 1952. I, 32-45.

Kenyon, Frederic. *Our Bible and the Ancient Manuscripts.* Rev. ed. New York: Harper & Brothers, 1958.

Lewis, Frank Grant. *How the Bible Grew.* Chicago: University of Chicago Press, 1919.

MacGregor, Geddes. *The Bible in the Making.* Philadelphia: J. B. Lippincott Co., 1959.

–––. *A Literary History of the Bible from the Middle Ages to the Present Day.* Nashville, Tenn.: Abingdon Press, 1968.

Margolis, Max L. *The Hebrew Scriptures in the Making.* Philadelphia: Jewish Publication Society of America, 1922.

–––. *The Story of Bible Translations.* Philadelphia: Jewish Publication Society of America, 1917.

O'Connell, John (ed.). *The Holy Bible.* Chicago: The Catholic Press, 1950.

Price, Ira Maurice. *The Ancestry of Our English Bible.* 3rd ed. rev. by William A. Irwin and Allen P. Wikgren. New York: Harper & Brothers, 1956.

Pritchard, James Bennett (ed.). *Ancient Near Eastern Texts Relating to the Old Testament.* Rev. ed. Princeton, N. J.: Princeton University Press, 1955.

Robinson, Henry W. *The Bible in Its Ancient and English Versions.* New York: Oxford University Press, 1954.

Rypins, Stanley. *The Book of Thirty Centuries.* New York: Macmillan Co., 1951.

Smyth, J. Paterson. *How We Got Our Bible.* Rev. ed. New York: Harper & Brothers, 1912.

Snaith, Norman H. "The Language of the Old Testament," *The Interpreter's Bible,* I, 220-232.

Wikgren, Allen. "The English Bible," *The Interpreter's Bible,* I, 84-105.

CHAPTER 3: THE FOUNDING OF THE HEBREW NATION

Barrois, George A. "Chronology, Metrology, etc.," *The Interpreter's Bible.* Nashville, Tenn.: Abingdon Press, 1952. I, 142-164.

Bright, John. Introduction and Exegesis to Joshua, *The Interpreter's Bible*. Nashville, Tenn.: Abingdon Press, 1953. II, 541-550 and 553-573.

Buber, Martin. *Moses: The Revelation and the Covenant*. London: East & West Library, 1946. Reprinted in paperback by Torchbooks (Harper & Row).

Marsh, John. Exegesis to Numbers, *The Interpreter's Bible*, II, 142-308.

Meek, T. J. *Hebrew Origins*. Rev. ed. New York: Harper & Brothers, 1960. Reprinted in paperback.

Micklem, Nathaniel. Introduction to Leviticus, *The Interpreter's Bible*, II, 3-9.

Rowley, Harold H. *From Joseph to Joshua*. New York: Oxford University Press, 1950.

Rylaarsdam, J. Coert. Introduction and Exegesis to Exodus, *The Interpreter's Bible*, I, 833-838 and 851-1099.

Simpson, Cuthbert A. Exegesis to Genesis, *The Interpreter's Bible*, I, 465-829.

———. "The Growth of the Hexateuch," *The Interpreter's Bible*, I, 185-200.

Wright, G. Ernest. Exegesis to Deuteronomy, *The Interpreter's Bible*, II, 331-537.

See also THE BIBLE: GENERAL BOOKS (p. 386) and THE OLD TESTAMENT: GENERAL BOOKS (p. 387).

CHAPTER 4: THE RISE AND FALL OF THE MONARCHY

Caird, George B. Introduction and Exegesis to I and II Samuel, *The Interpreter's Bible*. Nashville, Tenn.: Abingdon Press, 1953. II, 855-1176.

Muilenberg, James. "The History of the Religion of Israel," *The Interpreter's Bible*. Nashville, Tenn.: Abingdon Press, 1952. I, 305-335.

Myers, Jacob M. Introduction to Judges, *The Interpreter's Bible*, II, 677-687.

Robinson, Theodore. "The History of Israel," *The Interpreter's Bible*, I, 277-287.

Snaith, Norman H. Introduction and Exegesis to I and II Kings, *The Interpreter's Bible*. Nashville, Tenn.: Abingdon Press, 1954. III, 3-338.

Szikszai, Stephen. *Story of Israel from Joshua to Alexander the Great* Philadelphia: Westminster Press, 1960.

Welch, Adam C. *Kings and Prophets in Israel*. Nashville, Ill.: Alec R. Allenson, 1955.

See also THE BIBLE: GENERAL BOOKS (p. 386) and THE OLD TESTAMENT: GENERAL BOOKS (p. 387).

CHAPTER 5: ESTABLISHMENT OF A CHURCH STATE
AFTER THE EXILE

Bowman, Raymond A. Introduction and Exegesis to Ezra and Nehemiah, *The Interpreter's Bible*. Nashville, Tenn.: Abingdon Press, 1954. III, 551-819.

Elmslie, W. A. L. Introduction and Exegesis to I and II Chronicles, *The Interpreter's Bible*, III, 341-548.

Muilenburg, James. "The History of the Religion of Israel," *The Interpreter's Bible*. Nashville, Tenn.: Abingdon Press, 1952. I, 335-340.

Robinson, Theodore. "The History of Israel," *The Interpreter's Bible*, I, 287-288.

See also THE BIBLE: GENERAL BOOKS (p. 386), THE OLD TESTAMENT: GENERAL BOOKS (p. 387), and THE APOCRYPHA: GENERAL BOOKS (p. 388).

CHAPTER 6: THE MACCABEAN REVOLT

Charles, R. H. *Religious Development between the Old and the New Testaments*. New York: Oxford University Press, 1914.

Farmer, W. R. *Maccabees, Zealots, and Josephus: An Inquiry into Jewish Nationalism*. New York: Columbia University Press, 1956.

Pfeiffer, Robert H. *History of New Testament Times: With an Introduction to the Apocrypha*. New York: Harper & Brothers, 1949.

Robinson, Theodore H. "The History of Israel," *The Interpreter's Bible*. Nashville, Tenn.: Abingdon Press, 1952. I, 288-291.

See also THE BIBLE: GENERAL BOOKS (p. 386) and THE APOCRYPHA: GENERAL BOOKS (p. 388).

PROPHETIC LITERATURE: GENERAL BOOKS

Bewer, Julius A. (ed.). *The Prophets*. New York: Harper & Brothers, 1955.

Chase, Mary Ellen. *The Prophets for the Common Reader*. New York: W. W. Norton Co., 1963.

Fosbroke, Hughell E. W. "The Prophetic Literature," *The Interpreter's Bible*. Nashville, Tenn.: Abingdon Press, 1952. I, 201-211.

Hamilton, Edith. *The Prophets of Israel*. New York: W. W. Norton Co., 1936.

———. *Spokesmen for God*. New York: W. W. Norton Co., 1949. Reprinted in paperback.

Heschel, Abraham J. *The Prophets*. New York: Harper & Row, 1962.

Robinson, Theodore H. *Prophecy and the Prophets in Ancient Israel*. London: Gerald Duckworth and Co., 1953.

Scott, R. B. Y. *The Relevance of the Prophets*. New York: Macmillan Co., 1944.

CHAPTER 7: EIGHTH-CENTURY PROPHETS

Fosbroke, Hughell E. W. Introduction and Exegesis to Amos, *The Interpreter's Bible*. Nashville, Tenn.: Abingdon Press, 1956. VI, 763-853.

McFadyen, J. E. Commentary on Micah, *The Abingdon Bible Commentary*. Nashville, Tenn.: Abingdon Press, 1929. Pp. 791-797.

Mauchline, John. Introduction and Exegesis to Hosea, *The Interpreter's Bible*, VI, 553-725.

Robinson, H. Wheeler. Commentary on Amos, *The Abingdon Bible Commentary*, pp. 775-783.

———. Commentary on Hosea, *The Abingdon Bible Commentary*, pp. 759-767.

Rogers, Robert W. Commentary on Isaiah, *The Abingdon Bible Commentary*, pp. 628-654.

Scott, R. B. Y. Introduction and Exegesis to Isaiah 1–39, *The Interpreter's Bible*. Nashville, Tenn.: Abingdon Press, 1956. V, 151-381.

Wolfe, Rolland E. Introduction and Exegesis to Micah. *The Interpreter's Bible*, VI, 897-949.

CHAPTER 8: JUDAH'S PRE-EXILIC PROPHETS OF THE SEVENTH AND SIXTH CENTURIES

Bright, John (ed. and trans.). *Jeremiah*. Vol. 21 in The Anchor Bible Series. Garden City, N.Y.: Doubleday & Co., 1965.

Graham, William C. Commentary on Nahum, *The Abingdon Bible Commentary*. Nashville, Tenn.: Abingdon Press, 1929. Pp. 798-803.

———. Commentary on Zephaniah, *The Abingdon Bible Commentary*, pp. 809-814.

Hyatt, James Philip. Introduction and Exegesis to Jeremiah, *The Interpreter's Bible*. Nashville, Tenn.: Abingdon Press, 1956. V, 777-1142.

McFadyen, J. E. Commentary on Habakkuk, *The Abingdon Bible Commentary*, pp. 804-808.

Taylor, Charles L., Jr. Introduction and Exegesis to Habakkuk, *The Interpreter's Bible*. Nashville, Tenn.: Abingdon Press, 1956, VI, 973-1003.

———. Introduction and Exegesis to Nahum, *The Interpreter's Bible*, VI, 953-969.

———. Introduction and Exegesis to Zephaniah, *The Interpreter's Bible*, VI, 1007-1034.

Welch, Adam C. Commentary on Jeremiah, *The Abingdon Bible Commentary*, pp. 677-708.

CHAPTER 9: THE EXILIC PROPHETS

McKenzie, John L. (ed. and trans.). *Second Isaiah*, Vol. 20 in The Anchor Bible Series. Garden City, N.Y.: Doubleday & Co., 1968.

May, Herbert G. Introduction and Exegesis to Ezekiel, *The Interpreter's Bible*. Nashville, Tenn.: Abingdon Press, 1956. VI, 41-338.

Muilenburg, James. Introduction and Exegesis to Isaiah 40—55, *The Interpreter's Bible*. Nashville, Tenn.: Abingdon Press, 1956. V, 381-652.

Rogers, Robert W. Commentary on Isaiah 40—55, *The Abingdon Bible Commentary*. Nashville, Tenn.: Abingdon Press, 1929. Pp. 628-640, 653-667.

Wardle, W. L. Commentary on Ezekiel, *The Abingdon Bible Commentary*. Nashville, Tenn.: Abingdon Press, 1929. Pp. 714-745.

CHAPTER 10: THE POST-EXILIC PROPHETS

Dentan, Robert C. Introduction and Exegesis to Malachi, *The Interpreter's Bible*. Nashville, Tenn.: Abingdon Press, 1956. VI, 1117-1144.

———. Introduction and Exegesis to Zechariah 9—14, *The Interpreter's Bible*, VI, 1089-1114.

McFadyen, J. E. Commentary on Haggai, *The Abingdon Bible Commentary*. Nashville, Tenn.: Abingdon Press, 1929. Pp. 815-818.

———. Commentary on Malachi, *The Abingdon Bible Commentary*, pp. 832-836.

———. Commentary on Zechariah, *The Abingdon Bible Commentary*, pp. 819-831.

Muilenburg, James. Introduction and Exegesis to Isaiah 55—66, *The Interpreter's Bible*. Nashville, Tenn.: Abingdon Press, 1956. V, 381-422, 652-773.

Rogers, Robert W. Commentary on Isaiah 55—66. *The Abingdon Bible Commentary*, pp. 628-640, 668-677.

Thomas, D. Winton. Introduction and Exegesis to Haggai, *The Interpreter's Bible*, VI, 1037-1049.

———. Introduction and Exegesis to Zechariah 1—8, *The Interpreter's Bible*, VI, 1053-1088.

Thompson, John A. Introduction and Exegesis to Obadiah, *The Interpreter's Bible*, VI, 857-867.

———. Introduction and Exegesis to Joel, *The Interpreter's Bible*, VI, 729-760.

Watson, W. Gladstone. Commentary on Joel, *The Abingdon Bible Commentary*, 768-774.

———. Commentary on Obadiah, *The Abingdon Bible Commentary*, pp. 784-786.

CHAPTER 11: THE PSALMS

Chase, Mary Ellen. *The Psalms for the Common Reader*. New York: W. W. Norton Co., 1962.

Leslie, Elmer A. Introduction to the Psalms and Commentary on Psalms 1–72, *The Abingdon Bible Commentary*. Nashville, Tenn.: Abingdon Press, 1929. Pp. 509-554.

McCullough, W. Stewart. Introduction to Psalms and Exegesis to Psalms 72–92, 94, 97–99, 101–119, and 139, *The Interpreter's Bible*. Nashville, Tenn.: Abingdon Press, 1955. IV, 3-17, 379-502, 507-512, 521-532, 536-638, 712-717.

Shelton, W. A. Commentary on Psalms 72–150, *The Abingdon Bible Commentary*, pp. 554-601.

Taylor, William R. Exegesis to Psalms 1–71, 93, 95–96, 100, 120–138, 140–150, *The Interpreter's Bible*, IV, 17-378, 502-506, 512-521, 532-535, 638-711, 718-763.

CHAPTER 12: MINOR LYRICAL BOOKS

Jordan, W. G. Commentary on Lamentations, *The Abingdon Bible Commentary*. Nashville, Tenn.: Abingdon Press, 1929. Pp. 709-713.

Meek, Theophile J. Introduction and Exegesis to Lamentations, *The Interpreter's Bible*. Nashville, Tenn.: Abingdon Press, 1956. VI, 3-38.

CHAPTER 13: JOB

Crook, Margaret B. *The Cruel God: Job's Search for the Meaning of Suffering*. Boston: Beacon Press, 1959.

Jung, Carl G. *Answer to Job*. Translated by R. F. C. Hull. Cleveland, Ohio: World Publishing Co., 1965. Meridian Books paperback.

Kallen, H. M. *The Book of Job as a Greek Tragedy*. New York: Moffat, Yard and Co., 1918. Reprinted in paperback by Hill & Wang.

Lofthouse, W. F. Commentary on Job, *The Abingdon Bible Commentary*. Nashville, Tenn.: Abingdon Press, 1929. Pp. 483-508.

Pope, Marvin H. (ed. and trans.). Job, Vol. 15 in The Anchor Bible Series. Garden City, New York: Doubleday & Co., 1965.

Sanders, Paul S. (ed.). *Twentieth Century Interpretations of the Book of Job*. Englewood Cliffs, N.J.; Prentice-Hall, 1968. Paperback.

Terrien, Samuel. Introduction and Exegesis to Job, *The Interpreter's Bible*. Nashville, Tenn.: Abingdon Press, 1954. III, 877-1198.

CHAPTER 14: THE SONG OF SOLOMON

Gordis, Robert. *The Song of Songs: A Study, Modern Translation, and Commentary*. New York: Jewish Theological Seminary of America, 1954.

Jastrow, Morris. *The Song of Songs*. Philadelphia: J. B. Lippincott Co., 1921.

Meek, Theophile J. Introduction and Exegesis to The Song of Solomon, *The Interpreter's Bible*. Nashville, Tenn.: Abingdon Press, 1956. V, 81-98, 103-148.

Pfeiffer, Robert H. Commentary on The Song of Solomon, *The Abingdon Bible Commentary.* Nashville, Tenn.: Abingdon Press, 1929. Pp. 622-627.

CHAPTER 15: FOURTH CENTURY STORIES ADVOCATING TOLERANCE

Bickerman, Elias J. *Four Strange Books of the Bible: Jonah, Daniel, Koheleth, and Esther.* New York: Schocken Books, 1968.

Graham, William C. Commentary on Jonah, *The Abingdon Bible Commentary.* Nashville, Tenn.: Abingdon Press, 1929. Pp. 787-790.

———. Commentary on Ruth, *The Abingdon Bible Commentary,* pp. 377-380.

Smart, James D. Introduction and Exegesis to Jonah, *The Interpreter's Bible.* Nashville, Tenn.: Abingdon Press, 1956. VI, 871-894.

Smith, Louise Pettibone. Introduction and Exegesis to Ruth, *The Interpreter's Bible.* Nashville, Tenn.: Abingdon Press, 1953. II, 829-852.

CHAPTER 16: SECOND AND FIRST CENTURY STORIES ENCOURAGING INTEGRITY

Anderson, Bernhard W. Introduction and Exegesis to Esther, *The Interpreter's Bible.* Nashville, Tenn.: Abingdon Press, 1954. III, 823-874.

Bickerman, Elias J. *Four Strange Books of the Bible: Jonah, Daniel, Koheleth, and Esther.* New York: Schocken Books, 1968.

Jeffery, Arthur. Introduction and Exegesis to Daniel, *The Interpreter's Bible.* Nashville, Tenn.: Abingdon Press, 1956. VI, 341-549.

Pfeiffer, Robert H. Commentary on Esther, *The Abingdon Bible Commentary.* Nashville, Tenn.: Abingdon Press, 1929. Pp. 477-482.

CHAPTER 17: ETHICAL PRECEPTS AND CYNICAL PESSIMISM

Bickerman, Elias J. *Four Strange Books of the Bible: Jonah, Daniel, Koheleth, and Esther.* New York: Schocken Books, 1968.

Fritsch, Charles T. Introduction and Exegesis to Proverbs, *The Interpreter's Bible.* Nashville, Tenn.: Abingdon Press, 1955. IV, 767-779.

Gordis, Robert. *Koheleth, the Man and His World.* Rev. ed. New York: Schocken Books, 1968. Paperback.

Jastrow, Morris. *A Gentle Cynic.* Philadelphia: J. B. Lippincott Co., 1919.

Rankin, O. S. *Israel's Wisdom Literature.* Edinburgh: T. and T. Clark, 1936.

Scott, R. B. Y. (ed. and trans.). *Proverbs and Ecclesiastes,* Vol. 18 in The Anchor Bible Series. Garden City, N.Y.: Doubleday & Co., 1965.

Index

(Page numbers in **boldface** indicate the principal treatment of a subject.)

Aaron, 9, 65, 67, 69, **70-71**, 74-75, 146, 194, 360
Aaronites, 70
Abana River, 131
Abdon, 87
Abednego, 268, **312-314**, 332
Abel, 53
Abiah, 98
Abiathar, 96, 106, 109, 110
Abijam, 117
Abimelech, 86, 87, **91**, 105
Abinadab, 102
Abishag, 110
Abner, 105
Abraham (Abram), 5, 8-9, 13, 16, 50, 52, **55-57**, 58, 59, 70, 140, 259, 350
Abraham and Isaac, 58
Absalom, **108-109**, 140, 253
Achan, 82-83
Achior, 325-326, 328
Achor, 83
"Acrostic Dialogue on Theodicy," 274
Acts of the Apostles (book), 18, 20, 28, 164, 177, 232
Acts of Solomon, 111
Adam, 4, 46, **53**, 110, 140, 350, 360
Addison, Joseph, 248
Additions to the Book of Esther, 330. *See also* Rest of Esther
"Adonais," 264
Adonijah, 110
Adonis, 288
Aeschylus, 176, 273, 275
Aesop, 338
Agag, 100-101

Agagite, 331, 334
Agamemnon, 124
Agur, 340
Ahab, 11-12, 111, 112, 117, 119, 120, **122-125**, 126, 127, 128, 129, 130, 132, 139, 147, 164, 255, 271
Ahasuerus, 144, **330-335**
Ahaz, 116, 117, 168, 176, 181
Ahaziah, 12, 117, 119, 129, 132, 133
Ahikar, 307
Ahitophel, 108-109
Aholibah, 204
Ai, 82, 83
Ajalon, 83
Alcaeus, 207
Alcuin, 26
Alexander the Great, 5, 12-13, 24, 150, 154, 208, 317, 320
Alexandrian Sanhedrin, 25
Amaziah, 12, 117, 169, 172
"America," 21
American Standard Version, 16, 38-39, **40-41**, 43, 49
Amittai, 301
Ammonites, origin of, 57
Amnon, 108
Amon, 76, 118, 134, 185
Amos, 11, 127, 165, 167, **168-172**, 173, 176, 178, 181, 190, 193, 202, 219, 222, 223
Amos (book), 17, 60, 72, 164, 167, **168-172**, 186, 187, 232, 242
Anak, Anakim, 74, 84
Analects, 338
Anathoth, 190
Antigone, 92, 307
Antiochus III, 150-151, 154, 158

Antiochus IV (Epiphanes), 13, 23, 45, 150-151, **154**, 155-156, 158-159, 252, 268, 306, 312-314, 317-320, 325, 349, 358

Antiochus V (Eupator), 208

Apocalypse, 20. *See also* Revelation

Apocalyptic literature, 357-361

Apocrypha, origin and transmissions of, 27-28

Apollo, 278

Apology, 354

Apostles, 23

Aramaic Bible, 26-27

Arameans, 278

Ares, 16

Aristotle, 274

Ark of the Covenant, 70, 82, 98, 106-107, 109, 140, 245

Armageddon, Battle of, 232

Artaxerxes I, 138, 141, 143, 144-146, 148, 330-334

Artaxerxes II, 138, 141, 143, 330, 333, 360

Artemis, 278

Asa, 117, 141

Asaph, 241

Asenath, 63

Ashdod, 98, 146

Asher, 60

Asher (tribe), 88

Ashtoreth, 115

Asmodeus, 308, 310

Assideans, 152

Assurbanipal, 4

Assyrians, 11

Astarte, 288

Athaliah, 12, 116, 117, **132-133**

Augustine of Canterbury, 29

Aurelius, Marcus, 338

Authorized Version. *See* King James Version

Azariah (Abednego), 268-269

Azariah (Uzziah), 12, 117, 168, 175

Azarias, 268-269

Baal, baalim, 12, 90, 117, 118, 119, **122**, 124, 125, 126, 128, 129, 133, 164

Baal-zebub, 129

Baasha, 117, 119

Babel, Tower of, 55

"Babylonian Job," 274

Babylonian Exile (or Captivity), 12, **135-136**

Balaam, 75, 163, 327

Baladin, 134

Balak, 75

Barak, 88

Baruch, 191-192, **235-236**

Baruch (book), 27, 165, 219, **235-236**, 338

Bates, E. S., 274

Bathsheba, **107-108**, 110, 139, 140

Bay Psalm Book, 241

Beersheba, 6, 171

Bel, 236, 321

Bel and the Dragon, 27, 295, 311, 312, **320-322**

Belshazzar, 137, 312, **314-315**, 319, 334

Belshazzar's Feast, 314-315

Ben-hadad, 122, 124, 132

Benjamin, 60, 62

Benjamin (tribe), 10, 11, 49, 88, 99, 116, 137, 143

Benjamites, 95

Beowulf, 89 104

Ben Sira. *See* Jesus, Son of Sirach

Bensly, R. L., 359

Berechiah, 222

Bethel, 119, 126, 168, 169, 171, 226

Beth-horon, 145

Bethlehem, 103, 109, 298

Bethshemesh, 98

Bethulia, 325-326

Beza, Theodore, 32

Bible: classification of books of, 19-21; economic and social backgrounds of, 13-14; nature of, 18-19; origin and early transmission of, 21-29; sources of, 45-46. *See also* English Bible and names of particular Bibles and books of the Bible

Bible—An American Translation, 42

Bildad, 276, 279, 281-283

Bilhah, 60

Bishop's Bible, 33-34, 35
Blessing of Moses, 80
Blyth, Francis, 37
Boaz, 299-301
Book of Common Prayer, 32
Book of the Dead, 3
Book of the Kings of Israel, 267
Browning, Robert, 194, 275
Bunyan, John, 33
Bunyan, Paul, 92

Caedmon, 66
Caesars, 3, 5
Cain, 53
Calchas, 124
Caleb, 74, 76, 87
Calvin, John, 32, 241
Cambyses, 223
Canaan, 74, 81-84. *See also* Palestine
Canaanites, origin of, 54
Canticles, 37. *See also* Song of Solomon
Carchemish, 184, 190
Carlyle, Thomas, 273, 347
Carmel, Mount, 128, 170
Cervantes, Miguel, 304
Chaldeans, 4-5. *See also* Babylonian Exile
Challoner, Richard, 31
Chanukah, 156. *See also* Hanukkah
Charlemagne, 26
Chase, Mary Ellen, 99, 105
Chebar River, 201, 209
Chemosh, 115
"Chicago Bible," 42
Christ. *See* Jesus Christ
Chronicler, 138-144, 148, 153, 267
Chronicles (books I and II), 19, 28, 30, 31, 133, **137-141,** 143, 148, 199, 263, 267, 301
Chronicles of the Kings of Israel, 23, 111
Chronicles of the Kings of Judah, 23, 106
Chronicon, 138
Cimmerians, 184
Cinderella, 60-61, 299
Code of the Covenant, 69, 78

Codes of the Pentateuch, 78
Codex Alexandrinus, 25, 241
Codex Ephraemi, 25
Codex Sinaiticus, 25
Codex Vaticanus, 25
Coffin, Henry S., 218
Colossians, Epistle to (book), 354
"Comforters," Job's, 229, 276, 279, 280-283, 286, 337
Complete Bible: An American Translation, 42
"Confraternity Bible," 37, 38
Confucius, 338
Coniah (Jehoiachin), 190
Connelly, Marc, 54
Corinthians I and II, Epistles to (books), 74, 91, 175, 198, 288, 358
Covenant, 16, **55-56,** 57, 70, 78-79, 107, 173, 191, 214, 221, 252, 259, 338
Covenant Code, 78
Coverdale, Miles, 31-32
Coverdale Bible, 28, 31
Cranmer, Thomas, 31-32
Cranmer's Bible, 32
Creation, 4; two accounts of, 52-53
Cromwell, Oliver, 33
Cromwell, Thomas, 31-32
Cromwell's Bible, 32
Crucifixion of Christ, 217
Cursive manuscripts, 25
Cyaxares, 5
Cyrus, 5, 12, 137-138, 141, 143, 144, 148, 210-211, 213-214, 219, 319, 321-322

D Document, 49, **50,** 51, 76, 85, 134
Dagon, 94, 98, 146
Damascus, 10, 14, 131, 167, 170, 171
Dan, 60
Dan (city), 119, 126
Dan (tribe), 80, 88, 95. *See also* Danites
Danel, 311
Daniel, 295, 311-324, 334, 338, 357, 302

Daniel (book), 20, 23, 164, 201, 203, 235, 268, 295, 306, 358, 362, **311-320**, 321, 323, 338, 358

Daniel Cycle, **311-324**

Danites, 86, 95

Darius I, 144, 148-149, 220, 223, 312, 334

"Darius the Mede," 315-316, 319

Darius III, 12

David, 10, 22, 46, 49-50, 56, 96-97, 99, 100-101, **102-111**, 115, 132, 134, 139, 140, 164, 180, 197, 200, 207, 221, 227, 234, 237, 241, 242, 253, 287, 298, 338, 340, 346, 350; and Absalom, 108-109; anointment and rise to fame, 103; and Bathsheba, 107-108; decline and death of, 109-110; and Goliath, 103-104; and Jonathan, 104-105; and Michal, 106-107; public achievements of, 105-106

David's Lament of Absalom, 109

David's Lament for Saul and Jonathan, 105

Dead Sea Scrolls, 14, 22, 29, 306

Debir, 87

Deborah, 87, **88-89**, 90

Deborah's Song, **88-89**, 187, 237

Dedan, 179

Delilah, 94

Deluge, The, 54-55

Dentan, R. C., 357

Deutero-Isaiah. *See* Isaiah (book)

Deuteronomic Code, 50, 78

Deuteronomic reforms, 185, 191, 193

Deuteronomist, 50, 64, 76, 79, 81, 85-86, 229, 337

Deuteronomy (book), 16, 19, 20, 50, 56, **76-80**, 84, 85, 153, 229, 250, 298, 299

Dialogues, 338

Diaspora. *See* Dispersion

Dibhre Hayyamin, 138

Dies Irae, 186

Dinah, 60

Dinsmore, C. A., 242, 248

Dionysus, 164, 288

Dispersion, 191, 197, 230, 313, 329

Divided Kingdom, history of, **10-12**, 14, **116-120**

Domitian, 359

Don Quixote, 304

Douai, 34

Douay Bible, 28, 34, **38-39**, 311, 314, 320, 330, 348

Dramatic literature, 271-294

Driver, S. R., 274

Dunsinane, 102

E Document, 49, **50**, 51, 68, 85

Earlier Prophets (section of Bible), 19

East Aramaic Old Testament, 26-27

Ecbatana, 307, 308, 309

Ecclesiastes (book), 19, 23, 31, 237, 338, 339, **346-348**, 352

Ecclesiasticus (book), 20, 27, 194, 338, 339, **348-352**

Eden, Garden of, 53

Edomites, origin of, 58

Eglon, 87

Egypt, 3-4, 136; Abraham in, 56; Hebrew bondage in, 9, 63; Hebrew escape from, 9-10, 65-66; Joseph in, 61-63; plagues of, 65-66

"Egyptian Hallel," 247

Ehud, 60, 87, 88

Ekron, 98, 129

Elah, 119

Eleazar (scribe), 159-160

Eleazar (son of Aaron), 74

Eleazar (son of Mattathias), 154, 155

Elhanan, 104

Eli, 54, 97-98, 164

Eliakim, 118, 135, 190

Eliashib, 146

Elihu, 274, 276, 277, 284-285

Elijah, 11, 97, 111, 119, 122, 125, **126-130**, 139, 163, 164, 230, 350; and Ahab, 129; and Ahaziah, 129; ascension of, 129-130; contest at Mt. Carmel, 128; drought prophesied by, 127-128; Elisha anointed by, 129; second exile of, 128-129

Elijah Cycle, 126-130

Elimelech, 298, 299

Elisha, 11, 111, 119, 126, 128, 129, 130-132, 163; children cursed by, 131; miracles of assistance performed by, 130-131; Naaman healed by, 131-132; nature of, 130; Syrians confounded by, 132

Elisha Cycle, 130-132

Eliphaz, 273, 276-283

Elizabeth I (Tudor), 33, 34

Elkanah, 97

Elkosh, 186

Elon, 87

Elysium, 354

Endor, 102, 140

English Bible, 20, 23; before 1611, 29-34; modern versions of, 34-44

English Revised Version, 38-39, 40-41, 42, 258, 360

Enoch, 357

Ephraim, 60, 63, 259

Ephraim, Mount, 84, 95

Ephraim (tribe), Ephraimites, 10, 79, 88, 90, 140, 145, 174

Ephraim (state), 109, 145

Ephraim (wood), 109

Episcopal Committee of the Confraternity of Christian Doctrine, 37

"Epithalamion," 289

Esarhaddon, 307

Esau, 58-59, 140, 227

Esdraelon, 6

Esdras, 359-360. See also Ezra

Esdras I-IV (books), 27-28, 137, 147-149, 359-362

Esther, 328-335

Esther (book) and The Rest of Esther, 19, 20, 23, 31, 46, 295, 306, 328-335

Ethan, 241

Euripdes, 92, 274

Eusebius Hieronymus. See Jerome, Saint

Eve, 4, 46, 53

Evil-merodach, 136

Ewe Lamb, Parable of, 107-108

Exile. See Babylonian Exile

Exilic Prophets, 199-217

Exodus (book), 16, 19, 50, 51, 63-70, 72, 74, 78, 84, 88, 95, 130

Exodus (Caedmonian poem), 66

Exodus (period), 9-10, 63-80, 259

Ezekiel, 185, 194, 199, 200-210, 211, 222, 228, 271

Ezekiel (book), 19, 31, 32, 164, 165, 194, 199, 200-210, 220, 227, 232, 271, 311, 357-358

Ezra, 12, 138, 141-147, 148, 150, 152, 220, 258, 297, 319, 350, 357, 359-362. See also Esdras

Ezra (book), 28, 137, 138, 141-147, 148, 153, 213, 214. See also Esdras (books I-IV)

Fable, 91

Fables, 338

Faerie Queene, 320

Fall of Man, 53

Feast of Booths, 143

Feast of St. Luke, 351

Feast of Tabernacles, 143, 233

Five Documents of the Hexateuch, 49-51

Five Rolls, 20

Flood (Genesis), 4, 17, 54

Four Codes of the Pentateuch, 78

Franklin, Benjamin, 338

Gabriel, 318

Gad, 60

Gad (tribe), 76, 88. See also Gilead, Gileadites

Galatians, Epistle to (book), 189

Gath, 98, 102

Gaza, 94

Gedaliah, 136, 190

Gehazi, 132

Genesis, 9, 15, 16, 19, 20, 30, 39, 46, 49, 50, 51-63, 72, 75, 128, 153, 227, 237, 250, 295

Geneva Bible, 32-33, 34

Genung, J. F., 274, 275

Gerizim, Mount, 91

Geshem, 145

Gibeah, 86, 95

Gibeon, Gibeonites, 83

Gideon, 10, 60, 87, **90-91**
Gilboa, 102
Gilead, Gileadites, 88, 92, 109, 127, 170, 195
Gilgal, 130, 171
Gilgamesh, Epic of, 17
Gnostic heresies, 354
Goël, 282
Goethe, J. W. von, 298
Gog, 208
Golden calf, worship of, 69-70
Goliath, 101, **103-104**, 140
Gomer, 174
Gomorrah, 57
Good Samaritan, Parable of, 304
Good Shepherd, 207
Goodspeed, E. J., 42
Gordon, A. R., 42
Goshen, 62
Gospels, 20, 28, 29, 30, 241. *See also* John, Luke, Mark, Matthew
Great Bible, **31-32**, 33, 35
Greece, Greeks, 5, 150
Greek Old Testament, 24-25. *See also* Septuagint
Green Pastures, 54
Grendel, 104
Gulliver's Travels, 320
Gyges, 208

H Document, 48, **49-51**
Habakkuk, 184, **188-190**, 322
Habakkuk (book), 165, 184, **188-190**, 246, 265
Hagar, 56
Haggai, **220-221**, 222
Haggai (book), 219, **220-221**, 222
Ham, 54
Haman, 329, 334
Hamlet, 69
Hammurabi, 4
Handel, G. F., 92, 177, 314
Hannah, 97
Hannah's Song, 97
Hanukkah, 151, 156. *See also* Chanukah
Haran, 9, 55, 59
Hasidim, 152

Hasmon, Hasmoneans. *See* Maccabees
Hazael, 129
Hazor, 84
Hebrew Bible, 22-24; (1917), 39, **41-42**
Hebrew language, 21-22
Hebrews. *See* Israelites, Jews
Hebrews, Epistle to (book), 207
Hebron, 50, 56, 57, 105, 108, 140
Heliodorus, 158-159
Heman, 241
Henry VIII (Tudor), 31-32
Hercules, 92
Hereford, Nicholas of, 30
Hermon, Mount, 6, 150
Herod (the Great), 152
Herodotus, 96
Hexateuch, 19, **49-51**, 63, 74, 76, 80, 85, 138, 259
Hezekiah, 12, 116, 118, **133-134**, 141, 168, 175, 180, 181, 185, 210, 267, 339
Hieronymus. *See* Jerome, Saint
Hilkiah, 134
Hiram, 115, 140
History and biography, 45-161
History (section of the Old Testament), 20
Hitler, Adolf, 108
Hittites, 4, 107, 147
Holines Code, **50-51**, 71, 78, 208
Holofernes, 325-327
Homer, 307
Hophra, 204
Hor, Mount, 74
Horeb, Mount, 67, 78. *See also* Sinai, Mount
Hosea, 11, 163, 165, 167, 168, **173-175**, 176, 181, 185, 193, 218, 301
Hosea (book), 17, 20, 73, 164, 167, **173-175**, 187, 203
Hoshea, 120
Housman, A. E., 347-348
Hugo, Cardinal of Saneto Caro, 32
Humman, 329
Hur, 67
Hushai, 109
Hyrcanus, John, 151

Ibzan, 87
Iddo, 222
Idumea, 228
Ikhnaton, Pharaoh, 249
Iliad, 124, 307
In Memoriam, 264
Iphigenia at Aulis, 92
Isaac, 13, 52, 55, **57-58**, 59, 259
Ishmael, Ishmaelites, 56
Isaiah, 97, 111, 118, 133, 134, 164, 168, **175-181**, 185, 190, 201, 210, 218, 271, 301
Isaiah (book), 17, 19, 20, 22, 31, 165, 167, 168, **175-181**, 186, 187, 189, 199, 204, **210-218**, 219, 222, 224, 226-227, 232, 235, 265, 271, 357
Ishbosheth, 105
Ishtar, 288, 329
Israel, Israelites: conquest of Canaan by, 80-84; Divided Kingdom of, 10-12; early history of, 8-9; during the Exile, 12, 137-141; exodus from Egypt of, 9-10, 63-80; under judges, 10, 85-99; Maccabean revolt of, 150-151; under Macedonian rule, 12-13, 150-151; under Persian rule, 12, 141-149; United Kingdom of, 13-14, 99-116, 149. *See also* Jews
Issachar, 60
Issachar (tribe), 88
Issus, 12

J Document, **49-50**, 51-52, 68, 85
Jabesh, 102
Jabesh-gilead, 95
Jacob, 9, 13, 52, 55, **58-59**, 61-63, 80, 133, 172, 216, 227, 259
Jael, 60, 88-89
Jair, 87
Jakeh, 340
James, Epistle of, 338
James I (Stuart), 33, 35
Jamnites, 160
Japheth, 54
Jason (brother of Onias), 159
Jason of Cyrene, 157
Jastrow, Morris, 346

Jebusites, 105, 147
Jehoahaz, 117, 118, 119, 120, 135, 190, 205
Jehoash (Joash), 12, 117, 120, 133
Jehoiachin, 118, 135-136, 138, 184, 190, 199, 200, 201, 204, 205, 220
Jehoiada, 133
Jehoiakim, 12, 118, 135, 190, 192, 193, 218
Jehoram (Joram), 12, 117, 119, 126, 132
Jehoshaphap, 117, 124, 139, 141
Jehosheba, 133
Jehovah, 16, 41
Jehu, 11, 117, 119, 125-126, 129-130
Jephthah, 87, **91-92**
Jeremiah, 27, 141, 165, 185, **190-198**, 199, 200-201, 202, 206, 218, 219, 235, 262-263, 318, 337
Jeremiah (book), 9, 19, 31, 60, 161, 165, 184, 187, **190-198**, 199, 203, 204, 206, 235, 236, 265, 318, 337
Jeremiah, Epistle of, **161**, 236
Jeremias (Jeremiah), 161
Jericho, 82
Jeroboam I, 10-11, 69, 116, 119, **121-122**
Jeroboam II, 11, 120, 167, 169, 172, 179, 301, 307
Jerome, Saint, 26, 27, 29, 30, 138, 330, 359
Jerusalem: fall to Babylon, 12, **135-136**; fall to Rome, 13; dirge for (Lamentations), 262-266; geography of, 6; made capital of United Kingdom, 105
Jeshua. *See* Jesus, son of Sirach
Jesse, 103, 180, 224, 299
Jesus Christ, 17, 23, 25, 45, 70, 74, 77, 144, 152, 161, 183, 193, 198, 217-218, 229, 234, 244, 255, 282, 288, 304, 338, 343, 355, 359
Jesus Ben Sira. *See* Jesus, son of Sirach
Jesus, son of Sirach, 27, 348-352
Jethro, 50, 64
Jewish Publication Society of America, 41-42

404

Jews: early religious views, 15-17;
summary of early history of, 7-12.
See also Israel, Israelites

Jezebel, 11, 12, 117, 119, 120, 122,
125-126, 128, 129, 132, 164, 255

Jezreel, 125-126, 128, 129

Joab, 106-111, 338

Joan of Arc, 164, 328

Joannan, 154

Joash. *See* Jehoash

Job, 189, 223, 254, **273-286**, 311,
337, 338, 360, 361

Job (book), 19, 20, 31, 188, 211,
215, 223, 229, 271, **273-286**, 307

Joel (prophet), 230-233

Joel (son of Samuel), 98

Joel (book), 165, 219, **230-233**, 358

John I, Epistle of (book), 354

John, Gospel of (book), 20, 127,
207, 229, 234, 355

John the Baptist, 56, 127, 230

John Hyrcanus, 151, 157

Jonah, 301-305

Jonah (book), 17, 30, 164, 295, 297,
301-305, 306, 326

Jonathan (son of Saul), 100-102,
104-105

Jonathan Apphus, 151, 154-155,
156

Joram. *See* Jehoram

Joseph, 52, 55, **60-63**, 75, 133, 208,
259, 350

Josephus, 28

Josiah, 50, 76, 111, 118, **134-135**,
141, 148, 185, 190, 191, 193

Joshua (high priest), 224-225

Joshua (son of Nun), 10, 49, 74, 76,
80-84, 85, 86, 130

Joshua (book), 15, 16, 19, 20, 21,
31, 49, 50, 51, **80-84**, 86, 130

Jotham (king), 117, 168, 175, 181

Jotham (son of Gideon), 91

Jotham's Fable, 91, 295, 338

Joye, George, 31

Jubilate, 246

Judah, 49, 60-62

Judah, Kingdom of (Southern Kingdom): establishment of, 12, 116;
fall of, 12, 135-136; history of,

11-12, 116-118, 121-122, 132-
136; sovereigns of, 117-118. *See
also* Israel, Israelites, Jews

Judah (tribe), 10-11, 49, 80, 105,
116, 137, 143, 144

Judas Maccabeus, 13, 150-151, 153-
154, **155-156**, 160-161, 325, 328

Judas (son of Simon Thassi), 157

Jude (book), 20, 358

Judith, 325-328

Judith (book), 27, **324-328**

Judges, 15, 19, 50, 56, 60, 72, **85-95**,
105, 138, 237, 295, 298, 320, 326,
338

Judgment Day, 228, 230-232, 261,
318, 353

Kadesh, 67, 74

Kallen, H. M., 274

Kassites, 4

Keating, Joseph, 37

Kedar, 179

King James Version, 1, 20, 28, 33,
34, **35-37**, 38-39, 40, 42, 43, 72,
176, 180, 236, 239, 247, 250, 255,
258, 277, 282, 288, 303, 346, 360

Kings (books I and II), 19, 23, 50,
54, 76, 85, **104-136**, 138-141, 153,
164, 167, 176, 177, 182, 199, 205,
206, 245, 255, 267, 271, 301, 339

Kishon River, 88, 89

Knox, John, 32

Knox, Ronald A., 37

Knox Bible, 37

Koheleth, 346-348

Koiné, 42

Korah, 241

Laban, 59

Laish, 95

Lament for Saul and Jonathan, 237

Lamentations, 19, 31, 164, 227, 235,
236, 237, 239, **262-266**

La Rochefoucauld, 338

Last Supper, 198

Latin Old Testament, 26. *See also*
Vulgate

Latter Prophets, 19, 301

Lattey, Cuthbert, 37

Law (section of Old Testament), 19-20, 23

Leah, 59-61

Lebanon, Mount, 6

Lemuel, 340

Lesbos, 207

Leto, 278

Letter of Jeremiah. *See* Jeremiah, Epistle of

Levi, 60, 119

Levi (tribe), 63, 69, 80, 121

Levites (Temple attendants), 65, 69, 70-71, 73, 76, 95, 127, 139-142, 145-147, 209, 229, 304

Leviticus, 16, 19, 50, 51, **70-71**, 72, 78, 208, 220, 298

"Lion's Den," **315-316**, 320

"Little Hallel," 247

Logos, 355

Lollards, 30

Lot, 50, 56-57; wife of, 57

Lowth, Robert, 237, 274

Luke, 351

Luke, Gospel of (book), 18, 56, 97, 127, 212, 232, 237, 304, 358

Luther, Martin, 241, 246, 273, 307, 325

Lycidas, 264

Lydia, 208, 211

Lyric poetry, 237-270

Macarthur, J. R., 176, 242

Macbeth, 102

Maccabean Revolt, 13, **150-151**

Maccabeans, Maccabees, 13, **150-161**. *See also* Judas Maccabeus

Maccabees, I and II (books), 13, 20-21, 27-28, 45, 72, **152-161**

Macduff, 102

Macedonia, rule over Palestine, 12-13, 150

Machir (tribe), 88

Magnificat, 97, 237

Magog, 208

Major Prophets, 20

Malachi, 127, **228-230**

Malachi (book), 20, 31-32, 127, 165, 219, **228-230**, 232

Mamre, 56

Manasseh (king), 76, 118, 134, 135, 175, 185, 218, 267. *See also* Manasses

Manasseh (son of Joseph), 60, 63

Manasseh (tribe), 10, 27, 80, 88, 140

Manasses, Prayer of (book), 27, 239, 262, 267-268, 169. *See also* Manasseh (king)

Manna, 67, 73

Manoah, 92

Marah, 67

Marduk, 236, 320, 321, 329

Mareshah, 181

Mark, Gospel of (book), 21, 60, 127, 183, 212, 229, 230, 232, 234, 310, 358

Martin, Gregory, 34

Mary (mother of Jesus), 97, 237

Mary I (Tudor), 32, 34

Masoretes, 23-24

Masoretic text, 23, 39, 41

Masti, 329

Mattaniah, 118, 135, 190

Mattathias (father of Judas Maccabeus), 13, 151, **154-155**, 156

Mattathias (son of Simon), 157

Matthew, 18

Matthew, Gospel of (book), 18, 20, 21, 70, 127, 183, 193, 207, 212, 232, 234, 304, 310, 339, 343, 358

Matthew, Thomas, 31

Matthew Bible, **31**, 32

Medes, Median Empire, 5, 184, 186, 211, 307, 308, 310, 311, 313, 316, 317, 325, 360

Meek, T. J., 42

Megiddo, 89

Megilloth, 20, 262

Melchishua, 102

Melkart, 122

Menahem, 120

Menelaus (priest), 159

Mephibosheth, 105, 109

Merab, 104

Merneptah, 9

Merom, 84

Meshach, 268, **312-314**, 338

Messiah, Messianic Age, 17, 25, 103, 127, 176, **180-181**, 197, 199, 207, 218, 221, 224-225, 233-234, 255-256, 313, 316, 338, 359, 361-362

Messiah (oratorio), 177

Methuselah, 53

Metzger, B. M., 268

Micah, 164, 168, **181-183**, 185, 190, 193, 202, 222

Micah (book), 167, **181-183**, 187, 232

Micaiah, 124-125

Michael, angel, 318, 319

Michal, 101, 102, **106-107**

Michelangelo, 70

Midianites, 89-90

"Mighty Fortress Is Our God," 246

Milcom, 115

Milton, John, 92, 176, 264

Minor Prophets, 20, 23

Mizpah, 100

Moabites, origin of, 57

Moffatt, James, 39, 41, 42

Moffatt Bible, 39, 41, 42

Molech, 115

Mordecai, 329, **331-334**

Moses, 9, 15, 49, 50, **63-70**, 71, 72, 75-81, 84, 127, 130, 133, 135, 146, 147, 152, 163, 164, 177, 193, 212, 218, 226, 241, 242, 260, 324, 329, 350, 351, 360; birth of, 63-64; Blessing of, 80; call of, 64-65; death of, 80; exile of, 64; Last Song of, 79; as leader of Hebrew Exodus, 66-79; plagues on Egypt brought by, 65-66; Ten Commandments and other laws received by, 67-68

Moulton, R. G., 274, 280

Naaman, 131-132

Naboth, 119, 125-126, **129**

Nabunaid, 137

Nadab, 119

Nahum, 164-165, 184, **186-188**

Nahum (book), 186-188

Naomi, 298-301

Naphtali, 60

Naphthali (tribe), 80, 88, 183

Nathan, 106-108, 110, 164

Nazarite, Nazirite, rites of, 72

Nebo, Mount, 80

Nebuchadrezzar, 4, 23, 116, 118, **135-136**, 137, 143, 149, 184, 190, 191, 197, 204-206, 213, 268-269, 309, **312-315**, 320, 325, 327, 333, 334

Nehemiah, 12, 46, 137, 138, 142, 143, **144-146**, 147-148, 220, 258, 297, 319, 350

Nehemiah (book), 19, 28, 137, 138, **141-147**, 219, 224

"New Covenant," 197-198

New English Bible, 44

New Jerusalem, 201, 208-209, 227, 233, 361

Nicanor, 151, 156, 160-161

Nicanor's Day, 151, 156, 158, 160-161

Nicholas of Hereford, 30

Nineveh, Ninevites, 12, 134, 184, 186-187, **301-304**, 307, 309

Noah, 17, **53-54**, 55, 311

Noah (mystery play), 55

Noah, Mrs., 54

Northern Kingdom. *See* Israel, Israelites

Numbers, 10, 50-51, 54, **71-76**, 78, 84, 194, 327

"O God, Our Help in Ages Past," 260

Obadiah, 227-228

Obadiah (book), 165, 219, **227-228**, 230

Obed, 299

Oedipus, 320

Oedipus at Colonus, 274

Oholah, 204

"Old Hundred," 246

Old Latin Bible, 25, 29, 359

Omar Khayyám, 194, 347

Omri, 11, 119, 122, 126

Onias, **158-159**, 160-161

Ophir, 14

"Orphan Psalms," 241-242

Osiris, 4, 288

Othniel, 87
Ozias, 326

P Document, 49, **51**, 52, 220
Palestine: geography of, 3, 5-8; history of, *see* Israel, Jews
Paltiel, 106
Parable, 91
Paraleopomena, 138
Parallelism in Hebrew poetry, 237-238
Parker, Matthew, 33
Parker's Bible, 34
Parmelee, Alice, 96
Passover, **65-66**, 118, 127, 135
Paul, 74, 152, 175, 177, 189, 207, 343, 351, 354
Pekah, 120
Pekaliah, 120
Pentateuch, 19, 22, 24-25, 27, 42, 49, 71, 72, 78, 80, 351. *See also* Hexateuch
Pentecost, 232, 308
Perizzites, 147
Persia, rule over Palestine, 12, **137-138**
Persians, The, 275
Peshitta, Peshitto, **26-27,** 42
Peter, 232
Peter, I and II, Epistle of (books), 207, 358
Phaedo, 354
Phalti (Phaltiel), 106
Pharaoh, 3; in time of Ezekiel, 204; in time of Joseph, 61-62; in time of Josiah, 135; in time of Moses, 9, 61, 63, **65-66,** 164
Pharisees, Pharisaism, 77, 151, 152, 157, 160, 350
Pharpar River, 131
Philistines: and David, **98-99,** 105; and Samson, 87, **89-90**
Philo Judaeus, 355
Plagues of Egypt, 65-66
Plato, 353
Poe, Edgar Allan, 195
"Poem of the Righteous Sufferer," 273-274
Poetics, 274

Poetry (section of Old Testament), 20. *See also* Lyric poetry
Pompey the Great, 151
Poor Richard's Almanac, 338
Potiphar, 61; wife of, 61
Potter and the Clay, Parable of, 194
"Praise of Famous Men," 350
"Praise of the Physician," 351
Prayer of Azariah, 268
Prayer of Manasses (book), 27, 28, 239, 262, **267-268,** 269
Price, I. M., 41
Priesthood, establishment of, 69
Priestly Code, 78, 220
Prodigal Son, 304
Prometheus Bound, 273, 275
Prophetic literature, 163-236
Prophetism, origin of, 163-164
Prophets (section of Old Testament), 307
Prophets, Earlier, 19, 164
Prophets, "ecstatic," 164
Prophets, Latter, 19
Proverbs, 19, 31, 114, 238, 239, 260, 307, 337-338, **339-345,** 346, 349-354
Psalms, 19, 29-33, 38, 73, 77, 122, 192, 196, 199, 202, 207, 210, 211, 215, 227, 238, 239, **241-261,** 269, 281, 307, 338, 349, 353
Psalter, 29, 32. *See also* Psalms
Pseudepigraphs, 27
Ptahhotep, 338
Ptolemies, 13
Ptolemy II (Philadelphus), 24, 150
Purim, Festival of, **328-329,** 332-334
Purvey, John, 30

Qohéleth. *See* Koheleth
Qumran Scrolls, 22

Ra, 4
Rachel, 59-61
Raguel, 308, 310-311
Rahab, 81-82
Rameses II, 9
Raphael, 308-309, 311
Rebekan, 58-59
Red Sea, 66-67

Reformation, 25, 28
Rehoboam, 10, 11-12, **116**, 117, 141
Requiem Mass, 186
Rest of Esther, 27, 295, **328-335**
Resurrection of Christ, 218, 304
Reuben, 60-61
Reuben (tribe), 49, 76, 80, 88
Revelation (book), 20, 28, 29, 209,
    210, 232, 234, 237, 288, 358, 359,
    361
Revised Standard Version, 29, 37,
    38, 39, **42-43**, 236 258, 268, 291,
    318, 345
Rheims, 34
Rheims-Douay Bible, **34**, 37, 38
Rheims New Testament, 34
Rimmon, 131
Rogers, John, 31
Roman Catholic Bible, 20, **34**, **37-38**,
    43-44
Romans, Epistle to (book), 20, 60,
    156, 189, 194, 232, 343
Rome, Romans, 5, 20, 60
Rubáiyát, 194, 347
Ruth, 298-301
Ruth (book), 19, 46, 295, **297-301**,
    396, 327

Sabbath, institution of, 52, 69
Sabeans, 278
Sacrorum Bibliorum Concordantiae,
    32
Sadducees, Sadduceeism, 151, **152**,
    153, 157, 160, 349, 351, **352**
Saint-Saëns, Camille, 92
Salathiel, 359-360
Samaria, 11; made capital of Israel,
    119
Samaritan Pentateuch, 24
Samaritans, origin of, 144
Samson, 46, 56, 72, 87, **92-95**, 320,
    326
Samson (oratorio), 92
Samson and Delilah, 92
Samson Agonistes, 92
Samuel, 10, 13, **97-99**, 100-103, 126,
    139, 140, 164; administration of,
    98; anointing of David, 101;
    anointing of Saul, 99-100; birth

and childhood of, 97-98; prophet-
    ic activities of in retirement, 99
Samuel, I and II (books), 19, 28,
    50, 54, 56, 85, **95-111**, 138-140,
    164, 237, 242, 253, 338
Sanballat, 145, 146
Sarah (Sarai, wife of Abraham), 50,
    56-57
Sarah (daughter of Raguel), 308-
    310
Sargon, 11, 307
Saul, 10, 85, 97, **99-102**, 103, 104,
    105, 106, 140, 164; anointing and
    early victories of, 99; death of,
    102; decline of, 101; shortcom-
    ings and rejection of, 100
Satan (Lucifer), 223-224
Satan, The (in book of Job), 275,
    278, 279
"Saving Remnant," 179-180
"Sayings of the Seers," 267
Scythians, 184, 194, 208
Second Coming of Christ, 259
Second Isaiah. *See* Isaiah (book)
Seleucids, 13, 150-151, 153, 199,
    208, 306, 313, 319, 334
Seleucus, 13, 150
Seneca, 338
Sennacherib, **133-134**, 168, 246, 307
Septuagint, **24-25**, 27, 28, 42, 70, 96,
    111, 138, 148, 150, 241, 262, 314,
    322, 329-331
Sermon on the Mount, 338
Seven Brothers, Massacre of, 160
Shadrach, 268, **312-314**, 338
Shakespeare, William, 33, 69
Shallum, 120, 190
Shalmaneser V, 11, 307
Shamgar, 87
Shealtiel, 359
Sheba, 114, 115; Queen of, 114-115
Shechem, Shechemites, 10, 50, 91,
    116, 119, 121, 325
Shelley, Percy Bysshe, 264
Shem, 54-55
Shemaiah, 141
Sheol, 17, **152-153**, 172, 281, 354
Sheshbazzar, 137, 143, 220
Shiloh, 95, 97

Shishak, 141

Shinar, 225

Shushan, 144, 331

Simeon, 60

Simeon (tribe), 80

Simon (governor of Temple), 158

Simon (high priest), 350

Simon Thassi, 151, 154-155, **156-157**

Sinai, Mount, 16, 63, 66, 67, 69, 72, 73, 78, 207, 351. *See also* Horeb

Sira, Sirach, 27, 348, 349

Sisera, **88-89**, 338

Smith, J. M. P., 42

Smith-Goodspeed Bible, 37, 38, **42**

Sodom, 16, 56, 57

Solomon, 10, 11, 96, 108, **110-111**, 112, **113-116**, 117, 121, 139-141, 147, 241, 242, 245, 287, 293, 338, 339-340, 346, 352, 353; anointment as king, 110-111; apostasy and death, 115-116; building of Temple, 115; and Queen of Sheba, 114-115, reign of, 113-116; wisdom and riches of, 113-115. *See also* Song of Solomon

Song of Deborah and Barak, 88-89

Song of Moses and the People, 66, 88

Song of Solomon, 19, 20, 114, 271, **286-294**, 346

Song of Songs. *See* Song of Solomon

Song of the Sword, 237

Song of the Three Holy Children (book), 27, 239, 262, **268-270**, 295, 311, 314

Song of the Three Young Men. *See* Song of the Three Holy Children

Song of Vanity, 237

"Song of the Vineyard," 179

Sophocles, 92, 274, 307

Soul's Tragedy, A, 275

Southern Kingdom. *See* Judah

Spenser, Edmund, 289, 320

Spinoza, Baruch *or* Benedict, 64

Sprau, George, 274

Stoics, 353

Story of the Grateful Dead, 307

Story and Wisdom of Ahikar, 307

Succoth, 90

Suffering Servant, 211, **216-218**

Sukenik, E. L., 14

Susa, 144, 146, 331

Susanna, 322-324

Susanna (book), 27, 295, 311, **322-324**, 327

Swift, Jonathan, 304

Synagogue, founding of, 191

Synoptic Gospels, 212

Syria, Syrians, 116, **122-123**

Syriac Bible, 26

Taanach, 89

Tabernacle, 67-68, 70

Tabernacles, Feast of, 233

Tabor, Mount, 88

Tale of a Tub, 304

Talmud, 323

Tamar, 108

Tamerlane, 99

Tammuz, 236, 288

Targums, 26-27, 42, 256

Tarsus, 114

Tartarus, 354

Tatnai, Tattenai, 144

Taverner, Richard, 31

Taverner Bible, 31

"Teaching of Amen-em-Ope, The," 340

Tekoa, 168

Teman, 273

Temple: building of, 115; destruction of by Nebuchadrezzar, 136; rebuilding of by Zerubbabel, 138, 143-144

Ten Commandments, 46, **67-69**, 70, 78, 273, 323

Ten Lost Tribes, 362

Tennyson, Alfred, 264

Tetragrammaton, 16, 49

Thebes, 9

Thessa II, 358

Third Isaiah. *See* Isaiah (book)

Thomas of Celano, 186

Thompson, Francis, 251

Thor, 16, 92

Threnoi, 262

Thummim, 68

Tiglath-pileser, 118, 120, 173

Tirzah, 119, 120, 293
Tob, 92
Tobiah, 145-146
Tobias, 308-311
Tobit, 307-311
Tobit (book), 27, 295, **306-311**, 327
Tola, 87
Torah, 19, 227. *See also* Law, Pentateuch
Tower of Babel, 50, **55**
Tractate of Khons, 307
Transfiguration, 70, 127
Trito-Isaiah. *See* Isaiah (book)
Triumphal Entry of Christ, 234
Tyndale, William, 30, 31, 32, **38**
Tyndale Bible, 30

Uncial manuscripts, 25
United Kingdom, 10, 13, 17. *See also* Israel
Unknown Prophet, 17, 165, 199, **210-218**, 222. *See also* Isaiah (book)
Unleavened Bread, rite of, 60
Ur, 9, 55
Uriah, 107-108, 164
Uriel, 361
Urim, 68
Utnapishtim, 17
Uz, 277
Uzziah (Azariah), 12, 117, 168, 326, 327, 328

Vashti, 329, 331
Vulgate, 26, 27, 30, 34, 38, 40, 42, 70, 141, 148, 268, 314, 330, 359

Waterman, Leroy, 42
Watts, Isaac, 260
Westminster Bible, 37
Wetzstein, J. G., 289
Wild, Laura, 271

Wilderness, journey of the Hebrews in, 67, **73-74**
Wisdom of Jesus, Son of Sirach. *See* Ecclesiasticus
Wisdom Literature, 337-355
Wisdom of Solomon (book), 27, 194, 338, 339, 351, **353-355**
Witch of Endor, 102, 140
Woden, 16
Writings (section of Old Testament), 19, 23, 287, 297, 307
Wyclif, John, 30
Wyclif-Hereford Bible, 30
Wyclifite Bible, 30

Xerxes I, 144, 320, 330, 333

Yahweh: Hebrew concepts of, 15-17; worship of at Temple, 121
Yom Kippur, 71

Zachariah, 120
Zadok, 109, 200, 209
Zebulun, 60
Zechariah, 221-226
Zechariah (book), 165, 203, 210, 219, **221-226, 233-234**, 358
Zedekiah (king) 12, 118, 135, 136, 190-191, 193, 196, 204-205, 271
Zedekiah (prophet), 124-125
Zephaniah, 16, 184, **185-186**, 229
Zephaniah (book), 164, 185-186
Zerubbabel, 138, 143, 144, **148-149**, 220-222, 224-225
Zeus, 150, 154
Zilpah, 60
Zimri, 119, 125
Zion, Mount, 209, 232, 266, 360
Zipporah, 64
Zobah, 100
Zophar, 276, 279, 281, 283
Zorobabel, 143. *See also* Zerubbabel